W9-AYV-191

The Backyard Bird Lover's ULTIMATE HOW-TO GUIDE

More Than 200 Easy Ideas and Projects for Attracting and Feeding Your Favorite Birds

SALLY ROTH

For our children

Direct and trade editions are both being published in 2010.

Rodale books may be purchased for business or promotional use or for special sales. For information, please write to: Special Markets Department, Rodale Inc., 733 Third Avenue, New York, NY 10017.

Printed in the United States of America

Rodale Inc. makes every effort to use acid-free ♾, recycled paper ♻.

Book design by Christopher Rhoads

Illustrations by Christen Stewart/illustrationOnLine.com

Photography credits are on page 305.

Library of Congress Cataloging-in-Publication Data

Roth, Sally.
The backyard bird lover's ultimate how-to guide : more than 200 easy ideas and projects for attracting and feeding your favorite birds / Sally Roth.
p. cm.
Includes bibliographical references and index.
ISBN-13 978-1-60529-520-6 hardcover
ISBN-10 1-60529-520-5 hardcover
ISBN-13 978-1-60529-519-0 paperback
ISBN-10 1-60529-519-1 paperback
1. Bird watching. 2. Birds—Feeding and feeds. 3. Backyard gardens. I. Title.
QL676.5.R66834 2010
598.072'34—dc22 2010005137

Distributed to the trade by Macmillan

4 6 8 10 9 7 5 3 hardcover

2 4 6 8 10 9 7 5 3 1 paperback

We inspire and enable people to improve their lives and the world around them

Contents

A Whole New World

The big, wide world starts right in our own backyard.

Every time I buy a bag of seeds or a few blocks of suet for my backyard birds at the store, it seems someone will remark on it.

"Getting a lot of goldfinches?" the fellow in front of me asked the other day, as I slid a sack of niger onto the checkout counter.

"Just starting," I noted. "But I want to be ready when they come in."

"So far, mine are more interested in the cosmos flowers than the feeders," he laughed.

As we chatted about our birds, several people nearby and the checker herself joined in. What's the best food? What can I do about wasps at my hummingbird feeder? Do you think it's too late to plant zinnias for the finches?

Whether you've been feeding birds for a while or you're just getting started, it's easy to tell that the business is booming. New feeders, new foods, a whole aisle in the discount stores, and even entire shops dedicated to wild birds are all signs that we're a force to be reckoned with.

Unbelievable as it seems, one out of every four adult Americans watches birds in his or her backyard.

We number a grand total of 46 million, or one out of seven men, women, and children all across the country, according to 2009's *The US State of the Birds,* the first comprehensive report of US bird populations, coordinated by the US Fish and Wildlife Service with the help of many bird conservancy groups. No wonder we keep running into fellow bird lovers everywhere we go! Whether it's in my little hometown of New Harmony, Indiana, or the Boston metropolis, there are an awful lot of us feeding birds.

And, boy oh boy, do we spend the bucks: hundreds of millions of dollars on our seed, feeders, birdhouses, and other supplies, every year.

A force to be reckoned with? You better believe it.

And just in the nick of time.

All across the country, the woods right around us and in wild places, too, are becoming mighty bare of birds. Scores of species are in decline—wood thrushes, blue-winged warblers, chestnut-backed chickadees, and many others are dropping in such numbers that they've left a noticeable gap. May mornings just don't sound like they used to, and neither do the dusky evenings, when thrushes on every side once sang the day to sleep.

The grasslands aren't as full of lark song and bobwhite whistles as they once were, either. Field sparrows no longer fill our meadows of goldenrod and wild asters with their sweet twittering. And along creeks and around ponds, willow warblers and flycatchers are harder to find.

Our deserts, sagebrush, and other dry lands are even worse hit, with canyon wrens no longer echoing off every rock, and nearly three-quarters of species showing significant declines.

On the other hand, our feeders are booming. Though we're noticing some gaps—where are the white-crowned sparrows this year?—most of us are hosting more birds than ever before. We're even seeing some new kinds of birds come to visit our feeders for the very first time.

What's happening?

The world is changing. And birds are feeling the effects, big-time.

Success Story: Eastern Bluebird

Problems: Lack of nest sites; food shortages

Solutions: Birdhouses; feeders

Bluebirds are so beloved—and so noticeable—that they quickly got attention when their numbers dropped dramatically after a few bad winters in the South in the 1950s and a couple of big blizzards in the mid-1960s.

An unusually severe late-winter storm takes its toll on bluebirds because they're very early nesters, and insects are their food of choice. The cold itself can kill the birds outright, and the lack of food can starve the adults or nestlings.

Bluebirds usually rebound after a bad year, but numbers kept dropping because another factor was at play: habitat destruction. The birds nested in cavities in dead wood, and dead wood was fast becoming an endangered species itself.

Old apple trees, one of the birds' favorite nesting sites, were being tidied up, decaying limbs removed. Wooden fence posts were being torn out and replaced by metal. And introduced starlings and house sparrows, who also nest in cavities, were competing for the ever-scarcer homesites.

Simple solution: birdhouses, and lots of them.

Lawrence Zeleny started the North American Bluebird Society (www.nabluebirdsociety.org) in 1978 and began an energetic educational effort to spread the word about bluebird trails. He and other friends of the bluebird campaigned tirelessly to increase nest sites by building "bluebird trails." The trails of nest boxes have proved a big success. In 1978, bluebirds were so few and far between that many people had never seen one. By 1998, just 20 years later, they were being seen frequently wherever the habitat suited them.

Today, these lovely birds are common visitors to our own backyards if we're lucky enough to live near bluebird country. Whether your bluebirds are residents or only passing through, you can help them by providing the soft foods they like best: mealworms, peanut butter dough, and other bluebird feasts.

Tipping the Balance

Every day, an incredible balancing act is going on all around us. Jiggle the balance, and countless other plants and animals have to readjust because every living thing on Earth is connected to everything else.

Change is natural. Nature is always shifting, as plants and animals grab their share of space and resources. It's been going on for ages on our planet, in countless big and small ways.

Nature's been doing a great job of balancing things out. But as our own impact on Earth has become bigger and bigger, the changes have piled up. Too much change too fast causes that balance to swing in ways that can swamp whatever's in its path.

What's tipped the balance? Three factors add up to a great big loss of birds:

- Habitat destruction
- Pesticides and pollution
- Climate change

And now, many birds have started a slide that could be disastrous.

The good news? We can help Mother Nature tip the scale back the other way. Remember, there are 46 million of us bird-watchers.

Our humble backyards can save the birds.

Millions of Safe Havens

What a difference 46 million backyard bird sanctuaries would make to our friends!

We've already got a good start, with our feeders brimming with seeds and our birdbaths brimming with water for a refreshing drink. Many of us have added berry bushes for songbirds, nectar flowers for hummingbirds, birdhouses for wrens and chickadees, and other niceties that make our yards more welcoming.

Let's give ourselves a big pat on the back: Nearly all of our most familiar friends, the birds we see every day at our feeders or in our backyards, are thriving.

Birds of cities and towns, which are long accustomed to living right alongside us year-round or traveling only a short distance in winter, are doing fine, thank you.

Robins, blue jays, house finches, American goldfinches, black-capped and Carolina chickadees, downy woodpeckers, white-breasted nuthatches, and many others are all A-okay.

Why? Three big reasons:

1. Our backyards, city parks, and other "civilized" places have become part of the birds' natural habitat. Our feeders and plants, as well as the trees along our streets, have given them a helping hand or a place to call home, and they've made the most of it.
2. These birds are generalists, not narrowly focused specialists. They eat different kinds of foods or use a variety of plants and habitats as nest sites and can switch to other resources when they need to. If it's a bad year for acorns, they'll turn to other foods to take up the slack—including our sunflower seeds.
3. And—important factor!—these familiar birds don't migrate long distances or out of the country. So they don't face the rigors of an extended journey, with the possibility of scarce resources along the way or at the other end.

We must be doing the right things for these birds because they're holding their own, even with all the changes in the big wide world. Let's keep it up. And let's add even more bird appeal to our yards to make sure they continue to thrive.

As for the 251 bird species that are in decline or otherwise at risk (as of the March 2009, *US State of the Birds* report; let's hope that number hasn't gone up)—more than a third of the 654 native species in the continental United States, plus others in Hawaii—it's time to figure out how to give them the helping hand they desperately need.

These are the birds that visit our backyards only part of the time, not year-round. Many of them nest in our forests, grasslands, deserts, and other wild places, not in our backyards—not yet, anyhow. And many of them migrate to Central and South America or the islands offshore. Sometimes these two categories overlap, which spells double trouble, since these birds face challenges in both their summer and winter homes as well as while making the journey between them.

The numbers are sobering. The populations of many of these birds have declined by more than 50 percent in less than 40 years, and some by as much as 80 to 90 percent. No wonder our May mornings aren't as alive with birdsong as they used to be.

Some days I feel like Lewis and Clark must've felt, looking at the snowcapped Rockies piercing the sky and wondering, "How the heck do we ever get over this?"

Then I take heart. Because every incredible journey begins with a single small step, and those steps add up.

One backyard at a time, we can help make up for the staggering loss of wild habitat. And by

Success Story: Chestnut-Sided Warbler

Problem: Lack of suitable nest sites and habitat

Solution: Clearing forests to increase habitat

The wood warbler family includes many species that are at risk, but this pretty little bird is bucking the downward trend. The chestnut-sided warbler migrates to the tropics in winter, so it faces the same challenges there as other species do. The big difference? The very same destruction and fragmentation of forests that threaten other species actually benefit this one: It makes its home in "early succession" areas, the places where vegetation is growing back after land is cleared by logging, building, or farming. This warbler was a rare bird back in John James Audubon's day, when vast sweeps of forest covered the land. But today, it's among the most abundant breeding wood warbler species in its nesting areas in North America—around the Great Lakes, throughout the Northeast and New England, and down through the Appalachians. Because its population is doing well, you'll often see it during migration, too, in other areas. Listen for its happy call: *"Pleased, pleased, pleased-to-meetcha,"* says this bird that has benefited from human activities.

joining our voices and our dollars to conservation groups, we can have big effects on those wild places, too.

We already have some great success stories to point to. The bald eagle, osprey, and peregrine falcon have made amazing comebacks. Ducks and geese that were floundering are thriving again, thanks to the efforts of hunters and other conservationists. Pelicans, plovers, and other seabirds have made progress, too. Scientists know that conservation efforts work because the birds rebound.

There's no time to lose because hundreds of species of canaries-in-the-coal-mine are singing for their lives.

The first step? Looking at the big problems to see where we can make changes for the better.

Birds at a Glance

Number of bird species in the continental United States, including introduced species: about 700

Number of *native* bird species in the continental United States: 654

Number of bird species in North America in winter: 305

Number of bird species moving their range northward by an average of 35 miles: 183

Number of bird species in need of immediate conservation help: 176*

Percentage of forest birds significantly declining in population: 33

Percentage of grassland bird species significantly declining in population: 55

Percentage of desert, sagebrush, and other arid land bird species significantly declining in population: 75

Source: The US State of the Birds, 2009

**Per the 2007 Audubon WatchList, a joint project of the National Audubon Society and the American Bird Conservancy*

A 40-Year Slide

There's no telling exactly when the downturn in our bird populations began. Large, comprehensive counts of wintering or nesting birds didn't kick into gear until the 1960s, when the annual Audubon Christmas Count of birds began to gain steam. Nesting bird inventories, another important part of "citizen science," were undertaken then, too.

By comparing those early figures with the data from recent counts, scientists have a good snapshot of the state of our American birds.

Before these comparative reports were done, all we had to go on were anecdotal accounts, the stories told by observant folks who remembered when birds were abundant. There were plenty of warnings even then.

I heard some of those warnings from my friend Jimmie, an old man who lived very simply in a tiny stone house along a creek in Pennsylvania. Thirty years ago, we spent a lot of time roaming the woods and fields together. He'd often remark on the growing scarcity of birds, but I took his comments with a grain of salt.

Sometimes we'd hear the lovely plaintive song of a veery in the dim woods, or find ourselves in

Birds on the Brink

I can hardly believe the list of American birds in decline. I wouldn't have been surprised by seeing rare birds on the list, the ones I encounter only once in a great while. But, hey, these guys are my friends!

Bird species that face a shrinking home on both ends of their long migration journey—in North America and in Central or South America—are in the deepest trouble.

But even some of the birds that live in North America year-round are faltering, like the northern bobwhite, a bird whose call rang out from every field when I was a kid in Pennsylvania. Today, it's disappeared entirely from some areas and declined by 75 percent in the rest.

It's not only rare birds that are declining in numbers. Even familiar friends like this eastern meadowlark are becoming less common because of shrinking habitat, pesticides, and other pressures.

Many of the 251 species that are dropping fast are birds that are so familiar, it's hard to imagine our world without them.

No meadowlarks to whistle their poignant songs from a fence post? No eastern towhees to scratch up a storm in dead leaves, making me wonder if there's a bear over there? No wood pewees to imitate (*pee-oh-wee, pee-oh*)?

No wide-eyed field sparrows? No tree sparrows with their snazzy black stickpins to liven up our winter feeders? No chestnut-backed chickadees cracking sunflower seeds in the Northwest? No varied thrushes calling in a dim hemlock forest? No rufous hummingbirds?

Unthinkable. We've got to do something, and we can. By nurturing birds in our backyards, we can help them adapt to changing times. We can help turn the trend around.

To find more details about which birds are in trouble and why, read the entry Population Decline. You'll find other info about the situation throughout this book, particularly in the entry Habitat Destruction. And you'll find hundreds of ways that you can help birds in your own backyard in the other entries in this book, as well.

the middle of a wave of migrating wood warblers, or stumble upon a woodcock that rocketed up from under our feet in a heart-stopping rush.

Jimmie would join me in marveling over whatever wonder we'd come across, and then he would sigh deeply and say, "Boy, you hardly ever hear a veery anymore."

Or, "When I was a boy, it took an hour for a wave of warblers to pass through, that's how many there were."

Or, "I remember when there were so many woodcocks, you could hardly walk for tripping over them."

I figured he was just telling a fish story. After all, I could still count on scaring up a dozen woodcocks every time I took a walk in wet woods in spring. Seemed like plenty of woodcocks to me. And veeries? Why, I heard one every time I went out wandering. As for wood warblers, it must've been a matter of timing, I figured, and we'd simply missed the peak of the migration.

I simply couldn't accept that the world of nature I'd always loved might be less than it once was.

Now that I have a half-century of perspective under my belt, though, I find myself singing the same sad tune as Jimmie.

No, there aren't as many veeries around. Nor woodcocks, nor wood thrushes, nor tanagers, nor just about any of the other woodland birds I've known my whole life.

And there's no mistaking the drop in wood warblers. I see only a handful in a group at the peak of migration nowadays, instead of the hundreds just 30 years ago—the blink of an eye in bird time.

But don't take my word for it, because now there's science to back up the stories. By comparing population counts from years past, we know without a doubt that birds are disappearing all over the place.

The voice of the veery once filled the forest. Like other beloved songbirds, it's declining, most likely because of forest fragmentation that gives access to predators.

What Happened to Home?

When I started hearing the words "habitat destruction" back in the sixties, I wasn't worried. The rain forests of Central and South America—I still thought of them as "jungle" back then—seemed light years away from the birds I saw every day in the woods and fields.

I sent a few dollars to a conservation group, slapped a sticker on my car, and felt pretty proud of myself. Oh, and, hey, that Rainforest Crunch nut brittle was pretty yummy.

Yep, I was young and dumb. Saving the Earth sounded good for a slogan, but as a teenager I was more concerned about who would be at the dance on Friday. Like most of us, I ignored the problem until it hit home.

Besides, the birds around me seemed to be doing just fine. I still saw plenty of birds when I went poking around in the woods and fields. The mornings were still filled with birdsong, and I'd spot a lot of nests.

Habitat destruction as a cause for concern for birds? The first warnings fell on my deaf ears.

For me, the day of reckoning came when a housing boom suddenly hit my neighborhood.

The little grove of poplars down the road that had always sheltered a flycatcher's nest, the acres of woods where I'd always spotted the first tanager in spring and watched thrushes eat dogwood berries in fall? Bulldozed flat in less than a week.

The overgrown meadow that had sheltered sparrow nests, raucous pheasants, bobwhite families, and field mice for the barn owls I'd watched at night? Gone in a flash.

Habitat destruction. Now I got it.

The simple fact: Our population has exploded to such a point that it takes more and more room and resources to produce the stuff we use. Two hundred years ago, there were 8 million of us in the United States; today, there are 300 million.

It takes an awful lot of stuff to keep us going. So our mountaintops are gouged out by mining, forests flattened for 2 × 4s, wild places carved up for subdivisions and vacation homes, western sagebrush turned into grazing land.

Success Story: Marsh Birds

Problem: Habitat destruction

Solutions: Habitat restoration; habitat conservation

The rebound of birds that dwell in marshy places is one of the biggest reasons for hope—it proves that measures we take can quickly reverse a downward trend. Nearly one out of every four North American birds—from ducks and geese to rails, soras, and tiny, chattering marsh wrens—depends on wet areas (not salt marshes, but freshwater marshes, ponds, and other wetlands). When wetland conservation and restoration became high priorities, the birds that had been suffering from the loss of their natural habitat bounced back. The efforts of Ducks Unlimited and other conservation groups paid off in a big way, and many other species benefited right along with the teal, wood ducks, and other waterfowl that their measures were designed to aid. The sale of US Fish and Wildlife "Duck Stamps" and other fund-raising efforts added billions of dollars for purchasing wetland areas as sanctuaries. At least 139 species of wetland birds have been on the rise since the late 1970s, when their homelands began to get attention. The passage of the North American Wetlands Conservation Act in 1989 boosted the effort big-time, helping this story have a happy ending. Some wetland species are still in trouble, including the green heron, rusty blackbird, and spotted sandpiper, but all in all, our efforts prove we can reverse the trend.

Farm fields paint a pretty picture from above—but not to birds. Only the small areas of weedy brush and hedgerows give them a safe place to forage and raise a family.

Instead of family farm fields ringed with brush and hedgerows, we've shifted to "clean farming" with giant fields worked by giant machines. Every time the brush and hedgerows around the old fields have gotten turned into another strip of soybeans, we've eliminated more bird habitat. No wonder the numbers of our meadowlarks, horned larks, and other grassland birds have been dropping like a rock.

Turn to the entries Cowbirds and Predators, too, because there's another huge factor in the decline of our forest birds: the destruction of nests and young.

Cowbirds, which lay their eggs in other species' nests, shun deep forests. But because we've opened our forests with roads and houses, cowbirds are now able to reach the nests of many forest birds and wreak havoc.

In some areas, the forest fragmentation is so widespread and the cowbird problem so severe—30 to 90 percent of migratory songbird nests are parasitized by cowbirds in the forests of Illinois—that some of these songbirds can't raise enough young to maintain their populations.

Cats and raccoons, too, can now saunter through the access routes we've created and prey on birds along the way.

The destruction of habitat both on our continent and on others has reached critical levels.

Once "my" birds in the woods and fields of Pennsylvania were put at risk, I got educated in a hurry. I learned that the flycatchers, tanagers, and thrushes that had lost their homes to developments near my house were "neotropical" birds that wintered in faraway rain forests. It wasn't only the bulldozer down my street that was causing them problems.

All our beautiful neotropical migrants—

tanagers, wood warblers, vireos, thrushes, some grosbeaks, and other migrating species that head for Central or South America—are highly at risk, because they face habitat destruction on both ends of their journey. These species are mostly birds of the forest, and like the veeries my old friend Jimmie and I listened to, their numbers are dropping fast.

In Central and South America, countless acres once used by wintering migratory birds now churn out products we clamor for instead, from beef for fast-food burgers to coffee beans for our morning cuppa joe. With every acre that's destroyed, birds' food supplies get tighter and their shelter scantier. You'll find more details about who's in trouble and what we can do to help in the entries Habitat Destruction and Population Decline.

What We Can Do

You probably already have a feeder or two (or ten) and a birdbath. Maybe you've planted some flowers for hummingbirds or a berry bush for bluebirds, so you're already making a difference. Now let's think about building on those basics, so our millions of backyard sanctuaries can nurture and nourish the many birds that are having trouble keeping up with changing wild places.

You'll be surprised at how effective it is to create a more welcoming habitat for birds in your own yard, how much fun it is, and how fast it works.

Take a look at your grassy lawn. Any birds on it? Not many, unless there's a mob of starlings settled in for some serious grub-eating or a handful of robins pulling worms.

Most of the time, our lawns harbor only a few robins, grackles, starlings, a cowbird or two, sometimes a flicker, maybe even a crow or raven.

We're accustomed to prizing that sweep of green, but whether it's a little patch or a vast estate, lawn is mostly wasted space to most birds, including every species that's in decline.

Breaking up your lawn is a great way to start creating bird habitat. Planting just a single tree will help. But if you include a variety of trees, shrubs, berry bushes, and flowerbeds, your birdlife will blossom, too.

You'll get a slew of birds when you break up your lawn with plants, because you're creating the kind of habitat they're drawn to instead of the bare spaces they avoid. In fact, it's a pretty safe bet that you'll see a host of birds that are currently at risk, because your plantings will provide that all-important cover and the insects and other natural foods they need.

One of my favorite tricks is to make the most of what I've already got. To attract more towhees, native sparrows, and juncos, I link together isolated shrubs by surrounding them with shredded bark or chopped leaf mulch. The group of shrubs and bed of mulch gives these ground-level birds a larger, uninterrupted area where they can forage for food.

You'll find other bright ideas throughout this book to make the most of your existing plants and of the new plants you add to your property. Turn to such entries as Best of the Berries, Birds and Bush, and Hedge Hideout for shrubs with bonafide bird appeal. Check the entries Do Not Disturb and Layered Look for design ideas. And when it comes to all-important trees, get inspired by the entries Conifers and Broad-Leaved Evergreens, Fruit Trees, Small Trees, and Trees and Treetop Birds.

Native plants are important to birds, because birds have grown up with them through the ages. Birds know how to use their seeds, berries, and branches, and native plants are timed to coincide with birds' needs. In fact, natives are so closely connected to birds that many experts believe that "natives only" is the way to go.

Natives are great for birds, without a doubt, and I wouldn't be without them in my yard. But, in my opinion, they're not the be-all and end-all. You'll find out all of the reasons why I disagree with some experts in the entry Native or Not?, but here's a quick overview for starters.

Most birds get around quite a bit, so the native plants they're using are likely to be from several different regions. Hermit thrushes, for instance, eagerly eat the berries of native pondberry (*Lindera melissifolia*) when they arrive in Georgia in October. These very same thrushes may have stopped off in my Indiana yard along the way, and here they would have feasted on spice bush (*Lindera benzoin*), a pondberry relative that's native to my neck of the woods.

So, yes, plant natives in your yard, but add nonnatives, too, if you like them. Having a diversity of plants will help mitigate any diseases or insects that may move in. Many nonnatives have been eagerly adopted by birds as a source of food (think crabapples, hawthorns, Bradford pears) or for nest sites. Besides, all plants add to the protective cover your backyard has to offer.

Why It Will Work

Birds need plants, plants need birds—it's that simple.

And it's a nifty win-win exchange: Birds get food and shelter, and plants stay healthy and reproduce. Birds eat the insects that plague the plants, and they spread the plants' seeds via their droppings to ensure future generations. Birds that nip off tree buds for food help, too, by "pruning" the trees into new spurts of vigorous growth.

By changing our backyards to good bird habitat, we create mini-sanctuaries for traveling migrants as well as resident birds.

Once you start planting, you'll soon see that one backyard can make a difference. The additional plants will attract more birds, including more nesting birds, and the numbers soon start to add up.

And that's just in one yard alone. Multiply that by us 46 million bird lovers, and it's plain as the cardinal in that tree that we can be a mighty powerful influence on birdlife.

You probably already have some of the most familiar backyard birds raising a family at your place—robins, cardinals, jays, and others. But wouldn't you love to extend your helping hand a little further?

Of course you would. We all would, because it feels like a badge of honor when birds choose our yards to raise their brood. So let's put up birdhouses, or nest boxes as they're also called, for feathered friends who could use some more real

Keep a varied menu at your feeder, and you may be honored with a snazzy chestnut-sided warbler, one of the species that is beginning to use our backyards.

Guaranteed to Please

When I moved into my house in Indiana a couple of years ago, the yard was nothing but some big shade trees (a major plus, right there) and a thick "lawn" of English ivy. In spring, a colony of Virginia bluebells fought their way through the ivy, then died back to sleep until next year.

I had a big head start, thanks to the trees around my place. But except for that, there wasn't much to interest birds. Besides, every cat in the neighborhood—more than a dozen in all—had taken to hanging out here.

That first nesting season, I found five nests in my yard: a blue jay's, a robin's, a Baltimore oriole's, a song sparrow's, and a chimney swift's in—where else?—the chimney.

But not one of their babies made it. Cats picked off all of the nestlings or fledglings, even the swifts, and the mama song sparrow, to boot.

Two years later, it's a whole different story. This June, I watched the successful fledging of robins, blue jays, cardinals, gray catbirds, Baltimore orioles, warbling vireos, Carolina wrens, house wrens, Carolina chickadees, tufted titmice, downy woodpeckers, hairy woodpeckers, red-bellied woodpeckers, golden-shafted flickers, great crested flycatchers, chimney swifts, chipping sparrows, song sparrows, American goldfinches, cedar waxwings, and ruby-throated hummingbirds. That's 21 species, with at least two fledglings from each nest! And many of the birds raised at least two broods.

And, no, I don't live on a grand estate—I have a small in-town yard that's about 70 × 150 feet, including the house.

So what made the incredible difference in such a short time? Better habitat, which brought many more birds to my yard. And cat control, which allowed the birds to nest here.

As soon as I settled into the house, I dug right in on planting, adding shrubs and young trees that I transplanted from the wild, courtesy of generous land-owning friends—and barely spent a dime. I planted in groups, creating an understory beneath the shade trees, just like in the woods a mile away, with wide, inviting paths for strolling. I added a hedge of berry bushes, briars, and a tangle of vines, and a vegetable garden to tempt house wrens. I got rid of the English ivy, too, and replaced it with a mix of native plants and other bird favorites, including plenty of nectar flowers for hummingbirds.

Sound like a million-dollar effort? Not at all. I did the whole yard for practically nothing, by asking friends and neighbors for plants (gardeners love to share!), shopping the bargain corner and end-of-season sales at nurseries, and snapping up bargains at local plant sales.

It took surprisingly little effort to train the cats to stay away. I just gave them a blast with my trusty supersquirt gun whenever I saw them. Persistence paid off fast.

Every place I've ever lived, I've done the same thing (and that's maybe a dozen yards in various regions of the country). And every time, it's worked like a charm. When it comes to attracting birds, plants are sheer magic.

estate, including great crested flycatchers, flickers, and other migrating birds. You'll find details in the Birdhouses entry.

And let's not forget to add a one-stop shopping center for nest materials, too, particularly those that are getting scarcer because of the tidiness trend in farms, along roadsides, and in many yards. A basket of fluff and fibers can help birds replace natural nesting materials, and it may lure them into nesting in or near your backyard.

What about birds that don't nest in backyards? As difficulties mount in their usual wild habitats, they may turn to our yards to help meet their needs. Even chickadees and robins weren't always backyard birds—they learned that our yards were good places to visit or live, and they became regulars.

In recent years, other species, including gray catbirds, thrashers, some wrens, and cedar waxwings, have begun to make the same shift.

It's not only habitat that turns the tide: The offerings at our feeders can help encourage birds to consider our backyards as a place to call home. For most of the birds at risk, seeds alone won't do the trick. But there's now a whole menu of enticing options that may soon have vireos, warblers, wrens, and tanagers stopping in regularly at our backyard restaurants.

Success Story: A Pair of Chickadees

Problem: Expanding human population

Solution: Adaptation

Black-capped and Carolina chickadees have been keeping company with people for hundreds of years, probably before the first Europeans ever set foot in North America. Quick to take advantage of a food source, they easily made the shift from foraging in forests to exploring the possibilities around nearby homes. The destruction and fragmentation of forests affected these species much less than their cousins, the boreal and chestnut-backed chickadees, which have taken a hit from habitat destruction.

Today, the Carolina and black-capped chickadee are dependable visitors to feeders, and our backyards are now simply part of their natural habitat. It's easy to entice chickadees to your feeder, but getting them to nest in your yard is a different story. Many still retreat to the woods to raise their families, or they may move from winter feeding range to breeding grounds that don't include our particular yards. But they're quickly learning about new housing possibilities, too. Putting up a chickadee-size birdhouse can be a great inducement to a nesting pair of these perky birds, so give it a try. Carolina chickadees are beginning to show declines in some areas, and house wrens are one of the culprits: The wrens destroy chickadee eggs or baby birds in backyard boxes. You can help the situation by mounting your chickadee nest box higher, to about 9 to 10 feet, which won't be nearly as attractive to competing wrens. You'll know you've helped when the parent chickadees bring their lineup of babies to your welcoming feeder.

What's to Eat?

Insects are even more sensitive than birds are to their surroundings. A change in weather patterns, even if it's just an unusually cool and rainy spring, can cause native bees or butterflies to nosedive, and they'll often require a couple of years to recover.

Usually, the ups and downs run in cycles, with plenty of other insects to take up the slack, as far as birds' diets are concerned. When the natural balance gets really out of whack, though, it can have devastating consequences.

I'll never forget when gypsy moths marched through the East, devouring the leaves of every tree in their path.

Success Story: Bald Eagle

Problems: Pesticides and pollution; lead shot poisoning; illegal shooting; habitat destruction

Solutions: Banning of certain pesticides, including DDT; river and lake cleanups; banning of lead shot; enforced protection of the birds and their nest sites; adaptation

The bald eagle is a success story we can all be proud of. Today, tens of thousands of regal eagles perch and hunt along our rivers, lakes, and oceans. But just a few decades ago, the eagle population was on the brink of collapse. Experts estimated in 1963 that only 412 nesting pairs remained in the Lower 48 states.

It would've been pretty embarrassing to lose our national symbol to extinction, but the bald eagle is back from the brink. Look for the regal bird along rivers and lakes.

Polluted lakes and rivers and the tainted fish in them had sickened or killed many eagles. The waterfowl they preyed on were often contaminated with lead shot, another poison. Illegal shooting had wiped out even more of the big birds. Even though the eagles had been covered by the Bald Eagle Protection Act of 1940, the law was rarely enforced. Pesticides and other toxins caused sterility and produced fragile eggs that cracked under the weight of the parent on the nest. DDT often gets the blame, but new research is pointing to a lethal cocktail of pesticides and pollutants.

The state of affairs was looking mighty grim. But help was on the way. In 1972, DDT was banned, and efforts to curb other toxic pesticides and clean up pollution got underway. In

It was the strangest June landscape I'd ever seen. The bare trees looked like they did in winter, but birds were sitting on their nests—in full view, instead of hidden in greenery. And spring wildflowers were blooming a second time, pulled out of dormancy when the denuded trees allowed the sun to beat down on the summer forest floor.

Unless those birds were mighty fond of gypsy moth caterpillars (many birds avoid hairy 'pillars), they had to fly quite a distance to find food for their families.

Food shortages for birds go hand in hand with habitat destruction. When forests, grasslands, and other habitats are wiped out, the insects and wild fruits that birds depend on are gone, too.

1978, our national symbol came under the protection of the Endangered Species Act. Anyone who killed one of the birds now faced a stiff fine and jail time. And finally, in 1991, lead shot was banned nationwide.

Eagles were more numerous in a few states, and young birds from nests there or from a captive breeding program were "transplanted" to other areas of the country.

The method, called hacking, worked like a charm. The eaglets were kept in a cage atop a tall tower and hand-fed until they were able to fly and hunt on their own. Even without parents to show them the ropes, the young eagles learned to fend for themselves just fine. The very first eaglets were hacked in 1976 in Montezuma, New York. Four years later, the birds built their first nest nearby and hatched two chicks.

Eagles themselves aided their own recovery by adapting to the human presence. Once, they nested only in remote areas. Nowadays, they nest near houses, thoroughfares, and marinas, as well as in the wilderness. I've watched nesting pairs that seemed completely unfazed by human activity.

Success built on success, and on July 29, 2007, the bald eagle was officially removed from the List of Endangered and Threatened Wildlife and assigned the risk level of "Least Concern."

There's more good news, too. The measures taken to help the bald eagle, including the innovative hacking technique, have also reversed the steep decline of peregrine falcons and ospreys, two other magnificent birds of prey.

Yet the coast isn't completely clear for the bald eagle. A new neurological bird disease, avian vacuolar myelinopathy (AVM), cropped up in Arkansas in 1994, killing 29 bald eagles and many American coots, one of the many waterfowl species that eagles prey on. The sickness has spread to other lakes, and more than 100 eagles have succumbed to it as of 2007. The suspected cause is a neurotoxin produced by a bacterium on the leaves of a nonnative water plant (*Hydrilla verticillata*). The waterfowl eat the tainted plant, the eagles eat the waterfowl, and the disease does its dirty work. Prognosis? We just don't know yet. But at least we're now paying attention to our birds.

Pesticides have worsened the problem of bird food shortages. Controlling insects and weeds with chemicals so we can have perfect apples from our backyard trees and acres of waving grain seems like a miracle solution. But chemicals have turned out to be a great big *oops,* as far as birds are concerned.

The billion—yes, billion—pounds of pesticides we use every year kill insects, and insects are what birds eat. Sometimes the pesticides kill the birds themselves: *67 million birds a year* in the United States alone, as concluded by the landmark study by David Pimentel and others in 1992.

Pesticides are one of the main reasons that meadowlarks, horned larks, native sparrows, lark buntings, and other birds of open spaces are in big trouble. And these toxins affect migrants of all kinds, too, who look for sustenance and safe harbor along the way.

Hmm, suddenly that perfect shiny red apple doesn't seem so tempting. Uh, no thanks, I'll take the one with the small brown spot instead.

Climate change, the third major player on the scene, doesn't help matters, as far as food is concerned. As our weather patterns change, plants and insects feel the consequences, and so do the birds that depend on them.

A massive die-off of pinyon pines in the Southwest in 2002, the result of high heat following a severe drought—climate change—is one reason why pinyon jays are now on the birds-in-decline list.

Creating habitat in our backyards will help with the supply of natural foods for birds, whatever climate change brings down the pike. And our feeders are quickly becoming a vital factor on the scene, too.

How We Can Help

When the pinecone crop isn't up to snuff in the Far North, pine siskins, purple finches, crossbills, redpolls, red-breasted nuthatches, and other seed eaters skedaddle south in an event that bird-watchers call an irruption.

It's a red-letter winter for us when that happens, because many unusual visitors end up at our feeders, where they're perfectly content to substitute sunflowers for pine seeds.

So why didn't the pretty blue pinyon jays turn to feeders when the pinyon trees in the Southwest were hit hard by drought?

An occasional cone-crop failure is a pretty regular occurrence in the North, so those irruption birds have had thousands of years to figure it out. They've adapted to the situation and adopted a behavior that allows them to survive it.

The pinyon jays, on the other hand, weren't accustomed to a sudden cutoff of their food supply. Many of them did turn to feeders in the area, which helped to avert a massive die-off of the jays right along with the pines. But these jays typically collect and cache tens of thousands of pinyon seeds—pine nuts—per bird in a good year, and the lack of that food source took its toll.

I'm curious how the pinyon jays around Flagstaff, Arizona, where the die-off was centered, adapted to the loss of their special trees. Although the population of these big, bold birds took a hard hit, the species quickly reacted to the challenge. Researchers who studied 3,700 jays in the area learned that larger birds, males, and adults did best. Pinyon jays are intensely social and usually stick tight with members of their own family. But after the drought, some jays actually left their own little bands and joined other groups, which took in the hungry birds. Jays are clever birds, and my guess is that the species will gradually start to climb again in numbers, especially as the birds learn to substitute other foods.

When change comes gradually, most birds seem able to adapt their habits to make up for it. But when there's a sudden shift, birds are often at a loss. Snowy owls in the Arctic, for instance, are now having a hard time because the lemmings they depend on for food are getting flooded out as the Arctic ice melts.

Will we soon see snowy owls regularly in the Lower 48? Maybe, although I wouldn't start hanging mice from the feeder just yet. These birds need big stretches of open land to hunt the

Success Story: Wild Turkey

Problems: Overhunting; habitat destruction

Solutions: Reintroduction; food plots; managed hunting

Wild turkeys almost went the way of the passenger pigeon and for the same reason: There were so many that it seemed impossible that we'd ever wipe them out, even with uncontrolled hunting.

But turkeys were facing another hurdle, too, as the great hardwood forest was chopped down wholesale to make room for settlements and farms. By the time the American chestnut blight hit in the early 1900s, wiping out one of their major foods, the turkeys were already nearly gone.

Today, thanks to hunting groups and other conservationists, turkeys are gobbling again in every state in the Lower 48.

The birds were bred in captivity (in the wild, more than half the chicks commonly die in their first 4 weeks of life) and released into the woodsy, brushy habitat they like best. Transplants from those first flocks expanded their range, and then the turkeys did the rest themselves.

Conservation plots of oaks for acorns, grain, and other turkey foods gave them a boost, too.

Now the wild turkey is back with a vengeance, scratching for seeds and insects in forests and traipsing through brushy edges and fields. Its population is so healthy that the birds are quickly branching out into suburbia and even city parks. My daughter in Boston reports seeing a flock in her neighborhood every now and then.

In recent years, wild turkeys have taken to feeders with alacrity, with entire flocks showing up at times. My sister Mary in Pennsylvania, who had no wild turkeys on her place when she moved in 30 years ago, now feeds a regular flock. She's named her favorite bird "Gobble."

I imagine it won't be too long before we start seeing anti-turkey tricks for our feeding stations. These big birds may turn out to be too much of a good thing when they come into our backyards.

rodents they depend on, and I haven't noticed much tundra around my place, have you?

Still, snowy owls do visit us in winter, settling for a while in airports, pastures, and other big stretches of grassland. We can only guess whether they'll ever relocate year-round, instead of on rare occasions in winter when some of the great white birds make their way south.

Why It Will Work

Over time, many birds have learned to associate our backyard feeders with a good meal, even if the foods we offer aren't the same as they eat in the wild.

Chickadees, jays, and other year-round regulars have been cadging handouts for a couple of centuries, but now they have some new friends joining them.

Several species that once never gave our feeding stations a second glance have become regulars at our trays and tubes. You know how you look forward to that day in April when the brilliant indigo bunting that takes your breath away arrives, looking for a handout of millet? Thirty years ago, that bird wasn't even a possibility at a feeder. As for that waxwing at the mealworms—well, I never thought I'd see the day. Only a few years ago, waxwings simply ignored my feeders.

Since we never know who might show up tomorrow, it's a great idea to keep our feeding stations stocked with foods for every taste. Most seed-eating birds have been regulars at our feeders for a long time, but these new visitors specialize in soft foods. I can see that I'd better stock up on cornmeal and suet for my homemade bird doughs, because I have a feeling that soon I'll be feeding more soft foods than seeds.

You'll find lots of mouthwatering ideas for feeding your backyard birds throughout this book. Mouthwatering for them, that is, unless you've acquired a taste for wiggly mealworms or a nice chunk of lard. Mmm, yum.

New Foods and Feeders

When I wrote *The Backyard Bird Feeder's Bible*—can it really be 10 years ago already?—I thought I had the subject covered. I'd crammed in every bit I knew about every commercial feeder food on the market, and I'd included a ton of recipes that I'd dreamed up myself to bring in even more birds.

Nowadays, my big mixing bowl of cracker crumbs, cornmeal, and melted beef fat (not to mention my collection of empty pudding cups, cottage cheese containers, and other bird-feeders-to-be) is starting to feel more than a little quaint.

With all the buying power behind bird-watching, manufacturers have jumped on the

If you haven't tried mealworms at your feeder yet, don't wait another minute. Carolina wrens, bluebirds, catbirds, and a host of other interesting birds will soon come to sample them.

New Friends at the Feeder

A few decades ago—and for some species, even just a few years ago—the following birds were rarities at the feeder, birdbath, or other backyard attractions. Now they're showing up at our places with increasing frequency. Some of them have become such reliable regulars, it's hard to believe they once got all their food from the wild. Others are still unusual visitors, and a real treat.

- Baltimore oriole
- Bewick's wren
- Brown thrasher
- Bullock's oriole
- Carolina wren
- Cedar waxwing
- Chestnut-sided warbler
- Cooper's hawk
- Crossbills
- Gray catbird
- Hairy woodpecker
- Hepatic tanager
- Hummingbirds (all species)
- Indigo bunting
- Pileated woodpecker
- Rose-breasted grosbeak
- Scarlet tanager
- Scott's oriole
- Sharp-shinned hawk
- Summer tanager
- Western tanager
- Wild turkey

Notoriously standoffish cedar waxwings at a feeder? Not a chance, I would've said just a year or two ago. Now the birds do drop in on occasion, thanks to new foods that they've learned to associate with feeders.

bandwagon big-time. Look through any bird supply store, online site, or even big discount store, and you'll find some version of all the treats I've cooked up in my messy kitchen. They're sold neatly packaged now with catchy names like "Miracle Meal."

It's not just sunflowers, niger, and seed mix anymore, not by a long shot. Today, we can spend more than our weekly grocery budget keeping our birds in treats that are conveniently packaged for our feeders. Here's just a sample of what's available.

- Mealworms, live or roasted
- Other larvae, including waxworms and wireworms
- Soft foods, including plugs, blocks, and crumbles of various recipes, mostly based on cornmeal and fat
- Insect-enriched suet and soft foods

What's Going On?

Because of our changing climate, life on Earth is changing in all kinds of ways, big and small.

"Widespread climate-related impacts are occurring now and are likely to grow," says the comprehensive federal report on climate change that was released in June, 2009. The report, which you can download at www.globalchange.gov/publications/reports/scientific-assessments/us-impacts/download-the-report, lists pages of effects that are already occurring.

All of the changes affect birds . . . and eventually affect us, too. Here are some of the happenings we know about.

- Wildflowers are blooming earlier. Earlier snowmelt and late frosts endanger some mountain wildflowers.
- Birds are migrating earlier, perhaps adjusting their habits to keep up with the earlier flowers and insects.
- Insects are moving into new places—and moving out of old ones.
- Warming temperatures have caused entire populations of birds to move their range northward. Pine siskins, red-breasted mergansers, and three-toed woodpeckers are just a few of the many species that have abandoned homelands in the southern part of their range, some by 100 miles, and gone north.
- Even trees are marching up mountainsides, as the changing weather makes it possible for them to grow where once was snow and ice.
- Rain and snow are being dumped fast and hard in single storms, instead of being spread out over weeks.

- Waste-free seeds (no shells)
- Specialized seed mixes targeted to certain birds
- A variety of suet flavors to appeal to bluebirds, chickadees, woodpeckers, or other birds
- Nuggets and pelletized foods, such as berries and suet, and even vitamin-enriched pellets in seed mixes
- Dried fruits and berries for birds—even blueberries
- Walnut, almond, and other nut butters
- Molded seed and nut treats in decorative shapes, and with more appealing ingredients than the venerable "seed bell"
- Seed blocks to feed a crowd or just a few, made with a variety of ingredients to attract woodpeckers or other birds

- Creeks and rivers are drying up, or flooding fast and furious.
- Droughts and heat waves are increasing in frequency and severity.
- Millions of years' worth of ice is melting so fast that polar bears and the people of the Arctic are being forced out of places they've lived forever.
- Our oceans are feeling the impact, too. Warming water and the accelerating rise in sea level—after 2,000 years of stability—threaten many life forms, from tiny krill that form the base of the food chain to seabirds and human coast dwellers who face erosion and the risk of serious floods.
- Carbon dioxide levels are rising in the air we breathe, which could make life a tricky business for animals and plants. One plant that's favored in a higher CO_2 atmosphere: poison ivy.

Subalpine lupine springs into growth as soon as the snow melts, which happens weeks earlier these days. That head start doesn't help—the flowers are dealt a death blow when a late spring frost hits, so no seeds mature. As you can guess, this mountain plant is in trouble.

These new foods are welcomed by our old familiar birds, and they're quickly being adopted by the newer friends that are learning to use our feeders, too.

And where will we put all these different kinds of foods? Not to worry—feeder designers and builders have been busy, too. You'll find all kinds of nifty new designs on the market to add to your tried-and-true tubes, hoppers, and trays, from box feeders for bluebirds to fruit bars for orioles, catbirds, and waxwings.

You'll find advice, insider tips, and suggestions about all of these new foods and feeders throughout this book, including the entries À la Carte, Bite-Size Bits, and Doughs, among many others.

I'm hoping you like to be creative and resourceful—not to mention frugal—as much as I do. So you'll find an abundance of my bird-tested recipes to cook up in your own kitchen. And I've included some homemade feeders to put together out of odds and ends, if you're handy.

An Eye on the Weather

My birds know a big winter storm is coming even before I do. They begin gathering at the feeder the day ahead, eating more and staying longer. Once the snow starts to pile up, my feeders are bursting at the seams with birds. All day long, I have fun refilling the feeders and dreaming up special treats for all my hungry friends.

Drought brings more birds to our backyards, too, like the hundred hummingbirds that hung out at my place during the summer of 2007. Rain had been so scarce that even roadside flowers had given up the ghost, so the hummingbirds that might have feasted at trumpet vine and other blossoms turned to nectar feeders instead. Orioles, vireos, wood warblers, and other visitors took turns at the birdbaths from sunup to sundown, and the feeders were popular, too.

I'm a Weather Channel junkie, so I'm usually ready for the birds when snow, ice, or cold rolls in. But we don't need a meteorologist to know which way the winds of climate change are blowing. Big changes are in store, and some of them are already happening.

As weather patterns shift, food and shelter are likely to get even harder to find for birds. And as the world warms up, causing changes in insects and plants, birds are moving north, moving east, moving wherever it still feels like home. Experts tell us that climate change will increase the number and severity of snowstorms and droughts—in fact, that it already has.

All the more reason to make sure our backyard feeding stations are ready and waiting when the birds need them.

What We Can Do

Creating an oasis in your backyard, with welcoming plants for natural food, nesting, and cover, is the first step to helping birds face the challenge of climate change. As we've seen, our feeders can help birds in a big way, too. Climate change makes it even more important to stockpile an extra sack of seeds or suet cakes, so we're ready when the weather takes a dive.

And let's not forget about the most important part of an oasis—a birdbath.

The southwestern quadrant of our country, where water is already hard to come by, appears to be heading for a real water shortage as climate change continues. "Hotter than Hades," as my mom used to say, and dry as a bone is what seems to be in store, according to all of the predictions that experts have come up with.

The Northwest and Northeast look like they may be getting wetter, the Great Lakes snowier, the Southeast hotter. And the little town in Indiana where I live, well, it falls right on the dividing line—above, it looks like you guys will be getting a lot more rain. Below, it's getting drier, or so the experts predict.

I don't know whether to stock up on flippers to keep afloat, or start digging a pipeline to the river.

But whatever the changing climate brings to our backyards, and wherever our backyards are, there's one thing we can count on: Our birds need a reliable source of fresh water just as much as we do.

Why It Will Work

A reliable source of fresh water is as big a draw as a well-stocked feeder to most birds.

Our "regular" birds are used to visiting the classic pedestal birdbaths we've been putting in our yards for a hundred years or so, so start with one of those time-tested models. Good results are guaranteed, as long as you keep the water fresh and clean. For tips on choosing and using birdbaths, classic or artsy, turn to the Birdbath entries.

But don't stop there. With the possibility of other species showing up in our yards—birds that aren't used to the way we offer water—it's time to consider adding something that reminds them of home.

Many neotropical migrants are particularly drawn to water, but they're accustomed to creeks and lakes. Most fly right by a birdbath, maybe because they don't recognize its shape as a source of water.

A spring-flowering tree abuzz with tiny insects draws wood warblers like this black-throated blue. Put a naturalistic birdbath nearby for double the fun.

I've never quite gotten around to building a naturalistic recirculating creek in my yard, but I did add a fool-'em birdbath one spring, a molded plastic job that looked almost like a real rocky, shallow pool. Lo and behold, over the next few weeks of migration, a sprinkling of wood warblers, vireos, grosbeaks, and other neotropical birds dropped right out of the trees to visit the ground-level basin—the first time most of them had deigned to get a drink in my yard. It sure seemed to me that it was the look of the thing that caught their eye.

For another secret weapon, add a solar-powered fountain or battery operated "water wiggler" to any birdbath to stir up a bit of splishy-splashy water music to catch the ear of passing migrants and other birds. The entry Fountains and Misters will give you tips on setting it up.

Extra Added Attractions

Wherever I've lived, my backyard has been a work in progress. I'm constantly fiddling with things as I see what works for birds—and what doesn't. I look forward to spring and fall planting season, which includes transplanting—moving my bird bushes and other plants to better spots. And I'm always brainstorming new ways to make my backyard seem more like home to all of the birds that happen to come along.

You'll find lots of finishing touches throughout this book, from foods that add a little extra kick, like crushed eggshells to replace calcium during nesting season, to dust baths that help birds keep parasites at bay.

You'll also find tips that will help you support at-risk birds by targeting exactly the foods, feeders, plants, and other elements that they need. To support the eastern towhee, for example, you can add a good-sized area of native shrubs and a log that may entice this ground-nesting bird to tuck its deep cup of a nest in your backyard. If you're a fan of the great crested flycatcher, you can target your efforts toward mounting a nestbox high in a shade tree, letting dead wood remain as a perch if it's not a danger, and adding a butterfly garden. Just think about how your favorite birds live in the wild, and adjust your yard to include some of those elements.

A prominent dead branch on a shade tree may be all it takes to get a great-crested flycatcher to include your yard on its patrols. Add more butterfly plants for bird food on the wing, and sit back and enjoy the show.

Now more than ever, anything we can do to nurture the birds can make a real difference—even if it means just staying educated on issues that affect birds and appreciating what they bring to our backyards. And by offering nourishing foods, a reliable source of fresh water, and plants for cover, nesting, and natural foods, we can help our birds keep singing a happy tune.

As we watch birds eagerly eating at our feeding stations or from our berry bushes, as we see kinglets and flycatchers fluttering over our yard, as we listen to the first peeps from a nest of native sparrows, we can all give ourselves a great big pat on the back.

Birds can rebound, with our help. One by one, our backyards can become the first step on their journey.

One Small Step, One Giant Leap

Funny, but just as it is with our backyards, it's the small things that add up to make a really big difference. You've heard a lot about ways to make less of an impact on the world, and every one of them affects birds, too, whether directly or a few steps removed.

There are lots of little, easy changes we can make in our own daily habits that will have a big effect on birds. Here are some small steps that add up to a giant leap.

- **Buy shade-grown coffee.** This simple change directly affects the health and survival of our neotropical migrants. These birds have been severely affected by the destruction of their winter habitat—which was turned to monoculture coffee plantations to supply booming demand. For details on this important issue, see the Shade-Grown Coffee entry.
- **Switch to organic fruit and vegetables.** It's easy if you do it one kind at a time. Start with apples, for instance; the pesticides used to grow nonorganic crops directly affect the insects that spring migrant birds rely on.
- **Grow your own vegetables, berries, and fruits.** You can get a lot of good eating out of a little patch, and your wrens, catbirds, and thrashers will appreciate the insects in it.
- **Look for the seal of the Sustainable Forest Initiative (SFI)**, the Forest Stewardship Council, or other certifying agencies on lumber, teak patio furniture, and other products made of wood, whether it's pine from North American forests or exotic tropical hardwoods. The seal shows that the wood came from well-managed forests. There's an active movement toward sustainable logging, and it's vital for our birds' survival.

On the Front Lines

"Wish I'd lived a hundred years ago," I've always said. I'd have loved to be one of the explorers, seeing new lands for the first time, exploring nature firsthand.

Immersed as a kid in books by John Muir, E. H. "Chinese" Wilson, Jack London, and other explorers, I spent many an hour wishing I, too, could've been perched in the Sierras reveling in the peaks at sunset, or trekking narrow ledges in the Himalayas, or trying to keep my fingers from freezing in the Arctic. I'd dream about finding plants that were new to most of the world, seeing yaks and elephants, meeting people who lived in ways I couldn't imagine.

Instead, I've lived a very ordinary life. I'm a homebody at heart, so mostly, I just watch the goings-on in my own backyard and gradually get to know the natural wonders in the region surrounding my home.

I've been lucky enough to live in the East, the Midwest, and the Northwest, and I've definitely gotten a feel for those parts of the country. And everywhere I've traveled, I've dived in headfirst to check out wildflowers, birds, and all the other nature around me.

But is walking a dusty farm lane or jouncing along a rutted logging road really "exploring"?

It sure hasn't felt like it. I've still yearned for exploring on a grand scale, like gazing at the Rockies with Lewis and Clark.

But as my friends sometimes say, "Be careful what you wish for."

Today, I definitely feel like a big-time explorer, because the world we're living in is changing right before our eyes.

We're all explorers now, and explorers on the biggest scale imaginable.

Our changing climate is changing everything. Plants, insects, birds, weather—everything is shifting from what we once knew, and every day brings more changes. Most of them are so small that we don't even notice. Others make us sit up and say, "Hey! What's going on?"

It's a brand new world, whether we travel the world or watch our birds through the kitchen window.

There's plenty of exploring to do right in our own backyards. While it may seem that all we're doing is watching birds and filling our feeders, we're really on the front lines of this expedition.

What we see right in our own backyards can shed light on the rest of the situation, because birds are a bellwether that shows us what's going on.

When birds are thriving, we can rest easy, knowing it's a healthy world out there. But when they start to decline, we know that whatever's affecting them is bound to come our way, too.

Welcome to the frontier. What an exciting time to be a backyard bird explorer!

We're All Scientists

Citizen scientists, that is. The information we collect while watching our feeders or counting the nesting birds in our neighborhood is invaluable to science.

Without us, it'd be an impossible task to figure out what's going on with our birds—and what we can do about it.

So it's important to get the word out about what we're seeing. In the entry Citizen Science, you'll find the organizations that welcome—no, that *need*—your input. Those birds you're looking at in your yard are part of a great big picture, and only you have this missing piece.

Every bird count we take part in, every report of an unusual bird at the feeder—it all adds to the information that scientists need to interpret what's going on in the bird world. The comprehensive reports on how our birds are doing are a direct output from the data we "regular" people have helped collect over the years.

Fill the feeders together instead of making it an assigned chore, and kids will soon be bird lovers themselves, eager to help with bird counts for science.

One of the biggest citizen science efforts is Project FeederWatch. In 2008 to 2009, more than 15,000 of us took part in gathering data for this project, which counts birds that appear "because of something you have provided (plantings, food, or water)." You can participate as an individual, a family, or as part of a group; many schools, 4-H, and Scout groups are making it part of their education efforts and collecting priceless data in the process.

Get Involved

We've already seen the kinds of big changes we can bring about by banding together for the birds, because we've done it before.

When Rachel Carson sounded the alarm about DDT with her book *Silent Spring* in 1962, people joined their voices to demand that the deadly pesticide be outlawed. The birds—from our national symbol, the bald eagle, to the robins on our lawns—rebounded in a big way.

When hunters in the 1950s and 1960s noticed that the ducks they wanted in their sights simply weren't there anymore, they restricted daily "bag limits" and stepped up their campaign to acquire and restore habitat in all-important "prairie potholes" and other places where the birds sought refuge. Nearly every species of ducks recovered.

When bird lovers started the original Audubon Society back in the late 1800s, because egrets and songbirds were being killed by the millions for the feather trade and for food, they started a conservation movement that spread like wildfire. We wouldn't be seeing those pristine white egrets in our wetlands today if it weren't for those early bird lovers.

And now it's our turn. By adding our millions of voices to the effort, and putting our money where our mouths are, we can make changes that are just as vital as what we're doing in our backyards. We can encourage the development of refuges, change agricultural practices so our farms include room for birds, and save more wild habitat. So join, donate to, or volunteer at your local nature center and any national groups that catch your interest. You'll find many listed in the Resources section at the back of this book.

Many of us, including me, would like to pretend at times that our great big challenges don't exist. Habitat destruction may seem like something that we as individuals don't have any part in, or it may seem like a problem that's too big for us to solve. And climate change is even scarier to think about, because most of the predicted impacts seem too enormous to contemplate.

We'd like to just go on living the way we've been doing. So instead of looking the challenges in the face and asking ourselves, "What can I do?," we're tempted to comfort ourselves by pretending they're not happening, by staying uninformed, or maybe even by joining those who insist that the challenges don't exist.

But when we start looking at these big problems, we find out that there are lots of ways we can start making changes for the better.

Small changes in the way we live, including taking care of the birds in our backyards, are a great way to feel hopeful about the future.

So why not start a trend? Spread the word by talking to your friends and neighbors about the little things you're doing and why they're so important. Have a bake sale or a plant sale to benefit a conservation group. Get together and mix up a batch of homemade soft-food goodies for the new visitors at your bird feeders. Talk to the kids you know about what they can do and why it's vital. Start your own "block party" for the birds by enlisting your neighbors to making bird havens in their own backyards.

It's a whole new world.

Together, we can make a difference.

Spread the word about bird conservation and raise a little money with a plant sale "for the birds." Dig up samples of your own extra plants, put them in recycled pots, and make it an annual springtime party!

A

ACCESS ROUTES

I cringe when I remember one of my first bird feeder setups. I'd been watching birds my whole life, so I knew that most of them spend a lot more time in the trees or bushes than they do out in the open. And I knew that they rarely make a beeline to get from one place to another. Most of them travel in hops, skips, and jumps, flying from one perch to another.

So what did I do? I put my feeder right out in the open, smack-dab in the middle of a big expanse of lawn. That way, I figured, I would have a great view of the birds that came to eat.

I had a great view, all right—a view of nervous-jervis birds that dashed in to grab a quick bite and then darted away. No wonder they didn't want to stick around: They were sitting ducks for any hawk that happened along, and they knew it.

Once I planted a clump of birches by the feeder, the birds began to relax, and my feeder traffic picked up. And after I broke up that wide open lawn with some other young trees and added a hedge, birds spent a lot more time in my yard.

Happy Trails to You

Even ground birds, such as native sparrows, juncos, and quail, move in on a feeder by fits and starts, working their way from one sheltering plant to the next. It's a survival habit, because using staging areas along the way allows birds to stay safe from predators.

An abundance of cover will bring more birds to your yard. But there's no need to go for the jungle look in your landscaping. Just give the birds paths of plants, plant corridors if you will, so they can move about in safety.

Corridors don't have to be a solid line of shrubs and trees; staggered rest areas work great as bird trails. Aim for a mix of trees, tall shrubs, and maybe a vine-covered arch or two. Plants about 6 to 15 feet tall provide the perching places that appeal to the largest number of birds.

Happy Landings

If your feeding station is out in the open, plant a tree close by so that birds have an inviting place to land as they approach or leave the feeder and while they wait their turn. The ready cover will make them less apt to panic, and they'll be quicker to settle back down to eating after a false alarm. Birches (*Betula* spp.), flowering dogwoods (*Cornus florida*), flowering crabs (*Malus* spp.), redbuds (*Cercis* spp.), and serviceberries (*Amelanchier arborea* and hybrids) offer lots of places to perch and a bonus of bird-approved fruit or seeds.

Group your plants to boost their bird impact. A close trio of young trees is way more appealing to birds than the same trees dotted far apart.

You'll be amazed at how much your feeder traffic increases once you put in some rest stops along the way. Extra cover, even in a small yard, increases your chances of attracting the more wary birds, such as great crested flycatchers, catbirds, and tanagers. And cover will make your other guests more comfortable so that they're apt to visit more often.

The same plantings will serve your birds as waiting areas when your feeders are crowded. Goldfinches can settle on a vine-covered fence or trellis while they wait their turn for niger, downy woodpeckers can scout tree bark for snacks until there's a place at the nut feeder, and titmice can take to the branches until the mealworm feeder is free. You'll get to watch the natural habits of your feeder birds, with a bonus of free pest control.

ADVERTISING

My biggest feeder is a tray filled with a mix of seeds, a scattering of mealworms, and an occasional handful of peanuts or sunflower chips. A lively crowd of mostly house sparrows gathers there, and blue jays, cardinals, titmice, and all my other regulars drop in now and then to snatch a bite.

Red berries shine out loud and clear to foraging birds. The high-fat berries of a flowering dogwood are irresistible to fall migrants like this hermit thrush, which need to pack in plenty of calories for their journey.

The open tray works like a charm to attract bird attention to my feeder setup. It's not the food that's the key—it's the presence of the other birds. That big tray is the most visible of my feeders, so that birds flying overhead can easily notice the activity. A bunch of birds, busily eating, is the best kind of advertising you can get. Their presence means there is food and plenty of it, and that your feeder is a safe place to enjoy a meal.

Want hummingbirds? Advertise with a big splash of red. Six blazing red geraniums, planted in one patch or in a big container, will definitely ignite their interest in your yard. Put your nectar feeder nearby and you'll have daily hummers in a hurry.

Red berries are a great advertising trick to bring not-so-common songbirds to your yard.

Even passing migrants will stop in to take a closer look. Add a fast-growing cherry tree (any sweet or sour cherry *Prunus* cultivar) for summer, a flowering dogwood (*Cornus florida*) or mountain ash (*Sorbus* spp.) for fall, and evergreen hollies (*Ilex* spp.) or hawthorns (*Crataegus* spp.) for winter, and your yard will be an easy sell as a year-round destination for waxwings, bluebirds, tanagers, grosbeaks, orioles, thrashers, and thrushes.

AESTHETICS

Let's face it: Our beloved bird feeders can sure make our backyards look junky. Our eye is naturally drawn to these unnatural objects, especially if the feeders are dotted here and there around the yard. Even feeders made of wood or green plastic catch our eye. Throw in some colorful plastic or artistic glass, and they make even more of a higgledy-piggledy effect.

Oddly enough, the simple solution to feeder aesthetics is "more is less." Collect your feeders into a single group and that messy hodgepodge will instantly become a coherent focal point.

A multi-armed metal pole makes it easy: Just hang your tubes, domes, and the rest of your

To reduce the cluttered look that feeders can give a yard, use a multi-armed pole to corral your collection of bird feeders.

Hey, What Are Those Guys Eating?

If you're new to bird feeding, make sure at least one of your feeders is in plain sight. Birds will find it faster. No matter what kind of birds those first arrivals are, their interest and visible activity will draw others to your feeding area.

Pretty Sweet

To keep your hummingbirds hanging around longer, and to beautify the pole that holds your nectar feeder, plant seeds for cypress vine *(Ipomoea quamoclit)* at its base. The vines will soon spiral their way upward, cloaking the pole in greenery and adding a finishing touch of red flowers for natural nectar. You can also use scarlet runner beans for this trick, but be prepared to unwrap your feeder from this more vigorous vine's twining stems.

feeder assortment from the hooks, and you'll instantly create order out of chaos

You can do the same thing with an 8 foot tall 4 × 4 and four long-armed metal hangers sold for hanging baskets. Use a posthole digger to make a hole about 2 feet deep, insert the 4 × 4, and use your feet to refill and firm the soil into place around it (or add concrete to really secure the post). Attach the hangers to the four sides of the post with sturdy screws, and your custom seed feeder holder will be ready to use.

Add a second pole in another part of your yard for nectar and fruit offerings; the hummingbirds and orioles that are regulars at these feeders won't be interested in your seed selection.

AGASTACHE

Whenever people mention that they can't seem to attract hummers to their feeder, I hand over a starter seedling of one of my favorite hummingbird magnets.

"Plant this, and I guarantee you'll get hummers," I promise.

The joys of hummingbird gardening are addictive, and it's great fun to see my friends' surprise when they learn that it really is as easy as "Plant it and they will come."

Until a few years ago, my top choice for a pass-along plant was bright red bee balm (*Monarda didyma*). It's irresistible to nectar-seeking hummers, and my friends always got the zippy little birds they were craving.

They also got a fast-spreading plant that can take over an entire bed if you turn your back on it. Bee balm often comes down with unsightly mildew, too, and it looks pretty scraggly by the end of summer, unless you whack it back hard to make it branch out with fresh growth.

Bee balm is still a sure bet for hummers. But nowadays, I have another trick up my sleeve for friends who want hummingbirds: agastache (say "ag-uh-STAY-kee"), a plant with much better manners.

You're Getting Warmer

Blue-flowered agastache, or anise hyssop (*Agastache anisata*), has been around as a garden plant for a couple of decades. While it's a good hummingbird enticer, it's not quite of "magnet" rank for the buzzy guys. Instead of hummingbirds, bumblebees swarm the flowers and goldfinches can't resist the seeds.

Orange- and pink-flowered agastaches, though,

are a whole 'nother story. When I first encountered "hummingbird's mint" while exploring the Southwest's canyons many years ago, a swarm of western hummers were so intent at its flowers that I practically had to shoo them away to get a closer look.

When species and hybrids of these Southwest natives (*A. aurantiaca, A. cana, A. rupestris*) hit the market in recent years, I couldn't wait to get my hands on them. Plant breeders are playing with cultivars and crosses of our native agastaches, and hummers adore all of them.

Pink and orange agastaches (this one is 'Firebird') work like a charm to draw in hummingbirds. The flowers bloom for months, and hummers visit them day after day.

Slow Start, Fabulous Finish

The trick with orange and pink agastache is to give it plenty of room; don't let neighboring plants crowd it. It's easy to grow, but it looks very unpromising at the start—just a feeble stem or two that seems too delicate to make much of a show. Don't be fooled. By the height of summer, it will have filled out, and the following year it'll be a real star. In its native home in the dry Southwest, its roots grow under and among rocks where moisture remains, so don't think of it as a true "xeric" desert plant that can get by with just a drop of water. Give your plants a good weekly drink for better growth and more bloom.

These agastaches are way more adaptable than their Southwest heritage suggests, thriving in regular garden soil and conditions from Zones 5 or 6 through 9, as long as they have good drainage. They bloom later than bee balm, and the plant never runs rampant. It stays in a loose, airy clump, with yummy licorice-scented foliage and abundant spikes of orange or pink flowers—and hummingbirds!—from midsummer through frost.

Like all Mint family members, agastache benefits from a little tough love. Cut it back by about a third if it starts to look spindly, and it'll bounce back with a whole new burst of bloom.

AGGRESSION

One of the most traumatic experiences of my childhood was a fight between two male common grackles that I witnessed one day on the walk home from grade school. The birds were along the curb of a busy street, fluttering and pecking fiercely at each other. I thought one or the other would give up and fly away, but they kept at it. All of a sudden, one of the birds went limp and died, right before my eyes.

I'd seen male birds fight with each other before, but I'd never known it could be to the death. Years later, I watched helplessly as two male coots attacked each other in a pond until the stronger bird actually drowned his foe by holding its head underwater.

Usually, it's the male bird that defends his nesting territory—and his mate—by driving off competitors of the same species. Sometimes he even battles his own reflection when he spots this "competitor" in a window or car mirror.

One of the most notorious bullies at the bird feeder, the northern mockingbird will drive away all competition. Give the bird its own tray of raisins, far away from other feeders, to keep it occupied.

If you've ever wondered why a robin or cardinal batters himself against your window, that's what's going on in his little bird brain. Often the bird becomes so fixated on the persistent "trespasser" that he even attacks the window when the reflection is invisible. The only way to put a stop to this behavior is to cover the window on the outside until the bird loses interest.

Mine, Mine, All Mine

A reliable source of food can also be a bone of contention among birds, and fights over food aren't limited to nesting season or to the same species of bird. We've all seen squabbles among sparrows, juncos, finches, and many other species at the feeder, which usually last just a few seconds until the birds give each other a little elbow room.

While most birds call a truce when it comes to feeders, some simply refuse to share. Few birds will stick around when a jay comes screaming in, although I sometimes wonder if they fly the coop because they associate the jay's cries with danger, not because the jay is aggressive.

I don't have any doubts about my red-bellied woodpeckers, though, because they are definitely territorial at the feeder. I wouldn't drop in for a bite, either, when there's a big bird crouching low in a tray feeder, flaring its wings, and jabbing the business end of its long, pointy bill toward anybody that dares to alight.

Thank goodness, only a few birds are real bullies—the kinds that claim food as their territory, even when they're not eating themselves. Northern mockingbirds are notorious for their aggressive behavior; once they claim a nesting or feeding territory, they tirelessly attack trespassers, including people (which has led to a lot of amusing videos—well, "amusing" unless it was *your* head being unexpectedly dive-bombed).

The other biggest bullies on the block? Hard to believe, but it's those itty-bitty hummingbirds. Hummers have an aggressive streak a mile wide when it comes to food, whether the war is over feeding rights to ocotillo (*Fouquieria splendens*) in bloom in the desert or to a nectar feeder in your backyard.

The ruby-throated hummers in my yard, male and female alike, seem to have a particular vendetta against the Carolina chickadees. Maybe it's a matter of similar size, because the hummers don't chase the larger titmice, cardinals, and others. But every time a chickadee ventures out of the treetops, a determined hummer is instantly on its tail, pursuing it 'round and 'round the house like in a comedy routine.

But the real battle royal at my place took place last September, between the hummingbird who had summer-long rights to a nectar feeder and a mockingbird who came for some nearby berries. Guess who won? The tiny rubythroat, in a rout. The mocker was simply no match for the hummer's speed, agility—and needle-nose weapon.

Out of Sight, Out of Mind

When an aggressive hummingbird or mockingbird claims a feeder in your backyard, a quick solution is to add another feeder, out of view, for your other birds. Unfortunately, that's not always as easy as it sounds. Both mockers and hummers often adopt a high perch as their lookout post and they may simply claim the new feeder, too. In that case, it's time for Plan B: Remove the feeders for a few days so that the feathered tyrant moves on.

À LA CARTE

If you want to attract more birds and more kinds of birds to your yard—and who doesn't?—add a few à la carte feeders to your backyard setup. Fill each feeder with a food that has high appeal and you're guaranteed to gain loyal customers.

You probably already have a couple of à la carte offerings: your suet feeder and your tube of niger seed. Certain birds strongly prefer these foods, so the feeders work like a charm to draw in loyal customers. Woodpeckers, titmice, nuthatches, and chickadees are givens at the suet, and goldfinches and other finches are givens at the niger.

These birds are feeder regulars, and they visit more often and stay longer when you give them a selection of feeders dedicated to their favorite foods. Using the à la carte trick is a great way to expand your cast of characters, too. You can fine-tune your offerings to attract tanagers, bluebirds, wrens, and other special birds you'd like to see by matching the food and feeder to the birds you want to attract.

I use hanging feeders for most of my à la carte items, because the instability of a swinging feeder tends to discourage unwanted house sparrows and starlings from congregating. Note that "tends to," though: If starlings decide to swarm my special foods, I remove the food for a while until they disperse. I don't use an anti-starling feeder for special treats because it would also bar larger perching birds, like the gray catbird and brown thrasher, that I'm so fond of seeing.

Better Than Basics

Most of our everyday feeder birds are seed eaters. Well, duh, as my kids would say: Since seeds are what most feeders have to offer, seed-eating birds are bound to be there.

See You Here Tomorrow

When birds can expect to find a favorite food in a certain feeder, their loyalty as customers increases. They can depend on that food source, and that's a big deal in the bird world. So be sure to refill your à la carte feeder with the same kind of food, and keep it in the same location. Try not to let the food run out, especially in summer, when lots of oh-so-appealing natural foods are beckoning from every direction. Once a bird learns that a particular feeder is a reliable source of a favored food, eating at your place will soon become a habit.

If you want to see more chickadees, titmice, woodpeckers, cardinals, and other favorite seed eaters, start by improving their access to sunflower seeds. Add an à la carte offering of black oil sunflower in a hanging feeder, so your friends don't have to compete with the mob of house sparrows or starlings that may be at your main feeder.

The next step is to add foods that your bird friends like even better than sunflower seeds. Add a nut feeder to your setup along with feeders of other treats, and your friends will visit off and on all day, every day, even in the doldrums of summer.

Here's what I keep "hanging around."

- A wire mesh cylinder or square, chock-full of shelled nuts for chickadees, titmice, nuthatches, and woodpeckers. It also attracts wrens.
- A tube filled with sunflower chips for those same birds, plus catbirds and thrashers
- A tube of safflower seed for cardinals and grosbeaks
- A hopper or large hanging wire mesh feeder of gray striped sunflower for big seed eaters, including cardinals, grosbeaks, red-bellied woodpeckers, and jays
- A tube of white proso millet for buntings; they'll eat niger, but they prefer white millet.
- A tube of niger for finches, redpolls, and pine siskins
- An extra-large tail-prop suet feeder for pileated woodpeckers; this one I mount to a post for stability because the pileated's a big bird. (A tail-prop feeder allows large woodpeckers to prop their stiff tail feathers against the feeder for extra support while they feed.)

Special Foods for Special Birds

Most of the really "special" birds, such as the catbirds, orioles, waxwings, wrens, and other species we don't usually see at our feeders, aren't seed eaters. If they were, they'd already be mixing with the finches and sparrows at our trays and tube feeders.

These special songbirds are soft food eaters. They depend on insects and fruits in the wild. Our menu of sunflower seeds, millet, and niger? No, thanks, they say.

Just a few years ago, attracting these interesting birds meant mixing up homemade treats that would lure them in. Peanut butter dough and other DIY recipes still do the trick, but nowadays, you'll find an ever-growing selection of commercially made soft foods tailored to their tastes.

Oddball foods like mealworms, fruit bits, and suet nuggets attract the birds we're all hankering to host, like the bluebirds, tanagers, orioles, and other colorful or unusual visitors. Nut doughs and peanut-butter-based treats have huge appeal, too, to both soft food eaters and seed eaters.

By adding soft foods to your menu, you'll attract more kinds of birds, including the cream of the crop. Old faithfuls will visit more often, too. So start exploring the world of soft foods with à la carte offerings in feeders such as these.

- A clear plastic domed mealworm feeder for catbirds, titmice, chickadees, orioles, tanagers, wrens, and thrushes
- A clamp-on cup-type mealworm feeder for wrens, titmice, and other smaller birds
- A couple of suet logs or wire holders for nut dough, enriched suet, and other molded treats, to attract bluebirds, catbirds, wrens, and thrashers as well as your favorite seed eaters

The gray catbird is almost common at feeders nowadays, a change in behavior as more of us feed birds and offer a varied menu.

- Small plastic feeders that stick to your window with suction cups, to proffer a handful of mealworms, suet nuggets, or other much-loved morsels to small birds
- A bluebird feeder, through which birds enter from a side hole that's too small to admit starlings
- An oriole feeder for nectar and another one for oranges and jelly, which may also attract waxwings
- A fruit feeder on a pole with hooks for grapes to attract catbirds, orioles, and waxwings
- A low tray for feeding raisins and other fruit to mockingbirds, robins, thrashers, and thrushes

ANT MOATS

My son and I were talking at the patio table one fine summer day when his attention suddenly shifted. Pushing back his chair, he headed for the hummingbird feeder, saying, "Check this out, Mom!"

"Yeah, I know," I said resignedly. "Ants."

"But come see them," he urged. "Pretty cool."

"Pretty cool" is high praise from a teenager, so I went to see what all the fuss was about. The wire and metal hook from which the feeder was hanging were covered with marching ants. Those going to the nectar ports were their usual slim

HOW-TO Make Your Own Ant Moat

Here's a quick and cheap way to block ants from your sugar water.

- 1 plastic cap from a can of spray paint or hair spray
- Pointed tool for poking hole
- 8- to 10-inch piece of wire (thick and plastic-coated preferable)
- Waterproof glue or caulk

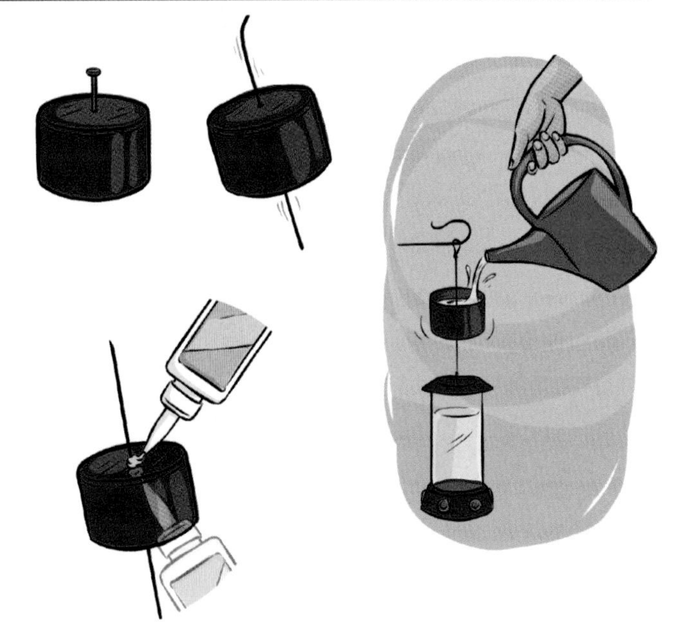

A recycled plastic spray-can cap becomes a freebie ant moat with a little glue and a sturdy length of thick wire.

1. Poke a small hole in the center of the plastic cap. I used an ice pick, but an awl, a nail, or a drill will work, too. Be sure to center the hole so that the moat hangs evenly when you fill it with water.

2. Thread the wire through the hole to make a hanger. I used a doubled length of green floral wire, left over from making birdseed wreaths; it was serviceable, but my moat tends to tilt. Use thicker plastic-coated wire for more stability. Twist each of the wire ends securely into an eye hook, for hanging.

3. Apply glue or caulk around the wire hole on both sides of the cap.

4. Let the glue or caulk dry thoroughly. Then hang your feeder below the moat, fill the cap with water, and say goodbye to your ant problems forever—as long as you remember to refill the moat when the water dries up!

selves. But those on their way back were so full of sugar water that their bloated bellies looked like translucent bubbles.

It *was* "pretty cool," but the cluster of ants at every port and the raft of drowned ones floating inside the feeder . . . well, as my son would say, "Not so much."

I'd been using the low-tech method of deterring ants—a thick glob of petroleum jelly on the wire hanger—and it had worked for a while. But the cool nights of southern Indiana solidified the Vaseline just enough so that the ants could walk across it with impunity. And during the day, the sun melted the greasy barrier, and it dripped off.

2-Minute Trick

You can turn any small waterproof container into a quickie ant moat, if you don't have a spray-paint cap on hand. Clear plastic cups from packaged snacks like pudding, applesauce, or fruit are a great substitute. It's easy to poke a hole in the cup, and you can trim off the top rim with scissors to disguise your recycling trick. A length of wire, a dab of caulk, and you're good to go.

Homemade Moats

It was time to get serious about ant control. Ready-made plastic ant moats are reasonably priced at about $6, but with several feeders to protect, I figured I could rig something up myself rather than shell out more than $30. How hard could it be to fashion some sort of contraption that would hold water to block the ants?

Answer: not as easy as it sounds. The trick is that the cup of water has to sit on the wire above the feeder. And that means devising a leak-proof hole in it somehow.

After a few false starts, I came up with a workable model that takes just a few minutes to put together. All you need is a plastic spray-can cap, wire, and quick-drying waterproof glue, such as Liquid Nails, or clear acrylic caulk. See "How-To" on the opposite page.

ANTI-PEST FEEDERS

"I have a very unusual bird in my yard!" an excited caller told me a few years ago. "He has a really long beak and really long legs. He's beautiful."

I tried to get a better fix. Was it a heron? What size? What color?

"No, not a heron. Brown and green and purple. And big feet."

Wow, now I was getting excited. Sounded like maybe she had a purple gallinule, a waterbird that's highly unusual in the farmlands of southern Indiana.

"I've been feeding birds for years and I never saw anything like it." She was getting impatient with me. "Can you just come tell me what it is?"

"Is it there now?"

"Oh, it's dead. It's in my yard."

Running through every possibility I could think of—gallinule, least bittern, maybe even a duck—I drove to her country home, wracking my brain for unusual birds.

"Here he is," she said proudly, leading me to a small dark lump on the lawn.

"Oh, he *is* beautiful," I agreed, admiring his iridescent feathers and long yellow bill.

"Look at his legs," she noted. "They're so long. And such long toes."

"I love the speckles all over him," I said. "Don't they look like little stars? And, see, if you look close—they're really the white tips of his dark feathers."

"They do look like stars," she agreed. "So what is he?"

"A starling," I replied, and let it sink in.

"A . . . *starling?*" she queried, in disbelief.

If starlings only showed up one at a time and only every now and then, we'd be fixing their favorite food, hoping to coax them in. They *are* beautiful birds.

But there are simply too many of these boisterous birds with big appetites, so that many of us never give these "pests" a second glance. Same with house sparrows and even house finches, at times. As for squirrels, even a single one can keep all birds away from a feeder while the animal eats and eats and eats some more.

Depend on Design

Choosing feeders that are designed to keep out pests—or at least make it more difficult for them to get to the goodies—goes a long way toward protecting your bird food budget. A deer can vacuum a seed tray clean in just minutes, and I've already observed that squirrels don't exactly have dainty appetites.

HOW-TO Instant Anti-Starling Guard

Here's a 2-minute solution to discourage starlings from gobbling your hanging suet. Just poke a hole in the center of a 12-inch-diameter clear plastic plant saucer, and thread it upside down onto the chain or wire on top of your suet cage. Push it down so that it rests on top of the wire cage. Woodpeckers, chickadees, titmice, and nuthatches won't have any problem accessing the suet from below, but starlings—which like a secure perch when they fly in—will be prevented from landing on top.

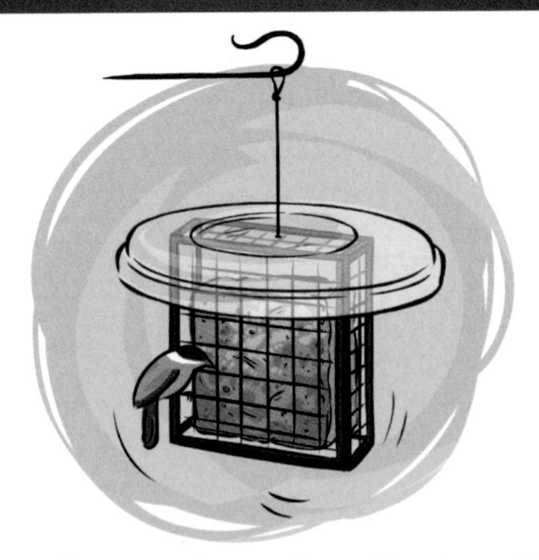

Shield your suet from starlings with a cheap, thin plastic plant saucer.

You'll not only save money by keeping out the feeder hogs, you'll also make sure your invited birds are able to dine in peace.

Manufacturers have come up with some ingenious designs, and some of them are just plain fun to watch. The Yankee Flipper Roller Feeder, for example, offers great entertainment as well as protects bird food—it revolves under the weight of a squirrel, sending the surprised animal harmlessly to the ground.

Shop at bird supply stores or online, and you'll find lots of squirrel-resistant feeders and a few that are marketed as anti-starling. Keep in mind that "resistant" doesn't mean 100 percent pest-proof. If your squirrels are as smart as mine, they won't have any trouble outwitting some of these models. My "No-No" collapsible wire mesh feeder, for instance, is touted as a squirrel-resistant feeder. But it's no challenge at all for my bushy-tailed pals. It only took them a few days to figure out how to hang on while they munch.

Squirrels aren't interested in plain suet or mealworms, but they may go after suet and soft foods with seeds or peanut butter in them. And starlings will greedily scarf up all of these treats. Starlings need a secure landing place, so a domed feeder discourages them. Feeders protected with sturdy wire cages are a safe bet against starlings and squirrels, too. They keep out deer, squirrels, and larger birds including starlings, so you can safely serve up nuts and other higher-priced foods without worrying that the gluttons will get them. The bad news? Caged feeders that bar starlings may also keep out grosbeaks, cardinals, mockingbirds, thrashers, and other desirable larger birds.

A big reason that starlings wear out their welcome in a hurry—they usually arrive in a horde that can gobble your bird food in no time flat.

You'll find specific recommendations of anti-pest feeders as well as other tips to reduce pest problems in the Deer Deterrents, Squirrels, and Starlings entries.

ASSOCIATION

I was so excited about seeing all of my old bird friends when I moved back to Indiana after years in the Northwest—cardinals! blue jays! tufted titmice!—that I put up my first feeder before I even finished moving in. As I hurriedly whacked the wooden tray to a post and poured in the seed, I could hear a big migrating flock of goldfinches twittering away in the trees overhead. Oh boy, I thought, picturing the tray crowded with 100 sunny yellow birds just like when I lived here several years ago.

By the end of the day, a happy crowd of titmice,

That Looks Familiar

Include feeders of typical designs at your station to draw in birds that recognize them as the source of a happy meal. For quick results, include as many of these styles as you can in your feeder collection: a tube feeder; a wire suet-block cage; a hummingbird nectar feeder with red plastic trim; an oriole nectar feeder and fruit feeder with orange-colored trim; a cylindrical wire-mesh nut feeder; a roofed "fly-through" feeder; a domed feeder; and a small, stick-on, clear plastic window feeder.

house sparrows, and cardinals had found the feeder. But to my chagrin, only a few goldfinches had come down to check it out. Not enough niger among the sunflower seed and millet? I poured in another big scoop but had no takers.

A few days later, I added more feeders to my setup, including a skinny tube of niger and a wide tube of sunflower. In minutes, both tubes were swarmed by goldfinches, noisily squabbling over perching rights. Dozens of finches fluttered back and forth to the tubes or waited impatiently for their turn, while my big open tray—a mainstay for many years—went ignored.

It was a real eye-opener. During my 6 years away, the goldfinches in this region had become accustomed to tube feeders and now associated them so strongly with a preferred food that they were reluctant to visit the tray that held the same seed.

If you feed hummingbirds, you know that the buzzy little guys get so fixated on a feeder's location that they return to the same spot each spring, whether or not there's a nectar feeder hanging there. Orioles, too, have learned to associate nectar and fruit feeders with foods they crave. And backyard birds quickly recognize a pedestal-type birdbath, while nontraditional models may take a while to attract bathers.

Now that millions of us are feeding birds, it makes sense that our feathered friends are learning to recognize the visual cues that say "Good Eats." By supplying the kinds of feeders they recognize, you'll increase the drawing power of your yard.

AZALEAS AND RHODODENDRONS

Hugely popular, these evergreen or deciduous shrubs (which all belong to the genus *Rhododendron*) put on a display of flowers that can stop traffic. Not just the human kind—some of these shrubs attract fabulous butterflies, including big, gorgeous swallowtails, and also serve as favorite pit stops for hummingbirds.

With all the azaleas and rhododendrons stocked by garden centers, you'd think at least some of them would be our own native species. Not the case. Even though North America is home to at least 25 wild beauties that range from the Atlantic (*R. atlanticum*) to the Pacific (*R. macrophyllum*) and from Montana (*R. albiflorum*)

to Mississippi (*R. viscosum*), most of the plants at garden centers and in our yards have their roots in China, Japan, and other Far Eastern countries.

What's the problem? True, some natives are a little more finicky than the drop-it-in-a-hole foreign hybrids. But others, including the gorgeous flame azalea (*R. calendulaceum*) I first met along the Appalachian Trail in Georgia, the intoxicating honeysuckle azalea of Florida (*R. austrinum*), and the delicate pink pinxterbloom (*R. periclymenoides*) that lights up the early spring woods in the eastern third of the country, easily adapt to backyard life in a wide range of zones.

With all of the interest in native plants these days, I'm betting that native azaleas and rhododendrons will soon be sharing the aisle at the garden center. In the meantime, you can get to know them at botanic gardens, in the wild, and in native plant nurseries like those listed in the Resources section at the back of this book.

Read Your Soil

You'll need soil on the acid side to grow azaleas and rhododendrons, so if your yard is dotted with limestone outcroppings, you probably won't have much luck. Limestone is alkaline, so keep your plants away from crushed limestone paths or driveways, too. If you're not sure about your soil, buy a pH soil test kit for less than $10 at any garden center and do a quick test of your planting area. The lower the number, the more acidic your soil. A reading of 5.0 to 6.0 is great; 6.5 is getting iffy. Mulch with pine needles or lawn-mower chopped oak leaves to help keep your acid-loving shrubs happy.

Made in the Shade

Whether native or not, azaleas and rhodies offer benefits to birds simply by increasing the amount of cover. Their flowers show off best when the bushes are planted in a group, and birds like them better that way, too, because it makes a bigger sweep of cover. Chipping sparrows, cardinals, and other species hide in them, sleep in them, nest in them, and stay dry under the overlapping leaves when a storm comes along. Towhees, native sparrows, and thrushes scratch in the leaf litter beneath them, and warblers and vireos pick small insects off them.

As for hummingbirds, they visit native and nonnative species alike. But from what I've seen, both in backyards and in the wild, the appeal of the natives is higher. Besides, it's fun to have plants in my yard that remind me of watching hummingbirds in the Appalachians, the Piedmont, on the slopes of Washington's Mt. Rainier, and along the banks of Georgia's Chattahoochee River.

It's easy to get addicted to rhodies and azaleas because there are so many kinds and colors to pick from. Plant a selection of different kinds, and you can have bloom from the first breath of spring to early summer. Most thrive in shade and part shade, but many manage to do fine in sun; read the label to pick the right plant for your spot.

BARK

My kids and I went treasure hunting a lot when they were young. Shells along the Jersey shore, garnets in North Carolina, fossils in the Pennsylvania coal regions. My kids were always way better at it than I was, even though I thought I was pretty quick at noticing things.

After yet another humbling experience, I had to whine.

"How come you find all the good stuff?" I complained to my son who was about 6 years old at the time.

"I'm closer to the ground than you are," he replied.

Good point. And that's exactly why nuthatches, brown creepers, and other short-legged birds are tops at finding bugs on bark.

The furrows and plates of tree bark make a great hiding place for insects in all stages of their

The three-toed woodpecker helps keep trees healthy in western mountains and New England. It clings just fine, although it's one toe short of the typical woodpecker foot.

Spread It Around

Bark-clinging birds are real suckers for peanut butter and other soft spreads. To ward off less agile starlings, I serve the greasy stuff on my homemade bark feeders. The "feeders" are nothing more than pieces of bark hanging vertically; I hammer two nails through the top corners of the bark to attach wire "handles." Five-minute-to-make feeders and free—you gotta love it! Each bark piece is roughly 6 × 10 inches and about half an inch thick, and its ridged surface holds the spread securely. Oh, and as for what kind of bark: Mine happens to be from a tulip poplar (*Liriodendron tulipifera*), Indiana's state tree.

lives, from egg to larva to pupa to adult. Ants, spiders, beetles, and certain moths all depend on the "habitat" of tree bark to shelter them from birds' prying eyes and hungry beaks.

Built for Bark

Songbirds, which pluck insects from leaves or off the ground, aren't equipped to forage for bugs in or on tree bark. The birds' feet are built for perching, not clinging. So you won't see a song sparrow, a catbird, or a cardinal searching for moth eggs on a tree trunk, although they may flutter up to grab a full-grown moth from its resting place.

Nuthatches and brown creepers, on the other hand, are perfectly designed for the job. Their stubby legs, clinging feet, and scuttling style give them a close-up view between bark ridges. And their long pointed bills fit neatly into crevices to extract insect eggs or other tidbits.

Bark is no haven for insects when a woodpecker's around, either. With their keen sense of hearing, downies, hairies, red-bellieds, and other hammerheads zero in on insects beneath the bark and chisel them out with alacrity. The birds' bodies, too, are built for the work, from strong, clinging feet to a stiff tail for a prop.

Whenever I hear bits of bark falling, I look up to find the woodpecker that's flaking them off. It's a great clue to the presence of hairy woodpeckers, which make bark flipping a habit. In the Rockies and other mountain ranges, including the Adirondacks, I often find a three-toed woodpecker above the shower of bark bits.

Hummingbird Herb

It's a cinch to grow basil from seed, as long as you wait until "corn planting time," when the soil warms up in late spring to early summer. Plant the seeds in a big pot to bring hummingbirds right onto your sunny patio, or tuck a few plants into a flowerbed. Once the plant gets big, basil will start to form buds. Instead of nipping out the tips of the branches to encourage more leafy growth for your own use, let some of the plants go to flower. They'll keep putting out new blooms until frost stops the plant in its tracks—and by then the hummers will be well on their way to Central and South America.

BASIL

My gardening style strongly leans toward the casual cottage jumble, but one year some sort of fit of orderliness overcame me, and I actually laid out a formal herb garden. It was a new backyard for me, with nothing but patchy lawn and plenty of sun, and I had a lot of fun setting out brick "spokes" from a homemade sundial at the center and then filling in the wedges with fragrant herbs. Seems like I never get enough pesto, so around the garden I planted a hedge of basil.

In just a few weeks, the tidy layout was looking great, and I was feeling mighty proud of myself.

Then the Bermuda grass moved in. I'd never seen it before, so I had no clue what a notorious bad actor I was dealing with. All I knew was that the more I yanked out, the more of the snaky-rooted grass came back.

Despite my best efforts, the herb garden was soon buried alive in Bermuda. The only plants that didn't get totally swamped in the onslaught were the tallest of them all—the basil hedge around the border. Well, good, I thought, as I mowed the turf that had grown right over my lovely brick paths—at least I'll get some pesto.

Twenty basil plants, it turns out, are enough to make pesto for an army. When I fell behind on harvesting, the basil burst into bloom. And that's when I got the real payoff—an incredible harvest of hummingbirds!

I'd never thought of basil as a hummingbird plant, but then again, I usually pinched out the flowers to keep fresh leaves coming. Basil is in the Mint family, and its flowers are tubular—big hummingbird-appeal hint—and evidently rich in nectar. As late summer migrants stopped in, the crowd of hummers in my herb, er, hummingbird garden grew even faster than the Bermuda grass.

BEST OF THE BERRIES

"Look at your berries!" exclaimed a friend in June, touching a heavily laden branch of one of the three shadblow trees (*Amelanchier arborea*) I'd planted the previous fall.

"These are my $7 clearance trees," I gloated. "I can't believe no one snapped them up. Remember how pretty they were in spring, with those white flowers? But just wait'll those berries ripen—I'll have waxwings eating out of my hand in a week."

Oops—I'd forgotten just how enamored birds are of shadblow, which also goes by the names Juneberry and serviceberry. The very next morning, while the berries were still red, not yet the deep blue-black of ripeness, a couple of catbirds and three robins moved in for the kill.

I'd also forgotten just how fast birds can strip a crop of berries. In less than an hour, they'd plucked every red berry off the small trees. "Wait!" I told them. "Save some for the waxwings!"

Fat chance. Shadblow berries are way too tempting to share, so it's first come, first served.

Luckily, all of the berries hadn't reddened at once, so the waxwings did eventually get a taste. A passing flock spotted them from the air and quickly descended to clean off the last few.

My hand-feeding plan didn't have a chance, because the scattered berries weren't enough to keep the sleek, semi-tame waxwings hanging around long enough to get used to me. But I did get to enjoy a visit from birds that usually don't grace my backyard.

Good Birds Galore

That's the best thing about planting berries: They attract the birds we all yearn for, better than any feeder does. You may see thrushes, bluebirds, waxwings, flickers, orioles, and a host of others. And the flowers that mature into berries attract birds, too—including vireos, wood warblers, and flycatchers—thanks to the swarms of small insects that feast on the nectar and pollen of the blossoms.

The only drawback is that the most appealing berries don't last long. It's funny how frustrating it can be to see the fruit disappearing like lightning,

(continued on page 50)

Best-Bet Berries

Birds eat dozens of different kinds of berries, but some of their favorites are plants that most of us would hesitate to invite into our yards. If I had an acre, I'd nurture a mulberry tree (*Morus* spp.), start a choke cherry (*Prunus virginiana*) hedge, and let some poison ivy grow—you can't beat 'em for bird appeal. But in my small yard, I stick to plants with better manners. Squeeze in as many kinds as you can to extend the appeal over a longer season. Here are enough choices to keep your yard alive with birds from early summer through winter.

SEASON	BERRY	DESCRIPTION	COMMENTS
Early summer	Shadblow, also called Juneberry or serviceberry (*Amelanchier* spp.)	Shrubs or small trees, depending on species, with fragrant white spring flowers, striking red and orange fall color, and dangling clusters of bountiful blueberry-like berries. Zones 3–8, sun to shade	Many shadblow species sprout suckers around the base; prune them off if you prefer a neater look or to keep the clump from spreading.
Midsummer; plant several varieties for a season that can last 6 to 8 weeks	Blueberry (*Vaccinium* spp.)	Deciduous shrubs with hummingbird-attracting flowers and irresistible berries. Glowing red fall color and bright orangish-red stems in late winter. Choose a cultivar suited to your area; those sold at local nurseries and garden centers are usually a safe bet. Zones 3–8, full sun	Blueberries need moist but well-drained, acid soil; if you're not sure, check your soil pH. A pH of 4.0 to 5.0 is ideal; if yours is too alkaline (a higher number), amend the soil with sulfate before planting.
Late summer to early fall; fruit of some species may last into winter	Elderberries (*Sambucus* spp.)	Arching deciduous shrubs with big, flat or conical sprays of tiny creamy flowers, followed by clusters of countless tiny black, blue, or red berries. Bushes usually sucker and spread. Zones 3–9, sun	Explore species that are native to your area for guaranteed bird appeal, or go with those sold for making wine and jam. Plant the bushes as a casual hedge along a fence to help support their stems and to add cover.

SEASON	BERRY	DESCRIPTION	COMMENTS
Early fall	Redtwig dogwood (*Cornus sericea*; may also be sold as *C. stolonifera*)	Deciduous multi-stemmed shrub, reaching 4 to 8 feet tall. Striking red bark in winter. Clusters of small white flowers later followed by white berries. Zones 2–8, sun to part shade	Redtwig dogwood will gradually spread into a thicket unless you prune off unwanted stems. Cutting back old stems in early spring leads to a flush of new growth that will have brighter winter color.
Fall	Arrow-wood viburnum (*Viburnum dentatum*)	A tall deciduous shrub, to about 10 feet, with stems that are so straight they were used by Native Americans as arrow shafts. Fall color varies from one plant to the next; many turn a soft burgundy. Fragrant white flowers, followed by clusters of blue-black berries. Zones 3–9, sun to part shade	'Blue Muffin' sounds like it should be a little cutie, and that's how it was advertised as a dwarf version. It's not. In most gardens, it grows into a tall, large shrub.
Fall	Flowering dogwood (*Cornus florida*)	Small deciduous tree to about 25 feet tall, with a graceful spreading crown. The famed white or pink flowers in spring mature into tight clusters of elongated, shiny red berries. Zones 5–9, sun to shade	The dreaded dogwood blight has simmered down, and both wild and cultivated trees show signs of being able to shake it off. Take a chance; this tree is tops for attracting fall migrants.
Fall through winter	American hollies (*Ilex opaca*)	Evergreen trees, eventually reaching 20 to 50 feet tall, with dense, prickly leaves, fragrant white flowers, and a multitude of Christmasy berries. Zones 5–9, sun to light shade	Deciduous hollies, or winterberry (*Ilex verticillata*), were once a guaranteed way of attracting birds, but some new cultivars—bred for prolific, colorful fruit—have lost their appeal, and the berries go uneaten. Seek out the unimproved species type, and you'll have better luck. All hollies require a male plant to pollinate the female, which bears the big crops.

Shadblow, shadbush, serviceberry, Juneberry are all names for our lovely native *Amelanchier* species. The drift of snowy flowers attracts warblers and vireos; the tasty berries, waxwings, catbirds, and many others.

even though that was the very reason you planted it. Still, as long as they last, the short-lived berries lure more birds of more kinds to your yard.

Teaching birds to associate your yard with food is a huge benefit of planting berries. With any luck, those birds may find something else to their liking—a birdbath, a mealworm feeder, or a later crop of berries—and become regular visitors.

Whether you plant your own favorite blueberries (so you can snitch a few handfuls, too!) or add a holly whose fruit is adored only by the birds, you can easily add weeks of bird watching fun to your backyard—and even more if you include two or three different kinds of bird-beloved berries.

The berries on different plants ripen at different times, and that means birds will keep coming back to check on the crop. A broader selection of berries will bring more bird visits to your backyard.

BILLS OR BEAKS

So, which is it—bill or beak? Either word is fine. Casual bird-watchers, especially those who grew up with the word "beak," still use it; more scientifically minded birders use "bill." I switch back and forth, although "beak" is still the first word that comes to mind when I look at a bird's schnoz.

Whatever you call it, that specialized tool on the front of a bird's head is a huge clue to the foods it likes best. Most families of birds share a similar style of bill, because they eat in similar ways: Think ducks, for instance, that sieve water with their flat spoonlike bills. Or woodpeckers that hammer, probe, and spear with their pointy chisels.

One glance at a bird's bill is usually all you need to determine which foods the bird's most likely to eat.

The Right Tool for the Job

SHAPE OF BILL	ADVANTAGE	BIRDS WITH BILL	NATURAL DIET
Tiny, thin	Pinpoint accuracy	Kinglets, chickadees, warblers, vireos	Small insects
Short, stout, triangular	Powerful nutcracker	Finches, grosbeaks, cardinals, titmice, sparrows	Seeds
Crossed	Extracting seeds from conifer cones; scissoring off fruit	Crossbills	Seeds, some fruit
Moderately long, nearly straight	Adaptable; good for reaching into leaf litter and grass	Robins, thrushes, orioles, blackbirds, tanagers	Insects, fruit, seeds
Long, curved	Ideal for crevices	Wrens, thrashers, catbird, mockingbird	Insects, fruit
Long, sturdy	Powerful grasp	Jays, crows, ravens	Just about anything—nuts, seeds, small animals, carrion
Extra long, extra thin	Accessing nectar in tubular flowers; picking insects out of spiderwebs or from plants	Hummingbirds	Nectar, insects
Large, flattened spoon	Sieving through water and muck	Ducks	Water plants, including tubers; fish and other aquatic creatures

BIRD AND BUSH

A "bird in the hand" is a real thrill. Whether it's a temporarily stunned victim of a window collision or a chickadee that's learned to check your hat for treats, actually touching a wild bird is an unbelievably special moment.

But birds in the bush are a pleasure, too. When you see towhees, thrushes, and native sparrows foraging beneath your shrubs, or hear a cardinal, brown thrasher, or catbird singing from their branches, you know your yard is getting a big thumbs-up. You've created the kind of surroundings that makes "birds of the bushes" feel right at home.

Planting shrubs is a great way to encourage birds to spend more time in your yard and to multiply your chances of attracting nesting birds, too. Remember "the bigger, the better" when it comes to providing cover: To make your yard more appealing to birds, plant your shrubs in groups, instead of dotting them as single specimens around your yard.

You probably already have some shrubs in your yard or around the foundation of your house. Build upon them by extending the plantings with shrubs of high bird appeal, like those you found in the previous entries Azaleas and Rhododendrons and Best of the Berries.

Shrubby cover may garner you a nesting pair of rose-breasted grosbeaks in the eastern half of the country; in the West, the closely related black-headed grosbeak.

Dense, layered plantings spell safety to birds. A garden like this one, with a sanctuary of sheltering shrubs and other plants, appeals to nesting catbirds, grosbeaks, cardinals, towhees, Carolina or Bewick's wrens, song sparrows, chipping sparrows, and other native sparrows.

Native shrubs are a can't-miss choice, because birds are already accustomed to making use of them. But old-fashioned nonnative flowering shrubs, including flowering quince (*Chaenomeles* spp.), weigela (*Weigela* spp.), mock orange (*Philadelphus* spp.), and lilac (*Syringa* spp.), are great additions, too. They're adaptable, fast growing, and trouble free. Birds appreciate their twiggy branches for cover, and their flowers offer a banquet of insects and nectar to songbirds and hummers. Plus the moist, humusy soil beneath the shrubs is prime territory for foraging towhees, native sparrows, juncos, brown thrashers, and gray catbirds.

BIRDBATH BASICS

I'm far from being the world's best housekeeper indoors, but my friends are very tolerant of my messiness (at least so far). When it comes to my birdbath, though, I make a point of keeping it spotless. I've learned from experience that birds won't put up with a neglected bath, and it's harder to regain their loyalty once they're let down.

Fresh water, believe it or not, can be even more of an attraction than the best-stocked feeder. Birds can find food just about anywhere, all on their own, but water's a different story. When natural puddles are scarce, or if birds live far from a creek or pond, your simple birdbath may be the most popular destination in your whole yard. Most backyard birds love a daily sip and an exuberant splashing bath. And once they learn that your water is reliably fresh and abundant, they'll make it a regular stop in all seasons.

So don't think of a birdbath as an accessory—if you want to attract birds, it's as vital as your

The more natural your birdbath, the more unusual species you'll attract. This western tanager isn't bathing in a rocky creek—that's a backyard rock that's been outfitted with a drip tube to attract birds.

Corncob Scrubbie

After your squirrels or woodpeckers strip the kernels from an ear of dried corn, don't toss that empty cob onto the compost pile. Snap it in half and toss the pieces near your birdbath instead. The abrasive cob will do a great job helping you to scrape off grime when your scummy basin needs a thorough going-over. The cob is long lasting, too; it'll serve you well for many scrubbing sessions. Just rinse it when you're done and toss it back onto the ground for next time.

Undercover Agents

Cover an area of at least 20 × 20 feet with shrubs, and you'll attract towhees and possibly thrushes. A smaller strip, about 10 feet long, or a hedge may become home to catbirds, mockingbirds, cardinals, Carolina or Bewick's wrens, and others. Take another tip from Mother Nature, too, and extend the inviting greenery by connecting your new shrub bed to an existing shade tree or conifer; plant the shrubs nearby or underneath it. Birds are drawn to yards where they can move about vertically—from tree to shrub to ground and bac k again—as well as horizontally.

favorite feeder. Keep it brimming, and birds will come flocking.

Naturally, there's a nice big payoff for us, as well as the birds, because it's just plain fun to watch birds taking a bath. Orioles, robins, catbirds, cardinals, and goldfinches are huge fans of bathing, so you can expect to see them splashing with abandon nearly every day. You're also likely to see thrashers, mockingbirds, wrens, bluebirds, blue jays, sparrows, grosbeaks, and dozens of others that relish a vigorous dip. Even starlings are a real joy to watch.

Songbirds don't give a hoot how pretty your handblown glass or gleaming copper basin looks. All they care about is that it offers a reliable source of fresh water.

The key word is "fresh:" A neglected, slimy birdbath will only be visited by birds that are truly desperate for a drink. When I treated my birdbath as an afterthought, scrubbing it out when I couldn't ignore it any longer, I had only a few visitors, and they were all English sparrows.

Once I got into the habit of serving up a sparkling fresh birdbath every morning, the number of daily visitors went through the roof. It seemed like every time I looked, another bird was taking a bath. Even in the dead of winter, my birdbath—a heated model I switch to when the weather turns cold—is alive with active birds.

BIRDBATH PLACEMENT

Choosing a spot for your birdbath setup isn't quite as simple as placing a feeder, because whether you use a simple pedestal style or the latest naturalistic rocky pool, you'll need an outdoor water source and possibly an electrical outlet to power a pump or winter heater.

Convenience to the hose (and electrical outlet, if you need one), a good view, and nearby cover are the three big considerations.

If you have to lug your hose across the yard or snake it around plantings, you're liable to let the birdbath go a little longer than it should between cleanings—or maybe that's just me. After I moved my bath away from my window view (where I used to have to drag the hose halfway across the yard) to a location that was a short, straight shot from my outdoor faucet instead, cleaning became a breeze. At first, I was disappointed not to be able to see much of the action from indoors. But once I carried my garden bench over there and created a nearby sitting spot, I had an even *better* view. And, as usual, a clean basin brought in a lot more bathers.

Make sure your birdbath has enough open space around it so that cats can't sneak up on your vulnerable bathers. A tall shrub or tree nearby will allow your friends to make a quick getaway if they need to and will give them a handy spot to fluff their feathers and preen after their bath, too. I like to plant a pussywillow at my birdbath; it loves the extra water it gets every time I dump the basin.

To slow the growth of algae, keep your birdbath in the shade. Some folks suggest adding a handful of copper pennies to discourage the green slime, but I haven't seen any difference; the coins themselves often get covered with algae, and that just means more to clean. Liquid and other algae inhibitors haven't worked well for me, either; besides, the water still needs freshening every day or two because of droppings, feathers, and other debris.

Fill 'Er Up!

To make birdbath refills more convenient, add a "hose bib," an upright pipe that works like an extension cord for your faucet. Hammer the bib into the ground near your birdbath, and connect it to your original faucet with a hose (you can bury that one in a shallow trench). Then all you'll need is another short length of hose to reach from the bib's faucet to your birdbath. This contraption will give you a handy outlet for refilling the bath. Prices start at about $20, and the setup is a snap.

BIRDBATH STYLES

Birds will accept any kind of container to drink from, as long as they can get a grip on its edge. I've seen them stretch their necks to sip from buckets, wheelbarrows, and deep stock troughs, while keeping a firm hold on the rims. So they'll happily adapt to any style of birdbath you choose—at least to drink from.

Bathing is another story. You'll get nearly instant results with an old-fashioned pedestal birdbath, because birds have learned to associate its shape with water. The basin is at a safe height, too, where the bather can keep an eye out for cats and other dangers.

A container that's reliably full of water will attract thirsty birds, whether it's an artsy glazed birdbath or the ant moat above your hummingbird feeder.

But why stop there? The stores and catalogs are full of beautiful birdbaths that you can add to your lineup, from hanging glass saucers to three-tier fountains. It may take your birds a few days to discover them, but once they do, they'll be back.

Ground-level birdbaths are popular with some birds, too, especially quail. The raccoons that visit my yard were forever knocking the basin of my pedestal birdbath off its stand when they scrambled up to get a drink. A ground-level bath solved that problem by giving the thirsty 'coons, squirrels, and other animals a secure place to get a drink.

If birds are drinking but not bathing in your bath, it's either too deep or too slippery. When it comes to bathing, birds prefer secure footing and shallow water. Lay a brick or a piece of sandstone or other non-slippery rock in the water, so they can wriggle and flutter with abandon, throwing out spray like 3-year-old kids in the tub.

BIRD CONSERVATION

Ever wonder why the Audubon Society uses a great white egret as its emblem? The bird is a symbol of the Society's success. When its ethereal breeding plumes were so in demand for adorning women's hats back in the late 1800s that the entire species was nearly wiped out, a major conservation act spurred on by the brand-new Audubon Society enabled the protected egret to make a comeback.

A great egret in full breeding plumage displays the reason this species was hunted almost to extinction—its feathers were once the height of fashion on ladies' hats.

Birds were already getting a lot of attention before the idea of conservation ever kicked into gear. Bird clubs and societies were popular in Eastern cities and other long-settled areas of the country. For years, boys and grown men had been out climbing trees, sloshing through swamps, and beating the bushes to see who could gather the biggest collection of bird eggs. Ornithologists prided themselves on the size of their specimen collections, with some having "collected" tens of thousands of birds—using guns.

Other people had a more basic interest in birds: They were eating them. An old book in my collection includes a photo of an empty robin's nest which was "knocked to the ground by an Italian," along with a photo of the feathers of two nestlings, "which were taken from it and plucked for the pot."

People shot sandhill cranes for Thanksgiving dinner, and songbirds as well as passenger pigeons were killed by the millions and shipped by boxcar loads to meat markets. Robins were a popular target, because they often gathered in huge flocks that could be netted en masse.

Factor in the fad for feathers, wings, and even entire bird bodies as decorations on the hats every smart woman wore, and the pressure on birds was enormous.

Winter Water

Fresh water is a great lure for birds during cold winter months. Natural sources are likely to be frozen stiff, and birds need clean feathers now more than ever, because dirt reduces the insulating abilities of their feathery parkas. You'll find a variety of heated birdbaths, from a solar model covered by a heat-absorbing black top, to a plug-in heater you can lay in the water, to a pedestal birdbath with a built-in heater. Read the labels or talk to the staff at a bird supply store to choose the right one for your climate and your budget. And if you want the lowest-tech model of all, just set out a clay saucer of fresh water every day at about the same time; birds will soon get used to the bathing hours at your backyard spa.

Conservation Takes Wing

Eventually, it began to dawn on people that they weren't seeing nearly as many birds as they used to. The catastrophic collapse of the passenger pigeon from billions—yes, billions—to zilch was hard to miss. But even robins and cedar waxwings were disappearing, and white egrets with their lovely plumes were just about gone.

Lots of people were talking about it, but George Bird Grinnell, an appropriately named New York naturalist, did something big. As the influential editor of the popular *Forest and Stream* magazine, he started the Audubon Society in 1886, aiming his pitch at the high-society women who were setting fashion trends by wearing the barbaric hats.

His brilliant marketing strategy was an instant success, and with the money and power of the social elite behind it, the new fashion for *not* using feathers caught fire. Grinnell soon gave up the club to focus on other things, but the Audubon Society had quickly developed a life of its own, and people around the world were joining the cause.

Grinnell—who hunted buffalo with the Pawnee, served as the naturalist on Custer's Black Hills gold expedition in 1874, and hung out with Teddy Roosevelt—chose the name of his society to honor the great bird painter and observer John James Audubon, a friend of his family. (The honor seems a little ironic, since all of the birds Audubon painted were shot dead so he could wire them into poses.)

By the time the very last passenger pigeon, Martha, dropped dead off her perch in the Cincinnati Zoo in 1914, the conservation movement was in full swing. Four years later, the Migratory Bird Treaty Act was passed, and America's birds—the great egret among them—finally had legal protection from exploitation.

Strength in Numbers

Conservation societies are even more vital today than they were during the darkest days of the passenger pigeon and great egret. Your membership dollars—whether $5 or a million bucks—help the effort to keep our birds alive and well, so pitch in whatever you can. Get educated about the problems birds face, too, so you can make choices in your daily life that won't contribute to their decline. I buy shade-grown coffee, for instance, because shade-grown coffee plantations help the very same scarlet tanagers I look forward to every May. I avoid buying beef that comes from South America, where rain forests that are vital to our planet's survival, as well as to birds, are cleared for grazing. Every little bit helps.

A Changing Scene

Legally protecting birds from overhunting and the feather trade was a great start, but it wasn't enough to shield them from other dangers. The pesticide DDT almost demolished birds all by itself, because it weakened eggshells so that they crumbled when the mama bird sat on them. Other pesticides poisoned insects that birds depended on, or killed the birds themselves.

Rachel Carson sounded the popular alarm on the pesticide problem with her stirring book, *Silent Spring*, in 1962. The thought of no more birds roused people everywhere to action, and once pesticides were brought under better control, the birds rebounded.

Whew. Big sigh of relief everywhere—until the next problem cropped up: habitat destruction. This one is tougher, because it's caused by simply too many people in the world. As forests are bulldozed, logged, or carved up around the globe, and as fields and meadows are turned to agribusiness, birds by the millions lose their happy homes and their sources of food.

The conservation network has been working on this problem for decades already, investigating alternatives that may spare our birds. Shade-grown coffee, certified tropical lumber, grazing mitigation, sanctuaries and reserves, and a whole slew of creative ideas are being tried. Every little bit helps, but we need some big ideas, too, and conservationists around the world are working together on them.

Just when we thought habitat destruction was the worst thing that could happen to birds, a "perfect storm" began to hit home: Climate change is happening even as we speak, and what the effects will be on birds is anyone's guess. For more details on the threats our birds are facing, turn to the entries Climate Change, Dangers, Habitat Destruction, and Population Decline. And for how our humble backyards can make a difference, read on.

Backyard Sanctuaries

I'm convinced that our backyards are one of the biggest bright spots of hope when it comes to bird conservation. Yes, the kinds of birds we see and how many of them visit will change over the coming years; they're already changing. (See the entries Population Decline and Range Shifts for more details on the big picture.)

But if we do our best to nurture birds right at home, we can make a real difference. We backyard bird-watchers are more than 46 million strong, and that's quite an army to put to work on birds' behalf.

Our feeders, birdbaths, birdhouses, and most of all, the habitat we create in our own backyards can really help if we all work together. And if we add our voices to the conservation cause, we can influence legislators and organizations.

Every single living thing on Earth is connected. Whatever we do for birds will have resounding effects on insects, earthworms, plants . . . everything on our planet. By protecting birds, we all win. The place to start? Our own backyards.

BIRDHOUSE BIRDS

The best birdhouse tenant I ever had wasn't a bird at all. It was an adorable flying squirrel that slept all day and ventured onto the birdhouse roof at dusk, ready to swoop around my yard from tree to tree in smooth, gliding flights. Flying squirrels are unusually tame creatures, and this one wasn't afraid of me at all. When I held out a nut, its huge dark eyes calmly sized me up before it delicately reached for the treat.

Until I saw the squirrel, I'd wondered why this lone birdhouse, of the four I had put up around my little yard, hadn't gotten any takers. Chickadees were in the wren house (the house wren had chosen an old sprinkling can hanging from a hook); tufted titmice were in the maybe-just-maybe-I'll-get-a-bluebird box; and a great crested flycatcher had proudly claimed the giant-size screech owl box. But the flicker birdhouse stood empty—or so I'd thought.

Only a select handful of bird species—plus a few animals—nest in cavities, which is what your birdhouse is. That's the bad news. The good news is that nearly all of those birds eagerly take to a readymade home, so your nest box is likely to have residents almost as soon as you put it up.

So what can you expect to see? About 85 species of the 654 native to the continental US nest in cavities. But don't worry, there's no need to start nailing up the high-rises to accommodate them. Of the 18 species of woodpeckers on the list, you're likely to attract only one or two; ditto with the 7 species of flycatchers, the 12 owls, and so on.

Who-o-o-o's that knocking? An appropriately sized nest box in your backyard may attract a single small screech owl or a pair. Your feathered tenants will help control any mice that scurry about at night in search of spilled birdseed.

Exactly which birds you'll attract depends on which cavity nesters breed in your area and what kind of habitat they prefer to call home.

- In a typical, relatively small backyard with maybe a shade tree and some shrubs, you have a good chance of attracting titmice and wrens, and you may get chickadees or a pair of woodpeckers, including downy, hairy, red-bellied, and flickers. Starlings and house sparrows are likely, too. And you may even attract a screech owl.
- A woodsier backyard, or one that borders a natural woods, boosts your chances for chickadees, nuthatches, brown creepers, other woodpeckers, great crested flycatchers, and owls. Mount your nest boxes at the edge of the woods, not in the dim interior.
- If your yard features or adjoins a large area of open space with mature trees, a woods' edge, or a golf course, your birdhouses may attract bluebirds, great crested flycatchers—and if there's water nearby—tree or violet-green swallows, purple martins, or maybe even wood ducks.
- Do you live in a desert? Look for woodpeckers and ash-throated flycatchers checking out your boxes.
- If your house is on stilts in the middle of a cypress swamp or anywhere nearby, don't forget to put out your nest box for prothonotary warblers.

BIRDHOUSES

I was paging through an old magazine at a local flea market, trying to decide if it was worth the $5 asking price, when my eye fell on an ad that made me reach for my wallet immediately.

"The important part of a birdhouse—It's inside" read the headline for the "Sure Nest," a hollowed-out section of log "copied from the woodpeckers." It promised to suit all hole-nesting birds "from Wren to Bluebird, Chickadee, and Downy Woodpecker."

For only $1.90, including shipping—35 cents extra, west of Mississippi—the birdhouse was a real bargain. Unfortunately, I was about 70 years too late, because the magazine was an issue from 1938.

Still, I snatched it up in hopes that I could finagle a woodworker friend into duplicating the

Chickadees are quick to snag a birdhouse in the backyard, which means you'll get the fun of seeing the fuzzy-headed family. Go for higher quality even though it costs more; a sturdy, well-built birdhouse will last for years.

HOW-TO Five Easy Pieces

Grab one of those old license plates out of your garage, and use it to cover the roof of this fun A-frame wren house. Who knows, that old plate may "drive" a pair of wrens right to the door. And the license plate will help make the little house weatherproof. If you don't have workshop space or tools at home, have the wood cut to size at the hardware store; the cost is very reasonable.

- 2 triangular 6 × 6 × 10-inch pieces of 1-inch-thick untreated pine (for A-frame front and back)
- 6 × 9-inch piece of 1-inch-thick untreated pine (for floor)
- 7 × 8-inch piece 1-inch-thick untreated pine (for roof)
- 7 × 8¾-inch piece of 1-inch-thick untreated pine (for roof)
- Metal license plate
- About 20 5d (5-penny) nails
- 2 eye hooks, any size
- Length of wire, for hanging
- Drill with 1-inch bit for making entrance hole
- Saw

An old license plate makes a rain-shedding roof for a house wren's little home.

1. Drill the entrance hole into one of the triangular pieces, centering it about 3 inches from the bottom.

2. Nail or screw the roof pieces to the slanted sides, overlapping the longer roof section at the top.

3. Nail the floor to the bottom of the birdhouse.

4. Bend the license plate in half over the sharp edge of a sturdy table, and nail it over the roof.

5. Screw in the eye hooks about 1 inch below the peak of the front and back walls.

6. Attach the wire and hang your newly licensed birdhouse.

Three's the Charm

Your local bird supply shop will have a selection of birdhouses that are tailored to the needs of the cavity-nesting species in your area. Instead of dreaming about bluebirds, start with a trio of houses sized to fit three easy targets: house wrens, chickadees, and downy woodpeckers. All of these delightful, friendly birds are very easy to attract to a new homesite in just about any backyard.

illustrated design. It had been invented, I found out, by Count Hans von Berlepsch, a German ornithologist who put up nest boxes on his wooded estate in Thuringia back in the early 20th century, when birdhouses were a new idea.

I get a kick out of seeing the egos that were on display during the glory days of the early 1900s, when attracting and studying birds was a fiercely competitive sport. The von Berlepsch birdhouse caught my eye, because it looked so natural and seemed so inviting. Still, the count's invention was sniffed at by E.H. Forbush, an American bird man, who deemed it a failure in trials.

Forbush didn't get much support for his anti-Count von B campaign. Paul Riis, the superintendent of Rockford, Illinois, parks at that time, was puzzled by Forbush's remarks, because he'd seen the birdhouses work like magic. And the high-society Meriden Bird Club of Plainfield, New Hampshire, set up shop to manufacture its own version after seeing how well the boxes worked.

Interest in birds was at a peak then, and birdhouses were the hottest thing around. People rushed to publish their plans or presented them at bird club meetings, and experimenting was part of the game. ("No bird was seen to enter it," one source reported at the end of the season, about a birdhouse made of roofing paper.)

An old photo in the weighty 1915 *Annual Report of the State Board of Agriculture, Massachusetts* proudly shows "The first red-breasted nuthatch known to breed in a nesting box." If I were a red-breasted nuthatch, I'd have moved right in, too, because the box was beautiful: an arm-thick length of white birch log, bark still on, hollowed out and topped with a flat roof.

I'm still looking for a woodworker willing to experiment with Count von Berlepsch's birdhouse, which apparently is harder to make than it looks. In the meantime, I get fine results with the houses favored by the snarky E.H. Forbush: simple wooden boxes made of sturdy 1-inch-thick pine boards.

BIRDHOUSE MATERIALS

When it comes to birdhouses, there's just no substitute for real wood. It's weatherproof, waterproof, and just as safe for birds as the tree it came from. It's the best choice by a mile thanks to its insulating abilities, too.

On chilly spring nights or at high altitudes, wood will keep out the cold so that your birds stay cozy and warm. On sunny June afternoons—which is when nesting season is at its peak—wood will insulate your little family from

Turn your birdhouses into focal points with flashy paint if you like, or let the wooden box weather naturally to be less visually obtrusive. It's the cavity itself that attracts birds, so your feathered friends will use them, either way.

Barking Up the Right Tree

Inexpensive birdhouses, including many of the models sold at craft shops and flea markets, are often made of thin wood or plywood that's too flimsy to provide good insulation. Here's a simple trick to doctor up those cheap boxes so they better serve your backyard friends: Just glue good-size pieces of bark to the sides and roof of the house. A fast-drying waterproof glue, such as Liquid Nails, will do the job in minutes. If you can't find enough bark shed by trees in your own yard, check with a sawmill, a tree-removal service, or your neighbor who chainsaws firewood; usually they'll have way more than you need, free for the asking.

the heat. Look for birdhouses that are made from wood at least ½-inch thick, or they'll be too thin to provide much insulation.

I like my birdhouses to fade into the background rather than grab the spotlight as yard art, so I buy unpainted wood and let it weather naturally. But if you want to spruce yours up, go right ahead—birds don't mind a plain or fancy paint job on their Home Sweet Home.

Be sure your birdhouse has a roof that completely covers all four sides of the box, with an overhang above the front door. My sister, whose Pennsylvania yard is blessed with bluebird tenants every year, was dismayed one rainy spring because one of her birdhouses had a roof gap that let the rain in. The two bluebird nestlings inside, she sadly told me, had drowned. To prevent disasters like that—which feel even worse because we've invited the birds to use the box—examine the roof of your house to make sure it fully covers the box.

Baby birds, bird eggs, and sometimes even a parent bird on the nest are popular targets of predators. Raccoons, snakes, and your neighbor's cat may all try to enter the little domicile. To keep your new family safe, invest in a predator guard. Visit a bird-supply store to find baffles to mount on the post or tree or tubes to insert into the entrance hole to make it hard for a paw to reach—and buy or make your own. You'll find more info about keeping birds safe in the entry Predators.

BIRDHOUSE PESTS

It's not always easy being a backyard across-the-board bird lover. When starlings or house sparrows take over a birdhouse meant for other friends, it can be mighty hard to feel warm and fuzzy toward them. Both of these introduced species are cavity nesters, and you know what that means—they'll soon be trying out your new birdhouses for size themselves.

Even though starlings look a lot bigger than house sparrows, both birds can squeeze through an entrance hole that's 1½ inches in diameter.

Uh-oh. That's the exact size that eastern bluebirds prefer and very close to the usual specs for western and mountain bluebirds, as well.

It's usually house sparrows that kick out the bluebirds from a backyard birdhouse. Unless the area is really short on nest sites, starlings usually prefer a higher home and roomier quarters than the usual bluebird box. With a little luck, starlings may take over a natural hole rather than force their way into your bluebird box.

But don't bet on it. Western bluebirds, which seem to go for a slightly larger 1⁹⁄₁₆-inch entrance hole, often get displaced by starlings.

If you decide to put up the "Keep Out" sign for starlings and house sparrows, you'll have to say goodbye to the possibility of bluebirds, flycatchers, most woodpeckers, owls, and other bigger birds. Starlings may move into any box with an entrance that's big enough for their bodies, even an extra-large owl box.

But you'll still have plenty of delightful birds to watch. A summer brood of house wrens, chickadees, or titmice is a joy, and you may also attract a pair of downy woodpeckers, nuthatches, or brown creepers. All of these little friends use birdhouses with entrance holes that are 1⅛ inches or smaller. Swallows, too, are still on the list of tenants, because you can use a box with a horizontal slit entrance that's wider than it is tall to accommodate their svelte bodies.

It's up to you whether or not to slam the birdhouse door on starlings or sparrows. Some bird lovers welcome a chirpy family of house sparrows, while others will be driven to distraction by their pushy habits. If you think you'll be irritated instead of charmed, then limit your accommodations to smaller birds that you know will be a pleasure.

I follow the open-door policy myself, and the birds seem to have worked it out so that only my bluebird box hosts a family of house sparrows. It wasn't going to attract any bluebirds anyway, since they live a mile away in summer, but I still groused about the sparrows taking possession.

Sorry, Squirrels

Got a gnawing problem? If squirrels try to enlarge the entrance of your nest box, block their efforts with an inexpensive metal squirrel guard, sold at bird supply shops or from the mail-order sources listed at the back of this book. There's even a classy model made of slate (just $5.99). You can improvise a guard with a piece of sheet metal cut to size, or by gluing on an extra large metal washer that matches your hole.

Aggressive house sparrows drive out favored tenants, like this poor tree swallow, to grab nest boxes for themselves.

Meanwhile, despite all my grumbling, I've also managed to develop quite a soft spot for those fluttery fledgling house sparrows at the feeder. One look at the soft yellow corners of their big, wide beaks, and I'm glad I scattered a few of their favorite mealworms on top of the seed mix. And, because my birdhouses are a variety of sizes, I still get to go "Awww" at the sight of a lineup of young chickadees or titmice and laugh out loud at the goofy fledgling woodpeckers, with their tufts of head feathers sticking up in all directions.

BIRDHOUSE SIZES

Cavity-nesting birds choose their homes in the wild the same way you or I might pick out a new T-shirt: They search through what's available to find one in their size. And because the birds that nest in cavities use sizes from XS through XXL, there's usually one that's a perfect fit.

Birds try out the front door first, because when it comes to the entrance, size matters. Most cavity nesters seek an entrance hole that is just big enough for the parent birds to squeeze in and out. If the hole is too big, larger birds may fight for possession, and predators may enter more easily.

Chickadees and house wrens, for instance, choose an XS tree cavity, perhaps where a branch died off. Titmice and nuthatches are more in the S category, while bluebirds, swallows, and downy woodpeckers go for the M-size holes. Wood ducks look for a size L entrance, like an abandoned flicker home, and owls hunt for the XL or maybe the XXL. Pileated woodpeckers use an XL or XXL home, with a rectangular entrance of 3 × 4 inches.

Small, Medium, or Large?

Keep the T-shirt method in mind when you shop for nest boxes. If you want more kinds of birds in your boxes, just buy (or build) a selection of sizes. Don't want to deal with sparrows or starlings? Stick to size S, about 4 × 4 × 8 inches, with an opening of 1⅛ inches to 1¼ inches, designed for house wrens, small nuthatches, downy woodpeckers, and chickadees. To expand your tenant list, add a birdhouse that's size M (about 5 × 5 × 10 inches, with an entrance 1½ inches to 1⁹⁄₁₆ inches) for white-breasted nuthatches, flycatchers, titmice, swallows, hairy woodpeckers, and bluebirds. To get all but the biggest birds, try a size L box (about 6 × 6 × 12 inches, with an opening of 2 inches to 2½ inches) for flickers and other larger woodpeckers.

A birdhouse adds a touch of homey charm to your yard. You can find nest boxes to suit any style of garden, from the most formal pedestal-mounted showpiece to this one in a rustic meadow setting.

Woodpeckers and other birds that chisel out their own homes can custom-peck the opening to exactly the right size. Those that aren't big on major excavation work, like wrens and flycatchers, look for an opening that's already there. They may try out several before they find one that's just the right fit, or they may re-use the same cavity year after year.

As for the size of the cavity itself, you'll attract most birds with a nest box that is taller than it is wide and that has the entrance nearer the roof than the floor. Most birds can adjust the space to their liking by adding nest materials, or, in the wild, by taking out a little more of the dead wood inside.

BIRDSEED BASICS

Boy, talk about feeling like a dinosaur—when I spotted a bag of big striped sunflower seed in a local farm store last spring, my whole long birdfeeding life flashed in front of my eyes. Suddenly, I felt really old.

Way back in the Dark Ages before birds became big business, when I first started buying seed, there was only one choice: a bag of mixed seed, mostly millets and grains, with a measly scattering of striped sunflower seeds.

I vividly remember how thrilled I was when I found out I could buy just sunflower seed by driving 40 miles to the nearest feed mill. The big seeds were first choice for cardinals, jays, nuthatches, titmice, chickadees, and woodpeckers, and they disappeared long before the rest of the seed mix. To be able to buy sunflower alone felt like a real luxury, and the ready supply meant my feeders were suddenly booming.

Gray-and-white-striped sunflower seeds were once the only kind on the birdfeeding menu. Now, black oil sunflower is the undisputed favorite among birds.

Speaking of aging brains, try as I might, I can't remember when black oil sunflower first came on the scene. I recall being reluctant to try it—why change something that worked great? It turned out that my birds liked it even better. It wasn't only the strong-beaked birds that chowed down on it, either; sparrows and goldfinches were cracking it, too. And the shells didn't make nearly as big a mountain under the feeder as those of the striped kind.

Gradually, black oil sunflower seed managed to become such a standard that it shoved the striped kind right off the shelf.

Fast-forward, oh, 40 years, and that 10-pound bag of striped seed looked like gold to my sentimental eyes last spring. I happily paid the price, which was higher than for the black kind, and took it home to see what my birds had to say.

Painted buntings as bright as parrots (and an indigo bunting) are perfectly happy with a serving of white proso millet. These vivid creatures, native to the lower central part of the US and the Southeast seaboard, were once sold as caged birds.

The Lowdown on Height

Instead of making a mix of your sunflower and millet, serve these basics in different feeders that suit the habits of the birds they attract. Most millet eaters, like juncos, native sparrows, and doves, prefer to eat on the ground and aren't very adept at perching on tube feeders. Use a tray or a hopper feeder, where they can scratch and peck. They'll find plenty to pick up beneath your feeders, too. Chickadees, finches, and other sunflower seed eaters prefer to eat at higher levels, not on the ground, so serve up their seed in hanging tubes or wire mesh feeders.

The finches turned up their noses at it and happily continued picking up the black oil seeds. The cardinals seemed to like it just as well, but if a black seed was closer, they ate that instead. Same deal with chickadees and both white- and red-breasted nuthatches.

But there were some birds that showed a distinct preference for the bigger striped seeds: blue jays, tufted titmice, grackles, and red-bellied woodpeckers.

Since all of these birds had been regularly coming for black oil seeds, too, it didn't make much sense to spend more of my precious pennies to serve them the striped kind, even if I did feel sentimental about it. I put the bag into the metal trash can that holds my collection of bird treats and faced facts: Black oil sunflower seed is No. 1 for feeding birds.

Feeding a Crowd

A big majority of our feeder birds, both in number of species and number of individuals, are seed eaters. Of the 80 or so birds in and around my feeding station in summer, only 6 of them aren't interested in seeds: the pair of Carolina wrens, the Baltimore oriole, the catbird couple, and the robin. In winter, those numbers get even more lopsided, as crowds of juncos and native sparrows move in after migration.

Black oil sunflower is okay for small seed eaters, like white-throated sparrows and their kin, and for our favorite gray-and-white snowbirds, the juncos. But these little birds have to really work at it, or sort through it to find bits of nutmeat dropped by birds with stronger beaks.

Seed mix will satisfy those birds with smaller beaks, but I usually don't bother with an inexpensive basic mix, since there's a single seed that's just as appealing: I buy white proso millet, a common ingredient in seed mixes, by the 50-pound sack, because it's so popular that you don't need to offer anything else besides sunflower.

Now, if your neighbor is serving up the latest specialty seed mixes—the ones that cost almost as much per pound as a steak used to—your birds may go where the grass is greener. But for basic bird feeding, it's hard to beat millet and sunflower. These basic seeds will satisfy a crowd.

Feeding Wild Birds, a landmark study on preferred bird foods published in 1998 by Drs. Aelred Geis and Peter Bromley, compared more than 700,000 observations of birds by volunteers in Maine, Maryland, Ohio, and California.

You'll never guess what they concluded: "Rather than buying mixes," wrote the researchers, "the bird feeder will spend his money more effectively by buying black, oil-type sunflower and white proso millet separately, in bulk from seed or animal feed dealers. Depending on the kinds of birds present, the amounts of these two best foods can be varied to attract the birds you want to see."

Couldn't have said it better myself. Of course, adding special foods to the menu of basics is part of the fun, so you'll find plenty of suggestions in other entries throughout this book.

BIRDSEED GARDENS

Birds have their own ideas about what makes a good garden. This winter, the most popular spot in my yard wasn't around those fancy-schmancy shrubs I had planted just so among the rocks. And the exotic perennials I'd searched high and low to find had zero appeal for the juncos, white-crowned sparrows, and towhees that came calling in the cold months.

What drew them in best was a bunch of dead stems that looked like the "before" photo of a garden that needed help in a hurry.

That unpromising patch was where I spent hours watching finches, native sparrows, towhees, thrushes, and more than a dozen other kinds of birds from early summer right through winter. And it cost me only a couple of dollars to get started.

You can make some birds happy with a "birdseed garden" of nothing but sunflowers. But to attract ground feeders, including native sparrows

A casual spill of 'Sensation'-type cosmos is all it takes to coax goldfinches to come to your yard. Look hard to spot the little birds on bending stems, plucking seeds as soon as they ripen.

and juncos, cottage garden flowers are the secret. These old-fashioned annuals—bachelor's buttons, cosmos, marigolds, zinnias, and others—produce multitudes of seeds, and their branching stems, even when dead, give birds cover while they forage.

"Cottage garden" sounds delightfully romantic, but the historic reality of cottage life was no bed of roses. The flowers that thrived around those cottages of yore were favored because they were cheap, easy, and trouble free. Better yet, they came back every year, sprouting from seeds that dropped to the ground. I add a couple of perennials to the casual mix: blue agastache (*Agastache foeniculum* and other spp.) and purple coneflowers, whose seeds attract goldfinches by the dozens.

Birds home in on all of these plants not because they're pretty, but because they offer nourishing food. Crush a cosmos seed with the back of your thumbnail against a piece of paper. See that greasy streak? Oily seeds are a big hit with birds. A single cosmos flower matures into multitudes of seeds, enough to keep a beak busy for weeks.

Watch for an airy cosmos plant moving when there's no breeze and you'll find goldfinches at work. They cling to the bending stems, extracting seeds as soon as they ripen, even if the petals are still hanging on the maturing flower. At least once a summer, I'll brush past a patch of cosmos and flush out a whole gang of goldfinches I didn't even know was there.

In fall, when seeds really hit their stride, that cottage garden will become just as popular as your bird feeder. Plump black-headed and evening grosbeaks seek out garden balsam (*Impatiens*

Orioles aren't interested in seeds, but they will visit flowers for nectar, insects, and sometimes entire blossoms.

Birdseed Garden Mix

A birdseed garden of sorts may sprout beneath your feeders every spring, but a prettier patch that turns to seeds will draw birds, too. The easy-to-grow plants listed below sprout fast from seed and keep on blooming for months, and they produce so many seeds that there are always plenty falling to the ground for the start of next year's garden. Good thing, because your birds are waiting.

- Agastache (blue-flowered varieties)
- Asters (any kind)
- Bachelor's buttons
- Calendula
- Celosia (any kind)
- Cockscomb (any kind)
- Cosmos
- Garden balsam *(Impatiens balsamina)*
- Marigolds
- Purple coneflower
- Zinnias
- Lettuce (any kind)
- Birdseed mix (any kind)
- Millet
- Safflower
- Sunflowers (any kind)
- Buckwheat

balsamina), snapping up the pudgy, spring-loaded pods before they can explode their seeds in every direction. Pine siskins gather in flocks on the dead stems of cosmos, zinnias, and bachelor's buttons, while purple finches seem to prefer the marigolds.

If you can manage to restrain your tidying-up impulses, let some of these dead plants stand through winter. You'll see golden-crowned sparrows, fox sparrows, song sparrows, and just about every other sparrow in the book scratching about below them, gleaning any seeds that have dropped. Towhees, juncos, doves, quail, and varied thrushes are likely to check out the pickin's, too, if these birds are in your area.

BITE-SIZE BITS

More kinds of birds than you'd expect are big fans of suet and other fats. The trouble is, these birds may not be able to access your suet feeder. Some of them, like catbirds and robins, have a hard time hanging onto a wire cage long enough to grab a bite. And others, like juncos and native sparrows, never even try.

I'll never forget how surprised I was the first time I saw a junco eat suet. I had no idea they ate anything but seeds. Yet this one was eagerly snatching up the bits of chopped beef fat I'd put in the tray feeder on a wicked cold day, when I was worried there was too much competition at the suet cage for my chickadees to get their share.

What an eye-opener—juncos, sparrows, cardinals, grosbeaks, just about everybody except the finches, wanted to, um, chew the fat. Every bite-size piece was cleaned off the tray and the ground as fast as the birds could find it.

Bite-size foods, particularly pelletized food or "bird nuggets," are the latest craze in bird treats. Bird supply stores and online sources offer a whole line of flavored bits, and they're sometimes included in seed mixes, too.

Nuggets and other bite-size bits are a big hit with birds that eat soft foods. If you're lucky enough to have bluebirds in your neighborhood, you'll find that nuggets are another great incentive for these pretty friends to pay a visit to your feeder.

In my yard, robins, catbirds, thrashers, mockingbirds, wrens, and woodpeckers are the main customers for bird nuggets, with an occasional warbler, tanager, or oriole sampling the treats. In winter, when the nearest bluebirds expand their feeding territories from their usual range a mile away, they always stop in for a bite. And any wintering thrushes in the neighborhood, including robins, eagerly snatch them up from low-level feeders.

Seed eaters show an interest, too, especially when the weather turns cold. Titmice, chickadees, and nuthatches all get their share, and juncos and native sparrows pick up even the tiniest bits.

I've had good results with the store-bought kind, but they can get pricey when you're feeding a crowd. Besides, it's fun to make your own.

Unless you have some sort of extruder machine (Would a Play-Doh Fun Factory work? I haven't tried it.), your "nuggets" will look a lot less perfect than the commercial kind. You'll make lumps and bumps and shreds instead of nice, neat cylinders. Still, birds will eat them just as eagerly, and that's what counts.

The technique is simple: All you do is roll the dough between your palms, like you're making

Weed Blocker

A birdseed garden sounds great, but here's something that sounds even better: a no-weeding birdseed garden! Here's how to grow one.

1. After you loosen the soil in your sunny patch, cover the entire area with newspaper, four sheets thick.

2. Soak the newspaper with your hose as you work, so it stays in place, and overlap the edges of the sections.

3. Cover the paper with about 2 inches of weed-free compost, then scatter your collection of seeds (see "Birdseed Garden Mix" on opposite page) onto the compost, willy-nilly, for that cottage-garden charm.

4. Keep the bed moist, and you'll see sprouts in just a few days.

The roots of your seeds will easily penetrate the wet newspaper, but weed seeds in the soil below the paper won't get the light they need to germinate. The only weeds that pop up will be those from seeds that blow in on the wind or are dropped by birds.

Flavor to Savor

Make your own flavored varieties of bird bites by playing with the ingredients in the Corn Nutty Bird Bites recipe. Instead of using ground nuts, try cracked corn or sunflower chips; woodpeckers love them. Or don a pair of rubber gloves and pour a cup of roasted mealworms into the mix for what I call Buggy Bites. Bluebirds, robins, and catbirds appreciate chopped dried fruit in their bite-size treats; add ¼ to ½ cup of just about any kind, from gourmet dried blueberries to run-of-the-mill raisins.

"snakes" of clay. If you're Pennsylvania Dutch like me, you may have used the same motion to make the little ragged lumps of dough called rivels in chicken soup. Your bird nuggets will look a lot more like rivels than clay snakes, because the dough is crumbly, not smooth and elastic.

All of my "recipes"—and I use that term loosely, because usually I throw in whatever I have on hand—begin with a semi-solid fat, like rendered beef fat, vegetable shortening, lard, peanut butter, or a mix of any or all of these. Then I throw in chopped nuts or dried fruit, sunflower chips, or anything else that looks good, and add coarse cornmeal or flour until it all sticks together.

The basic method is the same, no matter what you put into the recipe: Mix up the glop so it's about the consistency of cookie dough. Then break off a small piece of the dough and roll it between your palms while little bits and pieces fall onto a waxed-paper-lined cookie sheet.

I like to keep a few gallon-size bags of homemade bird bites in the freezer in winter, when backyard birds can really use a high-fat handout. But rolling all those lumps at one time is a daunting task. So I keep the dough in the fridge, where it will keep for at least a week, and work at the rolling for about 10 minutes at a stretch.

You'll be able to tell right away if your recipe needs adjusting. Too sticky? Add more cornmeal or flour. Too powdery? More grease, please.

I suspect that the reason bite-size bits are so popular is that they look sort of like an insect or a larva, at least enough to cause a bird to investigate. One nibble, and they're hooked.

CORN NUTTY BIRD BITES

1 cup Crisco or lard
1 cup chunky peanut butter
3 cups cornmeal
1 cup flour
1 cup ground nuts, any kind

1. Line a cookie sheet with waxed paper.
2. Mix all ingredients. Take a small chunk of dough and, holding it over the cookie sheet, roll it between your palms. Small lumps will fall off, which is exactly what you want to happen, because those little lumps are your bird bites.
3. Keep doing this until you have rolled all of the dough into lumps.
4. Serve some of your nuggets in a tray feeder or a mealworm feeder.
5. Spread out the leftovers on the cookie sheet so that they're mostly separated, and put the tray in the freezer for about 3 hours. Once frozen, transfer the nuggets into a zip-top plastic bag and store in the freezer.

BLUEBIRDS OF HAPPINESS

I'm convinced that color alone is the biggest reason we love bluebirds so much. The blue of a male eastern bluebird is so intense, it leaves even me speechless. "He carries the sky on his back," wrote Henry David Thoreau, who was enchanted with the birds.

Bluebirds are harbingers of spring, another reason that they hold a special place in our hearts. Here's Thoreau again, in his February 28, 1859, entry in *The Journals of Henry David Thoreau*, sounding a little grouchy about those who don't share his admiration for the birds: "If there is no response in you to the awakening of spring, . . . if the warble of the first bluebird does not thrill you, know that the morning and spring of your life are past." But that early arrival hasn't always served bluebirds so well. They begin nesting soon after they return, in February or March, and a setback in the weather can starve or freeze both parents and nestlings.

That's where our feeders come in. We can't do anything about the cold, but we can give bluebirds a full belly. And we can boost their daily calorie count with high-fat foods that help their bodies generate heat, even when it's frigid outside.

The trick to attracting bluebirds is to live near where they do. Bluebirds aren't backyard nesters, unless your yard includes or adjoins a big pasture bordering woods. They like open, grassy spaces with some trees, as well as orchards, hedgerows, and woods' edges, so you won't usually see them perched on a privacy fence in suburbia—unless your yard is near their native haunts. Then, it's pretty easy to lure them to your yard by serving up the soft foods they like best or by putting up a nest box.

If your property is big enough to mount a whole bluebird trail of boxes, then, sure, get your landlord business in gear. Bluebird trails, mounted away from house sparrow habitat and monitored for pest birds, have done a world of good for the species.

But if you've got house sparrows chirping at your feeder already, then save yourself some grief. Stick to feeding bluebirds instead of trying to house them.

Ready When You Are

It used to take a special incentive to bring bluebirds to your yard, because these birds don't usually hang out near houses. A bush of ripe berries may catch their attention, or a deep snow may send them looking for food. But now that bluebirds are learning to associate our feeders with desirable

In a tender act of courtship, a mountain bluebird feeds his mate. With three American bluebird species, every one of us has a chance to enjoy these beloved birds, even though most of us have to travel a few miles to find them.

If You Can't Beat 'Em . . .

Putting up bluebird nest boxes in a small-to-middlin' size backyard can be more frustrating than fun. First, you've got to attract bluebirds, which only works if your yard is near their natural habitat. And then you have to deal with house sparrows. Trying to keep the sparrows from taking over the nest boxes isn't easy, even with the new models that supposedly keep them out. If house sparrows are in residence at your place, forget the birdhouses and focus on your feeder. You and your bluebirds will be a lot happier that way.

food, the activity of other birds at your feeding station may be all it takes to get their attention.

Once they flutter in, it's easy to keep them coming back. Just make sure you have their favorite foods on hand. Catalogs, Web sites, and bird supply stores are brimming with all kinds of foods that are tailored to bluebird tastes, including peanut butter dough, special suet cakes, bite-size bird nuggets, and nut butters. It's fun to mix up your own versions of these treats, too.

But the biggest temptation is one that just came onto the market a few years ago: mealworms. I call these creepy critters my secret weapon because they're so irresistible, the birds will practically take them out of your hand.

All three of our bluebird species—eastern, western, and mountain—are year-round residents in many areas, and in winter, their territories stretch out to include a much wider area. If you offer mealworms, nut butters, cornmeal concoctions, and other bluebird favorites, these beautiful birds may keep you company all winter.

Bluebirds Only, Please

Sometimes I'd like to grab my bluebirds and say, "Hey! How about some assertiveness training?" These gentle souls hardly ever put up any kind of fight at all. Even when a house sparrow is kicking them out of their happy home, or a titmouse is being greedy at the mealworm feeder, the bluebird will just sit back and not make a fuss.

Too bad, because that means it's up to us to protect their food from other birds. And that's not easy, since both seed eaters and soft-food birds crave their stuff.

I started with a domed feeder, which worked great at excluding starlings—but left plenty of space for English sparrows. Next, I tried caged feeders, with metal grids or bars that kept bigger birds out.

That's when I realized it wasn't bigger birds that discouraged bluebirds: It was *any* birds. As soon as a chickadee alighted on the grid, the bluebird departed, as if saying, "Oh, no, please—after you!"

Like I said, assertiveness training. In the meantime, though, I finally broke down and shelled out nearly 30 bucks for a "bluebird feeder."

Ahhh. Instant relief.

I'd had my doubts about the feeder, which looks very much like a birdhouse with a clear plastic front and an entrance hole on the side. But it worked like a charm. Within a week, I was hosting two small families of bluebirds, seven birds in all, every day, and going through mealworms faster than the local fish-bait shop could keep up with. Ask about these feeders at your bird supply store, or see the Resources section near the back of this book for mail-order sources.

With their gentle personalities, bluebirds won't mind waiting their turn while other birds use their feeder. Wrens, nuthatches, and downy woodpeckers frequently go in and out of the entrance to grab a few bites of whatever treat I've put in it that morning.

The bluebirds often sit inside the feeder while they eat, perfectly at ease. But the other feeder users enter singly, quickly fill their beaks with choice morsels of chopped nuts, peanut butter/cornmeal dough, or whatever happens to be on the menu, and then make a hasty exit.

It takes a week or two for birds to become accustomed to using the feeder. But once they do, you'll realize it's one of the best investments you've ever made.

Bluebirds range farther afield to find food in winter, so catch their eye with lingering berries on a bush. Bite-size blue juniper berries are a favorite; so are deciduous and evergreen hollies and, late in winter, staghorn sumac.

BLUE TIMES TWO

Blue's an unusual color in backyard birds, so any flash of those feathers makes us sit up and take notice. You can count the true blue birds of North America on one hand: bluebirds, jays, buntings, and a couple of wood warblers, the cerulean and the black-throated blue. (I'm cheating a little bit: bluebirds, buntings, and jays include at least eight mostly blue species.)

Jays and buntings are the blue birds you're most likely to welcome at your feeder, so I've combined them in this entry to give you the blues times two. If you're looking for those "Bluebirds of Happiness," turn to the entry by that name; for more about the warblers, see the Cerulean Warbler and Wood Warblers entries.

From the Sublime to the Strident

While bluebirds are gentle, quiet, and deliberate, jays are raucous, cocky, and full of fire. Whether you love 'em or hate 'em, jays sure liven up the feeding station when they come shrieking in.

What's with the attitude? Maybe it has something to do with their role as the cops of the bird world. They're always alert for any dangers and they scream out a warning that other birds instantly heed. Other backyard birds may not appreciate their habit of grabbing an egg or nestling on occasion, but when it comes to leading a charge against a marauding black snake or kitty cat, there's nothing like having a bunch of noisy, courageous jays on your side.

In their home life, jays are silent and secretive. I'm always extraordinarily pleased to spot a jay's nest, because it's not easy to pinpoint the location, even if you have a strong suspicion they're nesting in your yard. Stealth is their motto when they're building their home and caring for their brood.

Several species of jays patrol North America and nearly all of them wear some shade of blue. They're not as catch-your-breath beautiful as bluebirds, but I look forward to their blue wings flashing toward my feeder.

I even had to rearrange my personal list of most beautiful birds, once I saw the western Steller's jay. I used to think the cedar waxwing deserved the crown of "Most Elegant" American bird; those red dots of wax and that dashing black mask were the perfect accessories for its svelte, sleek body. Then I met the dark and handsome Steller's, with its black crested hood and deep blue body. Oh, boy, talk about smitten—the brooding beauty of this jay is straight out of a romance novel. Move over, waxwings, we have a tie.

Peanuts in the shell are guaranteed to capture the attention of any jay, including the crestless scrub jay.

The stunning Steller's jay has a raucous, grating voice that clashes with its elegant good looks. You'll hear these birds long before you see them.

When I first encountered the crestless jays of the West—scrub, pinyon, and Mexican—their smooth, rounded heads looked mighty odd to this Easterner. Jays? These guys looked more like overgrown bluebirds than blue jays. Next time you visit Disney World, check out the Florida Scrub-Jay Trail (www.scrubjaytrail.org), east of the park, for a look at—one guess—the Florida scrub jay, a bird that's limited to only a part of that state.

Your feeders are bound to attract jays—in fact, it's getting rid of them that may be more on your mind. But why not enjoy your jays? Peanuts in the shell are the No. 1 way to go. Sunflower seeds and other nuts do the trick, too. But jays are omnivores and eat all kinds of other stuff, as well, including bird doughs and nuggets, suet, corn, and other handouts. For making them loyal visitors, though, nothing beats peanuts in the shell.

Loyal Friends—For a While

I always get really excited when I see the first indigo bunting at my feeder (or the first lazuli bunting, when I lived in the Northwest), because I know they're just the start of great things to come.

Buntings arrive early during the spring migration season. And hot on their heels, over the next month or so, will come more fabulous birds: rose-breasted and western grosbeaks, orioles, and tanagers.

There's no missing the arrival of a male indigo bunting at the feeder. Those stunning electric-blue feathers stand out like a spotlight, looking so unreal among the quiet gray juncos and brown sparrows that you may doubt your own eyes.

In the western half of the country, though, you might get fooled by the first lazuli bunting—it looks a lot like a small bluebird, with a ruddy chest and white belly.

A seasonal treat for most of us, the incredible indigo bunting spends a few weeks at feeders every year, during spring migration. Females are quiet brown in color, easy to mistake for a sparrow.

Gardening Jays

The jays of my acquaintance have always shown a strong preference for carrying off nuts and seeds in the shell, rather than eating at the feeder. The habit comes naturally to these birds, which play a vital role as reforesters, stashing nuts and acorns under leaf litter or in the ground. Those tight clusters of multiple sunflower seedlings that spring up in your flowerbeds or elsewhere in your yard—they're the work of jays, which stuff as many seeds into their beaks as they can and then poke them into a likely spot. Let some of those seedlings grow, and you'll get goldfinches when the seeds ripen.

Buntings are a regular treat in spring, when they're flying north on migration, until breeding season begins. You'll see a single male first; if you're lucky, he'll be joined by others in the coming days as more birds filter in.

These incredible birds are only a temporary pleasure, so enjoy them while you can. In a few weeks, once the brown females arrive, they'll pair off and leave our backyard feeders to take up residence in the fields and roadsides where they make their nests.

Indigo buntings are a relatively new phenomenon at feeders. They've only been regulars for a couple of decades, unlike, say, chickadees, which people have been befriending for more than a century.

You won't have to spend a bundle to make buntings happy. Their top choice is humble white proso millet, which they'll nibble for hours. They'll also eat niger and black oil sunflower, but so far, at least, millet is tops. Tray, hopper, and tube feeders suit their style just fine, and they may also eat on the ground beneath your feeders.

Indigo buntings have an interesting penchant for using plastic wrappers in their nests. So if you spot a neat, deep cup attached to a low crotch of a bare winter shrub while you're out exploring the fields and byways, check to see if any trash has been woven in. If it has, you've probably found the summer home of an indigo bunting family. My favorite find was a bunting nest that had an old potato chip bag woven in right along with the grasses.

BOTTLE BRUSHES

Practical Pipe Cleaners

A classic chenille pipe cleaner works just as well as a tiny bottle brush when it comes to getting the gunk out of the skinny tubes and feeding ports of your nectar feeder. Pipe cleaners are terrific for working the dead insects and other crud out of plastic-grid bee guards, too. The pipe cleaners are longer and more flexible than those itty-bitty bottle brushes, so you can pull them through the guard instead of just poking at it. To use a pipe cleaner as your bottle brush, just wet it, put a drop of dish soap on it, and run it back and forth through all of those small openings. For extra scrubbing power, use a jumbo pipe cleaner; it'll swab off all the goo in a single stroke. You can buy generous packs of pipe cleaners for about $1 at craft stores or in the craft aisle of a discount store.

Sometimes there's just no substitute for the right tools. Take the task of cleaning hummingbird feeders, for instance. Oh, sure, you can shake a bunch of dry rice into your feeder bottle to help scrape off the gunk, or you can swab the inside by poking around a bit of paper towel with a chopstick. But nectar feeders need a lot of cleaning, and makeshift methods lose their charm mighty fast when you're cleaning feeders three times a week.

I'd been making do for a while after misplacing my trusty bottle brush. I was living 40 miles away from the nearest bird supply store, and no one else had nectar feeder brushes. Then I shopped online and bought a set of three assorted brushes for the very reasonable price of $5.99.

Congratulating myself on finally having the right tools for the job, I filled the sink with soapy water, set the disassembled feeders in to soak, and picked up the first bottle to start scrubbing.

Oops. The brush didn't fit. No matter how hard I tried to cram the bristles into the opening of the tall glass jar, they simply wouldn't go past the bottleneck.

I looked at the other two brushes: One was a mini brush for cleaning the feeding ports. The other was perfect for my flying-saucer-style feeders, but way too short for the glass bottles.

The hummingbirds were waiting, I knew, and their nectar was already mixed and cooled. Grabbing my scissors, I snipped the long, stiff bristles down to a quarter-inch crew cut all around the wire and finished my cleanup job.

I still use the skinny feeder-port brushes that came with my set. But I replaced the stiff, scratchy, crew-cut bottle brush with a $3 bottle "mop" made of non-scratch foam flaps. It swipes out the crud with a few easy strokes—and slides easily into the necks of my bottle-type feeders. You'll find mail-order sources for bottle brushes of all types near the back of this book in the Resources section.

BRADFORD PEARS

A tidy upright tree with neat, dense branches, a cloud of cloyingly sweet white flowers, and lovely burnished red fall foliage, the 'Bradford' pear (*Pyrus calleryana* 'Bradford') has been a big hit with homeowners and city landscapers alike. Thousands have been planted to line streets and driveways or accent the corner of a house.

These pretty flowering trees can reach 50 or 60 feet tall, but most of them never make it. The neat, upright growth habit creates weak crotches, and once the limbs get big and heavy, the tree can split apart without warning, especially when a windstorm gives them a little extra push. In recent years, 'Bradford' pears have been torn out from along many city streets, so the branches don't conk passersby or crush cars.

There's more than one variety of what most of us lump together as "Bradford pears" or "Callery pears," including 'Chanticleer' and 'Aristocrat'. All were developed from a tree that's native to China, but only the original 'Bradford' has the not-so-nice habit of falling apart when it reaches maturity.

The true 'Bradford' became a popular street and backyard tree in the 1960s, but it's been grown in the United States since the early 1900s. Robins and other birds have always given its small fruits an enthusiastic thumbs-up, and except for its splitting problem, it hasn't caused any problems.

Newer cultivars, such as 'Chanticleer' and 'Aristocrat', which were developed to create a

The Softer, the Better

Ever wonder why birds are attracted to certain fruits and berries only in winter? In most cases, it's because the fruit needs a period of cold to soften it or to increase its palatability by sweetening its taste. Bradford pears of all varieties are an instant hit with songbirds, thanks to the multitudes of small fruits. But you won't see birds at the trees until after the hard little fruits have become mushy. Once they're softened, you'll see waxwings, robins, bluebirds, mockingbirds, and others gather at the trees for weeks, until every fruit is gone.

tree with stronger structure, are a different story. These more recent introductions don't have the splitting problem, but they do have one gigantic red flag: Unlike old 'Bradford', their seeds are viable.

Why's that bad news? Because any plant that attracts birds has the potential to become an invasive pest. Many of the seeds in "Bradford pear" fruits will pass through the birds without being digested. Not a problem with the non-sprouting seeds of the original 'Bradford', but it's a growing concern with other varieties.

When a hermit thrush heads into the woods after gorging on the newer cultivars (including the popular 'Chanticleer', also sold as 'Cleveland Select'), the bird's droppings may be the start of a new seedling tree—or 10 or 20 trees.

The same thing has been happening for decades with Japanese honeysuckle, autumn olive, multiflora rose, Oriental bittersweet, bush honeysuckles, and wintercreeper euonymus. Their fruits are all hugely attractive to birds, and the plants are now crowding out native plants in many places across the country.

Up until recently, ornamental pears didn't contribute to the problem. But now "Callery pears" are on the invasive lists of many states, including Tennessee and Georgia, where the pretty trees are ubiquitous in suburban subdivisions—and rapidly infiltrating fields, woods' edges, and even the native dogwood-and-redbud woods.

If you share the concern, plant a native flowering tree for birds instead, such as shadblow (*Amelanchier* spp.), redbud (*Cercis* spp.), or dogwood

Birds love the fruit of 'Bradford' pears, which is causing a problem of invasiveness with newer varieties. Correctly called Callery pears, the recent hybrids aren't sterile like the true 'Bradford' cultivar.

(*Cornus florida* or western *C. nuttalli*). You may even want to have your newer pear variety removed, to avoid contributing to the invasive problem. And if you already have a true older 'Bradford' pear, enjoy it while it lasts. You'll see swarms of birds at its stinky-sweet blossoms in spring, including vireos, warblers, flycatchers, and others that come for the insects at the flowers, and a whole crowd of characters will seek out those tasty fruits from fall through winter.

BRAZIL NUTS

Some of my discoveries for birds happen entirely by accident, not by design. Take the day I discovered I had run out of shelled peanuts to refill my nut feeder—which happened to be the very day my downy woodpeckers had brought their youngsters to the feeding station for the very first time.

I was feeling a lot like poor Old Mother Hubbard as I dug through my pantry shelves, because my usual stockpile of peanuts was completely gone. Then I came up with a plastic-wrapped tray of shelled Brazil nuts I'd bought for some exotic dish or other and had never opened. With no other recourse, I poured the giant-size nuts into the wire mesh feeder and hung it back in place.

Wow, wow, and wow! I'm pretty sure the downies had never seen a Brazil nut in their lives. But you'd never have guessed that by the way they fell upon the things. The nuts were a solid inch thick of oily meat, and the parent birds could hardly believe their luck. Within minutes, the fledglings had had their first taste, too, and they were yammering for more.

My red-bellied woodpecker bullied his way in to see what all the fuss was about, and soon a hairy and a flicker showed up, too. The little cylindrical feeder was set to swinging as woodpeckers flew in and out, and titmice, nuthatches, chickadees, Carolina wrens, and catbirds grabbed any opportunity they could find to snatch a bite.

I was a little trepidatious because I've known humans with severe allergies to Brazil nuts. But I also trust birds' ability to determine when something is or isn't safe to eat.

Sure enough, there were no ill effects. And, ta-da!, I had a new feeder food that even managed to beat the unbeatable peanuts and pecans that had topped the list for nut eaters up 'til then.

A World of Possibilities

Most of our feeder staples are actually pretty exotic themselves. Niger seed hails from Africa, millet from Asia, and even sunflower seed is only native to birds of the Southwest and Plains states. So experiment with whatever nutritious seeds, grains, and nuts you happen to have on hand—you, too, may happen to hit upon a new food that's an absolute bird magnet. Offer the food in a feeder that birds are already accustomed to visiting, one that you stock with similar, more usual foods, and you may discover that your backyard friends eat the new food with relish.

Brazil nuts aren't cheap ($5.99 a pound in these parts), but because they're so meaty, a pound lasts a while. Besides, a few dollars seems like a reasonable price to pay for a food that keeps the feeder hopping with wonderful woodpeckers day in and day out. I've even used the nuts to tempt downy woodpeckers to eat from my hand.

Now and then, when I hear the raucous holler of a pileated woodpecker in the neighborhood, I race to set out a few Brazil nuts in my open tray feeder and watch to see what happens. Sure seems like a fair exchange for the pleasure of seeing a huge pileated woodpecker who's pretty priceless himself.

BRIAR PATCH

When I grew up back in the '50s, even the new brick ranchers that sprang up in our neighborhood soon each had a berry patch—a little group of red or black raspberries tucked into a corner of the yard, often beside the garage.

Our yard was bigger and so was our berry patch. My mom had planted tart red wineberries she'd transplanted from the woods' edge, as well as blackcaps and everbearing red raspberries, and they'd knitted together into a thicket.

Big or small, the briar patches almost always had a bird in residence—a brown thrasher or gray catbird, with a nest hidden deep in the thorny stems. Bramble fruits bear a prolific crop, and there was always plenty to go around for both us and the birds.

"Watch out for the thrasher—she's on her nest," my mom would warn when we went to pick a few handfuls of berries to top our breakfast cereal. We'd steer clear of the nest, but I'd always sneak a peek, hoping to catch a glimpse of a bold golden eye staring back at me.

Thrashers and catbirds aren't as abundant as they were when I was a kid, but I had sometimes heard a thrasher singing in my neighborhood, although it had yet to come for a visit. Hoping to attract the bird, plus the robins, catbirds, and wrens that are also fond of berries, I planted six red raspberries in a little patch. They came into their own that summer, and the 5-foot-square briar patch was loaded with berries.

Carolina wrens discovered the ripe berries before I did. But with a fresh carton of vanilla ice

Backyard Berries

Any variety of bramble fruit will attract birds, so plant the ones whose tastes you like best or whose growing habits fit your yard. Red raspberries are shorter plants, so if you want an easy care, less rampant briar patch in a small space, give them a try. 'Autumn Britten' produces tons of big, flavorful berries; 'Caroline' is sweet and tasty. Wineberries and black raspberries, such as tried-and-true 'Jewel', are more vigorous growers, good in a bigger space. Raspberries and wineberries grow long canes that bend over and root where they touch the ground; prune them back to about 5 feet to keep your patch in bounds.

A brown thrasher is so secretive around its nest, you may never even know it raised a family in your backyard until the leaves fall.

cream in the freezer and guests coming for dinner, I went to claim my share of the harvest.

I had my arm deep in the thorny bushes, stretching for a fat cluster of berries, when a big rusty bird came rocketing out. My bowl of berries went flying as I leaped back.

Once my heartbeat settled down and the thorn scratches on my arm stopped smarting, I felt mighty honored: The brown thrasher had come to call.

Getting a bird to make its first visit to your yard is the hardest part of attracting birds. For thrashers, catbirds, larger wrens, and robins, a briar patch is one of the most tempting features you can add to your backyard habitat.

BROCCOLI

I used to wonder why little brown house wrens were so interested in my broccoli—the birds weren't vegetarians, were they? One day I finally took a closer look at the lovely broccoli crop I'd already been proudly serving to friends. With a lurch of my stomach, I discovered that some of the "branches" supporting the budding head were actually caterpillars: slim, green larvae perfectly disguised as broccoli stems. Not a find I wanted to share with my previous dinner guests.

"Broccoli worms" are the offspring of the dainty white butterflies that look so pretty fluttering over our flowerbeds all summer. Those are European cabbage butterflies, and, boy oh boy, do their larvae love broccoli. Adult butterflies lay their eggs on the plants, and before you know it, there's a nice crop of protein nibbling the stems.

But wrens are real experts at finding caterpillars. These active little birds forage at mid to low

A Thousand Little Flowers

Later in the season, when the tight buds of your broccoli heads open into a loose spire of small yellow flowers, the plants attract more butterflies—not to lay their eggs, but to sip nectar from the blossoms. To birds, butterflies are simply food on the wing. Just by tucking a few broccoli plants into your yard and letting them bloom, you may attract flycatchers, phoebes, mockingbirds, bluebirds, sparrows, cardinals, and grosbeaks, which'll come to snatch the butterflies right out of the air.

Growing broccoli without pesticides? Look close, and you'll see why wrens and other birds are so interested in the plants—they're likely to be infested with broccoli worms, the larvae of the European cabbage white butterfly.

levels, not in the treetops, so they're great for keeping your vegetables and flowers free of free-loaders.

If you've ever fed a bunch of teenage boys, you have an idea of how hard a pair of birds must work to keep food on the table. It takes an unbelievable amount of food to keep those growing bodies nourished. And 5 minutes after the youngsters chow down, they're hungry again.

No wonder parent birds zero in on caterpillars. Compared to itty-bitty aphids, a meaty, protein-packed 'pillar is like tucking into a 16-ounce steak.

Nowadays, I keep my eating crop of broccoli safe under floating row covers. But I tuck a few extra plants here and there in both my veggie and flower gardens, just for the caterpillars. That simple trick helped convince a pair of house wrens to adopt my yard as their headquarters, thanks to the cornucopia of cabbage worms.

BRUSH PILES

If you've got the space for a good-size pile of fallen branches, you'll find a brush pile is a surprisingly effective and pretty much effortless way to draw in towhees, Carolina or Bewick's wrens, hermit thrushes, pileated woodpeckers, white-crowned sparrows, fox sparrows, and other birds that often forage at low levels.

All you're doing is re-creating an element that reminds them of wild places—and that offers the same sorts of natural food that they like best. These birds are accustomed to looking for food on the ground in the woods or along its edge, so a loose pile of slowly decomposing sticks makes them feel very much at home. They'll find plenty of tasty sow bugs, centipedes, snails, slugs, beetles, and other crunchy critters that dwell in dark, damp places.

The wilder your yard, the better, as far as most birds are concerned. But that doesn't mean you need to turn it back over to Mother Nature. Just borrow some of the elements that duplicate a natural setting and fit them into your space.

I have a small yard, so my brush pile is a little one, about a foot high, 3 to 5 feet long, and 2 feet across. I keep it in a shady back corner, alongside the passive compost pile where I put my fall leaves, pulled weeds, and kitchen scraps.

It actually started because of sheer laziness: After a big winter ice storm, I piled the sticks and branches I collected around the yard and dropped

A loose pile of sticks and branches is just the kind of place a towhee likes to call home. A brush pile will also attract other ground-foraging birds, including wrens and thrushes.

them there, intending to bundle them for curbside pickup.

Out of sight, out of mind. By the time I was ready to tackle hauling away the branches, the pile was already being used by birds. A song sparrow had its nest deep in one side of the pile, and Carolina wrens and catbirds were regularly foraging among the sticks. In fall, a hermit thrush and a wood thrush visited the pile for a few days, and later, a rufous-sided towhee moved in, scratching for food and sheltering there all winter. In spring, blue jays, cardinals, and other birds sorted through to find just the right twigs for nest building.

I've made good use of my discarded sticks, too. The twiggy branches make ideal props for floppy perennials and garden peas. A brush pile is also a perfect place to stash the tough stalks of sunflowers, as well as clippings from shrubs, both of which take forever to break down in a compost pile.

Sticks with a Secret

Start your brush pile in a shady, undisturbed part of your yard, because that's the usual habitat of the thrushes and other birds that will make use of it. Simply pile the dropped sticks and branches from your trees in one spot. You can lay them all in roughly the same direction for a neater look, or drop them helter-skelter; birds will manage to hop about in the pile either way. Rabbits and other small animals may also use the pile for shelter, and the box turtle that took up residence in my yard often headed there on hot days. The branches will slowly decompose, adding nutrients to the soil and feeding the army of critters that live on and in the soil.

BUDGET SAVERS

A penny saved is a penny you can spend on something else for your birds, so why not cut corners wherever you can? Over the years, I've found lots of ways to trim the cost of feeding birds. Here are some of the budget savers I depend on.

- Use your telephone or browse online to check prices at local stores before you stock up on seed. No-frills feed stores usually have the lowest prices, especially soon after the harvest.

Minimize Spillage

Wasted seed is wasted money. Tube feeders are the most parsimonious about doling out seed, because birds withdraw the seeds one at a time. Look for a feeder with a tray attached beneath the tube to catch any overflow, or fashion your own by gluing a plastic saucer or plastic dinner plate to the bottom of the tube. Mounting your tube solidly to a post or pole will prevent it from swinging in the wind and help you save seed from spilling, too.

- Watch for sales at bird supply stores and other outlets; they can be a real deal. Most stores run sales at the beginning of prime feeder season, in fall.
- Bulk seed costs less per pound than smaller packaged bags, but hauling a 50- or 100-pound sack can be a real chore if you have no strong-armed pals to call on. Take along a few extra-sturdy trash bags and a seed scoop, and split up the bag right there at the store.
- Make friends with your closest meat market. Butchers are an unbeatable source for cheap, pure fat.
- Watch for sales on nuts during the prime baking seasons: Thanksgiving and Christmas. Stock up and store those walnuts, pecans, and other nuts in your freezer so they don't go rancid.
- If you live in a region with plentiful nut trees—pecans in the South, hickories in the North, filberts in the Northwest, walnuts just about anywhere—keep an eye out for folks who make a little cash by collecting, shelling, and selling wild nuts. Look for notices on community bulletin boards or in newspapers or for roadside signs and stands. Chances are you'll find a real bargain.
- Even cheaper: Collect and shell those nuts yourself!
- Practice the art of "gleaning:" Ask a farmer if you can look for leftovers in the field. Even the most modern harvesters often miss some ears of corn, and your woodpeckers will appreciate them.
- Start a scrap bag or put a lidded bucket on your kitchen counter to collect any leftover bits of bread, cereal, or crackers (and don't forget the crumbs). Mixed with peanut butter or oils, they're a useful—and free—ingredient in homemade bird treats.
- Increase your feeder collection by making your own holders for special treats. Wide, shallow cottage cheese containers are good for suet and doughs; net bags are fine suet feeders; milk jugs or coffee cans (with their lids cut in half for an entrance) are perfectly usable feeders. Dark brown or dark green spray paint will improve their looks, if you like. Drill holes to insert a hanging wire.
- If meal moths or beetles get to bird food first, your birds won't bother with it. Check a sample of sunflower seeds from the bag you intend to buy to make sure it's not riddled with insect holes.

BUTTERFLIES FOR BIRDS

Birds eat insects. Butterflies are insects. Birds eat butterflies.

I know that's the natural way of things, but I still have some qualms over the question of whether it's fair to invite butterflies into my backyard when I know they have a chance of ending up in some bird's stomach. I always feel a pang when I see the phoebe that sits sentry near the flowerbed snag a dancing butterfly in midair.

Like hummers, butterflies will drink nectar from any color flower, but there's one color that's a real grabber: purple. To a butterfly, purple appears to carry a strong "Come hither" message. Most purple flowers, from butterfly bush (*Buddleia davidii*) to larkspur to the sprawling verbena, are wildly popular with butterflies.

Second-best color: yellow. Think fields of wild mustard, or coreopsis, sunflowers, and other yellow daisies. A cloud of butterflies is always in attendance.

Most purple and yellow flowers are designed just right for the way a butterfly drinks: A cluster of flowers grows close together so that the insect can dip its drinking straw or proboscis into one after the other without leaving its perch.

Some do double duty, luring both butterflies and hummers with clusters of small purple flowers of tubular shape: butterfly bush, agastache (or anise hyssop), salvias, and verbenas.

"You have more kinds of purple flowers than I ever knew existed," a friend commented.

Heh-heh. It's all part of the plot.

With so many flowers to pick from, how do you know which ones are best for attracting butterflies? Easy—any in the big Composite, or Daisy, family, which is now called Asteraceae. Butterflies love zinnias, dahlias, coneflowers, tithonia, and other members of the Daisy family, because the little florets that make up the blossom are a whole bouquet of food.

But there's a trick, because not all composites look like daisies. Some are flat-topped or domed clusters of tiny flowers or florets (yarrow, dandelion, and marigolds), and others are fuzzy (thistles, ageratum, and Joe Pye weed).

So go by color and shape for starters: If the flower is purple or yellow, and clustered, classic, or fuzzy, you've got a winner.

A butterfly garden can bring you some fascinating birds. Flycatchers, phoebes, pewees, kingbirds, and cuckoos feast on butterflies, and so do bluebirds, robins, thrushes, and even woodpeckers.

Butterflies are just another insect food source for birds, although the sight of a great crested flycatcher nabbing one of your swallowtails can be a definite conflict of interests. If you can bear watching the natural food chain in action, plant a butterfly garden for the birds.

CACHES

Saving food for a rainy day is a natural behavior for chickadees, titmice, jays, crows, and acorn woodpeckers. Nuthatches and other woodpeckers indulge at times, too.

These food stores are called caches, and in our backyards they're often in crevices in tree bark, wooden fence posts, and other nooks and crannies where they're likely to go undisturbed. Jays often tuck their loot beneath rocks or leaf litter, or stab them into the soil itself.

But there are tons of good hiding places, and birds are adept at using them, even for a single bit of food. Chickadees may tuck a seed into the bud at the end of a spruce twig or under a bit of lichen or moss. Titmice may cement dozens of insects into a mass on a dead branch, with their own body fluids keeping the cache in place.

Both natural foods and feeder treats are squirreled away by our backyard birds. Boreal chickadees in Alaska hoard spruce seeds; tufted titmice in Mississippi store acorns. And all chickadees and titmice also tuck away sunflower seeds and chips, nuts, and even bits of fat.

The creepiest cache I ever came across was a collection of insects called snowy tree crickets: long-legged delicate critters that provide a throbbing backup on summer nights. Some bird—I never did find out who, but I suspect a chickadee or titmouse—had stuffed dozens of the bugs in the upper window gasket of my old pickup truck, which had sat idle for a few days. When I opened the door to climb in, I was showered with creepy, leggy bird food, some still feebly waving its antennae. I still shudder at the thought but admire the ingenuity involved.

When you see a bird stuffing its bill with seeds or nuts, but not swallowing them on the spot, it's probably planning to add them to its rainy-day fund. Our backyard birds are "scatter hoarders"—they hide their treasures in various places all over their territory, not in one big food bank. So how do they remember where they put it?

Scientific experiments have proven that's it the hippocampus—the part of the brain involved

Most of us never even notice the myriad of insects that live with us in our backyards. The snowy tree cricket is a constant and abundant presence on the summer scene and a favorite food for chickadees and other birds.

Saving for a Rainy Day

Foods that birds highly prefer are usually the ones that they cache. At my feeders, nuts win out over sunflower seeds by a mile. In fall and winter, I make sure to put out a daily handful of pecans, walnuts, and other high-fat nuts, so that my friends who "put food by" have a high-energy meal whenever they need it. To cater to the habits of jays, I offer nuts still in the shell, which are their favored food to, ahem, cache in on.

in memory—that birds call upon to retrieve the food. Birds that cache food have a significantly larger hippocampus than non-storing birds. And no, you really don't want to know how the researchers discovered which part of the brain was at work; sometimes science is not very kind to living creatures.

Chickadee caches have gotten a lot of attention from researchers. Turns out that the birds can remember where they hid their food for as long as 28 days. And not only do they have long memories about hiding spots; they also remember which cache has the highest-fat food, and they clean that one out first. That's a vital survival trick in cold weather, when calories count the most.

CANOLA

Would you buy a bottle of rapeseed oil for your kitchen pantry? Probably not, surmised Canadian growers, who coined the word "canola" (*Can*adian *o*il, *l*ow *a*cid) in 1978. The low acid distinction was an important part of the seed breeding and marketing campaign, because other, unimproved rapeseed was chock-full of erucic acid, which has a bitter taste.

My mother's canary seed mixes, back in the heyday of caged birds, listed rapeseed in the ingredients, and I always wondered what it was. Turns out it's a sunny yellow-flowered mustard, a relative of turnip, which is called *rapum* in Latin. No nefarious associations at all.

Rape (*Brassica campestris*) is one of the most oil-rich seeds around—and you can bet that birds love it, whether it's called canola or not. I scatter it among my flower gardens, to attract butterflies in summer and to nourish native sparrows, juncos, and other birds in fall and winter. You'll find mail-order suppliers of the seed in the Resources section near the back of this book.

Meanwhile, use that bottle of canola oil when you mix up kitchen concoctions for your birds. It's a great source of fat, and they readily eat treats containing it.

Like all fats, canola oil can turn rancid with age. To keep it fresh, store your bottle of oil in the refrigerator, where it will be shielded from heat and light, which can affect the oil.

When you make bird recipes with canola (or any other oil or fat), be sure to put the leftovers into cold storage so they don't spoil before your birds get to enjoy them. If you plan to use the extra mixture within a week or two, just keep it in your fridge. For long-term storage, put the leftovers in the freezer, where they will keep for months.

High-Fat Fix

EASY WINTER WARMUP

Woodpeckers, chickadees, titmice, bluebirds, catbirds, larger wrens, and many other birds will eagerly eat this soft-food treat, and the high fat content of the canola oil will help them keep warm. It takes just a couple of minutes to make.

- 2 cups whole-grain crackers, unsweetened whole-grain cereal, or bread crumbs
- ½ cup canola oil
- ½ cup chunky peanut butter

1. Crush the crackers or cereal. I put them in a sturdy gallon-size zip-top freezer bag, squeeze out the air, make sure the bag is tightly zippered, and step on it.
2. Stir in the canola oil and the peanut butter. I use a hand mixer to make quick work of the job. Depending on the absorbency of your grain-based ingredients, you may need to mix in a little more canola oil to make them stick together.
3. Offer the mixture in a feeder that suits the style of birds you want to attract: Spread it on tree bark or stuff it into a log feeder for woodpeckers, chickadees, and other agile birds; serve it to bluebirds in a bluebird feeder; or put it in a tray, a domed dish, or other accessible feeder for catbirds, mockingbirds, and other perching birds. Store extras in the freezer.

Traffic-stopping yellow flowers are the hallmark of canola, grown for human use. The seeds of canola and other mustards, including the wild ones that sprout in your yard, are sought by native sparrows and other small birds.

CARDINALS AND GROSBEAKS

It's easy to forget how special our common backyard birds really are, until we look at them with a fresh perspective. After living for several years in the Northwest, where cardinals and rose-breasted grosbeaks are nonexistent, I was stunned by the beauty of the birds when I returned to their stomping grounds in Indiana. Gosh, they were gorgeous!

The grosbeaks have remained a thrill, because they only stop in for a few weeks on migration. But the cardinals, I'm sorry to say, have soon faded into just another part of the everyday scenery for me.

Then a couple of filmmakers from England arrived. They were shooting a documentary on John James Audubon in the region, and someone had sent them to my door. The first words out of their mouths? "Your cardinals—they're fantastic!"

Of course they are. It's just that we get so used to seeing our regular birds, we forget how drop-dead gorgeous they actually are.

Grosbeaks are part of the Cardinal family, Cardinalidae. These big seed eaters are among our most colorful birds, with grosbeak species in mostly orange (the black-headed grosbeak), mostly yellow (evening grosbeak), mostly blue (yep, the blue grosbeak), and the dashing black-white-crimson of the rose-breasted. The cardinal and its cousin, the pyrrhuloxia of the Southwest, add red to the list.

A flash of cardinal red goes a long way to liven up a winter landscape in the eastern half of the country and into the Southwest. One of the most common and beloved backyard birds, it readily nests in shrubs and climbing roses.

Goober Gobblers

I didn't know how much my cardinals and grosbeaks loved peanuts until I happened to spill some when I was filling my nut feeder, a wire mesh cylinder. The big birds quickly fluttered to the ground to clean up the peanuts, which they couldn't access in my perch-less nut feeder. The lesson: Make sure you put your treats in a feeder that big birds can eat at. For these large perching birds, a tray or sturdy dish is best, because there's a secure rim to hold onto and plenty of room to maneuver. If you're offering cobs of corn to cardinals, you'll have better luck with a feeder that holds the ear horizontally, rather than vertically.

All of them have strong, heavy bills, made for cracking big seeds. They're big fans of fruit, too, and all of them now eagerly accept fruit at the feeder. Suet is of little interest—at least so far—except to the pyrrhuloxia, but mealworms are a real treat.

Sunflower seeds are the staple for these birds, but there are plenty of other temptations you can add to your list. If you've never tried a fruit feeder, these birds are a great incentive to add one to your collection. Apple is a big draw, but have fun experimenting—when I ran out of ordinary fruit, I served half a pomegranate, and they loved it. Shelled peanuts are another great way to grab their interest. Cardinals are big on corn, too, and will happily peck the kernels off a dried ear. I've never had much luck with safflower seed, but others swear by it; maybe my birds are just slow learners.

CAT AND DOG FOOD

A house a few blocks away from mine always seems to have more than its fair share of cardinals. The birds even congregate around the back door. So I was all ears when the homeowner stopped me on the street to share her secret for attracting the birds.

"The best cardinal feeder," she laughed, "is a bowl full of cat food."

Cat food? I knew blue jays adore pet food, but cardinals? "Absolutely," she told me.

Her bowl of Meow Mix had lured all of the cardinals for blocks around to her place. They were so fond of the stuff, they gathered at the back door if she was late putting out the chow.

Most cat and dog food is heavily based on corn and other grains with some added fats, so it's no wonder birds enjoy it. It may take your crew a while to try a sample, but once they do, you can add it to the menu for an inexpensive dish. It's also great in a decoy feeder to deter starlings, although these soft-food specialists prefer it moistened rather than crunchy. If you've done a good job discouraging cats from prowling your yard (see page 94 for cat-control tips), you won't have to worry about felines eating the birds attracted to the pet food. And if you haven't discouraged cats, your birds will be kitty chow whether or not you put out pet food.

Small pieces are easiest for birds to swallow. But starlings and jays like the stuff so much, they'll gulp down even large kibble.

Cheap Eats

Dry cat and dog foods are packed with nutrition for wild birds, too, so keep a bag on hand in a rodent-proof metal trash can. It's a good budget-stretching alternative in winter, when your feeders are extra busy, and especially when snow drives even more birds to your backyard. Cardinals, jays, and crows or ravens will choff it down whole, or crunch it in their strong bills. To feed a crowd of native sparrows, juncos, towhees, doves, and other small ground feeders, grind the dry pet food in your blender or food processor so it's in smaller pieces that they can readily eat.

CAT CONTROL

My relationship with cats is "complicated," as they say on Facebook. It's a love/hate deal: I love a purring lap cat, but when a stray kitty stalks my backyard, I whip out my anticat device in a hurry. The effect cats have on birdlife is so enormous, it boggles the mind. They prey on adult and young birds, even in the nest, to such an extent that they're considered one of the main reasons birds are declining.

Most people are so used to letting their cats roam free that suggesting they keep their pet indoors instantly arouses resentment. Since I'd rather have good relations with my neighbors, I simply took responsibility for cat control into my own hands.

I start with clapping my hands to scare them off, which usually works for a while. Chasing them a few feet ups the ante, at least temporarily.

But cats aren't dummies. They quickly learned that my bark was way worse than my bite, and as soon as they'd leave the yard, they'd sit down on the sidewalk and lick their paws to show their disdain.

Time to call in the reinforcements. A $15 long-range squirt gun goes a long way to encourage cats to change their habits, and it's totally harmless. As long as you're consistent for the first few days of training, it'll work like a charm. The cats simply couldn't believe I had such a weapon at my com-

Send Cats Skedaddling!

If you don't have the time to personally train cats with a squirt gun "discourager," consider an automated device. The Scarecrow (see the Resources section), a well-made contraption that hooks up to your garden hose, has an electric eye that sends it whizzing into action whenever an animal interrupts its beam. Poke its supporting stake into the soil near your feeding station, and your birds will be able to eat unmolested. To prevent getting sprayed yourself when you refill the feeders, attach a valve with an easy on/off switch between the end of your hose and its connection to the automated sprinkler, and turn off the water before you step into range.

A sprinkler near your feeders will help deter cats and other predators, but birds will usually be unfazed by the "shower." Aim the spray away from the seed itself.

mand, and they ran like the dickens. (If the weather is cold, I aim behind the cat rather than right on the mark, so it doesn't get soaked. I don't want to harm them; I just want to train them to stay away.)

Look for a super squirt gun with a range of at least 20 feet. Mine shoots a strong stream of water to almost 30 feet, and that's enough to encourage cats to make a wide berth around my yard. Repeat the shock treatment whenever a particularly persistent pussycat needs a reminder.

CATBIRDS AND THRASHERS

Here's another shift in bird habits: More and more of us are enjoying regular feeder visits from gray catbirds and brown thrashers, as well as other species of thrashers. The birds do eat some seeds, but mealworms, suet specialties, fruit feeders, and other soft foods are the big attraction. As these foods have increased in popularity with feeder fillers, the birds seem to have learned to associate a feeding station with good eats.

Our landscaping is a big part of the draw, too. These are birds of the bush—the more cover, the better, as far as they're concerned. As our backyard plantings mature, they attract attention from these skulkers, who are hesitant about crossing wide open spaces. Bird-friendly yards that offer hedges, maturing vines, shrubs, and other step-by-step approaches to the feeder put them at ease. And fast-growing fruits—best bet: elderberries—are a huge attraction, because they offer a favorite meal as well as good cover.

Thrashers are large birds, but skilled at balancing themselves on feeders. Soft foods are hugely popular with these long-tailed birds, but they'll eat some seeds, too.

Go with Grapes

If your yard is mostly lawn, a grape-covered arch or arbor will magically increase its appeal to catbirds and thrashers. Grapes grow like lightning; by the second year, they'll cover the arbor with a tangled web of leafy branches. Not only will you get fast cover, you'll also get a crop of fruit that attracts orioles, grosbeaks, bluebirds, and other songbirds to join the catbirds and thrashers. Any kind of grape will work; I'm partial to old reliable 'Concord', but birds like them all. You won't need to worry about special pruning for a bird arbor, either. Just give the vine a once-a-year trim in late winter to keep it in bounds.

CATERPILLARS

Caterpillars are fascinating critters: All the potential of an ethereal winged butterfly or moth in a very unlikely looking package. Birds look at them a little differently: These larvae are food.

With her usual fine sense of timing, Mother Nature has arranged things so that caterpillars are at their peak at the same time bird nestlings are squawking for food 24/7. It takes a lot of grub—or should we say grubs?—to fill a baby bird's belly, so soft, juicy caterpillars are a prime target of parent birds.

That's one of the reasons that climate change can wreak havoc on our natural world: If caterpillars (and butterflies) decline, birdlife is likely to suffer. It's already happening in England, where butterfly numbers have dropped like a rock (by 80 percent for some species) after a series of "freakishly soggy summers," as lepidopterist Patrick Barkham put it in an April 2009 edition of *The Guardian*. ("Once there were swarms of butterflies in our skies," he wrote.) The wet weather wasn't kind to butterflies, but two other factors have also made an impact. Habitat destruction has been rampant in England; Barkham estimates 97 percent of England's natural grassland and wildflower meadows are gone. And a parasitic fly whose larvae eat caterpillars from the inside out has recently invaded England; previously, it was confined to Europe. Climate change is considered the reason its range has expanded. Too bad for Britain's tortoiseshell butterflies, its main target. And too bad for any birds that depend on caterpillars.

We can't stave off all the changes that are already in motion, but we can take a few simple steps to boost the caterpillar populations in our own backyards. Here's where planting native trees and shrubs will really pay off; nearly all of them provide food for some species of caterpillar. Oaks that are native to your area are a top-notch choice, because they're hosts for all kinds of crawly larvae that birds adore.

No need to worry about being inundated with caterpillars, because most of them will be snatched by birds long before you notice them. Imported pests, like the gypsy moth, are another story. But even then, it's best to avoid pesticides because they'll kill other, desirable caterpillars as well as the pests.

Fuzzy Feast

If you have an outbreak of gypsy moth or tent caterpillars in your yard, hold off on the pesticides—you're likely to spot some super birds coming to the feast. Hairy, fuzzy 'pillars aren't popular with many birds (maybe they tickle, going down the hatch), but others eagerly devour them. You'll spot your friends the nuthatches and chickadees taking their share, and jays removing pupae from the cocoons to feed their nestlings. But you may also see sinuous, streamlined cuckoos, both black-billed and yellow-billed, and beautiful bay-breasted or green-throated wood warblers. The possibility of those special birds is enough reason (for me, at least) to tolerate the caterpillars until my feathered cleanup crew arrives.

Fuzzy gypsy moth caterpillars have become a good food source for some wood warblers and for the elegant black-billed and yellow-billed cuckoos, all birds of the forest that may visit your yard for these many-legged morsels.

Caterpillars are eating machines, so your host plants will have a ragged look until new foliage replaces the gnawed leaves. And, boy, do these larvae eat a lot. Here's Etienne Leopold Trouvelot, who was raising silkworms in Medford, Massachusetts, in 1867, when he wrote this in *American Naturalist*: "[O]ne who has had no experience in the matter could hardly believe what an amount of food is devoured by these little creatures.... What a destruction of leaves this single species of insect could make, if only a hundredth-part of the eggs laid came to maturity! A few years would be sufficient for the propagation of a number large enough to devour all the leaves of our forests." Mr. Trouvelot, in case his name doesn't ring a bell, was also the person who introduced gypsy moths to America. After his gypsies escaped into the forest, he gave up on lepidoptera and turned to astronomy instead.

CERULEAN WARBLER

A rare treat, and getting rarer: The tiny cerulean warbler, a pretty turquoise-and-white bird of the Eastern treetops, could be the poster child for the decline of American birds. Its numbers are sinking faster than any other species of bird in North America, and many bird experts fear the trend is irreversible.

Considering what this bird is up against, it's a wonder there are any ceruleans left at all. Its forest habitat both in this country and on its wintering grounds has been bulldozed, logged, and otherwise made to disappear. And what's left has been carved up into chunks that give the parasitic brown-headed cowbird a chance to lay eggs in cerulean warblers' nests.

The beautiful cerulean warbler is a victim of our own practices. It's a common target of brown-headed cowbirds, which parasitize its nest, due to forest fragmentation.

Got the Blues?

Wood warblers can show up anywhere during the flood of spring migration. Watch for the cerulean and the black-throated blue in the trees in your own yard in April, and keep an eye on your soft-food feeders, especially the mealworm dish, for a flash of precious blue feathers.

Maybe being forced to take care of those baby cowbirds has exhausted the cerulean warblers to near-endangered status. The impostor nestling is at least twice the size of its diminutive parents, who probably wear themselves to a frazzle finding bugs to shove down its gaping maw. Worse yet, the cerulean couple aren't raising any offspring of their own because the cowbird has usurped them.

Another reason we'll probably never see ceruleans at our mealworm feeders is because of that morning cup of cappuccino we so enjoy. Coffee plants bear most abundantly in sun, and that fact has led to the leveling of the Central American forests where this warbler used to spend winter. The increased popularity of coffee means more land stripped of trees, and that means fewer warblers. You'll find more details about these problems in the entry Habitat Destruction.

Meanwhile, if you want to catch a glimpse of this little blue bird, listen for its high-pitched buzz in tall forest trees near water in the eastern half of the country during nesting season. Or watch for the sky-blue cerulean and its dark cousin, the black-throated blue warbler, as waves of warblers—a phenomenon I hope we never see the end of—pass through during spring migration.

Cuppa shade-grown coffee, anyone?

CHICKADEES AND TITMICE

These little gray bird cousins have been friends of humankind for hundreds of years—much longer than most feeder birds. Old books refer to them as "confiding," a quaint way to describe their trusting nature.

While they do keep a little bit of distance between us and them, they don't panic when they spot a human, even in the wild. Instead of fleeing out of sight, they're apt to come close to investigate, swinging from a nearby branch tip to check us out.

Five species of chickadees and five titmouse species give everyone across the country enough to enjoy, and two more species add to the fun in the extreme Southwest and in Alaska. Whatever species you host in your region, you'll find that these friendly little birds are easy to please at the feeder. Nuts are No. 1 with them, but they eagerly eat sunflower seeds and suet, too. If you want to entertain a crowd, add sunflower chips, seed blocks, peanutty treats, bird doughs, nut butters, and mealworms to the menu.

"Tits," an old word for small birds that's still used for European cousins of our chickadees and titmice, are popular research subjects for scientists, so we know more about their lives than those of most birds. For more fascinating tidbits about these little high-energy friends, check the entries Caches and Cold.

Eating Out of Your Hand

Chickadees are among the easiest backyard birds to hand tame, if you're so inclined. (Red-breasted nuthatches and redpolls can be even more "confiding," to the point that they'll take food from your hand the first time you encounter them.) All it takes is patience—and a little bit of trickery.

A bird in the hand is an incredible thrill, and all species of chickadees are among the most trusting birds around. All it takes is a handful of temptations and some patience. This little guy is a mountain chickadee.

1. The trick? Remove or empty all of the feeders that your chickadees visit, except for one that they favor.

2. Stand quietly beside the feeder, with your hand outstretched and a few walnut pieces in your palm. If it's a cold, snowy morning, it may take just a few minutes to win a chickadee's complete confidence, but if the weather isn't frightful, you may need an hour's worth of patience. If standing is hard on you, settle yourself in a patio chair by the feeder. Rest your hand in or on the feeder to be more comfortable.

3. Remain very still, and watch your eye movements, too; keep looking down instead of meeting the bird's bright black eyes.

4. Once the chickadee alights on your fingers, you've made the big breakthrough. Let the bird eat all the nutmeats and then try it again. Rehang the feeders you removed.

5. Repeat the trick frequently, so chickadees learn to associate you with food. Once they do, you'll know it—they'll be eagerly waiting as soon as you step out the door, and you'd better have the walnuts ready!

Another aid to hand-taming your chickadees is keeping a schedule: Serve a small helping of their favorite nuts at the same time every morning, and soon the birds will learn to anticipate the breakfast hour. They'll be waiting when you step out the door. Then it's usually a cinch to entice them to take the treats from your outstretched hand.

Treats for the Tree

Try these bird-approved "gifts" to decorate your outdoor Christmas tree.

- **Chickadee treat baskets.** Craft stores sell tiny baskets, just a couple of inches in diameter, for pocket change. Stuff the baskets with suet or with your favorite soft bird food dough, and tie them to the branches with snippets of red ribbon or jute twine.
- **Bedecked pinecones.** Smear peanut butter or suet between the scales of pinecones, and hang them for titmice, chickadees, woodpeckers, and wrens. Keep the suet to the bottom half of the cone, so birds can land on the top.
- **Goodie bags.** Save your festive red plastic mesh onion bags to cut into squares and fill with dried fruit, nuts, or suet. Tie the ends together tightly with twine, and knot them onto the branches.

Hang bird-approved "ornaments" on an outdoor tree to celebrate the season.

- **Christmas corn.** Break ears of dried corn into halves or thirds, wrap florists' wire around them, and hang for jays, woodpeckers, and cardinals.
- **Stars 'n' bars.** Shape some stars, bars, and hearts out of a mixture of sunflower chips or other seeds and gelatin; you'll find the recipe in the entry Molded Treats.
- **Apple slice garland.** Forget the popcorn; birds won't eat it. Instead, thread slices of dried apple onto a long piece of jute twine at about 6-inch intervals; knot the twine to the branches so that catbirds, wrens, robins, and other fruit eaters can use the string as a perch while they work on the apples.
- **Mini sunflower heads.** Save the small seedheads from your garden sunflower plants to hang on your Christmas tree. Even a 2-inch seedhead will keep goldfinches and chickadees busy for hours. Dry the seedheads in an airy room after you clip them, and store in a tightly lidded box 'til 'tis the season. To hang, poke a piece of florists' wire through the head, make a loop, and hang with twine or a narrow red ribbon.
- **Holly sprigs.** Wire sprigs of berried holly to the branches for robins and mockingbirds.
- **Red and green grapes.** Attach small bunches of fresh green and red grapes to your Christmas tree; robins and other birds will enjoy them even if they freeze.

CHRISTMAS TREES

Real live Christmas trees are a dying breed these days, thanks to the convenience of artificial trees. For me, there's just no substitute for the real thing, sticky pine sap, crooked branches, dropped needles and all. I love the whole ritual, from picking out the right tree to the transformation of lights and ornaments. And once Christmas has come and gone, my well-loved tree gets to enjoy a second life—as an outdoor attraction for birds.

Decorating an outdoor Christmas tree is one of my favorite Christmas traditions. In fact, it's so much fun that I recommend buying a real tree for your yard, patio, or deck, even if you go the artificial route indoors. It's a fun family activity that puts the focus where we like it to be on Christmas—on giving.

The gift starts with the tree itself. Those branches are instant cover that'll last right through the cold months. The tree will shield your birds from the hawks that patrol our backyards in winter, and it'll help keep your birds cozy on cold nights or in bad weather.

But the fun part—well, that would be the gifts you make to hang on the tree for your birds. Just think about what birds prefer to eat and then deck the branches (see "Treats for the Tree" at left).

CITIZEN SCIENCE

Hi, fellow scientist, it's great to meet you!

Maybe you never thought of yourself as a member of the profession. But our simple backyard observations are shaping the research in the bird world in a big way.

Years ago, amateur observers were pretty much pooh-poohed. But now we're being courted by respected organizations and institutions, from the National Audubon Society to Cornell University, because there are millions of us. We're providing priceless data to help ornithologists, environmentalists, and lots of other "-ists" focus their research and come up with sound conclusions.

When conjunctivitis eye disease ran like wildfire through house finch populations, we backyard bird lovers were on the front lines, reporting our observations so experts could track the spread of the disease.

Science Needs You

Cornell's "Lab of O" channels citizen scientists like us into ongoing projects; go to www.birds.cornell.edu/NetCommunity/Page.aspx?pid=708 to see if one of them piques your interest and to sign up. This no-nonsense site tells you exactly what the project is, how big a commitment you're considering, and how much time you can expect it to take. Contact your Audubon Society chapter, too, and check with your local nature center; many welcome citizen scientists. Nearly all research is collected via computer, so this may be the nudge you've been waiting for to join the Tech Age.

Our counts of backyard birds and birds in the field at Christmastime, and in other censuses, have helped pinpoint species of concern and shown where the ranges of birds are shifting.

We're now "citizen scientists," and in these changing times, we're very much needed. Our work—whether it's counting birds at our feeder on one day a year, or tracking down nesting birds for an entire summer—is vital. We've already contributed invaluable data to many studies, including a landmark look at the shifts in the Northeast's birds.

We backyard bird-watchers are the "world's largest research team," says Cornell University's Laboratory of Ornithology, so why not be a part?

Cornell's "Lab of O," a mecca for serious birders, and the National Audubon Society are spearheading the charge. There are more than a dozen projects that need our help, and there's something for everybody.

You can start your citizen science efforts by keeping track of who visits your backyard in 4 days in February for the Great Backyard Bird Count—93,000 bird-watchers submitted checklists in 2009, totaling more than 11 million individual birds. Or you can track your birds all winter for Project FeederWatch.

If you're a city slicker, you can get involved with PigeonWatch to learn about and study pigeons, also known as rock doves. Love walking in the woods? Get involved in the project "Birds in Forested Landscapes."

Bird lovers of any age and any skill level, from brand-new beginners to old hands, are welcome. You'll learn a lot when you get involved and you'll gain a greater appreciation for the doings of your own backyard birds.

Quick Fix

Shells accumulate quickly beneath feeders, and so do droppings. I used to rake up my shells and add them to the compost pile, until I found out that sunflowers contain allelopathic chemicals that can inhibit the germination and growth of other plants' seeds. Now, I simply bury the shells (and droppings) with an inch-deep layer of shredded bark mulch or recycled wood chips from a tree-trimming service. Microbes and other soil critters do their decomposing work on the shells out of sight now.

CLEANLINESS

Our feeding stations invite birds to congregate in close quarters, and that can lead to problems if a sick bird joins the crowd. Birds in the wild don't usually get together in big numbers day after day, or in such a mix of species. Even when a prolific source of natural food—say, a fruiting mulberry—draws them in, the birds are spread out over the branches of the tree, not sitting cheek-by-jowl as they are at our feeders.

We've been really lucky so far, or birds are hardier than we give them credit for. Because even in such crowded conditions, outbreaks of disease are pretty rare. The conjunctivitis eye disease that spread through house finches a few years ago was one notorious outbreak, but even then, birds developed natural immunities and the disease ran its course. You'll find tips for recognizing a sick bird, and advice for dealing with the situation, in the Disease entry.

Even though birds seem generally unaffected by disease at our feeders, it's a good idea to give birds a hand by keeping their feeding area tidy. Empty and scrub the feeders every couple of months with a solution of 1 part bleach to 10 parts water and a good stiff brush, to remove droppings, old seed, and crusty dirt. Natural rainfall does a good job of diluting and washing away droppings from your feeder area, but if rain has been scarce, use a stiff blast from the nozzle of your garden hose to wash away the white stuff.

Hummingbird and oriole nectar feeders need even more frequent cleanup, because black mold builds up fast in and on a sugar-water feeder. Empty and disassemble your nectar feeders about every 3 days and clean all of the pieces thoroughly, inside and out.

CLIMATE CHANGE

I used to have a great little trick for remembering when to put out my hummingbird feeders in spring. Here in southwestern Indiana, the first hummers always arrived on April 15, give or take a day: exactly when I was finishing up my income tax forms.

Every year during my time in Indiana—more than a decade—that date was right on the money. And according to records, as well as firsthand reports from my neighbors, the hummingbirds had kept their date for much longer than I'd lived here.

In 2002, I moved to the Northwest for about 5 years. When I returned to Indiana, I was stunned to find out that the hummingbirds had updated their appointment book. Now, the first migrants arrive on April Fool's Day, with a few even making their appearance in late March.

That's a solid 2 weeks ahead of their former schedule. And the hummers are hanging around much longer, too. Instead of taking down my nectar feeders in late September, I now leave them up until Halloween because the little birds are still zipping through.

If it were only the fall migration that had shifted, I'd be tempted to believe it's because of our feeders. Millions of us are now feeding hummingbirds, so the birds don't have to zip out of here before frost kills the flowers. But an earlier spring arrival date doesn't match that theory—

It's hard to determine why birds are moving north, but many recent studies confirm that they are. Just 25 years ago, the Canada warbler was a fairly common resident of central New York. Now it's gone from that area, its range shifted to the north. Meanwhile, more southerly birds, including the tufted titmouse and red-bellied woodpecker, are moving on up.

many of us don't put out our nectar feeders until we spot the first hummingbird.

Our feeders may be a factor, but the biggest arrow points to climate change.

According to the Union of Concerned Scientists (UCS), a nonpolitically affiliated group, the Midwest growing season is getting longer. The date of the last spring frost is now a week earlier, according to the 2009 UCS report "Confronting Climate Change in the US Midwest," (www.ucsusa.org/global_warming/science_and_impacts/impacts/climate-change-midwest.html>) and the back end of the season is stretching, too.

Weather or Climate?

My two kids live a thousand miles away from me, one west and one east, which is why one of the first questions we always ask each other is "How's the weather?"

Weather has a big effect on our daily lives. Sweater or shorts? Gardening or a movie? Weather determines our clothes, our activities, and as we all know, even our moods.

Pinyon seeds, better known as pine nuts, were a Native American staple for centuries. In 2002, many pinyon pines in Arizona died because of severe drought and unusually high heat, and so did many of the pinyon jays that depend on these meaty seeds.

"Sunny and beautiful," my son might say with delight after a week of rain.

"Still gray here," my daughter may report. "Think I'll take a nap."

Weather is what happens every day. It's the rain, heat waves, windstorms, blizzards, and all of the other combinations of temperature, precipitation, humidity, and wind that affect our daily lives.

The cloud cover that makes us all cranky when it keeps up day after day? That's weather. And weather affects every other thing on earth, too.

A drought can take a heavy toll on every plant and animal that lived in or depended on a now dried-up creek or the seeds of plants that failed to mature. A late spring cold snap or an early frost can freeze flowers in their tracks and cause bees and other pollinators to plummet.

One thing we all know about the weather—it changes! The Midwest is notorious for sudden shifts from one extreme to the other, but I've heard our favorite saying in other places across the country, too: "Don't like this weather? Wait 5 minutes."

Some years, spring comes early and the wildflowers or garden flowers rush into bloom; some years, it seems like winter will never lose its grip. Some years, the butterflies are way down in numbers because of a wet spring; some years, the timing works just right and butterflies are everywhere.

Those kind of things are simply par for the course. They may take me by surprise, but they're to be expected. A change in the weather ripples through the natural world, and it may even affect the following year, too.

But when early spring follows early spring for year after year, so that we're planting peas in February instead of in March and hummingbirds are looking for my feeder in March instead of April, something bigger is afoot.

That "something" is climate. Add up decades' worth of weather events, find the averages of dates and amounts, and what you've got is climate.

Who Can You Believe?

I'm not a scientist. Not an official one, that is. I don't have a string of initials behind my name or papers published in scientific journals.

But I am a reader.

My walls are lined with books about every branch of the natural sciences, from plants and animals to rocks and weather. Stacks of scientific magazines cover more shelf space and the coffee table. And every day, I spend a couple of hours catching up on news from the world of science by reading the latest reports online.

I'm also an observer. I've been watching the natural world every day of my life for more than half a century now. It doesn't stop with just looking at pretty or interesting things, either—I'm always asking myself the big question: "Why?"

Over the years, I've seen for myself that Mother Nature is always changing. But in recent years, I've been seeing changes so dramatic that I can't assign them to weather anymore—they've got to be climate.

Southern butterflies that rarely strayed this far north now breed in my Indiana garden. Wildflowers reliably bloom 2 weeks earlier than they used to. Rain now falls in deluges of inches at a time, flooding creeks and rivers and keeping farmers from planting and harvesting. And the glaciers in the western mountains I love—they're shrinking right before my eyes.

Is climate change real or not? Only in the United States do we have a debate over whether

Deluges of rain are becoming a pattern in the East, South, and Midwest, with several inches of rain being dumped in a day or two instead of spread out over weeks. The flooding that follows takes a big toll on birds as well as people, both directly and indirectly, as insects, plants, and other organisms are disrupted.

climate change exists. Other countries around the globe are already taking steps to deal with changes such as rising sea level; they're not wasting time arguing over whether climate change is like the boy crying "Wolf!"

Climate Changes Everything

Climate change affects everything. Rainfall and drinking water depend on those shrinking glaciers. Ocean currents and dead zones mean fish will be harder to come by. Extinctions are occurring at an unprecedented rate—so far, most of them in smaller creatures and plants.

In short, all the stuff we've been trying to pretend isn't as bad as it sounds is happening, whether we believe it or not.

The trouble is that Nature's balance is a delicate one. One tiny tweak in any direction, and anything can happen. I keep thinking about a sci-fi story I read long ago, in which a time traveler, gone back to visit prehistoric days, accidentally crushes a butterfly. Her misstep echoes down the ages, affecting all sorts of connections, so that by the time the story returns to the present day, human beings are not part of the scene.

I'd love nothing better than to be wrong about all of this. Wouldn't we all love to just relax and keep living life the way we've known it? Sure we would. And sometimes, I do.

Worse yet, it's not climate change alone that's causing the decline of birds, insects, amphibians, bats, and the many other living things whose numbers are dropping. Habitat destruction and pesticides are to blame for many of the effects we're seeing. The combined effect of these three problems is unprecedented in our human history on the planet.

Yet for all the gloom and doom, I'm still an optimist. I have faith in communication. It's the ace card our species holds.

We can inspire each other. We can tell each other our stories. We can learn from each other. We can share. And not least, we can care.

We kicked into gear when the world united to defeat a common enemy in World War II, with retooled factories and Victory Gardens and tightening our belts. We can do it again, by minimizing our effects on the planet, by finding new ways of doing things, and by helping other species—like the birds in our own backyards—survive in these changing times.

COLD

It's always amazing to me how little we actually know about birds. Take chickadees, for example—these bright-eyed little guys have been familiar friends for centuries, and a welcome sight in winter. But we're only now learning exactly how such tiny bundles of feathers manage to survive the cold.

Turns out that chickadees have a whole slew of tricks up their sleeves for thriving in the cold, even in places like Vermont, Minnesota, and the frozen North, where temps regularly stay well below zero.

"Cold ecologists," a relatively new type of scientist, have learned that chickadees can drop their body temperature at night by more than 21 percent, from their usual 108°F to only 85°F. That means it takes less fuel to keep their furnaces stoked, so the little birds can make those

This blue jay's puffed feathers give it increased insulation, preserving body heat. Scientists are learning that some species, including chickadees, have some incredible tricks for staying warm in extreme cold.

high-calorie nuts from your feeder really last. Good thing, because winter cold comes hand-in-hand with shorter days, and that spells less time for foraging.

Only hummingbirds seem to share the chickadees' ability to go into a slow-motion state, according to what cold ecologists have discovered so far. That could be one big reason why many other songbirds freeze to death in a bad cold snap. Carolina wrens, eastern bluebirds, and swallows—which are early migrants—often fall victim when extreme cold settles in after they've migrated north in spring.

Chickadee feathers are different than other birds', too. They molt into a brand-new suit of clothes in fall, and those feathers weigh more than 25 percent more than the worn ones they shed. It's like adding a fourth down quilt to a three-blanket bed. Even the muscles that maneuver their feathers are better than other birds', so they can fluff that insulating layer to the greatest effect.

At night, chickadees seek out small, cozy natural cavities that they can warm with their own body heat. And here's an amazing thing that cold ecologists have learned—the birds often shiver through the night to generate a little extra warmth.

Of course you'll want to help your chickadees' natural advantages by supplying an abundance of high-fat feeder foods. And the birds that aren't so well-endowed for cold weather will benefit, too.

I pull out all the stops when extreme cold moves in, because I know that's when a feeder can make a big difference in bird survival. Nuts, nut butters, nutty bird doughs, cornmeal concoctions, suet treats—I unwrap or cook up any foods I can think of that have an extra-high ratio of fat.

Counting Calories

CHILL CHASER

Help your bluebirds, wrens, robins, chickadees, and other feeder friends keep warm during cold weather by mixing up this high-fat treat. The extra calories in every bite will make it easier for them to stay cozy through the long nights of winter or during an unexpected cold spell in spring.

3 packaged blocks of plain suet (about 11 ounces each), with no added seeds or other ingredients, or 2 pounds lard or suet
½ cup crushed peanuts, walnuts, or pecans (or macadamias, if your budget allows!)
½ cup chunky peanut butter
½ cup raw or oil-roasted unsalted peanuts

1. Melt the suet or lard in a pan over low heat.
2. Combine all ingredients, and mix thoroughly.
3. Spoon the mixture into a 9 × 13-inch baking pan, and let it solidify. (You can put it in your freezer to hurry it along.)
4. Put chunks of the mix in a suet feeder or log feeder for woodpeckers, brown creepers, chickadees, and titmice. Crumble it into a tray feeder or on the ground for catbirds, thrashers, mockingbirds, sparrows, juncos, towhees, thrushes, and robins. Serve chunks or crumbles to wrens, bluebirds, chickadees, and titmice in a domed or mealworm feeder.

COLD FRONTS

When I lived in the tiny town of Trexler near the foot of Hawk Mountain Sanctuary in Kempton, Pennsylvania, I quickly learned to recognize a cold front coming in. The buildup of low clouds, pushed by the wind in back that bullied the cold front along, was the signal to be ready to head for the lookout on the mountain the next day. Hawks riding the tailwind of the cold front would soon be pouring through along the flyway.

Migrating birds in fall often take advantage of the winds that accompany a cold front. Coasting on the moving air saves them energy and carries them far and fast.

Knowing about the effect of a cold front led me to great bird-watching at Cape May, New Jersey, too, when that kind of weather would drive hundreds of tiny wood warblers, flickers, and other birds to the jumping-off point for migrants at the shore of the Delaware Bay. I'd check the weather before planning the 4-hour trip from my Pennsylvania home, so I could get the timing right. Arriving a day or two after a front went through meant there'd be warblers chipping from every bush and tree, having stopped to rest and feed after the long flight. A day before the front, there'd be barely a bird.

Strong cold fronts pack enough oomph to blow migrants off course, too. The day after a front went through, a flock of robins 100 strong landed a few blocks from my house—and a varied thrush, hundreds of miles from its usual haunts, was among them.

Great Expectations

Pay attention whenever the weatherman says a cold front is coming in, and you'll have a heads-up for what to expect in your own yard. In late summer, when a cold front is forecast, start making extra nectar and consider adding another hummingbird feeder. That late-summer cold front won't just clear out the heat and humidity—it'll bring migrating hummers in on the wind. During spring or fall songbird migration (a little later than that of hummingbirds), stock your feeders with plenty of soft foods and put out extra mealworm feeders whenever you hear a cold front's on its way. That rush of air is likely to cause thrushes, tanagers, orioles, rose-breasted grosbeaks, and other migrants to alight in your welcoming yard, whether they've ridden a tailwind or are waiting out the storm.

Winds of Spring

In spring, a cold front has a different effect on migrants. That's when birds depend on warm fronts—wind blowing from the South—to carry them along. When a cold front roars in from the West, with its turbulent air and driving rain, it stops the migrants in their tracks. They stay grounded for days, feeding and resting right where they are.

If the birds are crossing a big body of water at the time the cold front comes in, they're out of luck—there's no choice but to keep flapping until they get to land.

If you ever happen to be along the Gulf Coast the day after spring migrants have fought a cold

Flowering trees like this redbud (*Cercis canadensis*) are a popular landing spot for scarlet tanagers and other spring migrants because of the abundant small insects that swarm around the blossoms.

front while crossing the water from Central America, you'll never forget the sight. Massive numbers of birds "fall out," exhausted, and remain for a few days to regain their strength.

As luck would have it, I arrived at the Gulf Coast one spring day just in time to see the phenomenon with my own eyes. Massive numbers of migrating birds had arrived on shore in the wee hours, after battling a cold front on their way across the Gulf.

The hard labor of beating their wings against the wind had taken its toll, and countless orioles and tanagers sat resting in every patch of woods and thicket and even on lawns like exotic robins. Indigo buntings and wood warblers filled the brush and scraggly trees. And in one short stretch, I saw more painted buntings than I'd seen in my entire life, combined. It seemed like every oriole, tanager, warbler, and bunting in America, plus plenty of other species, were all concentrated in a few miles of coastline.

Imagine what an incredible effort it takes to keep flapping for hours on end. Birds spend months building up fat stores before migration, and usually they make it before their reserves run out. Studies on hawks show that constant flapping—not even against a powerful wind, but on air that's still—can exhaust a bird's stored fat in just 5 days. But when the hawk glides along on helpful air currents, its stored fat can last 20 days.

Our migrant birds may travel 3,000 miles or more when they head for their seasonal home. There's some time for pit stops along the way, but research shows that the birds try to work with the winds, instead of against them. Get a handle on cold fronts yourself, and you'll be ready to serve up nourishing food when the hungry new arrivals land in your backyard.

CONIFERS AND BROAD-LEAVED EVERGREENS

Whether your evergreens are blue spruce, golden cypress, or green English laurel, they're worth their weight in gold to birds that are seeking shelter. Both conifers and broad-leaved evergreens block rain, snow, and ice, and that's a big benefit right there. Those with dense branches, especially plants with prickly foliage like hollies and junipers, provide a safe place to spend the night, too, because few predators will venture into the tree or large shrub.

Evergreens make your yard look better, too, because they keep it alive in winter. Aim for about one-fifth to one-third evergreen in your landscaping, and you'll strike a good balance. That doesn't mean one evergreen for every three to five deciduous trees or shrubs: It means a visual balance, a proportion of the whole. Just use your eyes to scan your yard in winter, and you'll see right away whether yours falls anywhere near that scale.

Too much green can feel oppressive in winter, unless you live in a region where evergreen is the law of the land. In the rainy Pacific Northwest, the usual proportion is tipped upside-down, with a much heavier balance of evergreen to deciduous.

Birds aren't nearly as particular as landscape designers. As long as your yard includes a few evergreens, they'll be happy.

Nurture a Native

If you can find the space, try to include at least one good-size conifer that's native to your area: a fir, spruce, pine, hemlock, or whatever fills your nearby wild places. Why native? Because your local birds already know exactly how to make use of the tree. They'll eat the seeds out of the cones, use the bark and needles in their nests, nibble the buds, gorge on the insects drawn to the tree, and nest in its branches.

In my part of southern Indiana, the choice is simple: The only native evergreen is the ouch-that's-prickly eastern red cedar, which is actually a juniper (*Juniperus virginiana*). Its vertical silhouette dots the fields and roadsides like a dark green exclamation point, and it draws roosting birds like a Hampton Inn sign. In fall, its small, frosty blue berries attract cedar waxwings, bluebirds, robins, yellow-rumped warblers, downy woodpeckers, and lots of other birds.

Whatever corner of the world you live in, you'll find homegrown evergreens that are just as tempting to birds as my juniper. Conifers seem to have higher appeal to birds than broad-leaved types, but any evergreen will get used in some way by your backyard birds. And when bad weather howls in, those sheltering leaves make an inviting haven, whether they're the big shingled roof of a rhododendron or the fine, short needles of a hemlock to break the force of the wind and rain.

Don't forget to explore the native broad-leaved evergreens of your area, too, or sample one from another American region. And get 'em while you can—some of our native plants most beneficial to birds are fading from the landscape. Red bay (*Persea borbonia*) is a beauty, with glossy aromatic leaves that have been used for ages by Southern cooks to flavor gumbo. The fruits supply high-energy food for many migrant birds traveling the Southeast or spending winter there, including tanagers, orioles, hermit thrushes, yellow-rumped warblers, and many others. Red bay thickets are the home of painted buntings, too. But the plant is under attack by the red bay ambrosia beetle, an Asian insect suspected of coming in on packing crates and infecting the trees with a fatal fungus. The same deadly bug is targeting spice bush (*Lindera benzoin*), sassafras, and the already rare pondspice (*Litsea aestivalis*), all highly valuable to birds.

It's impossible to stop the outbreaks of all imported pests and diseases, so all we can do is hope that plants manage to mount some natural defenses. In the meantime, help the birds compensate for losses like these by planting a diversity of evergreens and other useful plants in your yard, and keep those feeders stocked to help make up for the loss of wild foods.

An Evergreen Relationship

Many birds have a special connection to evergreens. Here's a sampling of the interesting birds that seek out evergreens to find their favorite foods, nest sites, or insects.

BIRD	TYPE OF EVERGREEN	ATTRACTION
Black-throated blue warbler	Rhododendron, hemlock	Nest sites, insect food
Black-throated gray warbler	Fir, manzanita, juniper, ceanothus	Nest sites, insect food
Chickadees, titmice	All conifers	Seeds from cones
Golden-crowned kinglet	All conifers	Insects at branch tips and in foliage
Hermit warbler	Tall conifers, especially Douglas fir and western red cedar	Nest sites, insect food
Hooded warbler	Rhododendron	Nest sites, insects at flowers
Hummingbirds	Azalea, rhododendron, salal, evergreen huckleberry	Nectar at flowers
Jays	Pine, spruce, fir	Nest sites, seeds from cones
Mourning dove	Pine, spruce, fir, hemlock	Nest sites
Nuthatches	All conifers	Seeds from cones
Ruby-crowned kinglet	All conifers	Insects at branch tips and in foliage
Ruffed grouse	Mountain laurel	Eats leaves (able to detoxify poisons in them)
Spruce grouse	Spruce	Eats buds
Swainson's warbler	Rhododendron	Nest sites, insect food
Townsend's warbler	Fir, pine, other tall conifers	Nest sites, insect food
Western tanager	Douglas fir, hemlock, lodgepole pine, ponderosa pine, white pine, whitebark pine	Nest sites, insect food
Yellow-rumped warbler	Many conifers	Nest sites, insect food

CONTAINER GARDENS

Watering Wisdom

Keeping up with watering is the hardest part about growing plants in containers, and nothing looks sadder than a lush planting that's gone limp. A soaking is needed almost every day in summer—unless you choose plants that can take the tough conditions. In a sunny site, your container's soil heats up, and so do your plant's roots. Even in the shade, your potted plants will dry out faster than your flowerbeds. Self-watering containers can help, but the best approach is to choose the right plant for the right place, just as you do in the garden. Old-fashioned geraniums are highly tolerant of heat and drought, and they'll bloom for months even if you forget to water. Just as important, their bright red flowers are a powerful advertisement to passing hummingbirds.

There's nothing like watching hummingbirds just inches from your nose, so include some container gardens for these pint-size entertainers on your patio or your porch.

Buy annuals in bud and bloom to fill your pots, so you have color to catch a hummer's eye from spring through fall. I keep my plantings simple, focusing on one or two kinds of flowers that I know hummers can't resist and that I also know will happily adapt to life in a flowerpot.

For guaranteed appeal, plant red or orange-red geraniums in containers for your sunny spots. In the shade, you can't go wrong with fuchsias, especially the erect, multistemmed 'Gartenmeister', and the new yellow impatiens varieties, including the 'Fusion' and 'Fanfare' series. The classic impatiens we all know and love has some hummer appeal, too, but not nearly as much as these new plants. Tuck a single plant of red or orange-red "regular" impatiens among your newbies, though, so its color can beckon hummingbirds. And add a colorful coleus to your planting for contrast; hummingbirds will visit the blue flowers when it comes into bloom late in summer.

CORN AND CORNMEAL

Who'd have ever guessed that cheap, plentiful corn is one of the best ways to entice birds to your yard? With some 70 million acres of it growing in the United States—that's more than 100,000 square miles—you'd think birds would've gotten their fill long ago.

Good thing birds still love corn, because I depend on it for the basis of most of my homemade bird doughs and other treats. It's got great nutritional value, with everything that birds need to keep them hopping, so no wonder it's a fave. Every tablespoon of yellow cornmeal is packed with about 50 calories of fat, carbs, and protein, and whole corn is just as nutritious.

The only problem with whole corn kernels is that many feeder birds can't eat them. Put out an ear of dried corn, and you'll only get a few takers: jays, cardinals, some of the larger woodpeckers, blackbirds, and our best friends, the ever-busy squirrels, who are likely to cart entire cobs of corn back to their dens.

I like watching red-bellied woodpeckers and cardinals work at removing corn kernels, so I make sure there's always an ear or two at the feeding station. My squirrels get their separate banquet at a feeder on a tree, where jays often sneak their own share. The empty cobs make great impromptu feeders: Just knot a piece of twine or twist a wire around a cob, smear on a suet or peanut butter mixture, and hang it up for chickadees, titmice, wrens, catbirds, and other friends.

Whole kernels of corn, on or off the cob, are too big for smaller birds to get their beak around and too hard for them to peck. But if you serve corn that's broken into bits, your list of customers will suddenly lengthen.

This cornstalk feeder holds the corn securely so that squirrels can't carry off the entire ear.

Get Cracking

Cracked corn is cheap and wholesome, and it's a standard in many brands of inexpensive seed mixes and in packaged suet blocks.

But it definitely has its drawbacks, so consider the consequences before you make it a staple at your feeder.

Lots of birds will eat cracked corn, especially if there's nothing better around. But the birds that are actually attracted by it are birds you probably don't want any more of. Mobs of house sparrows, platoons of starlings, and whole squadrons of grackles, cowbirds, and blackbirds will quickly descend on a handout of cracked corn. Rodents will come running, too.

Cardinals enjoy cracked corn, but they'll usually head for the sunflower seeds instead. Jays generally lose interest when the kernels are cracked, because they prefer their seeds and nuts whole, so they can bury them.

I keep a sack of cracked corn on hand, especially for snowstorms, because it's the cheapest way to feed a crowd in a hurry. And my heart goes out to any bird that's hungry, so I actually feel good when I watch the horde of house sparrows and starlings chowing down on a snowy day.

Instead of pouring cracked corn into your open feeders, you may want to save it for your homemade bird doughs, suet treats, and other soft foods. Then your catbirds, mockingbirds, thrashers, bluebirds, wrens, and small birds can benefit from the nutritional bites presented in a high-fat food they'll readily eat.

Happy Meal

Cornmeal is the best way to feed your birds corn. Mix it with peanut butter, suet, lard, or Crisco, and you have an instant treat for nearly all your backyard birds—including the most-wanted kinds, like

(continued on page 116)

Serving Style

All backyard birds are likely to sample your corny treats, if they can easily access the food. If you want to limit the clientele, serve these treats, and any others you cook up, in feeders that suit the style of the birds you want to attract. Stuff the treats into the holes of a log feeder, for example, for catbirds, Carolina and Bewick's wrens, woodpeckers, chickadees, and titmice; serve them in a tray feeder for cardinals, juncos, towhees, and other perching birds; use a feeder with bars or a grid to feed small birds; put treats in a mealworm dish or platform feeder for cardinals, orioles, tanagers, and waxwings. Store any leftovers in your freezer in zip-top plastic bags or other containers.

CORNBREAD CRUNCH

3 cups cornmeal
1 cup lard
3 cups water
1½ teaspoons baking powder
½ cup chopped peanuts or cracked corn
½ cup chopped raisins or dried currants

1. Grease a rectangular 9 × 12-inch baking pan, and preheat oven to 425°F.
2. Use a hand mixer to combine the cornmeal, lard, and water. The mixture will be very thin.
3. Stir in the baking powder.
4. Pour the mixture into the pan, and scatter the peanuts or cracked corn and fruit across it.
5. Bake for about 30 minutes. Let it cool in the pan, and then break it up with a spatula to serve to your birds.

BLUEBIRD BEST

1–1¼ cups suet
4 cups cornmeal
1 cup white or whole-wheat flour
1 cup dried currants
1 cup sunflower chips
1 cup chopped peanuts
1 cup chunky peanut butter

1. Melt the suet over low heat.
2. Combine the other ingredients except the peanut butter in a large bowl.
3. Mix in the peanut butter.
4. Pour the suet into the bowl while mixing. The mixture will begin to stick together into small clumps, like crumb topping for a pie. When all of the dry ingredients have been mixed with the fat, you're done.
5. Serve crumbled in small pieces about the size of peas or smaller in whatever feeder your bluebirds like best.

CATBIRDS GET CORNY

1 pound suet
1 cup crunchy or creamy peanut butter
4 cups cornmeal
1 cup white or whole-wheat flour
1 cup chopped fresh or dried apple
1 cup sunflower chips

1. Melt the suet over low heat. Stir in the peanut butter.
2. Combine the other ingredients in a large bowl.
3. Pour the melted suet and peanut butter over them, and mix well. Serve in a platform or tray feeder or any other feeder your catbirds are accustomed to using.

WOODPECKER BREAKFAST

1 pound suet
1 cup cornmeal
1 cup rolled oats, not instant
1 cup chunky peanut butter
1 cup chopped nuts
1 cup sunflower chips
½ cup dried fruit, any kind, chopped
¼ cup leftover cooked sausage, crumbled

1. Melt the suet in a large saucepan over low heat.
2. Meanwhile, combine the other ingredients.
3. Pour the melted suet over the dry ingredients, and mix thoroughly.
4. Spoon the mixture into molds, such as recycled suet block trays, or pour it into a baking pan.
5. Cool or freeze until solidified. Serve in wire cages, or cut into chunks to fill mesh onion bags or log feeders.

JUNCO MUNCH

1 cup chunky peanut butter
4 cups cornmeal
1 cup no-waste (no shells) seed mix
1 pound finely chopped or ground suet

1. Combine the peanut butter and cornmeal to make a crumbly mixture.
2. Stir in the seed mix.
3. Add the suet, using your hands to make sure it's distributed thoroughly. The mixture will be crumbly, just the way juncos and native sparrows like it. Scatter a few handfuls of it on the ground or in a low tray feeder.

wrens, bluebirds, thrushes, and woodpeckers. Cornmeal makes your fats stretch further, so you can feed more birds for less money. And it makes the mixes more palatable to native sparrows, towhees, juncos, and other feeder friends.

Yellow cornmeal is such a staple in my bird-friendly kitchen that I buy it in 20-pound sacks at the Mexican market. Cornmeal's a staple in the diet south of the border, and I've learned the prices at my local Mexican market are much less expensive than at my supermarket—less than $1 a pound, instead of more than $3 for the smiling Quaker-brand canister.

You can use cornmeal as an ingredient in just about any bird food recipe you can dream up. Fruit eaters, such as orioles, will eat it if you mix fat and fruit with it. Seed eaters enjoy it best when you mix it with sunflower chips, nuts, and fat. Woodpeckers gobble it with peanuts or other nuts, dried fruit, peanut butter, and some suet or solid vegetable shortening. Robins, towhees, catbirds, mockingbirds, varied thrushes, and many others eagerly eat crumbled cornbread and other treats, too.

That's a lot of bang for very little buck. So make nutritious, inexpensive cornmeal a staple in your own kitchen, and have fun cooking up your own bird-attracting treats.

Buy coarse yellow cornmeal if you can find it, instead of white or extra-finely ground meal. It's usually more nutritious and less expensive than white, and it's not as dusty as fine meal, so it's easier to work with.

COWBIRDS

I would've loved to see a flock of cowbirds in the old days, when the ground-feeding birds followed right on the heels of the massive buffalo herds that crisscrossed the country. As the shaggy beasts stirred up insects, these brown-headed blackbirds snapped them up.

The tiny chipping sparrow's nest is a frequent target of the brown-headed cowbird, whose large nestling will soon cause the demise of the baby sparrows.

Nowadays, though, I have mixed feelings when I see a group or even a pair of cowbirds in my backyard or elsewhere. Why? Because these birds are one of the big reasons our American songbirds have been declining so fast in recent years.

The brown-headed cowbird is a "brood parasite." Instead of building its own nest and caring for its family, it dumps its eggs in other birds' homes and immediately flies the coop.

In most cases, the other birds never notice the difference, and they raise the hefty cowbird baby as one of their own. Or, should I say, as an only child—the saddest part of the story is that the cowbird youngster shoves the other nestlings out of the nest, or demands way more of the food, causing them to starve.

It gets even worse. A single female cowbird can lay about 30 to 80 eggs every breeding season, dropping them into different nests one or two at

An Expanding "Herd"

Two other cowbird species are on the increase these days. The shiny cowbird of South America has expanded its range to the United States and is now breeding in Florida. The bronzed cowbird is also venturing far from its usual home in the deep Southwest; it's been spotted along the entire Gulf Coast and elsewhere. That spells even more trouble for our other birds, because these species, like their brown-headed cousin, are also brood parasites.

The shiny cowbird was the target of an extermination campaign in a teeny-tiny reserve for the pale-headed brush-finch, a rarest-of-the-rare bird that lives in the Andes in Ecuador. The finch's home covers less than 200 acres, so an eradication campaign was doable, and the cowbirds were wiped out. In 1999, there was a grand total of exactly 10 pale-headed brush-finches; by 2005, sans cowbirds, the reserve held 50 of them.

I can't see such a campaign working in the United States, because our songbirds and cowbirds are spread out so widely. And you can't take matters into your own hands, either, even if you find a songbird nest in your own yard with one or two of those highly suspect, brown-speckled bluish white eggs: The cowbird and its eggs are protected by the same federal law that protects their victims.

a time. *Just one cowbird can prevent 20, 30, or even 50 or more songbirds from raising families.*

Cowbirds in Changing Times

That's a great system for cowbirds, but not so good for the birds whose nests are parasitized. Still, songbirds have been able to live in balance with cowbirds for centuries, because the percentage of nest failures due to cowbirds was just a drop in the bucket.

That's not the case anymore.

As forest birds get crammed into smaller and smaller areas, and as the remaining stretches of woods get carved up for houses or access roads, the cowbird—which shies away from deep forest—can reach a lot more nests.

All those "drop in the bucket" cowbird effects are hugely multiplied today. Many of our American birds have dwindled to alarming numbers, and even disappeared entirely from many areas. So cowbird depredations have an exponentially bigger effect.

Cowbirds victimize 200 species (even hummingbirds!), and many are "neotropical migrants," the birds that migrate back and forth from the New World ("neo") tropics to North America. (For more about the problems these birds face, see the entries Climate Change, Dangers, Habitat Destruction, and Population Decline.)

It's not the cowbirds' fault that we're losing birds—it's ours. Cowbirds simply did what comes naturally, and they took advantage of the increased habitat we provided for them. Unfortunately for all of us, the numbers of wood warblers, thrushes, and vireos they zero in on have dropped like a rock. Eventually, that could turn out to be a problem for the cowbirds, too, because there won't be enough other birds to nurture their young. Maybe then things will once again reach a balance.

D

DANGERS

One of my son David's favorite bedtime books was an old western called *The X Bar X Boys*. His dad and I took turns reading the *very exciting* chapters, which always ended with a cliff-hanger. David's favorite, which we came to know almost by heart thanks to repeated readings, was the chapter titled "Many Perils." I vaguely recall dens of rattlesnakes, snarling bears, and who knows what else, but it was out of the frying pan into the fire every step of the way.

Today, our birds are in the middle of their own "Many Perils" chapter, facing the massive destruction of forests and other wild land. Pesticides and pollution kill millions of birds. Skyscraper windows and our cell phone towers break millions of birds' necks. Cats take a toll greater than any natural predator.

And look out, birds, there's an even bigger herd of ferocious grizzlies coming fast! Climate change is the biggest challenge that birds—and we ourselves—have ever faced. It's already happening, with Nature's careful web being ripped apart all over the world.

Food sources for birds are changing in availability and timing. Insects may hatch weeks before nestlings are ready to be fed, and flowers may be scarce when hummingbirds need them most.

Birds are already on the move, leaving the southerly parts of their homes and shifting their ranges northward to escape some of the changes, or to move along with the insects and plants they depend upon as the planet warms up.

What's a backyard bird lover to do when danger lurks in every direction? Plenty!

Riding to the Rescue

Start by tackling the dangers that are easy to handle: cats and other predators, and window collisions. The Windows entry will show you how to save your birds' necks, and you'll find plenty of practical suggestions for guarding your birds from predators in the entries Cat Control, Hawk Watch, and Predators.

Put down the pesticides, too, and go organic: Insects play an important role in a healthy backyard, whether birds eat them or not.

Counteract habitat destruction by creating your own habitat for birds at home. You'll find ideas throughout this book, including entries like Best of the Berries, Bird in the Bush, Birdseed Gardens, Do Not Disturb, Hedge Hideout, and many others.

Our nurturing backyards will help make up for some of the changes. And by banding together as bird lovers, we can be a powerful force for good, just like George Bird Grinnell's first Audubon Society group a hundred years ago.

We're almost certain to lose more species along the way. But if we all do our part, I have hopes that our children's children will still be listening to birdsong a hundred years from now.

DEAD WOOD

When a storm brought down a major limb of the hackberry tree across the street, I looked at it with longing. A curving, gray-barked, 10-inch-thick log was just what I needed as an accent piece in my shady backyard. I could envision the wood thrush pausing on top of it, the nuthatches scooting over the bark, the towhee scratching out tidbits from the moist earth underneath. Unfortunately, the limb was way too big for the spot I had in mind, not to mention about three times heavier than I could lift.

A few days later, the property owners showed up with a pickup truck and a chain saw. *Vvvv-VRRRRRAAAAAA* went the saw, kicking into life, as I hurried into my sneakers to run across the street. Chain saws work fast, and by the time I got there, there was only an 8-foot section left.

Standing well back, I cupped my hands around my mouth and hollered, "Can I have that?"

The chain saw sputtered to a halt.

"You want this log?"

I nodded vigorously. "For my birds."

Dead wood is a natural component of wild places, and it's one more element that'll make your yard appeal to birds. On the ground, a handsome log provides a perching place for low-level birds like thrushes, native sparrows, and quail, and supplies more food opportunities as the

Treasure from the Trees

When a storm sends a dead limb plummeting to the ground in your yard, see if it has possibilities for your bird-friendly landscape before you have it sawed up into firewood. If it's 7 or 8 inches in diameter or better, it'll make a fine log to settle into a shady spot for a natural accent that'll invite more birds to your yard. Landscape it like Mother Nature does, with ferns, hosta, heuchera, or other shade-loving perennials along its length, groundcovers, wildflowers, or impatiens around it, and a native hydrangea (*Hydrangea arborescens*), azalea, rhodie, or other shrub as a backdrop. You'll have a nice little nook that may tempt thrushes, towhees, and other woodsy birds to investigate your place. Or you can install the fallen limb vertically as a "feeder": Dig a 1½- to 2-foot deep hole to insert it into, firm it with soil into place, and spread your nut butters, suet, and other high-fat treats directly on the bark or bare wood.

Our shortest dogwood, bunchberry (*Cornus canadensis*), will snuggle itself against a dead log in your yard as a groundcover. Its bright red fall berries are a treat for migrating thrushes.

wood decomposes. In previous yards, I've had a song sparrow and towhee build nests against the belly of a log, where a stand of ferns provided cover.

You may not want to use a log in your landscape, but dead or dying wood that's still attached to the tree is even more of a magnet for birds. I let dead branches stay until they fall naturally, unless they're likely to take out a chunk of my roof or some utility lines when they finally keel over.

Whether it's a wrist-thin branch or a waist-thick stump, dead wood is one of the most popular attractions for birds in your yard. Beetles and larvae burrow through the bark and tissue, calling chickadees, titmice, and especially woodpeckers to the feast, and the dead wood is apt to soon be riddled with nest holes.

My old sweetgum tree (*Liquidambar styraciflua*) is slowly giving up the ghost, but its decrepit branches still work hard for birds. This spring, a dead limb of the sweetgum hosted three different bird families: downy woodpeckers at the bottom, flickers in the middle, and great-crested flycatchers in the penthouse suite. It was quite a circus to watch, but the birds were oblivious to each other's comings and goings.

DECOY FEEDERS

Right outside my desk window is a good-size wooden tray, filled with a basic mix of black oil sunflower, white millet, cracked corn—and a horde of house sparrows. The inexpensive mix keeps them from disturbing the à la carte feeders for my "special birds," which hang several yards away. The chirpy bunch of about two dozen birds is here from dawn to nearly dusk, with various individuals taking a break now and then to sip at the birdbath or loll in the dust. Occasionally a cardinal flies in to crack a few seeds, and sometimes a couple of chipping sparrows join in. But mostly it's all English sparrows, all the time.

I've gotten fond of my little flock, which often basks on the roof of my house, even on the hottest summer days. And I don't mind that the sparrows have taken over the tray feeder—they make for a lively view, and meanwhile, my "more special" birds have claimed other feeders.

About 20 feet from the tray stands a multi-armed black metal pole with half a dozen specialized feeders. Each one holds a favorite food for what I consider my "special birds." There's a mealworm dish for the wrens and catbirds; a tube of niger for the finches; a nut feeder for the woodpeckers, chickadees, titmice, and Carolina wrens; a hopper of sunflower seeds for cardinals, jays, woodpeckers, chickadees, titmice, and nuthatches; and a couple of homemade holders for peanutty treats for brown creepers, wrens, bluebirds, and anyone else who wants a bite.

All of those birds are free to eat at leisure, without competing with a mob of house sparrows. The tray feeder at which the sparrows congregate is a decoy that draws them away from the other feeders with the lure of abundance and easy pickings.

Decoy or Deter?

When it comes to feeder hogs like house sparrows and starlings, you have two choices: You can discourage them, by using inaccessible feeders or by serving only foods they aren't particularly fond of. Or you can join 'em, by putting out a spread designed to capture their undivided attention.

The theory is that the decoy feeder will keep the pesky birds so well satisfied, that they never

Pest-Bird Pleasures

Use an easy-access open tray for your decoy feeders, and fill them with the preferred foods of the birds you're trying to keep distracted. For house sparrows, that's cracked corn and millet. For starlings, try a big meaty soup bone, dog food, apples, oranges, suet, bird doughs, noodles, stale bread with bacon fat, and other kitchen leftovers. Put your sparrow decoy feeder about 20 to 30 feet from other feeders, or farther. Set up your starling decoy feeder as far away from your feeding station as you can, and make sure there's some shrubbery or other visual obstructions between them.

bother to investigate your other feeders. House sparrows are usually good about sticking to the decoy feeder. Just don't let the cracked corn and millet run out, or they may realize that your other feeders have good eats, too.

Because my feeders have always been "Come one, come all," I didn't think of my first decoy feeder as a decoy. I called it my starling feeder, and just as I do for all my birds, I filled it with their favorite foods. I put the tray on the opposite side of the house from my regular bird feeders, mostly to keep the noisy gang away from the other birds. Eventually, it dawned on me that their own personal feeder was keeping them so busy they didn't swarm the other feeders like they used to.

I've used the trick ever since—but I've also learned that it eventually tends to backfire.

Like those Japanese beetle traps that lure beetles to their doom with a pheromone, an irresistible decoy feeder will snag more and more of the sparrows or starlings in your neighborhood.

When those burgeoning crowds overflow your decoy feeder, they may spread out to see what else you've got to eat. Uh-oh, there goes the suet. Oops, that's the end of the peanut logs. Drat, how'd those mealworms disappear so fast?

No matter how tempting a banquet you make them, it's usually only a matter of time until starlings find the good stuff at your other feeders, especially once their numbers start to increase. When my local handful of starlings starts to bring along everybody and their uncle, I pull the welcome mat out from under them. I switch to a menu that they're not as interested in, and I put the foods they love best in inaccessible feeders, so that their choices are limited. Usually, they soon go elsewhere.

We play the decoy/don't decoy game all winter, until I give up and put out enough food to keep everybody happy.

DEER DETERRENTS

The first time a deer showed up at my niece's bird feeder in New Jersey, with a spotted fawn in tow, she was so charmed by the gentle creatures that she didn't mind at all when the doe vacuumed every bit of seed out of the tray. When my niece realized a few days later that she'd run through a month's supply of birdseed keeping up with Bambi and his mom's appetites, the pleasure of their company began to grow a little thin, especially once they learned to tilt her tube feeders and drain them, too, in less than 10 minutes. And when the deer turned to eating her flowers, she started looking for ways to keep deer out, not invite them in.

She's not alone. As we move into the wild places that once belonged to deer, the deer are adapting to suburban life with a vengeance.

Some of us choose to put up feeders just for the deer, like the beautiful, sturdy, reasonably priced cedar troughs offered by the Hurley-Byrd Bird Feeder Company (see the Resources section on page 297), which hold 25 pounds or more of corn, apples, or "deer chow." If you place the feeder, and perhaps an added salt block, far away from your bird feeders, the deer may leave your bird setup alone. Or not.

Many of us are going in the other direction, trying to encourage the animals to become "deerly departed." Here are some options, from sure solutions to cross-your-fingers ideas; you'll find product sources in the Resources section.

- A deer fence around your feeding station is the best surefire remedy; the lightweight plastic mesh is relatively inexpensive, easy to install as a DIY project, and it works. A 330-foot roll of 6-foot-high fence costs about $200.
- An automated blast of water may be effective in scaring the deer away from your feeder area. Check out the Scarecrow, which attaches to your hose; when an animal interrupts the beam of the electric eye, the water starts blasting. It costs about $60.
- Rugged metal deer-proof feeders, like the cast iron Feeder Hut Pest Proof Feeder by Songbird Essentials with a metal mesh seed cage, are available. They cost about $50 and up. From the photo of the product, it looks like deer would still be able to empty the feeder. But at least they won't break it.
- When the infrared motion sensor on an ultrasonic pest repeller, about $40 to $60, detects a creature (from mosquitoes and roaches, to cats, squirrels, or deer), the high-pitched sound allegedly drives them away. That's the theory, anyhow, but many

HOW-TO Reel It In

If you're tired of fiddling with anti-deer gadgets and repellents that don't work, try this simple solution: Just bring your feeders in every evening, before the deer come to visit. Or mount your feeder extra high, where deer won't be able to reach it even if they stand on their back legs. The trouble with this trick is that you probably won't be able to reach it either, when it's time to refill. So try this mechanical solution to keep your feeder out of harm's way: Rig up a simple pulley system so you can smoothly raise and lower your feeder whenever you want. Two pulleys from a home supply store and a length of cord will do the trick. It's a simple DIY job, but you'll need a ladder and some know-how, so ask a friend or neighbor for help to hang your feeder without a hitch.

Use a simple pulley to keep your feeder out of the reach of deer.

customers say it doesn't work. In 2001, the Federal Trade Commission issued a warning to manufacturers and sellers of the devices, stating that their claims must be supported by scientific evidence. Haven't seen any of that evidence yet.

- Try a "scent barrier" deer repellent product, such as Hinder or Liquid Fence. There are many on the market, including such substances as predator urine, dried blood, and other concoctions. Ask your wild bird supply store for a recommendation, or check with the staff at a farm supply or hunting store.
- Slice bars of Irish Spring soap into quarters and hang them around your feeder area and from the post or pole itself. Or do the same with scented dryer sheets. Supposedly, deer are disgusted by the smell.
- Collect human hair clippings (ask for some at a salon or barbershop), bag them in squares cut from a mesh bag or pantyhose, and hang them around the perimeter of your feeder area.

DEPENDENCY

Some people strongly believe that feeding birds is a bad thing. They argue against it on several fronts, such as:

- Birds become dependent on feeders and "forget" how to find natural food.
- Feeder choices are less nutritious than a natural diet.
- Mortality is higher at bird feeders because of the dangers of cats and collisions with windows.
- Birds, especially hummingbirds, choose nest sites because of the reliability of a nearby food source, so an empty feeder endangers their families.
- Feeders are affecting the migrations and ranges of bird species.

Answering these questions is a complicated task, since there can be so many other elements at play. Some studies have come up with conclusions that seem pretty unassailable, and if you pay attention to the birds in your backyard, the answers won't surprise you. Let's take a look at the objections, and see if we can figure out where the truth lies.

The Myth of Dependency

Do our feeders cause birds to forget how to find food on their own? An article in *Defenders of Wildlife* magazine back in 1982 raised the question, and some people have jumped on the bandwagon. With the popularity of the online world, the suggestion is still being spread as fact.

But it's simply not the case. All scientific studies so far, and everything I've seen with my own eyes, quickly shoot down the idea as nothing more than a myth.

You've probably noticed the same thing in your own backyard: Birds eat a lot of natural food, even when our feeders are brimming with the very best nuts, seeds, and other offerings.

Margaret Brittingham and Stanley Temple of the University of Wisconsin have done groundbreaking research on the question of dependency, through their work with wild black-capped chickadees in the North. Even in winter, their studies showed, the chickadees depended more

Birds balance a feeder menu with natural insects and seeds, too.

heavily on natural foods (79 percent of their daily calories) than feeder foods (21 percent).

Those proportions may be somewhat different in our backyards, because Brittingham and Temple's research took place in forest habitat, where natural food is plentiful. In a setting where lawn covers more space than a dense stand of evergreens with a beckoning crop of cones, the ratio may be tipped more toward the feeder side. But I haven't seen a bird yet that sat at a feeder 24/7 and never nibbled a natural morsel—and I've been watching for more than 50 years. Even house sparrows, the birds that stay the longest at the feeder, occasionally wander off in search of a change of pace.

Will removing your feeders or going on vacation and letting them go empty affect your birds? Probably not much, if at all, unless a bout of extreme weather hits your area. Chickadees and many other birds travel from one "food patch" to another, taking advantage of abundance whenever they find it, whether it's an outbreak of tent caterpillars, a bird feeder, or a stand of roadside weeds. Even in winter, say Brittingham and Temple, the effects of running out of sunflower seed probably would not "be as detrimental as is typically thought."

In winter, they point out, "a natural food patch may disappear suddenly as a result of a winter snow or ice storm or the foraging activities of other flock members." So birds can cope with the sudden unavailability of food at a feeder because they've been foraging this way, from place to place, for eons.

Are our feeders as beneficial to birds as we like to think? That's still up in the air. Brittingham and Temple found no differences in survival rates between birds that used feeders and those who didn't, except during the absolute worst weather. It seems we're merely supplying part of our birds' daily diet, and, so far, the biggest benefit is to us: our own pleasure at watching them.

Natural disasters, like hurricanes, floods, and ice storms, and habitat destruction are catastrophic for birds because they wipe out big areas of potential food sources all at once. After Hurricane Katrina, many folks in the affected area noted the absence of hummingbirds, because the flowers had been destroyed. When nectar feeders were distributed as part of the relief efforts, the birds were back in force—and this time, they *were* dependent on a human helping hand.

As the changing climate continues to affect insects, plants, and weather, and as habitat destruction continues, our feeders may become a bigger factor in the survival of bird species.

The Full-Meal Deal

There's no doubt that a feeder diet is different from a natural diet. Our foods are limited, compared to the huge variety of edibles in nature.

Take nectar, for example. In the Nectar entry, you'll learn that plants produce a variety of different kinds of sugars; our feeders offer only sucrose. Is that bad for birds? We simply don't know. But I see my hummingbirds zooming

After a snack of suet, this jaunty bridled titmouse will soon be off foraging for insects and conifer seeds.

from flower to flower in my yard for nectar and dabbing up insects for protein, in addition to lapping up the sucrose. Seems to me they can balance their diet on their own.

As for the seeds and soft foods at my feeders, I rarely see birds eating them exclusively. The usual scenario is that the bird helps itself to a handout and then flits from tree to tree, picking off insects and nibbling natural seeds. Birds use our feeders to augment their natural diet, not to supplant it. Even the birds that spend hours on end at the feeder—like house sparrows and juncos—wander off to grab a bite of natural food, whether it's a singing cicada or a weed gone to seed.

Although we don't provide the diversity of Mother Nature's larder, the nutritious foods we do offer are a boon to birds. High-fat suet and sunflower seeds provide a concentrated dose of calories, so the birds can fulfill their daily needs in less time than they would in the wild. In winter and during the nesting season and migration, that seems to me like a good thing.

With so many of us feeding birds, our backyards are likely to affect bird habits more than we know. But one of Brittingham and Temple's definitive studies done in 1988 on the effects of feeders proved that our nonnatural foods can mean the difference between life and death to chickadees in a harsh winter. And with the availability of natural foods declining swiftly thanks to all the dangers that birds face, my feeling is that our handouts help birds more than hinder them.

Fatal Attraction?

A front-page article by James P. Sterba in the December 2002 *Wall Street Journal* raised quite a hue and cry over feeding birds. Headlined "Crying Fowl: Feeding Wild Birds May Harm Them and Environment," it caused some people to take down their feeders and spread the message.

Only problem was, Mr. Sterba's conclusions were so off base that most bird organizations tried to counteract the article by getting out the truth—which is that feeding birds is a good thing, for us, for the birds, and for the environment.

Cars, cats, and collisions with windows killed many birds coming to feeders, asserted Sterba.

I haven't noticed a pile of dead bird bodies on

Wild cats live in balance with birds, taking a sustainable share of feathered food. But domestic cats, both pets and those gone feral, are a grave danger.

my street, and I get a lot of bird traffic and a lot of passing cars. The only place I've seen bird feeding result in death by car has been where misguided highway departments planted shrubs with bird-attracting berries in roadway medians. Backyard cats certainly take their toll on birds, more so than predators in the wild. And collisions with our windows can kill some birds, too.

But is that reason to take down the feeding station? Not if you minimize the dangers.

If you invite birds to your yard, whether by plantings, feeders, or water, you owe it to them to make sure your yard is as free of cats as you can make it. Keep your own pet indoors, even at night. Roosting birds are just as vulnerable to cat attacks as birds at your feeder. Chase off straying cats, too; you'll find out how in the entry Cat Control.

To prevent window collisions, keep your feeders close to the window, so birds don't have much speed when they panic. Cover large plate glass windows with lattice to break up the reflection. You'll find how-tos in the entry Windows.

Nesting Needs

Those who say no to feeding stations have a valid point about nest site selection. Birds tend to choose a nest site with plenty of food available, as there is near our feeders. It's common sense, because nestlings need a lot of chow, and their hard-working parents need fuel to keep going, too.

Our feeding stations do play a role in keeping parent birds well nourished—but only partially. The parents are still eating natural food as well as snatching the occasional sunflower seed from our feeders.

And as far as nestlings are concerned, well, up until recently, our feeders didn't offer much of anything that a baby bird could eat. Baby birds need soft foods, not seeds and nuts. Even cardinals and other strong-billed seed eaters feed their youngsters soft, juicy caterpillars and other insects. So, until most feeder keepers start providing mealworms, bread dough, and other soft foods on a daily basis, our feeders simply aren't a prime source for nestling food.

Most of us who feed birds have yards that birds like to nest in, because we pay attention to their needs for cover, roosts, and natural food like berries and flowers. And many of us choose our trees, shrubs, vines, and other plants with the hope of attracting nesting birds. So the presence of nesting birds in a yard with feeders probably has more to do with the habitat, and the natural food in it, than the feeding station itself.

There's one big exception to this theory, though: hummingbirds. A nectar feeder is such a boon to hummers that they may select their nest site because of the reliable source of sugar water. They drink it themselves, and they feed it to their young. That's another good reason—as if you needed one!—to plant more hummingbird flowers. Then, if your feeder runs dry, your little friends won't have trouble finding their next meal.

Range Effects

Are our feeders affecting the range of North American birds? In nearly all cases, the answer is a resounding no.

Birds are noticeably shifting their usual nesting and wintering grounds, but it's not because of feeders: It's because of climate change.

Well, except in one case. When it comes to rufous hummingbirds, it may be our nectar feeders are drawing them to places where they didn't used to go. You'll find more details in the entry Range Shifts.

DESERT BIRDS

Birds of the desert are full of tricks. Good thing, because it's those adaptations and behaviors that enable them not only to survive but to thrive.

The first trick is a simple one: avoiding the worst of the sun. In the heat of the day, desert birds find a cool spot to wait it out. Any patch of shade provides a welcome respite. Cactus wrens, black-throated sparrows, lesser nighthawks, and many other species rest quietly in the shade of desert shrubs; others head for a shady canyon or rocky ledge. The adorable elf owl hides out in a hole in a saguaro; the burrowing owl waits out the heat in a hole dug in the ground.

Feathers make a great layer of insulation against the brutal sun, and desert birds use them as built-in cooling devices, too. When the air is still, curve-billed thrashers and other desert birds pull each feather snug against the skin, sleeking their puffy coat so that the hot air can't penetrate. But when a breeze stirs the air, you'll see desert birds puff up and erect their feathers with special muscles, so that every bit of that cooling breeze can fan through them.

Desert birds have a habit of standing tall, too, stretching their legs straight and raising their bodies as high as they can. Meanwhile, they dilate the blood vessels of their bare, scaly legs. This nifty trick sends their body heat into the air, cooling the bird. Ever run cold water over your wrists on a hot day? Ahhh, refreshing.

A good, splashy bath is a welcome treat to this black-crested titmouse, a bird of Texas and northeast Mexico.

Speaking of water—well, who cares? The dryness of the desert isn't a problem for most of its feathered citizens because they get moisture from fruit, insects, and animal food.

"No water" doesn't mean "no liquid," though, even for the birds called xerophiles, which never seek water (though they're not above visiting a birdbath). The cactus wren's diet includes lots of juicy cactus fruit, and when a cactus gets injured and oozes juice, you're likely to see a wren arrive to lap up the liquid. Le Conte's thrasher and the ash-throated flycatcher are xerophiles, too, and like the cactus wren, their diet includes a lot of juicy food (lizard, anyone?).

King of the Oddballs

The best grab bag of tricks among North American desert birds belongs to a real oddball—the greater roadrunner (the lesser roadrunner lives in Mexico and Central America). For starters, it can zoom along at 18 mph, flinging out its long tail as a rudder when it makes a turn. It never bathes in water, but it loves a good dust bath. Sunbathing is a regular part of its morning routine, and its babies have black skin so they can soak up warmth after a chilly desert night. At courtship time, the birds go into dance routines that you'll have to see to believe. They're great actors, too: To distract predators from the nest, they run off and pitifully flutter a "broken" wing. And here's another odd thing—the roadrunner is classed with the cuckoos, those slinky, deliberate birds of forest treetops that don't even seem like distant cousins. But when the roadrunner opens its mouth, you'll hear the evidence: cooing calls that sound out of place for such a big, active bird.

What's the roadrunner running after? Lizards, snakes, spiders, you name it—it'll eat just about any living creature it can get its beak on. It's also adept at finagling under rocks and debris to pluck out scorpions and spiders, or grabbing eggs or babies from other birds' nests. It even eats bats that have fallen from the roof of their cave. To make larger prey easier to swallow, the roadrunner bashes the animal, slamming it against a rock, stick, or the ground, until softened and slimmed down enough to slide down the bird's throat.

Poisonous prey is no problem for the roadrunner, and neither are prickly creatures like the horned lizard (horned toad), which the bird swallows so that the animal goes down the bird's throat with its horns pointing away from the bird's vital organs.

Once, only people who lived or visited the Southwest and Texas—or watched Saturday morning cartoons—got to see this bird. But you can now see the roadrunner skimming along almost to the Mississippi River and north into Missouri. It's one of the bird species that is quickly expanding its range. That's not necessarily a good thing for backyard bird lovers, because other birds are high on its menu. Roadrunners nab hummingbirds and songbirds at feeders, and because this bird can fly a bit and perch as well as run, it's learned to raid birdhouses and even purple martin colonies.

Portable Spa

A birdbath is such a big attraction to most desert birds that you'll have more visitors than you can keep track of. Add a low-level bath to your desert yard for the charming quail that come to call; they're perfectly capable of fluttering to a pedestal bath, but they're more comfy near the ground. I've never had the pleasure of living in a desert area, but I like to visit. And when I do, I bring along a metal baking dish that does double-duty as a birdbath. Filled with water, it's an almost instant temptation for desert birds whenever I stop in parking areas with shrubs or wild land nearby. I'll never forget the Scott's oriole, with its yellow body and dramatic black hood, that came to my water dish within minutes in Arizona. The desert birds get a good drink, and I get a good look at the local birds.

DISEASE

If a sick bird joins the crowd at your bustling backyard restaurant, disease can spread like wildfire. Take action immediately when you spot a bird that's acting in an unusual way. Puffed feathers when it's not cold, unusual tameness, lethargy, or wobbly flight or gait are all signs of trouble. Remove and scrub the feeders with a solution of 1 part chlorine bleach, 10 parts water, and don't put them back up until the sick bird has moved on or met its fate.

If you find a dead bird in your yard, don't touch it with your bare hands. Call your local USDA

Cleanliness Counts

A good way to prevent disease outbreaks at your feeding station is to spread out your feeders, if you use a lot of them. Set up two or three areas, rather than just one. That way, the chances of a sick bird contaminating the rest of the tribe will be greatly reduced.

The threat of disease is another good reason to keep your feeding area tidy, by spreading bark mulch over the droppings beneath the feeders. And don't forget about your birdbath, either: Keep it sparkling clean. Nasty germs can grow fast in stagnant water if birds bring them in on their feet, feathers, or droppings.

extension agent, in case the experts in your region are tracking a disease, such as West Nile virus; they may want to come and collect the dead bird themselves. If not, pull on a pair of disposable rubber gloves and bag it securely for the trash.

Even if a bird doesn't look sick, its droppings may contain pathogens that can get mixed with seed and other feeder foods. Or the bird may carry germs on its body, feet, or beak. Most of the time, that's not a problem for other birds, but sometimes a virulent disease spreads through every bird at the feeder.

In 2007, backyard bird lovers in Washington State, where I lived at the time, started noticing dead and dying birds near their feeders. Testing showed that the problem was salmonellosis—the disease caused by the salmonella germ. This sickness is so serious, and can kill so many birds, that the Washington Department of Fish and Wildlife recommended that people temporarily discontinue bird feeding.

I hadn't seen any signs of illness in the black-headed grosbeaks, Bullock's orioles, lesser goldfinches, purple finches, and other birds at my feeders, but I was happy to comply. The thought of aiding the spread of an epidemic was unconscionable, so down came my feeders until the "All clear" was sounded a few weeks later. Sure, I missed the fun of watching my birds. But the disease was stopped in its tracks, thanks to the efforts of backyard bird lovers like you and me.

DO NOT DISTURB

Want to increase the number of birds that visit or live in your yard without doing a thing? That's it: Dedicate a part of your yard to not doing a thing. If you stay out of a shrubby area or let a flowerbed go a little wild, the birds will come in.

My most enticing spot is a back corner of my yard, where a wire fence joins an outbuilding. Wintercreeper and Japanese honeysuckle have covered the fence, and I've added shrubs that can take care of themselves. That undisturbed corner is my most popular attraction for catbirds, Carolina wrens, cardinals, brown thrashers, native sparrows, juncos, towhees, and more—and it's only about 6 × 10 feet.

In other yards I've lived in, I've let a little sunny corner take care of itself, too. Those areas drew doves, quail, white-crowned and golden-crowned sparrows, indigo and lazuli buntings, goldfinches of two varieties, and other shelter-seeking birds—and some came back the next year to nest.

DOORYARD BIRDS

Lots of birds are ready and willing to explore your backyard, especially if it includes abundant cover. With a shade tree, you're likely to see tanagers, purple finches, kinglets, vireos, several kinds of warblers, and other birds of the treetops. With an inviting planting of shrubs, you're apt to draw in thrashers, larger wrens, yellow-rumped and willow warblers, catbirds, mockingbirds, and a slew of others.

But most of these backyard birds will keep away from your house and lawn. They'd rather stay safe amid the sheltering foliage. "Dooryard birds," on the other hand, will happily explore right up to your front door, and they may choose nesting sites that are right in the path of your daily comings and goings.

That list of close-up birds includes some familiar friends and a couple that you may not have realized are living nearby. Here are the birds you're likely to see in your dooryard.

- Look for the flashy northern cardinal nesting in the climbing rose that covers your cottage or your mansion, or in the lilac that you planted near the door so you could revel in its fragrance. A nest of chirping cardinals is a great bonus.
- If you have a wreath on your front door to welcome visitors, you're likely to find that it's also welcomed a nest-building robin.
- Potted and hanging plants on your open porch? Good spot for a mourning dove or house finch to build its nest, and for the female house finch to charm you by singing while she's sitting on it.
- If your windows have an overhanging sill, a gentle phoebe may take up residence, constructing her nest where you can have a bird's-eye view of her babies.
- Hang a birdhouse that's sized for house wrens and chickadees on your porch or near your front door, and you may get an entertaining family to enjoy.
- The shrubs along your foundation or beside your front door might harbor a nesting chipping sparrow, a tiny chestnut-capped brown bird with a trilling song. Chippies often nest right near a well-used door. Maybe they've learned that our comings and goings mean that predators aren't likely to come close?

HOW-TO A Good Foundation

Robins and phoebes need a foundation for their nests, and if you provide one, you'll boost your chances of attracting one of these birds. (The eastern phoebe and Say's phoebe are possible nesters; the black phoebe prefers to live very close to water and often builds under bridges.) A simple shelf is all you need. Mount the shelf about 8 to 15 feet high on a wall of your house, where it's protected from rain, and see who takes you up on the offer.

DOUGHS

Soft foods are big news at bird feeders in recent years, and new products are springing up right and left. My bird supplies include an economy-size plastic bucket of Nuts 'n' Bugs, a commercial dough-type mixture that my titmice, chickadees, house and Carolina wrens, catbirds, and lots of other birds can't seem to get enough of. I smear it on bark, jam it into log feeders, and put chunks in three or four other feeders. It's been a hit since I started offering it.

Other products are just as attractive, so try out any that catch your eye and fit your budget. You'll find stiff, molded doughs to slip into feeders with cylindrical holders or log feeders, as well as blocks and pails of looser mixtures that will satisfy all your feathery friends.

Bird doughs are a combination of fats and grain-based foods (like cornmeal), plus nuts or fruit. The recipe varies from one product to another, but even the doughs that are filled out with cheap ingredients like cracked corn or seed mix will bring in the birds. Soft-food specialists like catbirds and wrens will gulp down the seeds right along with the rest. Nuthatches, chickadees, woodpeckers, and other seed eaters may pull seeds out to crack, swallow smaller chunks whole, or discard them while picking out the good bits of suet and other fats in the mix.

When it comes to attracting "special" birds, nothing works like bird doughs. But I've found two big drawbacks to these miracle meals: They attract starlings and house sparrows. And they cost a lot of scratch.

I solve the first problem by putting the foods in feeders that the pest birds can't easily access. I also put some in accessible feeders, too, where they can peck at it freely, because I don't want them to mount a concerted effort to outwit my deterrent feeders.

As for the second drawback, that's easy to solve, too: I buy the dough-type treats that include ingredients I don't have on hand, like the insects in Nuts 'n' Bugs. And I make the rest myself, for way less money than it costs to buy them. Of course, if your bird budget is a generous one, you may prefer the convenience of buying all of your bird doughs. But since it's even more fun to see birds eat something you've made yourself, why not give homemade a shot, too? It takes just minutes to mix up a big batch.

Bird Dough Basics

You don't need special recipes to make bird doughs—all you need is a feel for the product. If you can squeeze a handful of your concoction and have it hold together without crumbling when you poke it, you've got it made.

You only need three ingredients to make good bird dough, but you can add others to stretch it further or make it even more enticing.

1. Start with a **white fat**: any kind of solid or semi-solid fat, which is what'll hold your concoction together. Depending on what I have on hand, or what I remember to buy at the grocery store, that might be suet, chopped fat scraps from the butcher, lard, Crisco, or any other solid vegetable shortening. Another option, if you like: Save the fat when you cook a beef roast, pork roast, a batch of bacon, or even a roast chicken or turkey (sounds cannibalistic, but songbirds do eat bird fat), let it solidify, and add this softer stuff to the other fats.
2. Then, reach for another standard ingredient: **cornmeal**. That's what your fat will

stick to, so it stretches the fat to feed more birds, and it adds nutrition. Nearly all birds eat cornmeal when it's covered with fat, so it's a big part of nearly all my bird doughs.

3. Next, it's time for the third of the basic three ingredients, your secret weapon: **peanut butter**. Birds can't resist, so stock up on economy-size jars when you see them on sale. Chunky is the way to go, because those bits of peanuts are really enticing to birds. But they'll eagerly eat doughs made with creamy, too.

The Bird Gourmet

Making bird doughs isn't an exact science because the consistency of fats differs, and so does the gooeyness of peanut butter. Use your hands to gauge when the dough is ready: If it's too dry, add more solid fat or some oil; if it's too gooey, mix in more cornmeal or other dry carbs.

Start by melting the fat and peanut butter in a saucepan over low heat, then add the dry ingredients. After you thoroughly mix the ingredients, spread the dough on a cookie sheet or spoon it into molds to fit specialized feeders, and put it in your fridge or freezer to harden. Then put the molded dough into appropriate feeders for bluebirds, woodpeckers, chickadees, and all the rest, or cut the sheet of dough into pieces to serve and store. Extras will keep for months in your freezer in zip-top plastic freezer bags. Because bird doughs are heavy on fat, they can melt in summer heat. Try the "No-Melt" variation if your summers are steamy or your feeder is in the sun.

BASIC BIRD DOUGH

1 cup melted white fat, any kind
1 cup peanut butter
4 cups cornmeal
1 cup flour

NO-MELT BIRD DOUGH

1 cup melted lard
1 cup peanut butter
2 cups cornmeal
2 cups oatmeal (not instant)
1 cup flour

EXTRA-TEMPTING BIRD DOUGH

2 cups melted white fat, any kind
1 cup peanut butter
4 cups cornmeal
1 cup chopped nuts
½ cup chopped dates or currants

SEEDY BIRD DOUGH

1 cup melted white fat, any kind
½ cup peanut butter
1 cup sunflower chips
1 cup chopped peanuts
½ cup cracked corn

BIRD BALLS

1 cup melted white fat, any kind
1 cup peanut butter
3 cups cornmeal
1 cup flour
½ cup sunflower chips
½ cup finely chopped pecans or walnuts

4. Add more carbs, if you like, to make your dough stretch even further. Grab the flour, oatmeal, crushed crackers or breakfast cereal, or bread crumbs, and use them singly or together. They all help stiffen the mix.
5. If your mix feels too dry and you've run out of solid fats, add some oil. Corn, peanut, canola, or generic vegetable oil all work great; so do more expensive walnut and almond oil. I haven't had much success at my feeders with olive oil, when I've had to resort to using it after running out of the other oils.
6. And now the fun part: the extra added incentive! Throw in chopped nuts and chopped or bite-size dried fruit to make your dough even more tempting. And if you have a strong stomach, mix in roasted mealworms, waxworms, or other larvae for an irresistible bird treat.

DRIED BERRIES AND FRUIT

I doubt if my robins ever saw a papaya tree—come to think of it, neither have I—but the redbreasts that winter in my neighborhood snatch up those little orange bits at my feeding station like they've been eating them all their lives. Same with mango, cranberries, dates, and every other dried fruit I've tried. They still like fresh apples the best (see the Fresh Fruit entry for more on that), but dried fruit has won their favor, too.

I figure it's all because the robins have learned to associate my feeding station with food. The same behavior is happening all across the country these days, and with way more birds than just robins.

Once fruit-eating orioles, tanagers, catbirds, thrashers, flycatchers, wrens, pileated woodpeckers, and other birds learn to come to your feeder for a meal, you can give dried fruit a bigger place on your menu. Add it to your homemade treats, or offer a handful as-is in your feeders that serve these birds.

Your birds may peck at big pieces of dried fruit, like apple rings or peaches, but they'll gobble up bite-size bits more eagerly, maybe because they seem like wild berries. Experiment with any fruits you find. Apples, currants, and raisins—

Nonstick Tricks

I find it easier to use my kitchen shears, rather than a knife, to snip larger dried fruit into pieces. But even so, it can be a sticky business. Dates, prunes, nectarines, and other dried fruits are full of concentrated sugar, which quickly gums up your knife or kitchen shears. To solve that problem, just give your blade a spritz of nonstick cooking spray before you slice 'n' dice.

Keep a few apples on hand to feed any robins that show up at your feeder in winter. They'll peck out every bit of flesh, leaving a neat, empty shell.

which used to go uneaten at my feeder—are fast becoming a hit with the new birds that visit us, but I've found they'll eat prunes, mango, apricots, blueberries, cherries, and just about anything else I decide to share with them.

I've had great success with dried wild fruits I've collected, too. You can get a whole winter's supply by shaking the branches of a mulberry tree, and drying the fruits for a few hours in a 200°F oven. Or collect the fruits from Bradford pears, hackberries, sassafras, Juneberries, chokecherries, and other wild cherries, and give them the same treatment.

FRUITY FEAST

1 cup melted suet

2 cups cornmeal

2 cups of "trail mix" dried fruit and nuts, chopped

Mix all ingredients thoroughly, let it harden, and then serve in chunks and crumbles in suet feeders, log feeders, oriole feeders, or in mealworm feeders. Your woodpeckers, catbirds, wrens, and other fruit eaters will come flocking.

DROUGHT

I moved back to Indiana from the rainy Northwest just in time for the worst drought in decades. Corn and soybeans shriveled in the cracked fields, lawns gave up and went dormant or dead, and as for my garden, forget it. Even if I'd been willing to pay hundreds of dollars to keep it alive with water pumped from the Wabash River, the effort simply wasn't worth it. Seventy-four Indiana counties were declared agricultural disaster areas that year, and my dried-up garden was part of them.

My birdbath that summer was the most popular spot for miles, it seemed, with scores of birds depending on it daily. Even the wood thrushes came out of the woods a mile away to get a drink, and the bluebirds, which usually don't pay me a visit until winter, were there in force. Migration brought mobs of birds to the simple clay saucers of fresh water I'd set out all over the yard, including tiny wood warblers and vireos that dropped down from the treetops to enjoy a life-giving drink.

But it was the hummingbirds that were the most incredible happening that season. People from all across the drought-affected region sent me reports of more hummers than they'd ever seen—not just a few dozen, but hundreds, swirling around their feeders. I was going through 10 pounds of sugar a week—that's 5 gallons of nectar.

The effect of the drought didn't end in summer, either. Many wild fruits and seeds that nourish the birds through fall and winter had failed, too, so feeders were hopping. It was a pleasure to help take up the slack, even if I did have to rearrange my budget to find enough funds for all the seed I was going through.

By late fall, the rains were back to normal, thank goodness. But that's not always the case. If you live in the Southeast, you know what an extended drought can do: The drought of 2007 took a long time to loosen its grip.

When Water Dries Up

Droughts have occurred since long before the catastrophic Dust Bowl days. But they've been increasing in frequency and severity over the past

Juicy Fruit

Add fresh fruit to your feeders during a drought to provide moisture to all kinds of birds, from robins and wrens to flycatchers and orioles. Halved apples and oranges are a mainstay, but you can experiment with other fruits, too. During the drought of 2002 here in Indiana, the bunches of not-so-great grapes I got for free from the supermarket were more popular than any other offerings in my yard. All I did was hook the bunches over the branches of my shrubs and young trees, where the birds could dine on them as they would in the wild.

few decades, "coincident with rising temperatures," as the respected scientists who contributed to the federal government's *Global Climate Change Impacts in the United States* 2009 report put it. "In the future," they wrote, "droughts are likely to become more frequent and severe in some regions."

It's the Southwest that's expected to bear the Sahara-like brunt of future droughts, according to the maps in the report. But lots of other regions are apt to feel the pinch in water supplies, too. I've shifted my choice of hummingbird flowers toward those that will tolerate dry soil but thrive in deluges, too, just in case the rains do come. And I've added drought-tolerant amaranth and sunflowers, so there's some extra seed available, just in case.

The best thing you can do for your birds when drought sets in is to make sure your birdbaths are always filled with fresh water. It's absolutely vital for most birds, especially when drought dries up the usual crop of summer fruit that supplies moisture to birds and animals.

A ground-level birdbath will get lots of use by both birds and more unusual visitors during a drought, so be sure to add one to your offerings when the big faucet in the sky shuts off for an extended period. Just wait until you see the other visitors your water may attract: hummingbirds, crows, bats, rabbits, flying squirrels, possums, box turtles, toads, and even a whole bunch of snails availed themselves of the precious resource in my humble birdbaths.

You can make a big difference in the survival of your birds and other wildlife, just by offering a little water.

DUST BATHS

There's no doubt that house sparrows can be a pain—most of the time, they come in mobs, keeping other birds from the feeder and making gluttons of themselves. But at times, these chubby brown birds with the black bibs are an utter delight.

Muddy runoff collects at a low spot on my brick patio, and I'm not always good about getting out the broom to brush it away after it dries out. My lackadaisical housekeeping is a boon for the house sparrows, though, which quickly turn the dried mud into a dust bath. With wings fluttering and feet kicking, a dozen sparrows will cram into the little space, kicking up dust with abandon.

It's just plain fun to watch, because the birds look like they're heartily enjoying themselves. And it may even give you a new appreciation for house sparrows.

Not ready to add a dust bath to attract house sparrows? Okay, how about for a wild turkey? Believe it or not, these gigantic birds enjoy wallowing in a cloud of dust, too, just like chickens in a barnyard. In recent years, wild turkeys have quickly become regulars at many feeding stations, so if yours is on the list, add a dust spa to the facilities.

The dust probably shakes loose or suffocates tiny lice and other parasites between the birds' feathers, surmise scientists, and I'll bet it feels good to get rid of the itch. You'll be surprised at the variety of different birds that relish a good, dusty bath: titmice, doves, flickers, roadrunners, wrens, thrashers, quail, bobwhites, and horned larks, to name a few. (Next time you take an African safari, watch for oxpeckers and guinea hens taking a dust bath.)

Even the most dignified birds look mighty comical when they're lolling in the dust. After bathing, the birds shake themselves vigorously to get rid of it. And most of them make the birdbath their next stop, to finish freshening up.

HOW-TO Dust Bath Deluxe

Any area of bare, fine soil, extra-fine sand, or wood ashes makes a great dust bath, as far as birds are concerned. You can let the birds create their own au naturel spot, or you can build a dust bath so you can have the fun of watching. A sunny spot about 5 to 10 feet from your birdbath makes a good location, since most birds take a water bath afterward. Just clear a 2 × 2-foot square of soil (make it 3 × 3-foot if you have turkeys), and outline it with a low rim of bricks or concrete edgers. Pour in a layer of fine sand (sandbox sand), about 2 inches deep, and add a shovelful of wood ashes from your fireplace or patio fire pit for extra appeal. Don't worry about protecting the dust from rain: It'll dry out quickly, and your bathers will soon be back.

Mourning doves and other dust bath users really get into it, wriggling and shaking and fluffing their feathers with abandon. Must feel great!

E/F

EGGS AND EGGSHELLS

I first started learning about what birds need—and what they like best—from my mother's caged canaries, which she kept in a sunny kitchen window. Year-round, the birds lived on a seed mix that was heavy on canary seed and millet. In early spring, we added Hartz Mountain Song Food from a bright orange tin, which included such exotic ingredients as Indian thistle and sesame seeds, plus egg yolks and dehydrated milk solids. When the pair of canaries began courting, I noticed that the female nibbled on the calcium-rich cuttlebone much more than usual. Throughout spring, both birds eagerly ate the dehydrated egg yolk wafers we fastened to the cage.

The lessons I learned when I helped my mom with her canaries hold true for wild birds, too. After all, all caged birds were once wild things themselves.

A Cardinal in Your Kitchen?

Long before feeding wild birds became a national pastime, caged birds were all the rage. Canaries native to islands off of Africa were singing from cages in Europe by the 1400s. Parakeets from Australia and parrots soon joined the ranks. The birdlife of America was exploited, too—thousands of cardinals and other songbirds were sold in America and shipped to Europe in the 1800s.

"The males are charming songsters, and the demand for them lately has greatly increased," wrote George H. Holden about rose-breasted grosbeaks, in his 1888 book, *Canaries and Cage-Birds: Birds for Pleasure and for Profit.* House finches (then called linnets) and painted buntings were sold for pets as recently as the 1950s.

The bird trade, as you might suspect, led to the decimation of many wild species, a problem that continues with parrots and exotic finches today.

Nowadays, we'd never dream of keeping a cardinal in a cage. But we can still use similar foods and treats to nurture birds in the wild—and to tempt them to our feeders.

Not a wild American bird, the common canary, once a popular caged bird, taught me a lot about birds' preferences—including their appetite for eggs.

Easter Eggs

When Easter season rolls around, think eggs. Spring is prime breeding season, and eggs we offer in our feeders are appealing to nesting birds. The yolks are high in fat and protein, which is just what breeding birds need—it takes a lot of energy for a male to defend his family. The shells are rich in calcium, another essential element at nesting time when females are depleting their reserves to produce their own eggs.

Adding eggs and shells to your spring menu can attract birds you don't usually see, including martins and swallows, blue-gray gnatcatchers, warblers, kingbirds and other flycatchers, wrens, tanagers, and orioles. Other feeder regulars will enjoy eggs, too. You'll notice that it's the female birds that are most interested in the shells, while males tend to go for the yolks.

That's It Egg-zactly!

For a calcium boost during nesting season, offer crushed eggshells. Rinse the shells and bake at 250°F for about 10 minutes, until they're dry but not browned. They'll crumble easily by hand. Or you can put them in a zip-top freezer bag, press out the air and seal the bag, and step on it to crush the shells. Serve in a tray feeder, where birds can easily see and access the treat, or put a handful on your deck railing or on bare ground.

EGG CRUMBLES

3 hard-boiled eggs, peeled
½ cup cornmeal
1 cup nonfat dry milk

Mash eggs with the back of a fork. Pour in dry ingredients, and mash again until thoroughly mixed. Serve in small amounts in a tray, a mealworm dish, or a stick-on window feeder. Wrens, warblers, gnatcatchers, orioles, chickadees, and many other birds enjoy this treat in springtime because it's high in protein, fat, and calcium.

If starlings are a problem, serve in a domed feeder with the dome lowered to exclude large birds.

ENJOY

Birds are a pleasure, no doubt about it. Extending a helping hand, whether it's by planting a dogwood for berries, putting up a wren house, or cooking up a suet treat, makes us feel good. Watching our backyard birds is a treat, too, and so is listening to them on a spring morning or in the dead of winter. Our feathered friends make our yards come alive.

Sometimes, we need to remind ourselves to slow down and enjoy the little sanctuary we've created. That's why it's a great idea to include a window feeder in your lineup, or to set a garden bench near the birdbath so you can have a front-row seat. I like to plant hummingbird flowers near a window, too, so I can enjoy the little buzzy guys even when I'm busy in the house.

Visual Aids

These aren't my bird photos gracing the pages of this book—they're from pros who spend thousands of dollars and hours of time getting a good shot. My pics are almost always blurry, because birds don't usually sit still long enough for me to snap the shutter. Still, even with my very amateur results, I get a lot of pleasure out of taking bird pics.

Digital cameras make it easy for any of us to get candid shots of our backyard birds. Even my out-of-focus photos teach me a lot about birds, because they capture the details of behavior, flight, and anatomy that my eyes miss. Take the gray catbird, for instance—field guides point out the rusty-colored patch of feathers where the bird's tail joins its body, but it wasn't until one of my photos happened to catch a catbird from underneath that I realized how pretty that rusty patch is. Now, I make a habit of watching for it every time I spy a catbird.

Camera Catalog

Taking photos of your feeding station is a quick way to inventory who's at your feeders and to keep track of how your birds change with the seasons. During spring and fall, when the cast of characters is changing fast, I try to remember to snap some shots at least once a week. My photos help me remember who was here when—a scarlet tanager when the tulips were blooming; the horned lark during the ice storm; the last of the juncos when indigo buntings arrived in spring. Even if you don't use the photos to review your backyard routine, they're still a delight to look at and "remember when."

The more you watch your birds, the more little details of appearance and behavior you'll notice. Try for a look at the underside of a gray catbird's tail to see its patch of pretty chestnut feathers.

Those fine points are why I keep a pair of binoculars near at hand, too. My binocs are little lightweight cheapies, but they're good enough to zero in on birds from inside the house or when I'm out in the yard. The more you look closely at your pals, the better you'll get to know them. Besides, watching birds is good for you! Studies show it reduces stress as well as meditation does and can even lower blood pressure.

EXPECTATIONS

I don't think I'll ever have a bald eagle in my little backyard or spot a roadrunner coursing along the alley, but I'm not ready to rule out the possibility. Birds are changing their habits in lots of ways, and as they respond to climate change and shifting habitats, just about anything is possible.

In recent years, birds of the forest, such as Cooper's hawks, wild turkeys, and tanagers, have become a common sight in backyards, and great blue herons are now including backyard garden pools in their stop-off sites. Ranges are changing, too, and some species are leaving their more southerly locales to move northward. Others are going eastward after years of staying in the West, or vice versa—western hummingbirds show up east of the Mississippi, and cardinals have been spotted in Seattle.

I'm ready for anything in my backyard—wonder if the bird store will be stocking lizards when that roadrunner shows up?—but meanwhile, it's easy to make an educated guess at

The Regulars

Many birds are already backyard regulars, having adapted to feeding and/or nesting in our homey habitat. Wherever you live, you're almost certain to see most of these birds. Not all of them will visit your feeder; to see which birds are becoming interested in feeding stations as well as backyard habitat, check "The Newbies" on the opposite page.

- American goldfinch
- American robin
- Cedar waxwing
- Chickadees
- Downy woodpecker
- Flickers
- Grackles
- Grosbeaks
- House finch
- House sparrow
- Hummingbirds
- Indigo or lazuli bunting
- Jays
- Mockingbird
- Mourning dove
- Orioles
- Pine siskin
- Song sparrow
- Starling
- Titmice
- Wrens

The Newbies

Mostly insect eaters, these birds are adapting to visiting our feeders and backyards, and others will no doubt be joining them. Some of them are grassland birds, displaced by modern agriculture and pesticides. Keep an eye out for these less common backyard birds, and have mealworms, fruit, and soft foods ready and waiting along with your usual seed supply.

- American robin
- Baltimore oriole
- Black-throated blue warbler
- Bohemian waxwing
- Brown thrasher
- Bullock's oriole
- Cedar waxwing
- Dickcissel
- Eastern meadowlark
- Gray catbird
- Hepatic tanager
- Hooded oriole
- Horned lark
- Orange-crowned warbler
- Orchard oriole
- Pileated woodpecker
- Pine warbler
- Sapsuckers
- Scarlet tanager
- Scott's oriole
- Summer tanager
- Townsend's warbler
- Western meadowlark
- Western tanager
- Wild turkey
- Yellow-rumped warbler (both Audubon's and myrtle races)

which visitors will stop in. All I have to do is look around to see what kinds of habitat are nearby.

Most of us across the country share the same basic cast of characters at our feeding stations. But dozens of other birds may show up in your yard, depending on which part of the country you live in and what kind of wild places are near your home. Here's a sampling of the possibilities beyond the basic birds that you might attract.

Forest. If you live within about a mile of a patch of woods or a forest, look for tanagers, warblers, ovenbirds, vireos, blue-gray gnatcatchers, grosbeaks, pileated woodpeckers, red-headed and other larger woodpeckers, brown creepers, small flycatchers, towhees, juncos, and white-throated and other native sparrows. If you live near coniferous woods, you might spot grouse and wood warblers from that habitat.

Grassland. If you live near farm fields or meadows, you may attract bluebirds, eastern or western meadowlarks, horned larks, dickcissels, field sparrows, grasshopper sparrows, other

If your yard is nestled among the pine forests of the Southeast, a delightful pine warbler may drop in. No pines? You're not likely to see it, except during migration.

native sparrows, eastern or western kingbirds, scissor-tailed flycatchers, great crested or ash-throated flycatchers, barn swallows, quail, ring-neck pheasants, magpies, and in the right range, roadrunners.

Sagebrush. If you live in sagebrush country or chaparral, you may spot bluebirds, quail, sage and sharp-tailed grouse, sage thrashers, sage sparrows, black-throated sparrows, other native sparrows, and maybe even burrowing owls.

Wetlands and water. If you live within a half-mile or so of a river, lake, swamp, or other watery habitat, you may see herons, tree swallows, swamp sparrows, prothonotary warblers, water-thrushes, purple martins, and wood ducks.

EXPERIMENT!

"Oh boy! Are you making a concoction?" my kids would ask, whenever I'd pull out the biggest mixing bowl. "Can we help?"

"Sure," I'd answer, and we'd start ransacking the cupboards for stuff to throw into the mix. The jar of peanut butter came first, and cornmeal was a staple, but after that, just about anything was fair game: old cereal, stale crackers, bread crusts, dried currants left over from some recipe or other, and anything else that looked like it might be palatable to birds.

The guidelines were simple: If it started its life as a seed or a nut, it went into the mix. There were only a few exceptions—no rice or legumes (dry peas, beans, lentils), because most birds weren't interested, and nothing sticky-sweet, because it would draw wasps.

Most of my bird dough recipes today still start the same way: peanut butter to bind the stuff together, cornmeal for high calories, and whatever dry stuff I have on hand to bulk up the mix.

Maybe I've just been lucky, but birds have eagerly eaten all of the concoctions I've put together. I suspect it's peanut butter that's the magic ingredient. No matter what's coated with it, birds will choff it down.

Start with the recipes in this book to get a feel for the proportions of various ingredients, but don't be afraid to experiment. Out of cornmeal? Use flour, biscuit mix, or pancake mix—or, if you can afford it, ground nuts or almond meal. Running low on peanut butter? Mash in some shortening or a suet block to stick things together. Too dry? Work in a little cooking oil to stick it together.

I do a lot of experimenting with commercial bird foods, too, because you never know which one will be a real hit with the birds. But I start small, by buying the smallest size I can, before I go whole hog. Safflower seeds, for instance, are now packaged for birds, because cardinals are learning to appreciate them at feeders. My cardinals are slow learners, it seems—I've been using the same 5-pound bag for close to a year now. On the other hand, a product called Nuts 'n' Bugs (see Resources on page 297) has been a huge hit with my wrens, catbirds, brown creepers, titmice, nuthatches, and chickadees since Day 1, so I buy it by the 5-pound pail.

FALL LEAVES

Every fall, the whine of leaf blowers goes on for weeks in my small town, as fall leaves are removed and bagged at the curb for pickup.

At my place, it's a different story. Here, I get weird looks from the neighbors. Why? Because I rake leaves into my yard instead of out of it.

It's another trick I learned at my mother's knee. She let the wind take care of arranging the fall leaves around her rose bushes, perennial beds, and trees, so they had an insulating blanket for the cold weather ahead.

A Living Feast

Fall leaves make better soil, my mom used to tell me, and she was right. A whole civilization of chewing, creeping things, from earthworms and beetles, to slugs and snails, to tiny soil critters and microscopic bacteria, break the leaves down over winter, creating a loose, humusy compost right in place.

Ever wonder why towhees, sparrows, thrashers, thrushes, grackles, and wild turkeys spend so much time scratching in dead leaves? That blanket of leaves is a living banquet of creepy crawlies, as well as stray seeds, acorns, or other goodies. All that food will attract more birds to your backyard, especially when the neighbors' yards are raked bare.

The leaves' insulating property is another boon to birds. The humusy soil beneath a layer of leaves doesn't freeze as soon or as solid as exposed areas, so robins and other birds can still find food, even when the air is frigid, and even when they dig down beneath the snow.

Let the Wind Do the Work

Think about your last walk in the woods, and you'll realize that leaves decompose fast. A foot-deep layer decomposes to a thin scattering by the time spring rolls around, which is why you don't slog through neck-deep leaves when you walk a woodsy path. So put down the rake, and let the leaves blow where they will. The wind will nestle them around the plants in your yard and under hedges, where birds will be drawn to the food beneath them. If you're worried that leaves may harm your lawn, you can help the wind out with a few minutes of raking. Or, better yet, reduce those lawn areas for better bird habitat.

FATS AND OILS

Thanks to my solid peasant stock heritage, my body is really good at storing food. Potatoes and other starches go right to my hips, as insurance against hard times that so far haven't come.

As I've tried to get a handle on how my body works, I've learned a lot about nutrition, and some of it has been a real surprise. With the current focus on obesity, I'm reading more and more about how metabolism and foods work.

Fats and oils are higher in calories than any other foods, ounce for ounce. That makes them great for fueling birds on migration or in cold weather (and not so great for couch potatoes eating sour cream dips). These foods are easy to recognize, on both the bird and human menu, because they're super oily or greasy.

Best Bird Fats

Birds will eat all oils and fats, but in my experience, some are more appealing than others.

Solid or semi-solid fats, such as vegetable shortening (and suet, of course) win by a mile, because birds can take bites of pure fat. Hardened bacon fat or meat drippings are hugely popular, too.

First of the wood warbler clan to become a backyard regular, the yellow-rumped warbler is fond of suet and other soft foods in any season.

For use in homemade bird treats, plant-based oils are welcome, too, especially if you include a solid fat to bulk up the mix. I've found that sunflower and peanut oils are tops, as you might expect, since those are two of the most popular seeds at the feeder. Walnut and almond oils are a hit, too, although, with their high prices, I usually save them for my own baking. Canola oil, flaxseed oil, corn oil, and generic vegetable oil will work, too, and some folks even report success using olive oil in recipes, although my birds turn up their noses at it. But if your goal is to attract birds, why not go for their faves?

I usually reserve a bottle of cheap vegetable or corn oil for my starling decoy feeder (see Decoy Feeders entry). Softened kibble dog food, drizzled with cheap vegetable oil and set far from the other feeders, keeps these birds happy for hours.

Hidden Fats

Other high-fat foods aren't so easy to identify. Take dogwood berries, for instance. I've often wondered why dogwoods are so popular with fall migrating bluebirds, tanagers, thrushes, thrashers, and grosbeaks, which will descend on a berried tree by the dozens.

I used to think the berries must be extra tasty, but then I found out that birds don't have a sense of taste like ours. (That's why they aren't deterred by seeds treated with hot pepper sprays, although squirrels are sent running.) Maybe the berries smell good?

Maybe so. But birds can discern "umami," the taste of foods that are high in protein (see the entry Umami for more details on this interesting addition to our sense of taste).

It's the umami taste of those shiny red berries that draws birds to the trees. Foods rich in protein generally are also high in fat. Getting lots of calories down the hatch is the birds' goal during their grueling flights, and all of the berries favored by birds during migration have a high fat content.

Only about one of every five plants with fleshy fruits (berries, in other words) fills the bill, but fill it they do. Flowering dogwood (*Cornus florida*) is right at the top of the list, with spice bush, gray dogwood, silky dogwood, sassafras, black gum, Virginia creeper, arrow-wood, and poison ivy close behind.

All their berries have a high fat content—greater than 10 percent lipids, which is a lot when we're talking about fruit. Guess I won't be snacking on dogwood berries anytime soon.

Attention-Getting Berries

More birds than ever are learning to associate feeders with a meal, but natural food still gets their attention first. To attract bluebirds, tanagers, and other fruit-eating travelers, plant a high-fat berry shrub or tree to catch their eye during fall migration. Keep your feeders stocked with fatty foods that they can also investigate. Offer suet and molded treats in feeders that are accessible to perching birds, and try chopped suet or bite-size high-fat foods (see Bite-Size Bits entry) in your tray feeders.

FEATHERS

Feathers are an amazing creation, considering they're made out of the same substance as our own fingernails. That wonder material is keratin, a fibrous protein that forms other animal structures, too: bird beaks, horse hooves, porcupine quills, turtle shells, and grizzly bear claws, to name a few. Lots of animals have claws or hooves, but only birds have feathers, and all birds, except when newly hatched, have them. So, if it has feathers, it's a bird.

Without feathers, birds couldn't fly, and without feathers, birds might freeze or fry. The fluffy body feathers and down provide super insulation to keep the bird from getting too cold or too hot.

Once a feather is fully formed, the end of the mid-vein closes off, and there's no life in the feather, only in the muscles that hold it in place. Birds molt as their feathers get old and worn-out, usually after nesting season is finished. The molt lasts a few weeks, because only a few feathers are shed at a time.

A Marvel of Design

Grab a magnifying glass when you find a bird feather in your backyard, and you can see the deeper miracle of a feather. It's made of lots of tiny interlocking parts that hold together like zippers, so that the surface stays sleek.

When you see a bird running its feathers through its bill after a good splashing bath, it's realigning those barbs and barbules by zipping them back into shape.

While you've got that feather in your hand, see if you can figure out which bird it came from. It's a lot trickier than it seems!

Straight from the Source

You'll get a lifetime supply of feathers for nest material from a single feather pillow. Check a thrift shop or garage sale to find one for a bargain price. Or visit a poultry farm or duck pond, and collect a handful of stray feathers near the premises. Scatter the feathers on your lawn so the birds can choose their favorites, or include them in a basket of other nesting materials.

The striped wings of a downy woodpecker, for instance, are actually made of spotted feathers. The white and black sections of each feather align to create a stripe when the downy spreads its wings.

Feathering the Nest

Lots of birds make a point of including feathers in their nests. Waterfowl pluck their own down to create a soft, insulating lining, but other birds go treasure hunting to find feathers of other species for their nests.

They collect whatever suitable feathers they can find in their own neighborhood. Exactly which birds those come from will vary.

Tree swallows and violet-green swallows, for instance, which nest near water, gather soft white feathers from the ducks and geese that dwell in their usual homelands. Palm warblers, on the other hand, nest in woodsy wet places in the Far North, and their nests typically include feathers of the ruffed grouse, spruce grouse, barred owl, and robin, all birds that share their habitat.

Scatter soft white feathers on your lawn, and the svelte violet-green swallow may flutter down to collect them.

With all these birds, plus others, seeking feathers for their nests, it's a good bet that your offering of feathers at nesting time will tickle the fancy of your backyard birds. There's no need to worry about matching your feather offerings to the species in your neighborhood, because feathers are such a prize that most birds will eagerly snatch any kind you put out. Don't bother offering stiff tail or wing feathers; it's soft, curled body feathers or downy feathers that are the prize for nest-feathering birds. (To find feathers, see "Straight from the Source" above.)

Why do birds use feathers in their nest? The big reason is insulation, to keep their nestlings warm and cozy. Feathers help keep their babies dry, too, and can hide them from predators.

FEEDER CHOICES

Peruse any bird supply store or catalog, and you'll find so many styles of bird feeders, it's hard to tell where to start. If you're like most of us, you'll pick the one that you find prettiest, rather than comparing them for practicality.

I gnash my teeth every time I look at the boxful of nice-looking but frustrating feeders I replaced when their shortcomings became obvious.

In spite of the plethora of choices, most bird feeders boil down to a few basic designs—tube, hopper, tray, cage, or dish—with variations.

Function is just as important as style, so make sure your feeder works the way you want it to. To make sure you have the perfect match, take a look at it from both the birds' viewpoint and your own.

Scarlet tanagers scout treetop foliage for insects, but they'll happily visit your feeder if there's a comfortable place to perch.

Perchers and Clingers

Choose wire mesh feeders without perches for birds that are good at clinging—chickadees, titmice, nuthatches, woodpeckers, wrens, and brown creepers. For larger birds that prefer to perch, such as cardinals, grosbeaks, tanagers, bluebirds, jays, catbirds, thrashers, and thrushes, look for feeders that offer a perching area that's spacious enough to accommodate the birds.

- How many birds can it accommodate at the same time? Make sure at least one of your feeders can serve a crowd.
- Can birds perch at it comfortably? Avoid feeders that don't have enough room for birds to eat in a natural position.
- How easy is it to refill? Imagine it's a cold, rainy morning or a driving snowstorm, and pretend to fill the feeder in the store.
- Will you have to take down a hanging feeder to fill it, or can you do it one-handed while it's hanging in place?
- How much does it hold? Small feeders will need your attention more often.
- Will it discourage squirrels from making off with the goodies?
- Is there a roof to keep the food from getting wet and moldy?

FEEDER SITES

If it hadn't been such a job getting my multi-armed feeder pole into the ground, I'd rearrange it. But I was so focused on finagling it in among the tree roots that crisscross my backyard, that when I finally found a free space, I put it up without thinking about which direction the arms were pointing.

Only after I firmed the ground back into place and hung my feeders did I realize I'd robbed myself of a full view. One of the arms is completely hidden behind the pole and a front feeder, so I never get to see the birds at the rear feeder. Had I angled the post instead. . . .

That's why it pays to think through your view before you set up your feeders. Sure, you're doing this to help the birds—but, hey, you want a payoff, too. It's not nearly as much fun refilling feeders and buying or making treats when you can't see the birds partaking of your goodies.

Consider from which window and which angle you're most likely to watch, and mount the feeder so you get the best view.

Next to Natural

Right beside your feeder, add a shadblow, dogwood, spice bush, elderberry, or other native plant with berries that birds are fond of. When the berries ripen, the catbirds, thrushes, robins, bluebirds, waxwings, and other fruit eaters they attract can easily make the move from the natural food to the treats you have waiting.

Room with a View

The most important "rule" in feeder placement is to put your feeder (or birdbath) as close to a window as you can. Not just any window—make it one that you look out of a lot, like the one near your kitchen table or next to your living room chair. Putting the feeder about 4 to 10 feet from the window will give you a great view of the comings and goings.

With a close-up view, you'll feel more connected to your backyard birds, and you'll get to know your friends a lot faster. It's safer for birds, too, because they won't be able to get up much speed if—make that "when"—they panic. So any collisions with the window are apt to be less than lethal.

Notice how birds approach your feeding station: Often the bird will land on the top of your pole before it moves down to a feeder, or it may approach from an overhead branch.

That's why I always plant a tall shrub or small tree next to the feeder. The birds use it as a staging point when they enter and exit the feeding area or while they're waiting their turn. You'll find more details in the entry Access Routes.

Watch Out Below

Seed shells and other debris collect below the feeder, and droppings often decorate the surrounding foliage. Birds that scratch beneath a feeder can damage plants, too. So, if you're planning to put your feeder in an existing garden bed, avoid choosing a spot that's among delicate plants or prized specimens.

FENCES

"Something there is that doesn't love a wall," muses Robert Frost in his famous poem "Mending Wall," while his neighbor keeps insisting that "Good fences make good neighbors."

I'm not a fan of fences and walls, either, but sometimes they're a necessary evil. In my case, a neighbor's dogs and privacy were the motivation behind the fence I put up along one side of my backyard.

The raw new wood was rudely eye-catching at first. But in less than 2 years, the fence has become a valuable part of my overall habitat.

Last winter, a pair of Carolina wrens sought shelter every night in a tangle of vines that spill over it (until they retreated to the garage when bitter cold came in). In spring, a gray catbird raised two broods in a nest among the vines. In another year or two, rosehips, holly, and Virginia creeper berries will lure even more birds to what is now a sheltering wall of greenery.

Pretty and Practical

Ornamental miscanthus grasses don't have much value to birds for food or cover. Their growth is too dense for birds to penetrate, and the seeds get few takers. But the dry grass is sought for nesting materials, and birds can shelter from wind or snow on the lee side of the clumps. Plant the grasses about 6 feet away from your fence, and you'll create a sheltered nook for foraging native sparrows, juncos, doves, quail, and other ground-level birds.

Oh, Grow Up!

Just think of your fence as vertical planting space, and use it to add to the mix of bird-attracting cover. If your fence is solid boards without much space between, look for vines that cling with little sucker feet, like Virginia creeper or Boston ivy, to swiftly climb the expanse.

If you have a more open fence of spaced boards or wire, coral honeysuckle or Hall's honeysuckle would be a beautiful choice to clothe it quickly—and coax in hummingbirds at the same time. Or try the ultra-fast growing autumn clematis, which'll create a dense tangle of stems for wrens, catbirds, thrashers, and other birds to hide out in. Trumpet vine and wisteria are too rampant for a fence, but morning glories work great, and attract butterflies and hummingbirds.

I use my fence as a backdrop for shrubs, too, in keeping with the multi-layered theme of my yard (see the Layered Look entry). Roses are a natural with a fence, and I planted one that's a boon to birds but a bane of farmers: the multiflora rose that grows wild wherever birds happen to drop a seed. In fact, a bird planted the rose in my own yard; I simply transplanted it along the fence (that doesn't make me guilty, does it?). If you don't want the invasive plant police to come to your home, choose another climbing rose, such as trouble-free 'New Dawn'. I added a trio of hollies, too, for winter cover and evergreen color, and for their robin-tempting berries.

FINCHES AND FINCH MIX

The active little singers called finches are among the most reliable visitors to backyards and feeders. It doesn't take much to make them happy—a tube of niger or sunflowers and a basin of water will keep them coming back day after day.

Purple finches are a winter or migration visitor in most areas of the country; other finches, such as Cassin's finch and the lesser goldfinch, have a more limited range. Buntings are also members of the finch family, and they're usually a seasonal delight, stopping in backyards on spring migration. Redpolls usually visit in winter.

But American goldfinches and house finches are common year-round residents, so you can count on hosting these birds just about any day of the year. You'll soon notice that goldfinch numbers build to a sunny crescendo in spring and fall, when the birds settle in at feeding hot spots for a few weeks.

It's not all that unusual—but it is a real delight—to see 50 or more of these bright birds twittering in your backyard or crowding your feeders.

Special Seeds

Niger seed is the magnet for most finches, and tube feeders or seed socks are the way to go. These birds have learned to associate the seed with the feeder, so take advantage of that habit by serving them in the style to which they've become accustomed.

Finches also gladly eat black oil sunflower seeds, and buntings will gobble white proso millet if it's available. They like it even better than niger, at least at my feeders.

Weed seeds are a huge favorite with finches,

Purple finches are more dramatically colored and bulkier than the similar house finch. Tube feeders suit all finches to a T.

which is all the excuse I need to let an occasional plant of lamb's-quarters or pigweed amaranth have its way in my gardens. Speaking of gardens, little finches are also big fans of flower seeds. For more tips on particular plants to attract this happy tribe, see the entry Birdseed Gardens.

Because finches are easy to attract and beloved by bird-watchers, commercial companies have created a slew of seed mixes just for them. The basic seeds we've already talked about will win their loyalty, but if you want to give them a special treat—or if your finches have defected to your neighbor's yard—why not splurge on a bag of finch mix?

Ingredients are listed according to their proportion in the mix, from the most to the least. Canary seed is the real treasure in finch mix, so make sure it's up near the top of the list of ingredients. Canola seed, a tiny round black seed, is another popular ingredient in some finch mixes; it may take your finches some time to get used to it. You'll find more about this seed in the Canola entry. Sunflower chips and millets of various kinds (white, tan, or red) often round out the mix. Always read the label before you buy to see what you're paying for.

Specialty of the House

Most finch mixes sell for $2.50 to $3 per pound, in 5-pound bags. You can usually save some money by making your own mix of canary seed, niger, millet, and sunflower chips. Canary seed is not as widely available as the other ingredients, although I keep hoping bird suppliers will wise up and start stocking it all by itself. Meanwhile, you can ask your bird supply shop or feed store to order it for you, or buy from mail-order suppliers like those listed in the Resources section at the back of this book.

FLOCKS

It's always a bittersweet moment when I notice the first flock of birds in summer.

"Oh, the swallows are flocking," I exult, loving the sight of hundreds of birds behaving as if with one mind.

Next thing you know, I'm saying the same thing, but with a different inflection. "Oh, the birds are flocking," I mourn at the first sign of the changing season.

Even if I'm holding a sun-warmed tomato in my hand at the moment I spot that first flock, I know there's no stopping winter once birds start to gather in groups.

Once the breeding season is finished, some species of birds band together in ever-growing groups as they prepare and set out for their winter quarters. Swallows are the first to gather and go, with purple martins, grackles and other blackbirds, and chimney swifts soon following behind. Less widespread birds, including bobolinks and blue grosbeaks, also gather forces in late summer.

Boys Will Be Boys

Territorial aggression between male birds gets left in the dust when breeding season ends. For an early indicator that fall is on its way, watch for male cardinals, male orioles, and other former fighters serenely sharing the feeder. That behavior is a great reminder to get your feeding station in shape and stock up on seeds for the crowds that will soon be coming.

Starlings and crows flock, too, but they often hang around all year. They change their habits, though, to cover grain fields and other open areas while feeding en masse in fall and winter, and they join in communal roosts at night. (For more on starling flocks, see the Starlings entry.)

Flocking behavior starts small, but if you keep your eyes open, you'll notice the change. Instead of a pair of birds at your feeder, you'll start seeing family groups. They join with other families, and the numbers keep increasing until one day your feeding station is swamped with a crowd of, say, red-winged blackbirds.

In spring, the same big flocks return, but the groups get smaller instead of expanding, as individual birds drop out to return to their nesting grounds. At that time of year, a flock is always a welcome sight for me. Even the grating calls of common grackles are music to my ears then. Oh, joy! Spring is here.

Birds of a Feather

Most birds don't join together in such enormous and close-knit flocks. Instead, they congregate in smaller, looser groups at the end of breeding season, either to travel or to spend winter foraging over their feeding territories.

It's easy to notice a flock of robins or flickers when they descend on lawns during fall or spring migration. In the air, the birds leave a lot more elbow room between individuals, so they won't catch your eye as readily as a dense, black-pepper swarm of grackles will.

Evening grosbeaks will definitely grab your attention, though, when a migrating or wintering flock descends on your feeder to gabble and gobble. There's no mistaking what these big, pretty birds are saying: It's "Feed me!"

I often surprise a flock of native sparrows when I'm out exploring in spring or fall—or, I should say, a flock of sparrows often surprises me. Loose flocks of mixed sparrow species sneak through weedy fields and brush during fall and spring, scouring seeds near ground level. There's usually a flash of white tail feathers here and there in the group, because juncos often join them.

Close Companions

Like the Waltons on the old TV show, some birds don't seem to need much private time. Cedar waxwings, goldfinches, pine siskins, and house finches are gregarious by nature, keeping company with others of their kind nearly all year long. They often go about in companionable groups, except when they're busy tending their nests.

House or English sparrows, too, rarely show up one at a time—they usually arrive in our backyards in a big, chattering bunch. They even nest in close quarters, when they're available (like your purple martin house, perhaps?).

In winter, your backyard is likely to be part of

the route of a foraging flock—a band of chickadees, titmice, and nuthatches, with a downy woodpecker or brown creeper tagging along, and perhaps a few companionable kinglets. These birds travel together, exploring different niches of similar habitat: the trunks and branches of trees in forests or backyards. When mating season begins, the winter flocks break up as the birds pair off into couples and move to their nesting territories.

FLUFF AND FIBERS

My friend, Docey, a textile designer, travels the world seeking fibers used by indigenous people in their weavings, and then "translates" those fibers into exotic (and expensive!) wall coverings. She's worked with abaca, a fiber from the banana tree in the Philippines, and with Indonesian rattan and African cotton, to name just a few.

When she mentioned that she was trying to come up with something new and different for her next line of products, I suggested she investigate much closer to home.

"Just look at what the birds use in their nests," I say. "They already have it all figured out."

"Birds?" she asked, ready to laugh at my joke.

"Ever look at an oriole nest?" I countered. "Birds are incredible weavers."

Whether they're human or avian, weavers need fibers to work with, and that's where we come in. Offering materials that suit their nesting needs is a great way to attract any birds that may be nesting in the neighborhood. And a generous supply source may even convince them to build their home right in our own backyards.

Opportunity Knocks

Birds use the materials they find in their own habitat to make their nests. Moose hair may make the inner circle for a dark-eyed junco in the Maine woods, while Spanish moss softens the nest of a prothonotary warbler in Georgia. Birds work with what's around them.

It's fun to think about how birds recycle natural materials from their home grounds (you'll find more details in the entry Nest Materials), but our feathered friends are quick to substitute anything that serves the purpose. That makes it a cinch to offer them materials they can work with.

String and yarn are perfect for weaving, so orioles and robins will snatch them up. Thin strips of paper or cellophane will get takers, too. As for those clippings from your ornamental grass—

Early Birds Get the Fluff

Cavity-nesting birds like chickadees and titmice, which are fond of fluff for their homes, get started early, so have your nest materials out in late winter, when courtship begins. Stuff your treasures into a clean suet cage or a small wicker basket—let some of the stuff dangle or protrude invitingly!—and attach it firmly to a post or tree so birds can pull out their prizes.

Birds can cling securely to a clean wire suet cage while they pull out just the right bit of fiber or fluff.

stuff them loosely into a basket, and you'll be able to watch the builders come 'n' get it.

Fluff can be an even bigger draw than fibers, especially for chickadees, titmice, wrens, and other backyard favorites. So offer them anything that'll be nice and cozy: cotton balls, a tuft of unspun wool, a scrap of fur from an old coat collar, or the dry moss from a floral arrangement.

Last spring, I cut a 6 × 6-inch piece from one of those bulky mohair sweaters that were all the rage back in the 60s—a garage sale find—and tacked it to a tree. I had my first taker within an hour: a tufted titmouse, who made several return trips to pluck the fluff. Angora garments also make great raw material.

Add natural materials to your offerings, too, such as cattails, milkweed fluff, soft curled feathers, and horsehair, if you can find some. Even if the same stuff is common in your neighborhood, birds will still appreciate your one-stop shopping center.

Never offer dryer lint as nesting material. It may look soft and fluffy, but it's a pig-in-a-poke: The fibers are so short that they mat quickly as soon as they get moist, so the stuff has no use as insulation. If you've ever tried to peel lint off your damp hands, you know what a mess it is. It'll stick to eggs and nestlings the same way.

FOUNTAINS AND MISTERS

Ahhh, there's nothing like a shower. No matter how tired I am, standing in that exhilarating spray makes me feel like a new person—refreshed, energized, and ready for anything.

Birds love a shower as much as we do. Set up a garden sprinkler, and it won't be long before robins are wriggling in the "rain." Water your seedlings with a hose in your hand, and you may attract a hummingbird to dance in and out of the spray.

Installing shower facilities in your own backyard will pay off fast in "better" birds—the ones you don't usually see. Moving water can quickly entice migrating warblers, towhees, finches, and others into making a stopover at your place. And it's one of the best ways to lure tanagers, vireos, waxwings, and other birds that usually stay in the treetops to fly right down to eye level.

Fountains for the Birds

Don't bother investing in a classic garden fountain—the kind with tiered basins or a lion's head spouting water—in hopes of attracting birds. The basin is usually too deep, too curved, or too slippery for birds to feel comfortable using it. You may see an occasional thirsty bird sipping from the rim, but your backyard friends won't flock to it like they do to a model that's more their size.

Instead of investing in a sculptured masterpiece, put your pennies into a shower that's made for the birds. There's already a good selection of birdbaths with built-in fountains, and more are hitting the market every year (see the Resources section at the back of this book for mail-order sources).

Shop for a solar-powered fountain/birdbath instead of one that needs to be plugged in. Not only will you reduce your energy use and save money, you'll get the huge benefit of being able to put your new attraction anywhere you want, instead of keeping it tethered to an outlet. As long as the sun shines on your solar birdbath, your fountain will murmur along happily.

Birdbaths with fountains start at less than $100, which is reasonable considering how easy they are to set up and use, not to mention the priceless fun of watching birds a-splishing and a-splashing all day long. The sound of a fountain is another plus—the trickling water is music to our ears, too.

Maid of the Mist

Water is such an immense attraction that, all by itself, it can pull in birds that may never visit a feeder. So next time you're tempted to add another feeder to your repertoire, invest in your backyard bird spa instead.

Misters break water into an ultra-fine spray that hummingbirds can't seem to get enough of. They swing in and out of the spray or perch and preen beneath it. Goldfinches, robins, catbirds, and other songbirds love it, too. But the hummingbird circus alone is reason enough to give a mister a try. Look for one at your bird supply store, or check Resources on page 298; these devices cost about $20.

The yellow-throated vireo, which may nest in a woodsy backyard, appreciates both an offering of nest materials and a summer shower at your mister.

The Mechanics of Misters

A mister is a cinch to set up: Just screw the connector at the end of its thin black tubing onto your outdoor faucet, and attach the spray head to a thin branch or plant stake. It's essentially a teeny-tiny hose nozzle that uses very little water, so you won't see skyrocketing water bills, even if you let it spray for hours. I bought a model that's more of a focal point, with the spray head mounted atop a stack of faux slate slabs, because I like to invite friends to watch the hummers—they stay for half an hour at a time!

FRAGMENTATION

Clearing wild land for houses, shopping areas, industrial parks, or anything else means the remaining parts of that wild space are now in fragments. Instead of being one big, unbroken whole, the wild places are smaller and farther apart.

Fragmentation has been going on for centuries, ever since European settlers first began applying the ax and plow. Where once was forest is farmland, with patches of woods at the edge of acres of grain. Where once was grassland or sagebrush is now suburbia or second homes.

All of the birds that lived in that wild land have been squeezed into smaller areas, and not all of them have been able to adapt. Some have modified their habits and adopted our backyards as their new habitat. Sadly, some have checked out—the ivory-billed woodpecker, for example, which apparently couldn't survive without its native swampy home.

We'll never know for sure what the effect has been, but we can get an idea by reading old-timers like Thoreau, Audubon, and other observers who knew the wilderness before it was chopped into pieces. What we do know is that back in the 1800s, when the early naturalists were rhapsodizing about birds, those birds were a lot more common than they are today. Other factors helped bring about the decline of birds, too; the entries Habitat Destruction, Pesticides, and Population Decline will give you an idea of the big forces working against birds.

Are You Part of the Problem?

If you've yielded to the call of the wild and built your dream home in what once was forest, sagebrush, or other wild spaces, you can still help mitigate your effects on the birds around you. Use native plants in your landscaping to help knit the wild places back together. Stick to tube feeders, cage feeders, and dome feeders that exclude cowbirds; they're less likely to linger when there's not much to eat. And ***keep your cat inside!*** There's simply no excuse for letting Kitty roam free.

Making Inroads

Bulldozing an entire forest is disastrous for birds, but carving it up takes a huge toll, too. Every time one of us builds a house way out in the middle of nowhere, it separates bird spaces. Opening up a solid stretch of woods with an access road, whether it's for a driveway or for logging, further fragments the forest.

By making inroads into wild places, we've set the stage for predators to have a field day. Cats, raccoons, and cowbirds avoid the deep, dark woods. But they can easily prey on birds and nests along the newly opened edges.

Now that there are fewer birds—and fewer bird nests—each one counts way more than it used to when birds were super plentiful. There are more roaming cats than ever these days, and they're one of the biggest dangers all birds face. Raccoons, too, are thriving. And cowbirds—well, they've been the main reason for the catastrophic destruction of some species.

There's no way to stop our human population from continuing to climb, but we can make our voices heard about suburban sprawl and zoning issues. We can support organizations like The Nature Conservancy and investigate putting our own land into a trust, to try to keep as much wild space intact as we can.

Birds are doing what they can, too. After examining the wings of hundreds of forest bird specimens in museum collections, ecologist Andre Desrochers discovered major changes in their wings over the last century. The wings of birds from areas where forests have been disappearing had become longer and pointier, better for flying long distances to find a mate.

Meanwhile, whatever we can do to create mini bird sanctuaries in our backyards will help. Providing nourishing food and vital water, adding native plants, and planting trees for the future can help birds survive.

Getting Down to Business

Birds that eat a lot of fruit are accustomed to picking up berries that have fallen from the bush. Take advantage of that habit to set the stage for your first try at fruit feeding: When your berry crop begins to ripen, set a ground-level tray feeder below one of the bushes, and scatter that kind of fruit into it. Your first customer is likely to be a robin, since it's the most common and most abundant fruit fancier. The robin's presence will soon alert other birds to the food source. Once they associate the feeder with fruit, set up a similar low feeder at your main feeding area to coax them in that direction.

FRESH FRUIT

I'm old enough to remember when cherries were a seasonal treat. They showed up in the grocery store in June and stayed there as long as the harvest season lasted. Once they were done, they were done, and I had to wait until the next year to get my fresh-cherry fix. Apricots, peaches, and nectarines were short-lived delights, too. Apples were always plentiful, although we all knew that buying them in winter was risky—they could be mushy instead of crisp.

It wasn't too many generations ago that eating seasonally was a way of life. Instead of stopping at the supermarket to pick up fresh fruit in any month of the year, our grandparents savored each fruit in its season. Flying in a planeload of cherries from Chile, or apples from New Zealand, would've seemed like science fiction to them.

Of course they "put some by" for the winter months when each fruit was at its peak. Canned cherries or dried apples taste mighty good when you can't get the real thing.

Learning New Habits

When it comes to serving fruit at the feeder, most of us depend on dried fruit, whether it's in a store-bought treat or mixed up in the kitchen. Birds welcome it when natural fruit is scarce.

But when fresh fruit is ripe for the plucking, a dried berry—even if it did cost $8 a pound—is about as appealing as shoe leather. Orioles, waxwings, catbirds, and other fruit eaters forsake the feeder and flock to the wild or garden-grown blueberries, raspberries, and other bite-size fruits.

So why can't you simply offer fresh blueberries at the feeder to keep your birds hanging around?

To a bird brain, a berry that's not on the bush, where the bird expects to find it, seems to be unrecognizable as food. Pour a pint of perfect blueberries into your feeder, and birds usually ignore them.

You can help your birds learn to eat fruit at your feeders by planting raspberry, blueberry, or elderberry bushes in your yard, next to or very near your feeders. Eventually, some brave soul may make the connection between the berries on the bush and the fruit in your feeder and actually try a sample.

FRUIT TREES

"Want to see something cool?" I called to some tourists in my small town a couple of autumns ago. I motioned them over to an apple tree where I was watching one of my favorite happenings: a horde of butterflies getting drunk on the rotting fruit.

"What butterflies?" they asked, when I told them what I was watching.

The red-spotted purples, red admirals, and hackberry butterflies were hard to see, because they were sitting still with their wings closed, showing only the mottled undersides that are perfect camouflage. So I took a few steps toward them, causing a sudden fluttering of wings.

In a flash, a migrating flycatcher I hadn't noticed swooped in for the kill. Click! went the bird's beak as he swooped out just as quickly.

"Oh! An olive-sided flycatcher! Haven't seen one in years!" I pointed to the tip of a nearby tree, where the very unexciting-looking drab greenish bird was busily plucking the wings off his prize.

Now I had even more reason to shoehorn an apple tree into my own backyard. Like all fruit trees, apples are great at attracting birds, including those special ones we all want to see.

Year-Round Appeal

Fruit tree magic starts in spring. It doesn't matter whether you plant an apple, pear, plum, or any other fruit you like—its cloud of sweet-scented blossoms is going to attract a swarm of insects. Birds will be close behind.

Fruit trees bloom when spring migrants are moving through, and that means your tree is likely to attract warblers, vireos, orioles, rose-breasted grosbeaks, chickadees, kinglets, and flycatchers. Depending on where you live, you might also spot bluebirds, red-headed woodpeckers, or other fabulous birds helping themselves to the bugs.

As long as you don't douse your tree with pesticides, it'll also provide a feast in summer, as birds pick off insects among the leaves. Robins, chipping sparrows, or other backyard birds may nest in the branches. If your apple tree is an old one, you may even get bluebirds, which are highly attracted to dead wood where they can make their home.

When your crop ripens, birds will help themselves to a share without waiting for your invitation. A peach tree in one of my former yards was a prime target for house finches, which would puncture the ripe fruit to drink the sweet juice. Peaches with peck marks taste just as good as perfect ones, I quickly discovered. As for cherries, you'll have to be quick to get any for yourself. Once cedar waxwings spot them, your crop will simply vanish.

Fallen fruit in fall attracts insects, especially butterflies, ants, and wasps. Here come the flycatchers again, plus flickers and robins, which may alight in a migrating flock. Since the bugs are at ground level, treetop birds like vireos and warblers don't have much interest.

Now it's winter, and your fruit tree is still attracting birds. Chickadees, titmice, and nuthatches will scour the bark for insects, and robins, catbirds, and waxwings will show a keen interest in any fruit still dangling from the branches.

Pruning Is for the Birds

Fruit trees are easy to grow, as long as you're not aiming for perfection. Choose a variety that will resist diseases, and keep it pesticide-free for the sake of your birds. If you're worried about mastering the art of pruning, don't give it a second thought. Just cut back the tallest branches in late winter, so your fruit crop will be in easy reach. Or forego pruning altogether, and let your tree be entirely for the birds.

A possible visit from cedar waxwings is a great reason to plant a crabapple tree. Flickers, bluebirds, and other friends enjoy the fruit, too, and warblers, vireos, and orioles glean insects from the blossoms.

FUCHSIAS

You can never have too many hummingbird flowers, to my way of thinking, and fuchsias are right up at the top. All day long, the hummers in my yard patrol the fuchsia plants, hovering underneath to poke in their bill, tilt the flower slightly upward, and drink its nectar.

No wonder they're such a perfect match: Fuchsias are native from Mexico to South America, and that's where hummingbirds are, too. Like other hummingbird flowers, fuchsias evolved to meet the birds' needs and to match their habits. What's in it for them? Pollination—that's their payoff.

Nearly all fuchsias die without a backward glance in cold winters. They're hardy only in Zone 8 or 9, which is way out of my league here in Indiana.

Still, there's one fuchsia that survives in Zone 6, and with a little luck, even farther northward: *Fuchsia magellanica*. Believe it or not, it comes from as far south in South America as you can get—the tip of Tierra del Fuego, around which Magellan sailed. This fuchsia grows into a beautiful fine-textured shrub, reaching about 5 feet tall and wide, with dainty dangling "earrings" in classic red-and-purple. I treat it like my butterfly bushes, cutting it back to the ground if an extra cold winter kills the top growth. And I give it a 6-inch-deep mulch of fall leaves for extra insurance before the ground freezes, to help the roots survive.

If you live in a cold climate, the easiest way to keep fuchsias from one year to the next (other than the hardier *F. magellanica*) is to grow them in pots that you can bring in over winter.

When I run out of room, I follow my mother's trick so I don't have to invest in new plants every

Open to Temptation

Want to see hummingbirds right at your window? Hang a basket of fuchsias from a hook on your window frame or from a shepherd's hook just outside the glass. Any variety will do the trick, but those with some red usually get hummer attention the soonest. Notice the yellow dust on the hummingbird's head as it makes its way from flower to flower? That's pollen, which the bird unwittingly carries from one blossom to another—exactly the hidden agenda of these pretty flowers.

Snip some stems of fuchsia before frost hits and keep them inside in a jar of water. You won't have to buy new plants next year.

year. Before frost, I just clip off some stems, strip the lower leaves, and stick them in a jar of water for the winter. When the weather warms in May, I plant them back outside or in pots. It works for any tender variety except for erect, red-flowered 'Gartenmeister Bonstedt', which needs to come inside in a pot for the best chance of success.

Fabulous Fuchsias

There are 100 species of fuchsias in the world. All but 6 hail from Central and South America and some Caribbean islands, where hummingbirds are also highly abundant, serving as vital pollinators of the flowers. Our garden fuchsias are just a tiny sampling of the wild ones, but there are plenty to entice avid nectar-seeking hummers to our backyards. Here are some easy growers to delight your zippy little friends. All do best in shade to part shade.

NAME	DESCRIPTION	HOW TO GROW
Fuchsia magellanica	Medium-sized deciduous, multistemmed shrub, about 4 × 4, with fine branches and a graceful habit. Slender, dangling, red-and-purple blossoms.	Hardy to Zone 6b and perhaps colder. Mulch with 6 inches or more of dead fall leaves after frost, through spring. If top growth freezes over winter, cut back to a few inches above soil level, as you would with butterflybush (*Buddleia davidii*). Grows very fast and blooms profusely from early summer until frost. 'Maiden's Blush' has pale pink flowers.
F. magellanica 'Aurea'	Same as *F. magellanica*, but with unusual yellow leaves on red stems.	Hardy to Zone 7 and perhaps colder. Mulch with 6 inches or more of dead fall leaves after frost, through spring. If top growth freezes over winter, cut back to a few inches above soil level, as you would with butterflybush (*Buddleia davidii*).
F. magellanica 'Santa Claus'	Same as *F. magellanica*, but with lovely gray leaves streaked with cream and pink.	Hardy to Zone 7 and perhaps colder. Mulch with 6 inches or more of dead fall leaves after frost, through spring. If top growth freezes over winter, cut back to a few inches above soil level, as you would with butterflybush (*Buddleia davidii*).
Fuchsia 'Riccartonii'	This hybrid is a small to mid-sized shrub, about 3 × 3, with red-and-purple flowers.	Hardy to Zone 6b and perhaps colder. Mulch deeply in fall with dead leaves, and remove the mulch in sping. Cut back any winter-killed top growth to soil level. Grows very fast, and blooms profusely from early summer until frost.
Fuchsia 'Gartenmeister Bonstedt'	Developed from the species *F. tripylla*, this tender perennial grows 2 feet to 3 feet tall, with clusters of slim red-orange trumpets topping the erect, slightly arching stems.	Hardy in Zones 10 and 11, but worth growing as an annual anywhere. Water regularly. Multiply by clipping 6-inch to 8-inch stems, stripping the leaves, and poking a few inches deep into moist soil; keep moist, and you'll soon see new growth. Great in containers.

G/H

GOOD BIRDS

I was out bird-watching one day when I ran into a fellow with binoculars around his neck. "See any good birds?" he asked.

"What's a 'good' bird?" I asked right back. Did the starling I'd spent 10 minutes watching as he bathed his iridescent feathers in a puddle count at all? How about the common-as-dirt crow that was extracting some sort of leech thing from the pond mud? Maybe the equally common golden-crowned sparrows that were eating chickweed leaves, a behavior that was brand-new to me? How about the cedar waxwings dining on pollen-laden ash tree flowers?

He didn't get excited about any of that, so finally I gave him the answer I knew he wanted: "Saw the first hooded mergansers on the slough, and there's a lazuli bunting singing near the end of the loop road."

High five! He was off and running to get his "good birds."

A Matter of Perspective

To me, the good birds that day were those I'd gotten to know a little better by watching patiently as they did whatever it is they were doing. Sure, I love the thrill of the first returning migrants, the fun of an unfamiliar bird, and the surprise of an unexpected rare bird.

But I realized long ago that any bird can be a good bird, simply because of the connection we feel when we spend time watching them. That's why I'm even fond of starlings, grackles, house sparrows, and other birds that people call feeder pests. I find them just as interesting and just as entertaining as a—is that a bluebird?! 'Scuse me, gotta go!

Of course a beautiful bird will make us stop

New Wonders on the Way

The excitement of "good birds" is why the changing scene in backyard birding is so much fun. Ten years ago, the very thought of hosting an oriole would've seemed like a dream; now, they've become such regular friends that we can even buy special feeders and treats for them. Who knows which species will be the next to change its ways? As birds adapt to climate change and shifting habitat, and as they start to associate our feeding station with their kind of food, we're starting to see more and more "good birds" dropping in for a backyard visit. It's a great time to be a bird-watcher.

watching the ordinary gang at the feeder. Who doesn't say *Oooh* at a bluebird? Or hold their breath when an oriole arrives in his vivid orange-and-black finery?

Birds that are only occasional visitors or rarities at the feeder make me sit up and take notice, too, just as they do with most of us. Having lived in several distinctly different parts of the country, I know that a rarity in one area may be an ultra-common bird in another.

In fact, I've sometimes laughed at myself for reacting to these "good birds"—like the slate-colored junco that showed up among the usual mob of Oregon juncos at my Northwest feeder. I got so excited, you would've thought the little gray bird was an Amazon parrot.

GROUND LEVEL

Ever wonder why white-throated sparrows and juncos are more likely to scratch about beneath the feeders than actually eat out of them? That's because these birds are ground feeders by nature. They're used to foraging for seeds that fall to the ground, and the highest level that they usually reach to is only as tall as the weeds that they feed from.

Scattering seed right on the ground will make these birds feel right at home. Other native sparrows, grackles, blackbirds, doves, robins, flickers, towhees, pheasants, wild turkeys, and quail will feel right at home, too. But seed on the ground quickly absorbs moisture if it isn't eaten, leading to mold. And worse yet, it attracts mice and other rodents.

There's a neat solution to making ground-level birds happy while helping to keep your feeding station free of pests and mold: a low-level feeder. Mice are more reluctant to climb into a tray to eat than they are to nibble seed right from the ground, where they can swiftly make a getaway if danger threatens. You can buy or build your own low tray feeder, elevated from wet ground on low legs. Look for one with a roof to keep the seed dry, or try an unroofed feeder until birds get used to visiting the new setup or for a better view of your busy guests. If you build your own, use a stiff piece of wire screen for the bottom or drill drainage holes to help keep the seed from spoiling.

The same birds that forage on or near the

Predator Protection

Birds on the ground are more vulnerable to cats and hawks than birds at higher feeders, especially if they're bathing or wet. To reduce the risk, choose a site for your low-level bath or feeder that's near protective cover that the birds can reach in a hurry. Placing your bath or feeder under the sheltering branches of a tree will help block them from the view of hawks patrolling the air. If cats wander your yard, don't use low-level baths or feeders at all, and keep the area beneath your feeders tidy so that ground-feeding birds aren't tempted to forage there.

ground will also appreciate a low-level birdbath. A single basin set directly on the ground looks awkward to my eye, so I use a simple two-bath arrangement for a more appealing design. I put one large clay saucer on top of an upright, 12-inch-tall section of clay drainage pipe and position the second basin on the ground in front of this pedestal arrangement. You can also elevate your basin on a flat rock or a concrete block to make it look better.

GROW UP

Metal shepherd's hooks, at about $10 each, are a terrific value for the amount of use you'll get out of them, and inexpensive metal trellises (around $20 or less) are close behind. You can poke the trellises into the ground to add extra growing space just about anywhere.

The trellises are ideal for supporting fast-growing annual vines—the kinds that attract hummingbirds like a beacon. Scarlet cypress creeper (*Ipomoea quamoclit*), cardinal climber (*Ipomoea × sloteri*), and scarlet runner beans (*Kennedia prostrata*) are my top picks because hummingbirds zoom to the red flowers as if they're a homing device. Regular morning glories will also get attention from hummers.

As easy to grow as morning glories, cypress creeper (*Ipomoea quamoclit*) is a fast-growing annual vine that will lure every passing hummingbird.

Climbing the Walls

To catch the eye of cardinals, brown thrashers, catbirds, and others that are shopping for a homesite, plant a vigorous climbing rose against the wall of your house or over an arbor, where the canes can grow into a tangle that will keep out predators. One of my favorite roses for nesting birds is the old variety named 'Climbing Cecile Brunner'. It's fast growing (don't prune it for the first 2 or 3 years) and untroubled by disease. Looking at its fragrant waterfall of small pink roses in late spring, you'd never guess that this rose is tough as nails and thrives on neglect. Be sure to buy the climbing variety; there's also a bush form.

Use sturdier trellises of wood or metal to support permanent vines and climbing roses for your birds. Grapes are easy to grow, especially trouble-free 'Concord', and the delicious fruit will draw in catbirds, thrashers, orioles, robins, and other fruit eaters. Honeysuckle vines of any kind will attract hummingbirds.

HABITAT

Wherever I've lived, my backyards have always been welcoming to birds and other wild creatures. But this year I made it official. I applied for certification of my yard as a Backyard Wildlife Habitat, through a program run by the National Wildlife Federation. The application process, which I did online, didn't take very long, and my yard was approved quickly. But the best part was yet to come—the metal signs I ordered after certification, to announce to passersby that my yard is a haven for wild friends.

The signs were the reason I applied in the first place: I'm hoping they'll start conversations with passersby, so I can tell them how easy it is to create habitat and how much fun it is to have a yard that's alive with birds every day of the year.

Can You Count to Five?

For your yard to be approved as a bird habitat, whether it's through an official program or by the birds themselves, you'll need to supply five things.

1. Food
2. Water
3. Cover
4. Places to raise young
5. A "green" space, with native plants and no chemical pesticides

Providing these basics will bring birds to your yard. Put up a feeder, fill a birdbath, plant a tree, mount a birdhouse, and keep your hand off the pesticide spray bottle, and you'll get some birds. For that matter, a feeder alone will get you some takers.

But "some birds" isn't the goal for most backyard bird lovers—we want as many birds as we can possibly get. But not just any birds! We want to see "good birds," like bluebirds, orioles, tanagers, wrens, grosbeaks, and whatever other birds we like best.

Ticking off the five elements will get you approved by the Backyard Wildlife Habitat program. But it won't win you the award you really want—the seal of approval from birds themselves.

For that, you'll need to create inviting habitat, as well as pay attention to the menu at your feeders. You can accomplish these goals in an endless number of ways, depending on what you choose to plant and where you put it, but I find a natural-

An official sign from the National Wildlife Federation proves to passersby that your yard is a safe haven for birds and other wildlife.

istic gardening style works best for drawing out-of-the-ordinary birds to my backyard. After all, it's what they're used to, so they'll instantly recognize it in your yard, even if you live miles away from wild places.

Birds that are already backyard regulars—downy woodpeckers, jays, cardinals, and robins, for instance—will happily visit, no matter what your style of gardening is. But to lure in others, start by taking a look at your nearby wild places.

In my area, that's hardwood forest, so my yard now looks a lot like the wild places, with mulched paths winding through casual plantings of native wildflowers, shrubs, and understory trees beneath the big sugar maple and tulip trees I was already blessed with, and a mulch of decomposing leaves among the plants.

As soon as I put in the plants, the birds followed. Tanagers, warblers, flycatchers, thrushes, and towhees regularly visit, simply because I matched the gardening style of Mother Nature.

When you're ready to create bird habitat in your own yard, start by taking a walk on the wild side. Take a look at how closely together wild plants grow, even if you have no idea which plants they are. Notice how smaller trees and shrubs step up to taller ones, and how some plants create a small thicket or colony.

When you mimic that look in your own yard, you've made big strides towards creating good habitat. Be sure to include native plants, and increase the appeal with food plants that birds adore, like berry bushes for thrushes, a fruit tree for waxwings, nectar flowers for hummingbirds, and seed-rich flowers for goldfinches.

And don't forget about #5 on that list of requirements for the National Wildlife Federation's habitat certification program: a "green" yard. It's part of the plan for a very important reason. By going green in your own backyard, you're helping birds in the bigger picture, too.

Avoiding chemical pesticides keeps your yard free of toxins that definitely kill insects, which birds depend on, and may do other damage. Chemicals can seep into the soil and affect soil organisms we don't even know the importance of yet. They may wash out of your yard, too, with rain or blow away on the wind.

We're all part of the same big picture, and it all begins at home. If millions of us eliminated chemicals in our yards, the demand would drop, and the plants that manufacture the stuff would put out less pollutants, too. In a cleaner, greener world, our birds will sing a happier tune.

How to Get Certified

To apply for Backyard Wildlife Habitat certification, go to www.nwf.org/gardenforwildlife to learn about the online application process, or call the National Wildlife Federation at 1-800-822-9919. You can also write to NWF, 11100 Wildlife Center Drive, Reston, VA 20190, to ask for a form you can fill out and mail in. You'll need to answer questions that show you've followed the guidelines to make your yard welcoming. A simple click of a button for each question is all you do in the quick and easy online process. The fee for applying is $20; metal yard or house signs cost an extra $30 to $150 each, depending on which style you choose.

HABITAT DESTRUCTION

I vividly remember two things about my first airplane trip: First, how amazed I was by all the wild land down there, and second, how annoyed my seatmate was at my enthusiasm.

I'd been hearing for years about suburban sprawl and overpopulation, and I'd seen it firsthand around my home in Pennsylvania. Farm fields sprouting fast-growing crops of new houses; woods cut down for another highway or subdivision. My little world had changed from a sleepy rural byway to a congested, noisy part of the New York megalopolis.

So when I looked out the plane window—"Mind if I switch seats with you?" I'd innocently asked my neighbor, not knowing what a serious breach of airplane etiquette I was committing—and saw big stretches of woods below, just 15 minutes out of the airport I was stunned.

Towns and even cities looked insignificant compared to all the trees in Pennsylvania. Urban sprawl? It looked more like the forest primeval down below.

That plane trip was some 30 years ago, but the country still looks pretty much the same from the air. There are a lot of wild places left.

So what's the problem?

Appearances can be deceptive, for one thing. What I couldn't see from 5 miles high were all the little roads that now crisscrossed the forests, and what an impact even a single cleared homesite can have on birds. It's called fragmentation, and it's opened the land to predators and other dangers.

Other parts of America have undergone big changes, too. Logging in the West and Northwest has eliminated a lot of bird homeland. Housing developments have sprouted in the deserts and sagebrush country. And in the Midwest, instead of family farms with fields ringed with brush and

How many birds lost their homes when these hills and mountains of Madagascar were stripped of rainforest? Habitat destruction is happening right here at home, too, with equally stark areas where forest—and forest birds—once flourished.

hedgerows, we now have gigantic fields made to accommodate gigantic machines.

Trouble on Two Fronts

Another part of the picture isn't in this country: It's in Central and South America, where many of our birds spend the winter.

I haven't flown over those countries, but I have looked at lots of pictures, and the scenery is pretty grim. Big areas of land have been stripped of trees—and those are exactly the places our migrating birds spend their winters.

Destroying the forests and wild places means our birds face food shortages when they reach their wintering grounds—and that winter home doesn't look anything like it used to. Even the climate has changed because the trees that once created their own life-giving moisture—the cloud forest—have been leveled, leaving a barren moonscape instead of a thriving jungle.

The yellowest of the wood warblers and one of the most determined singers, the male yellow warbler pours out more than 3,000 songs a day! This little bird is under big pressure: Cowbirds parasitize its nests on North American breeding grounds, and its winter habitat is being rapidly destroyed.

We've been hearing about the destruction of the rain forests for decades now, so long that many of us barely pay attention anymore. But the situation is critical. Part of the problem is us—and that means we can help solve it, too.

The Coffee Connection

When I moved to the Pacific Northwest, I was surprised—and pleased—to find a coffee kiosk on what seemed like every corner. Soon, I, too, was pulling up to get a to-go cup of cappuccino for a pick-me-up every morning during the 6-month rainy season. The drizzly gloom didn't seem nearly as bad with a jolt of caffeine buzzing through my brain.

Those little kiosks, and the shiny, modern bistros that served coffee as a mainstay, started a boom that soon swept the whole country. Our coffee consumption went way, way up, and as it did, our birds started going down.

How can a morning cuppa joe possibly affect the survival of a scarlet tanager, a yellow warbler, a Swainson's thrush, or dozens of other birds? By habitat destruction, that's how.

Multiply your single morning wake-up cup by those of millions of people, and you have a hint of how the problem exploded. Whole hillsides in Central America were leveled quickly so that coffee could be planted to take advantage of the beverage boom. Unfortunately, that area happens to be exactly where many of our birds head to spend their winter.

Unbelievable as it may sound, one small change in our daily habits could mean the world to the birds wintering in this coffee-growing area. What's the change we'd have to make? Switching to organic coffee grown in the shade of the trees our birds need. You'll find more info in the entry Shade-Grown Coffee.

Accelerating Change

Changes in habitat have been going on for ages, sometimes by accident, sometimes by design, and usually without any consideration of the consequences.

Fast-moving blights took out two of our major tree species, the American chestnut and the elm, both of them highly valuable to birds. Long before the blights, those trees were just two members of a gigantic hardwood forest that once marched from the Mississippi all the way to the Atlantic seaboard. Tall, dark, and handsome, those great woods fell to the ax as we cleared the land to build houses and towns.

We're still leveling the woods and slicing roads through it to build cabins and houses. Every time we do, we divide it into still more fragments, and that spells trouble for birds of the forest. Most forest birds migrate to Central and South America, and the situation they face there is just as grim.

Grassland birds are having their own difficulties. For these species, it's the changes we've wrought right here at home, not the destruction in Central and South America, that threaten their survival most.

Habitat destruction for grassland birds started long ago, when the great Tallgrass Prairie was turned under the plow. Grasses so high that people got lost in them used to stretch across hundreds of thousands of acres, blanketing the belly of the continent.

Now the land is planted in corn, wheat, soybeans—and sunflowers, so we can feed some of the same birds that once feasted on the multitude of native prairie plants.

Adapting to Change

We're all part of an interconnected web, so the death of a widespread species ripples across countless other living things. Everything from soil bacteria to mushrooms to tannin-loving plants to birds to bears, and a zillion more species in between, would've been caught in the shock wave when the chestnut tree went under.

But eventually, the shock wave levels out, as it did with the chestnut and the elm. Baltimore orioles, which often nested in the graceful vase-shaped crowns of American elms, suspending their pendant nests from high branches, made the switch to sycamores and other tall trees without much problem when the elms died, one by one.

Animals and birds adapt, and Nature's balance is restored. It won't be the same as it was before, but most species will learn to live without the species that died out, and they'll survive.

Habitat destruction is a different story. We're talking about entire interconnected systems being wiped out, not just a single species. No wonder it's so much harder for birds to adjust.

Yet, even with the giant changes we wrought in habitats across our country, most of our birds managed to adapt and survive.

Only a handful of species, those that were so specialized that they had trouble adjusting to the new lay of the land, dwindled to rarities. Prairie chickens, for instance, sank like a stone when the prairie was plowed. Meadowlarks and horned larks, on the other hand, managed to make the transition to hay fields, wheat fields, and other habitat.

Many of the forest birds made do with their shrinking homeland. Some, including chickadees, titmice, orioles, and downy woodpeckers, even moved into our backyards.

Those changes were just the start for birds, though. As our impact on the planet has become bigger and bigger, the changes have piled up. Our birds may have been able to rebound from the habitat destruction we wrought in North America in the last couple of centuries. But when you add in the pressure they now are under in Central and South America, it's no surprise that many species are dropping at an alarming rate.

For more about the downturn in bird numbers, see "A Whole New World," as well as the entries Cat Control, Climate Change, Cowbirds, Fragmentation, Pesticides, and Population Decline. As you can see just from looking at that list, our birds are facing quite a whammy.

That's why our backyards are more important than ever. By creating mini-sanctuaries and offering appropriate food, we can help our beleaguered birds.

HAMBURGER

What does hamburger look like when you pull it apart? Why, worms, of course, or maybe caterpillars—and that means birds will recognize it quickly as a food for them.

It's strange to think about our backyard birds as meat eaters. Vultures and crows, sure. But house wrens and bluebirds? Yep, them too, as well as lots of other species.

You'll be surprised to see who turns up to feast upon your meaty treats. I've seen woodpeckers, chickadees, titmice, nuthatches, jays, thrashers, mockingbirds, and even wrens lining up for a chance to grab a bite. Even catbirds eat hamburger with, ahem, relish.

Cheap hamburger is soft, not stringy, so even small birds can manage to peck off a bite. And it's so fatty that it's not that far removed from suet. That makes it ideal for cold-weather feeding, not only because of nutrition, but because birds can still peck off pieces even when it's frozen.

Next time you see a good price on low-grade hamburger, stock up for winter. But before you toss the package in the freezer, mold it into whatever shape of treats you intend to serve, and then freeze them individually. You can also fork the meat apart onto a cookie sheet for freezing, and then bag the shreds for freezer storage. Bluebirds, chickadees, wrens, catbirds, and others will snatch them quickly from a mealworm feeder.

Seasonal Treat

Save hamburger for winter feeding only, when the weather is cold and your feeders are busy. In warmer temperatures, meat spoils quickly and attracts flies and yellow jackets. To serve your hungry winter birds in a hurry, just shape the raw hamburger into balls, plugs, or cakes to fit your feeders. Suet cages, log feeders, and molded-ball feeders will serve agile birds or those that are good at clinging, like woodpeckers and chickadees. For bluebirds, wrens, and other perching birds, crumble the burger and offer it in a mealworm dish or dome feeder.

MEATLOAF SPECIAL

Give your woodpeckers, wrens, chickadees, and titmice a change of pace by baking a meatloaf to fill their feeders.

1½ pounds hamburger (the fattier, the better)

1 cup 2% milk

½ cup bread crumbs

½ cup cornmeal

Mix all ingredients in a bowl, pack into an ungreased bread pan, and bake at 350°F for about an hour. Pour off any accumulated fat, and reserve. Refrigerate both meatloaf and reserved fat until cold, or overnight. To serve your birds, slice the meatloaf into pieces that will easily slide into a suet feeder, or cut off chunks to stuff a log feeder. Slice the rest of the loaf and freeze the extras in a zip-top bag for future use. No need to thaw before serving; birds will eagerly work at the frozen meat. Serve the solidified fat stuffed into a log feeder or slathered on tree bark.

HANGING BASKETS AND WREATHS

When front door wreaths and hanging baskets became an instant hit during the "country" decorating trend, birds soon adapted the lasting fad for their own use—as homesites, that is. Now, just a decade or two down the road, finding a bird nest in your decorations has become almost commonplace.

Even though it's not an unusual occurrence, it's still a thrill when it happens to you for the first time. Who wouldn't be charmed by a robin that takes up residence right in the grapevine wreath on the front door? Or a house finch that sits on its nest in your Boston fern basket, with its mate singing sweetly nearby?

The thrill of finding a bird at home in your hanging decorations can get dampened, though, as nesting birds show their messier side. Globs of mud, stray pieces of nesting material, and, last but definitely not least, bird droppings from parents and nestlings can soon make you wish the pair had chosen the neighbor's wreath instead. Still, hosing down the front walk or porch floor now and then is a small price to pay for the fun of watching birds care for their family. And when the babies leave the nest—well, it's almost as poignant a moment as when your own kids went off to kindergarten.

Don't be surprised if that lush hanging basket on your porch is chosen as a nest site by a mourning dove, robin, or house finch. These birds often nest very close to our own homes.

House finches, robins, and mourning doves are the most common nesting birds in dooryard decorations. Robins generally prefer a wreath, although they'll take a basket, too, while house finches and doves make hanging baskets their first choice. It doesn't seem to matter what kind of plant is in the basket, once the bird takes a shine to its location.

Why have birds taken to our wreaths and baskets? My guess is because of predators. Or, rather, lack of them. Except for house cats, few of the creatures that prey on birds or nestlings will venture right up onto a porch. Our own presence isn't a deterrent to the nesting couple—but it is to the hawks, 'coons, and other predators that might sniff out the nest. And even if a predator did brave coming close to the house, it still would be almost impossible for it to climb the door or get to the hanging basket.

Hanging Basket Home Repair

Your birds' nest-building and their traffic in and out of your hanging basket can leave your plant looking pretty battered, and your watering will be next to impossible, so cross your fingers and hope for the best. Nesting lasts about 4 weeks—2 weeks on the eggs, 2 weeks until the babies fly the coop. After the family leaves, cut your plant back to encourage new growth, give it a dose of fertilizer, and water it regularly. Then it should make a fine recovery from its nursery duties.

HAWK WATCH

Years ago, I lived at the foot of Hawk Mountain, a renowned location on the fall migration route for hawks of all kinds, as well as ospreys, eagles, golden-shafted flickers, ruby-throated hummingbirds, and monarch butterflies. The long-distance travelers followed the ridge, riding the warm air currents rising from its flanks. Lookout areas perched atop the ridge gave us watchers a terrific view of approaching birds, and I quickly became addicted to the excitement of spotting hawks.

At Cape May, New Jersey, long a favorite beach playground for my family, I discovered hawk-watching of a different kind. There, the birds were not only in the air, they were patrolling the scrubby thickets and perched everywhere you looked. Every patch of vegetation was full of other migrants, too: wood warblers, flickers, robins, and dozens of other birds, all trying for one last meal before they set out on a grueling stretch of their journey—more than 20 miles across the open water of the Delaware Bay. Hummingbirds and monarchs also abounded there, and they were busy fueling up, too.

Visiting those places gave me a great education in recognizing different hawks and in learning how they hunted and what they ate. I soon saw that the red-tailed hawks and small falcons called kestrels preferred to sit and spy out their prey, while the slimmer sharp-shinned and Cooper's hawks actually beat the bushes, darting through the trees and brush to scare out a songbird for lunch.

Big, plump flickers were popular prey, and I

On a fine fall day, the rocky outcrops at Hawk Mountain Sanctuary in eastern Pennsylvania are an exhilarating place to watch the migration of thousands of birds of prey.

found lots of feathers where the predators had plucked their kills. I'd seen the same thing at Hawk Mountain, in a different style: There, hawks sometimes snatched flickers right out of the air and plucked and ate them as they flew along. The drive-thru lane, I suppose.

Our feeders have become hawk hot spots in fall and winter, thanks to the abundance of their feathered food. You can see both the sit-and-wait and the dash-and-grab styles of hawk attack in your own yard.

Remove the "Food"

Once a hawk discovers the all-you-can-eat banquet of songbirds at your feeding station, it'll probably be back. If the predator becomes a frequent visitor, stop feeding your birds for about a week, until the hawk gives up. Empty the feeders, tidy up underneath, and hope the hungry hunter moves on to birdier pastures.

There's a Kind of Hush

Unless you happen to be looking at just the right moment, you're likely to miss the hawk attacks at your feeding station. But there's no mistaking the aftermath. The feeder birds simply disappear.

It can take an hour or more before they venture out again, finally convinced that the hawk is gone.

Often, the big bird hasn't left. It's merely sitting very still in some nearby tree, waiting for another victim.

If you notice your feeder is bare when it should be booming, take a look-see yourself. Try to avoid flushing your small birds out of the cover where they're hiding, but do scan the trees, the rooftop, and any nearby utility poles or other high perches to see if you can spot the hunter.

A hawk attack is just part of the natural cycle of things. Still, it doesn't feel good to see our feeder birds get nabbed. My heart breaks every time a chickadee gets snatched—these are my friends, doggone it!—but hawks don't usually put too big a dent in the feeder population.

If the predator becomes a daily visitor, though, I start to fight back. Clapping and yelling usually chase a hawk away, although you'll have to repeat the old heave-ho a few times until the hawk gets the message.

HEDGE HIDEOUT

For a hundred years or more, hedges were the only way to go when you wanted to mark the boundary of your yard and add a little privacy. Oh, you might have a little picket fence in front, but along the sides of the yard or across the back, it was hedges to hold the line.

What kind of hedge? You might opt for rugged, reliable, and delightfully cheap privet, or go for a whole waterfall of golden forsythia. If you wanted flowers, you planted azaleas, lilacs, rose-of-Sharon, or a wall of fragrant rugosa roses.

Add a few plants of prickly holly to your hedge to create an inviting homesite for Carolina wrens. Thrashers, cardinals, and catbirds may take you up on your offer, too.

You could go casual, and "mix it up" by planting a variety of bushes. Or you could take the formal route with boxwood, barberry, or good old privet clipped into shape.

What Happened to Hedges?

Once, every nursery sold bundles of bareroot "hedge plants," tough varieties that would look good and fill out fast. And it seemed like everybody knew that all you needed to do to start a privet hedge was to get some clippings from a neighbor to stick in the ground, where they'd root like magic.

Too bad instant gratification is so hard to resist. When prefab privacy fences came onto the scene around the 1970s—remember the fad for stockade fence, the first style available?—hedges quickly fell out of favor. Who wants to wait 2 or 3 years for a bunch of bushes to fill in, when you can block the neighbor's view in a weekend by putting up a fence?

Easy as 1-2-3

Planting a hedge is child's play, which may be one reason I'm such a big fan of these easy bird attractors. You won't need to figure out a landscape plan—just dig the holes in a straight row, and you're good to go. If you plan to let the shrubs grow au naturel instead of shearing them, plant only one kind of shrub, or create a mix of plants that mature at about the same height.

Then arborvitae entered the picture, and that was pretty much the death knell for the old-fashioned hedge. If you didn't like the look of a raw new fence, you could hire a crew or DIY, and line your boundary with a row of 5-foot-tall arborvitae planted shoulder to shoulder. Instant gratification all over again. Okay, so arborvitae was green, at least, but as far as birds were concerned, its too-dense branches made it almost as useless as a fence for cover and nesting sites.

If your yard is bordered by a naked privacy fence, just think of it as a trellis, to make it appealing to birds. Plant fast-growing grapevines or honeysuckle to cover it, and add bird-favored shrubs in front of it. If you already have a flower bed in front of the fence, the vines won't interfere (you may have to round up stray tendrils every so often), and you can dot the bed with blueberries, arrow-wood, or other bird-loved berry plants. Wait'll you see the transformation, as far as bird use: You'll still have your privacy, but now your fence will be attracting birds.

Big Benefits

Planting a hedge adds a lot of cover to your yard. Your new line of shrubs will give juncos, native sparrows, cardinals, thrushes, catbirds, wrens, and thrashers a safe corridor to travel along without being exposed to predators.

Once the bushes fill in, your planting will be a popular hideout in winter, too, when birds will gather among the branches in between visits to your feeders. At night, many of the same birds are likely to retreat to your hedge to roost for the night. My hedge is always filled with softly twittering white-throated sparrows and juncos from fall through spring.

A hedge can be a big source of natural food for your birds, too. They'll find plenty of insects to glean among the foliage and from the leaf litter beneath the bushes. And if you choose berry or fruiting plants in your mix, your hedge will practically become a neon sign when the crop comes in for waxwings, grosbeaks, and other fruit aficionados.

Nesting birds often choose a hedge for a homesite. Cardinals, catbirds, Carolina wrens, brown thrashers, robins—the list goes on. If your hedge includes prickly plants that deter predators, like roses, barberries, or holly, so much the better.

Loosen Up

Birds like a natural or only occasionally pruned hedge best, because they can easily move about within the branches. They're able to make a fast exit, too, instead of getting slowed down by a congested tangle of branches.

Pruning encourages denser growth inside the hedge, because side branches will sprout below the cut-off tips. If you don't like the au naturel look, limit your hedge haircuts to once or twice a year. If you frequently trim your hedge to keep it tidy, it may become so compacted that only house sparrows will use it. So try to live with a little shagginess for the sake of your birds.

If arborvitaes parade down your property, you can adapt them for better bird use by snipping off some branches to open up their dense interiors. It's amazing how many branches you can remove without affecting the overall appearance of your plants. And it's even more amazing how big a pile of clippings you'll end up with. Is it any wonder birds weren't too interested in fighting their way through that wall of green?

HONEYSUCKLES

There's nothing like the heady scent of honeysuckle. When Avon came out with a line of products many years ago that smelled just like the flowers, my mom stocked up on a lifetime supply.

Inhaling the perfume of blooming honeysuckle on a June night is one thing, but being surrounded by the heavy scent at breakfast, lunch, and dinner is a little much. Luckily, my mom got tired of it herself before we had to stage a honeysuckle intervention.

Yes, this is a honeysuckle, though its flowers aren't the long, slim trumpets we're used to. It's twinberry, a large native western shrub. Like all honeysuckles, it gets the seal of approval from nectaring hummingbirds and berry-eating birds.

Honeysuckle plants come in lots of shapes and sizes. Some, like the familiar yellow-and-white Japanese honeysuckle, are woody vines that are so vigorous that they can squeeze a living tree into a spiraling corkscrew as they grow up it. Others are medium- to large-size shrubs. As for that signature fragrance—some have it, some don't.

Hummingbirds love honeysuckle of any kind, because even if the flowers aren't heavily scented, they still carry a bounty of nectar. Songbirds and woodpeckers like honeysuckle, too: They eat the berries, and some songbirds nest in the branches or jungle of vines.

Too Much of a Good Thing

The big problem with honeysuckles is that birds like them a little too much. They eat the berries; they drop the seeds; and a new honeysuckle plant sprouts.

That was all well and good when the only honeysuckles in America were our native red-flowered vines and a few well-behaved shrub types. Birds were just a natural part of the distribution method for these plants.

A Quintet of Native Honeysuckles

To avoid contributing to the problem of pest plants, stick to the natives when you plant a honeysuckle vine or bush for the birds. We have about 20 native species in North America. Only a few are generally available from nurseries, but what a quintet they are! None are fragrant, but all are powerful . . . All are powerful hummingbird magnets and beautiful plants for your backyard. Goldfinches, purple finches, robins, thrushes, catbirds, and quail, among others, are fond of the berries.

HONEYSUCKLE	NATIVE TO	DESCRIPTION
Coral honeysuckle (*Lonicera sempervirens*)	Eastern half of the United States, from Texas and Florida to Maine	Semi-evergreen vine (evergreen in the South), climbing to about 10 to 20 feet, depending on cultivar. Clusters of downward-angled red flowers, yellow on inside. Bright red berries.
Yellow honeysuckle (*L. flava*)	Southeast, lower Midwest, and Central states	Deciduous vine, reaching about 10 to 20 feet high. Whorls of showy yellow clusters of outward-facing flowers. Orange to red berries.
Twinberry honeysuckle (*L. involucrata*)	Northwest, Mountain West, south into Southwest mountains	Deciduous shrub with large leaves and pairs of yellow flowers tucked where the paired leaves meet. Flowers are followed by nearly black berries in bright reddish purple bracts. About 4 feet tall and 6 feet wide, but can vary in size up to 8 feet.
Orange trumpet honeysuckle (*L. ciliosa*)	Pacific Northwest	Deciduous vine reaching, 15 to 20 feet high. Clusters of bright orange-red, orange, or yellow-orange flowers in spring, with a few more in summer. Bright red berries.
Pink or California honeysuckle (*L. hispidula*)	California	Loose, rambling deciduous "vine" that usually grows as a groundcover in native oak forests. Abundant pink springtime flowers; red fall berries.

	CULTURE	COMMENTS
	Plant in full sun for the most flowers; also thrives in part shade. Zone 4	This vine has gotten the most attention from plant breeders, so you'll find excellent named varieties for sale, as well as the "unimproved" species. 'Blanche Sandman' is an old favorite; 'John Clayton' and 'Sulphurea' have yellow flowers. But the 2009 introduction 'Major Wheeler' wins by a mile—it's absolutely covered in red flowers, and it's mildew free.
	Grows in full sun to shade; flowers best in sun. Prefers well-drained soil. Zone 5	Unlike coral honeysuckle, this one is delightfully fragrant, though not as heavily scented as the familiar Japanese honeysuckle.
	Grows best in shade to part shade, but adapts to sun. Does best in moist, humusy soil. Zone 4	This stately shrub with large, faintly glossy leaves and wide, rounded form looks nothing like a honeysuckle—at least not like the open, arching, kinda weedy bushes of the foreign species. It's a beauty, worth a special place in your yard as part of the shaded understory.
	Plant in open shade or part shade; also adapts to sun. Can withstand months of drought once established. Zone 7.	In its native home on the edges of dense conifer forests, this vine scrambles up through the dark branches, adding dots of eyecatching color that attract rufous hummingbirds, the plant's pollinator. It grows equally well on a trellis.
	Grows well in sun to shade and is drought-tolerant once established. Zone 8.	Let this species sprawl in a mound a few feet high and several feet across rather than training it to a trellis, which it will resist. Or let it wend its way up through a native shrub, another habit of this plant in the wild.

Native Know-How

Native honeysuckle vines aren't nearly as rampant as white-and-yellow Japanese honeysuckle or other imported types. The well-behaved native vines are perfect for an inexpensive metal trellis, a fence, or an arbor. If the plant gets mildewy or becomes badly infested with aphids, cut off the affected parts and dispose of them in the trash. The vine will quickly sprout fresh new growth.

Then foreign honeysuckles entered the picture. Some were brought here as ornamentals, and others were introduced by our own Department of Agriculture, which is notorious for introducing plants that have become real pests. Kudzu, autumn olive, multiflora rose, and Japanese honeysuckle are among their well-intentioned disasters. The agency touted the plants to farmers for erosion control or wildlife benefit and distributed them for planting by the thousands. Oops. Really big oops.

Regardless of how they got here, some of the foreign species quickly outgrew their welcome. Like wildfire, they spread out of control, thanks to those tasty berries.

Today, vining Japanese honeysuckle and the shrubs Amur honeysuckle (*Lonicera maackii*) and Tatarian honeysuckle (*L. tatarica*) are high on the list of unwelcome invasive plants.

Not as far as birds are concerned, though. Cedar waxwings, robins, thrushes, catbirds, downy woodpeckers, and other species are still enjoying the berries—and dropping the seeds willy-nilly.

HOOKS, HANGERS, POLES, AND POSTS

I'd love to give a great big hug to whomever came up with the idea of those sturdy, inexpensive black metal shepherd's hooks. They sure make it easy to indulge in bird feeders—instead of lugging out the posthole digger and laboring with a heavy wooden 4 × 4, all you have to do is push in the pole and hang your feeder from its hook.

Of course, when you have a whole collection of feeders, you're gonna need more than a two-prong shepherd's hook to hold them. Bird supply companies have come up with some great systems, including multi-armed metal poles; metal poles with screw tops; and metal poles that you can tailor to your needs with clamp-on attachments. Plus, there's always the old reliable 4 × 4.

Take some time to examine the systems for holding feeders before you invest a hefty chunk of change into one or another. Some require special mounts for your feeders, which'll add to the cost. Others only work with certain kinds of feeders.

Check garden centers, too, before you buy. I found similar well-made, sturdy, four-armed metal poles at both a rural supply store (for $15) and a big-box store's garden center ($30). Okay, so they only had colonial-looking finials atop the poles instead of a metal sculpture of a bird or flower, but they cost just a fraction of the price of poles sold by specialty bird supply stores.

If you're handy, you can substitute parts from a hardware store for the pricey ones at bird supply shops. When I visited my sister and brother-in-law last year, I admired the feeder pole and mount he'd made himself. He'd used a length of black pipe with a threaded end to which he attached a flat metal plate, or flange, to hold his heavy feeder. The whole setup cost him less than $10, not counting the feeder itself.

Before you install your feeder-holding pole or post, make sure it's lined up so that you'll have a view of as many of your feeders as possible. I made the mistake of putting mine in place without checking and then discovered that the feeders on the backside were completely hidden by those in front. Recruiting a helper to hold the pole in place while you check the angle—before you fill the hole with soil and tromp it into place—will make this part of the job much easier.

I like to give my hummingbirds something else to keep them busy when they buzz around the feeders, so I plant red-flowered vines at the pole's base. Just two or three seeds of scarlet cypress vine (*Ipomoea quamoclit*), cardinal climber (*Ipomoea* × *sloteri*), or scarlet runner bean (*Kennedia prostrata*) are enough to cover the poles in tempting flowers.

HOW-TO Double Duty

For a fast and easy feeder holder, you can't beat a pair of double-armed shepherd's hooks. Step on the horizontal foot bar to install the first pole, and stomp the bar about 2 inches below the soil surface. Then slide the double arm of the second pole over the double arm of the first, so that the arms cross at right angles, and stomp on the second pole's foot bar until it stops on top of the foot bar of the first pole. In just a few minutes, you'll have a sturdy holder in place for four separate feeders.

Feeding a multitude of hummers? Double up your shepherd's hooks to make a four-armed feeder.

HOT PEPPERS

Mammals can't tolerate the taste of hot peppers, but birds aren't deterred by the fiery tang. That's because birds lack taste receptors for the spicy capsaicin in the peppers. They can blithely eat the hottest peppers—more than 100,000 Scoville units—with complete impunity, and they do. Meanwhile, we're going "Whoo-ee!" and frantically fanning our mouths. (The hotness of chile peppers is rated based on Scoville units, a method developed by Wilbur Scoville in 1912.)

Birds are vital to wild peppers because they play a big role in dispersing their seeds. If an animal eats a pepper, the seeds are mostly digested. But in birds, they pass right through, surrounded by a dab of "fertilizer." Wild peppers often have tiny fruits, just the right size for a bird to nip off. They're bright red when ripe for the picking, just like a lot of other bird-favored fruits.

Walk on the Wild Side

The bird pepper, a plant that grows wild mostly south of the border, got its name because birds readily eat the tiny red fruits, supposedly even hotter than habaneros. In Texas, where wild bird peppers are known as *chile pequin,* I've watched wild turkeys and mockingbirds plucking the peppers as fast as they could. Who knows what other birds these fruits may attract. If you're into hot peppers, why not grow a few of these tough, bushy plants and see what your birds do with the fiery fruits? Just remember to handle them with care yourself—these things are rated extremely hot on the Scoville chile pepper heat scale.

Anti-Squirrel Sprays

Squirrels are mammals, so they're sensitive to capsaicin. This gives us another weapon to use in our ongoing battle against the feeder-hogging bushytails.

Back in the Dark Ages of bird feeding—oh, about 10 or 15 years ago—I made my own hot pepper deterrent through a messy process of soaking peppers, straining liquid, filling bottles, spritzing birdseed, stirring the seed, spritzing again.

It was, both literally and figuratively, a real pain. I was trying hard not to be a klutz, and I wore long sleeves and gloves, but I still managed to get burning hot pepper juice on my skin when I thoughtlessly rubbed an itch, and, even worse, in my eyes when the wind blew the spray.

Commercial pepper sprays are now widely available at garden centers. (My favorite name among these products is Cole's Flaming Squirrel Seed Sauce, which apparently you can also dip tulip bulbs into to discourage squirrels from eating them.) These ready-made liquids make it easier to treat your birdseed, but you'll still need to be careful when you're spritzing the stuff. Stand upwind, and keep your face away from the spray.

Finally, I'm happy to report, there's now a truly easy way to light a fire under squirrels: Just buy birdseed that's already been treated with hot peppers. You'll still need to wear gloves and stand upwind when you fill your feeder, but it's a whole lot simpler than the old methods.

Although the seed is higher priced than the untreated kind, it'll save you money by preventing squirrels from vacuuming your feeder. Squirrel Free Inc., a Buffalo, New York, company that developed and manufactures these products, says that after about 2 weeks, the squirrels in your yard should be trained to avoid the feeder, thanks to the deterrent. At that point, you can switch back to regular seed, saving the treated stuff in case your squirrels need any remedial lessons.

Ask your bird supply store for treated seed, or see the Resources section near the back of this book for a sampling of suppliers.

HOUSE SPARROWS

American cities of the 1800s were bustling with people and industry, but one thing was sorely lacking: birds.

Not yet accustomed to civilized life, the birds retreated to the forests and wildlands when the cities sprang up. Nary a pigeon flew over the smokestacks and houses, and even robins and cardinals kept their distance.

What to do? The answer seemed obvious: Why, just bring city birds over from Europe!

By 1850, bird lovers were enamored of the idea, and birds were being released all over the place. House sparrows and starlings, a cheerful presence in Jolly Olde England (that's where the name "English" sparrow comes from), were two of the most popular. In 2 years, the Cincinnati Acclimatization Society released more than 4,000 European birds so that "the ennobling influence of birds will be felt by the inhabitants of that fair city."

"Ennobling"? I don't know about you, but I don't exactly feel honored when a flock of house sparrows or starlings descends on my feeder.

On second thought, maybe we should appreciate them while they're here. Sad to say, these two species are declining so dramatically in England that protection efforts have been started to keep them from disappearing altogether.

House Sparrow Habits

Ever wonder why pest birds, including house sparrows and starlings, are so plentiful? It's because they're generalists: They can find food just about anywhere. French fries in the parking lot, birdseed at the feeder, seeds plucked from manure—just about anything is fair game.

Slip-Slidin' Away

Decoy feeders work great for keeping houses sparrows away from your other feeders—most of the time. But if the birds take a liking to something you've put in a tube feeder, not even a decoy feeder will keep them away. Shorter perches may discourage them from using the tube, but switching to a wire mesh model without perches, or to niger socks, works even better. The sparrows will have difficulty clinging to it, and they'll turn to a feeder that's easier to access, instead.

A natural cavity in a dead tree usually doesn't appeal to house sparrows, even though they'll avidly adopt a birdhouse. In Arizona, a stalwart saguaro cactus occasionally serves the purpose.

Hanging around in groups gives these adaptable birds another advantage—when one spots food, the others are soon behind, whether it's a few scraps in a Dumpster or a well-stocked feeding station. And if food is reliably available, they'll visit off and on all day, every day.

It's easier to block starlings at the feeder than it is to put up a "Keep Out" sign for house sparrows. Unfortunately, anything that deters the imported sparrows will also discourage native birds such as white-throated and other native sparrows, juncos, finches, and towhees.

The best solution is to put up a feeder just for the house sparrows, so your other birds can eat in peace. You'll find more details in the entry Decoy Feeders.

Home Sweet Home

Many folks despise house sparrows because they take over bluebird houses and martin condos. There's not much you can do to keep sparrows out, as you'll learn in the entry Birdhouses, because the entrance holes of these houses are big enough for them, too.

House sparrows nest in colonies when they can, which is why martin houses appeal to them. Interestingly, these birds don't nest in natural cavities in dead wood. Instead, they seek a niche on the outsides of buildings or within the vines on a wall. Old, ivy-covered buildings, like those on college campuses, often host a dozen or more pairs of nesting house sparrows.

If there's no suitable wall or niche, the birds

make do with whatever they can. The strangest colony I've seen so far was in the landscaping of an isolated McDonald's just off a highway in the wide-open plains. The few scrubby hawthorns clinging to life near the drive-thru were the only "trees" for miles, and house sparrows had filled each one with giant, messy, communal nests of twigs, trash, and other fixin's wedged and woven among the spiny branches. I bought an extra order of french fries just for them, in honor of their ingenuity.

HUMMINGBIRD FEEDERS

Put up a hummingbird feeder with some red on it, and you'll get hummingbirds. It may take a while for the birds to discover your setup, but they will. And once they do find the food, you can bet they'll be back.

Well, unless you live within the region that covers the western parts of Montana and Wyoming and the eastern halves of North Dakota and South Dakota. Sorry, folks, but hummers aren't common in those parts, for reasons that they haven't shared with us yet. Still, birds are changing their habits, and hummingbird ranges are expanding every year. The zippy little birds have been showing up more and more often in that part of the country, usually during migration. So put your feeder up anyway, just in case they decide to pay you a visit.

When should you put up your feeder? That depends on where you live. Your local chapter of the Audubon Society or a nearby nature center

A horde of Anna's hummingbirds bellies up to the bar at a nectar feeder in Arizona. If you're feeding this many birds, mix an extra-big batch of nectar and keep an extra gallon jug in the fridge for fast fill-ups.

can tell you when your hummer arrival date is. Or you can check the map on a Web site that tracks hummingbird sightings across the country: www.hummingbirds.net/map.

Selecting a Feeder

Hummingbird feeders come in a confusing array of shapes, sizes, and designs and in a wide range of prices, from a few bucks to $30 or more. Some have molded flowers at the feeding ports, some just have holes; some have bee guards, some don't; some have perches, some expect the birds to hover.

If you compare feeders side by side, you'll see that even the position of the perches and the ports varies from one to another. With so many differences in design, how do you know which one your hummers will like best? You won't, unless you experiment with all of the different models in a side-by-side setup in your yard—or use my handy guide.

Choosing a Hummingbird Feeder

FEEDER FEATURE	BENEFIT
Red trim	It's the magic color. If you're attracting hummers for the first time, the more red the better. If the birds already frequent your yard, even a tiny red tip on the feeding tube will get their attention.
Glass reservoir	Plastic bottles get cloudy and breed mold faster than glass ones do.
Perches	Hummers will feed without perching, but a feeder with perches will entice them to stay longer.
Large reservoir	You won't need to refill it as often as a feeder that holds less than a cup of nectar, which hummers can empty in hours.
Clear reservoir	A transparent reservoir makes it easy to see when the feeder needs refilling or is growing mold and needs cleaning.
Ports partly yellow	Hummers like a little bull's-eye so they know where to aim their bill. If the ports are highlighted in yellow plastic, it makes it much easier for them to find the feeding hole.
Base easy to clean	Mold will build up in the base of the feeder, so you'll need to be able to reach all the nooks and crannies with your bottle brush.
Ant moat	Some feeders have a moat built in; for others, you can buy or make the water-filled device (see the entry Ant Moats).
Stick-on window feeder	Add one to your lineup so you can enjoy an amazing close-up view of your hummers.

Use these guidelines to select a feeder that's good for you and your birds.

And the Winner Is . . .

Over the years, I've tried just about every hummingbird feeder on the market. But the Perky Pet hummingbird feeder with the pinched-waist-shaped glass bottle plus perches has been a mainstay in my yard since I bought my first one years ago. Hummers gave it the seal of approval from Day 1, and their opinion hasn't changed.

It seems to me that the perches and feeding holes are spaced just right for the birds to eat in a comfortable position. Other models that look very much the same at first glance actually have slight differences in the position of the perches in relation to the feeding holes. Although the differences seem minor, hummers have to eat in an unnatural position or hover.

Maybe the feeding port construction has something to do with it, too, or the level of nectar in the ports, because even the orioles, downy woodpeckers, house finches, and other birds that visit my nectar feeders prefer this model.

When I don't put out my Perky Pet feeder, the hummers make do with whatever feeders are available. But as soon as I hang their favorite back up, the other feeders are quickly forsaken.

I've added saucer feeders, fancy feeders, and many other models to my backyard, just to give them a fair try. I've switched places, so the other models hang where the Perky Pet usually is, and vice versa. But it's easy to see the hummers love this one best.

Unfortunately, wasps and bees love it, too. They can be a problem during summer and even worse in early fall, when bad-tempered yellow jackets join them.

Twice as Nice

A hummingbird will often lay claim to a nectar feeder and vigorously drive away any other hummers that try to steal a sip. If your feeder gets its own "guard dog" hummingbird, just put up another feeder. But make sure you put it where the territorial bird can't see it or where it's too far away for the bird to guard both at once. If your yard is mostly lawn, or your hummer is especially pugnacious, you may need to put the second feeder around the corner out of sight.

Bees, Be Gone!

Bees and wasps are a real pain around a hummingbird feeder. They're aggressive to hummers and to humans, and often they end up having the feeder all to themselves. Even a few of these sugar-seeking insects can cause you problems—they crawl into the feeding tubes and end up floating in the reservoir, fouling the nectar.

Many feeders are outfitted with plastic-grid bee guards, or you can buy the guards to stick on your feeder. They're a help at keeping wasps and bees away from the nectar, but they aren't foolproof: A determined insect can wriggle right through. And when wasps and bees are at their peak, the guards will barely slow them down.

Once, in desperation, I tried a decoy feeder: a saucer filled with sugar water that I set well away from my feeders. Hoo-boy, was that asking for trouble! Now I had aggressive bees and wasps on the feeders *and* in my garden. I gave up on that idea fast.

Next I sprang for a pricey flying-saucer-type feeder because it touted special bee guards—tight-fitting plastic inserts inside the ports. No luck there, either. My wasps apparently hadn't read the catalog copy, and they easily outwitted the devices.

Part of the problem is that wasps and bees have long tongues that can reach through the guards. They also gather at drops of nectar that spill when the wind blows the feeder or when liquid leaks from the ports because of expansion.

A Bee-Free Feeder

After 30-some years of battling bees and wasps and several boxes filled with various discarded feeder models that attracted more bees than hummingbirds, I was ready to give up.

Then I found the one that works: the Perky Pet "Our Best" Model 209. It has a deep base attached to the jar with feeding ports on top of the base. The liquid is too far down for bees and wasps to reach, and the feeder doesn't leak or drip. In fact, I fill it inside and carry it out without worrying about spilling—it's never sloshed even a single drop.

This is a big feeder. The straight-sided glass cylinder holds 30 ounces of nectar, which means it's great for the big rush of late summer, when hummers are passing through in droves. It's easy to assemble, and although it's one hefty feeder when it's filled to the brim, it's not too heavy for a shepherd's hook.

I was amazed at the difference when I tried my first one last summer. The bees and wasps that were swarming the feeders came to check it out, but they gave up in just a day or two, and never bothered it again.

That was all the evidence I needed. I bought three more of the big feeders, hung them from a pair of double-armed shepherd's hooks, and enjoyed a constant stream of hummingbirds for the rest of the season—and not a single bee.

The only drawback is that the deep base can't be disassembled for cleaning after you unscrew it from the jar. Still, 5 or 10 minutes of fiddling with a bottle brush is a fair exchange for a feeder that doesn't attract stinging insects.

I still use my hourglass Perky Pet feeders early in the season, before bees get interested in the nectar. But once the insects become real pests, I replace the smaller feeders with the big bee-proof model.

Nectar Tips

One part sugar to four parts water is the recipe for hummingbird nectar. Filling a small feeder? Mix 1/4 cup of sugar with 1 cup of water. Giant-size bottle? Then 1 cup of sugar to 4 cups of water will give you the right proportion. You'll find more info, including preparation shortcuts and storage tips, in the Nectar entry.

Don't use red dye in your nectar. Hummers don't need to see red liquid to be attracted to your feeder; its red plastic trim will catch their eye all by itself. Using dye is completely unnecessary, and no research has been done to see how it affects hummingbirds. So why risk it when you don't need it?

A big bottle of sugar water can go bad in just a few days, especially in summer. When hummer traffic is slow, fill your feeder only partway. Or buy two feeders—one with a smaller reservoir and another with a bigger one for boom times. Use the small feeder in early spring until traffic picks up, and then replace it with the economy-size model. When the rush is over, switch back until the next big rush in late summer.

HUMMINGBIRD FLOWERS

In Mother Nature's grand scheme, flowers use color, shape, and scent to attract certain pollinators. By targeting their audience, the plants make sure their flowers are tickled in just the right way so that they can set seed.

The musky aroma of skunk cabbage, for instance, draws in the flies that pollinate it. Blue flowers tend to attract bumblebees to do their duty. Sweet-smelling blossoms catch the scent receptors of butterflies and honeybees.

Flowers that beckon to hummingbirds use a color that stands out from a long distance—an important benefit when your target audience moves fast. Unlike bees and other insects that seek the ultraviolet spectrum, hummers head for red wavelengths of visible light. To put it in plain English, it's the gaudiest flowers that catch their eye—red and orange-red, as well as fuchsia. These hues are impossible for the zippy birds to overlook.

Once hummers are in your yard, they'll take their cue from shape, too. When they spot slender, dangling bells, tall spikes, or flaring tubes, they're Johnny-on-the-spot.

It's easy to suit the style of these feathered pollinators in your own backyard. Start by using color to grab their attention, and follow through with blossoms of the best shape.

Red and Orange-Red

Hummingbirds immediately investigate anything that's red or orange-red, which is why my yard is splashed with those zingy colors. The entire garden is one big advertisement.

Flowering quince snags the early crowd, followed by wild columbine and azaleas. By May, there's a whole parade of hummingbird flowers kicking into gear and a whole parade of hummingbirds visiting them.

Any flower in orange-red or red will attract hummingbirds, so try any plants you find appealing. Here's a sampling of vivid flowers that hummingbirds can't resist.

Agastache 'Orange Flare' and other warm-colored varieties (*Agastache* hybrids)

Asiatic lilies (*Lilium* hybrids)

Bee balm (*Monarda didyma*)

Cardinal climber (*Ipomoea* × *sloteri*)

Cigar plant (*Cuphea* spp.)

Coral honeysuckle (*Lonicera sempervirens*)

Cypress vine (*Ipomoea quamoclit*)

Daylilies (*Hemerocallis* spp. and hybrids)

Fire pink (*Silene virginica*)

Believe it or not, there's a fuchsia that's almost as tough as butterfly bush (*Buddleia davidii*). Meet *Fuchsia magellanica*, a hummingbird magnet that survives even in Zone 6.

- Fuchsia (*Fuchsia* spp. and hybrids)
- Geranium (*Pelargonium* hybrids)
- Gladiolus (*Gladiolus* hybrids)
- Indian pink (*Spigelia marilandica*)
- Jewelweed (*Impatiens capensis*, spotted touch-me-not; *I. pallida*, pale touch-me-not)
- Maltese cross (*Lychnis chalcedonica*)
- Mexican sunflower (*Tithonia rotundifolia*)
- Nasturtium 'Empress of India', 'Vesuvius', or other hot colors (*Tropaeolum majus*)
- Red-hot poker (*Kniphofia* spp. and hybrids)
- Salvias (*Salvia* spp. and hybrids)
- Scarlet gilia (*Ipomopsis aggregata*)
- Scarlet morning glory (*Ipomoea hederifolia*)
- Scarlet runner bean (*Kennedia prostrata*)
- Trumpet vine (*Campsis radicans*)
- Zinnias (*Zinnia* spp. and hybrids, especially red-flowered varieties)

Tubes and Spurs

Hummers don't waste much time visiting flowers that have had their nectar emptied by other pollinators. They know that red or orange-red flowers will suit them to a T. But when it comes to blossoms of other colors, shape clues them in.

How do they tell which blossom is a good bet? They go for the flowers whose petals form long tubes or which carry an extended "spur" behind the flower. The nectar in these kinds of flowers is out of reach of most insects, so it's a safe bet that the hummer's probing bill will get a sweet reward. Dangling trumpets are a safe choice, too, because insects need a landing platform that those blooms don't have.

You'll find tons of possibilities in every color of the rainbow to draw in hummers. The nodding bells of foxgloves and fuchsias are tubular flowers. So are the big single blossoms of daylilies and morning glories. Peer at a spike of salvia or

Tubular flowers are the trick to attracting hummingbirds. Their nectar is out of reach for most insects, but arranged just right for hummingbirds to collect the payoff.

agastache; it's made of thousands of tiny tubular flowers. The eye of a daisy and the center of a rose are packed full of little tubular flowers, too, and so is a spire of butterfly bush or lilac.

It's a long list, but don't worry, you won't need to memorize it. Just think like a hummingbird, and you're bound to pick plants that are the perfect fit. Keep in mind, too, that hummers need room to buzz their wings while feeding. Flowers that are held on a tall spire, like delphinium or hosta flowers, or in spikes, like salvias, give them plenty of room to maneuver.

Long-spurred flowers are a big hit, too, because nectar waits in the base of the spur. That's why columbines, impatiens, larkspur, delphinium, and nasturtiums are always a temptation, no matter what color they are.

The Grand Plan

More than 8,000 species of flowers in the Americas are tailor-made for the hummingbirds that pollinate them, from desert ocotillo to tropical bromeliads and bird-of-paradise. You gotta love the way Nature works—the plants are concentrated where hummingbirds are thickest, or maybe it's vice versa. You'll find tons of great hummingbird flowers in the Western mountains and even more in Peru, where hummers are thick as flies, but only a few in Alaska.

Not only that—the plants have evolved to exactly match the hummingbird species they intend to attract. That's pretty incredible fine-tuning, considering that hummingbird beaks and bodies vary in shape and size by only fractions of an inch.

And there's still more! The bloom time of the flowers is exactly timed to the needs of hummingbirds. In spring, a red flush moves up from the South to nurture the birds' long migration; in summer, there's a virtual feast; in fall, the bloom moves southward.

Scientists call it coevolution and coadaptation: the development of characteristics for mutual benefit. Just another one of Mother Nature's countless miracles.

Only in America

You won't find hummingbirds in Australia, Africa, or anywhere else besides the Americas. Those humming wings never developed on other continents.

Yet some of the best hummingbird flowers for our gardens—red-hot poker, gladiolus, and agaves from Africa; eucalyptus and kangaroo paw from Australia—come from other continents. What gives?

No, there aren't any hummers in Africa or Australia, where most of these plants come from. There are, however, long-tongued bees, flies, and moths, as well as gorgeous sunbirds and honeyeaters. Like our hummingbirds and sphinx moths, all of these pollinators have long bills, or in the case of insects, extremely long tongues or proboscises that can reach into the flowers.

Do It with a Dot

If a fiery garden isn't your style, dot your yard with gaudy flowers to draw hummingbirds from one bed to another. A single bright red or red-orange plant is all you need to get the birds to the bed. Then your other tubular or spurred flowers will keep them lingering.

ICE AND SNOWSTORMS

Whoo-eet! Whoo-eet! All hands on deck! Emergency!

Don't waste a minute when an ice storm or a blizzard hits. Birds need help, and they need it now. So get going: Shovel off your feeders, scatter seed right on the ground, and make sure there's plenty of food available as long as the weather lasts.

Ice storms are so dangerous to birds that they can kill off thousands in a couple of days. It's starvation that's the threat. A coating of ice makes it nearly impossible for birds to get at the seeds and insects they so desperately need.

All birds suffer in an ice storm, but ground-feeding birds like native sparrows, juncos, doves, quail, towhees, and blackbirds are most at risk. Their foraging areas are completely inaccessible.

Big snows mean tough times, too, and again, it's access to food that's the problem. Fortunately, many of our backyard friends are well adapted to snow, and most manage to find enough food to keep body and soul together. The seedy heads of weeds, grasses, and other plants are still available for foraging, and the birds can comb tree branches and bark for wintering insects, seeds, or cones.

Snowstorms that arrive earlier or later than usual, however, are the biggest troublemakers because birds that depend on insects are often around. Bluebirds and Carolina wrens sometimes suffer catastrophic losses when that happens, and catbirds, orioles, robins, and other birds can get caught by the weather, too.

No matter when the weather hits, birds sure appreciate a helping hand during snow and ice storms. Your feeders will be bursting at the seams.

Winter Storm Feeding

Now's no time to be stingy with the seed. Once the snow or ice stops, serve the stuff with a generous hand, so you don't need to step outside very

Free the Feeders

It's tempting to hole up inside your snug house when a snowstorm hits, but haul out the long johns and grab the broom: Keeping your feeders clear is the most important part of helping birds through a storm. If you can't get outside to clear them frequently, pour seed and other foods under the sheltering branches of an evergreen shrub or tree, where the food will remain uncovered longer than it would out in the open. In an ice storm, I put bird food anywhere and everywhere—including right on my front porch. Neatness doesn't count when it comes to keeping birds alive.

Keeping your feeders cleared is vital during a snowstorm. To make sure a hearty breakfast is ready and waiting for the early birds, sweep off and refill the feeders at night.

often. When you come out to refill the feeders, you'll scare the birds away, and that means wasted energy when they need to preserve all the calories they can.

If it's still snowing or the freezing rain is still coming down, serve your birds smaller helpings, because the seed will soon be buried. Add extra in the afternoon, though, because the birds will be up the next morning before you are, digging their way down to it.

There's nothing worse than scraping the bottom of the barrel when there are dozens of hungry birds trusting you to take care of them. Running out of seed when a storm hits is all the incentive you'll need to keep an extra sack on hand, if you aren't already doing so. Of course, that's when ingenuity kicks in. If you run out, start ransacking your pantry shelves and serving crumbled crackers, cereal, or any other grain-based foods. Cook up a bunch of treats, too, like those you'll find in the entries Bite-Size Bits, Doughs, Dried Berries and Fruit, and Fats and Oils.

Soft fruits and foods like those homemade recipes, as well as store-bought nuggets, cakes, and balls, are vital now, too. Stock your feeders with suet cakes and chopped suet, and keep your mealworm dishes and nut feeders filled. These foods are high in fat and exactly what your bluebirds, wrens, catbirds, thrashers, robins, and waxwings need to help them weather the storm. Your regular winter birds will be grateful, too.

IDENTIFICATION AIDS

Learning which bird is which can be confusing at first—and downright maddening even for experienced birders when it comes to lookalike species like female wood warblers.

When I was a beginner, I practiced immersion methods to learn bird identification. One of the biggest helps was the cheapest: an inexpensive poster of backyard birds that I bought at a national wildlife refuge gift shop. I mounted it right by the door I used the most, so I could look at it often. Soon, I'd bought the whole set of posters—birds of the forest, grassland, marshes—so I could learn even more.

The more you watch your birds, the better you'll get to know them—and the faster you'll spot an unfamiliar one in their midst. So pour yourself another cup of coffee, and take an extra half-hour to enjoy your breakfast crowd.

You're not being lazy, you're doing research!

A field guide is a huge help, too. Start by learning to recognize the families into which birds are grouped—finches, jays, thrushes, and so on—so you can quickly flip to that part of the book when you're trying to peg a bird's name. I wouldn't be without my *Sibley Guide to Birds* because I think it's the best one ever produced. It includes bird calls, illustrations of female and young birds as well as adult males, and range maps that show not only nesting and wintering areas, but where the birds might show up on migration.

Sometimes, it's a very small characteristic that makes the difference in figuring out which bird you're looking at. Does it have an eye ring? A pink bill? Hard to tell unless you get a good look at the details through a pair of binoculars. Binocs will give you a better appreciation for the unique beauty of even the most common birds in your yard, too. Ever notice the starry feathers that give a starling its name? With binocs, you won't miss 'em. No need to step outside to use your field glasses. Binoculars work just fine through a window, so you can observe your birds from the comfort of your easy chair. An inexpensive pair of 7 × 35s is best for beginners, and it'll serve you well for years of backyard bird-watching.

A Foundation to Build On

Winter is the perfect time to start learning your birds. The cast of characters is more limited than it is in other seasons, the trees are bare, and best of all, most of the birds are right at your feeders. Learning your regulars will give you a great foundation of 20 or more species. When newcomers begin to arrive during spring migration, you'll already have a solid head start.

IMPATIENS

Everybody knows the bedding impatiens sold at garden centers, but did you know there are two native species and lots of other exotic ones besides? If you want more hummingbirds in your yard, branch out beyond the typical impatiens to bring these birds in buzzing.

Start with the old-fashioned nonnative annual called balsam (*Impatiens balsamina*), an erect plant that blooms in sun to shade. It comes in a mix of bright colors, from fuchsia to red, as well as pastels, and blooms all summer. It'll self-sow, so you'll have more of the 1- to 2-foot-tall plants next year. Like all impatiens species, it's very easy to transplant, so you can move the seedlings wherever you want them or share them with friends.

Our two natives are jewelweed (*I. capensis*) and pale touch-me-not (*I. pallida*). Both of these 3- to 6-foot annuals are best in naturalistic gardens, because both self-sow prolifically to make a thick stand of plants. Named for the way water beads up and looks like silver on its leaves, jewelweed has dangling spurred flowers in rich orange with dark freckles; it's irresistible to hummers. The pale version is light sulfur yellow, and bumblebees as well as hummers sip from the dangling blossoms.

Flowers for Free

All impatiens, even the garden center type, are super easy to grow from seed. To collect the seeds from your plants for next year, capture the fat, ripe pods in your hand so the seeds don't escape, and drop them into a small paper sack. In spring, after the weather is reliably warm, sow your seeds—yes, even those of the bedding type!—directly in the soil. You won't believe how fast they grow and bloom, calling to hummingbirds all over the garden.

Anchored by New Guinea impatiens, at lower right, this scrumptious container overflows with hummingbird appeal. Dangling fuchsia, fiery cannas, and red begonias all act like a neon sign to attract the zippy birds, while a dark spot of ruby chard and a spill of lime-green *Lysimachia* make it look good to our eyes, too.

All impatiens have seedpods that are spring-loaded. Touch a plump one and you'll see where the name "touch-me-not" comes from—it'll make you jump when the seeds explode. They're more than generous at spreading themselves around.

That's a problem with a plant I once grew, Himalayan impatiens (*I. glandulifera*), also known as policeman's helmet. It's a gorgeous specimen, growing to almost the size of a small tree (10 feet), with many clusters of dangling rose-pink flowers. Unlike the common bedding impatiens, its seeds manage to survive cold winters.

When I saw that its far-flung seeds had leaped the bed and were spreading into nearby woods, I yanked out my plants and hoed out the seedlings. It's now on invasive plant lists in the Pacific Northwest and other areas, but hummers still visit the renegades.

For other impatiens, including a gorgeous true-blue one from Tibet (*I. namchabarwensis*), you'll have to track down seeds or mail order plants; check the Resources section near the back of this book.

INDIVIDUALS

We love our birds, but we love 'em even better when we can tell them apart as individuals. How do you tell one chickadee from another? It's not easy, unless an individual bird has something that makes it stand out from the others.

That's why it's so much fun when, say, a robin

with a white tail feather turns up. All of a sudden, that bird takes on special meaning. "Hey, there's my robin," we say when the bird comes back to visit.

White feathers are the usual distinguishing mark, because albinism is fairly common in birds. You may even see an all-white robin or other bird, and, boy, is that weird! It's amazing how hard it is to tell what species a bird is without its usual colors.

You usually can't tell birds apart by behavior alone, unless you take the time to hand-tame them. This is easier than it seems, because your birds already associate you with food: They've seen you filling their feeders. Some birds are just naturally tame, especially those that come down from the Far North. Approach the feeder very slowly and make no sudden movements, and you may have good luck getting evening grosbeaks, redpolls, and red-breasted nuthatches to take sunflower seeds out of your hand in just a few minutes. You'll quickly learn to tell one individual from the next, just by the way they behave when you offer them food. Once the bird rejoins its flock, though, all bets are off; it'll blend right in with the rest of the bunch.

Sometimes, you'll have a bird in your yard that sounds different than its kin. For years, I welcomed a blue jay that could imitate the scream of a red-tailed hawk almost perfectly. The bird was so good at this trick that I spent a lot of time scanning the skies for Mr. Hawk until it finally dawned on me that it was my jay. Just as with any bird that you get to know as an individual, you'll feel a lot warmer toward that bird with the idiosyncratic voice.

Up Close and Personal

Chickadees, titmice, and nuthatches love nuts and sunflower seeds, and they're among the easiest birds to hand-tame. On a cold or snowy morning, when the birds really, really want your food, grab a handful of nuts or seeds and stand quietly beside a feeder with your hand in the tray, holding out the tempting food. After a while, birds will begin to approach the feeder, and if you're patient enough, they'll take a nut or seed from your hand. "It only took about 15 minutes to get a nuthatch to eat out of my new 'feeder,'" says bird lover Matt Bartmann, whose home is 8,000 feet high in the Rocky Mountains. After a March snowstorm, he tempted the red-breasted nuthatch shown here with a handful of birdseed and stale cake—and even managed to snap a photo at the same time.

Once you gain the trust of your little friends, repeat the trick frequently to reinforce the behavior.

INSECT FOODS

Insect foods are one of the big leaps forward in bird feeding over the last few years. At least one specialty supplier (Oregon Feeder Insects, which specializes in houseflies) has been selling insect foods for years, but now these products have hit the mainstream. With greater availability, it's easy to add this long-missing ingredient to the lineup at our feeders, and, wow, does it pay off.

All birds eat insects, but some depend more heavily on them than others—and those are exactly the birds we want to see more of! Bluebirds, tanagers, waxwings, vireos, warblers, catbirds, flycatchers, wrens, and brown creepers aren't much interested in seeds. But put out a pan of mealworms, and now we're talking!

Bluebirds of all species, including this male western bluebird, adore mealworms. Serve them sparingly but regularly. If you're using live larvae, put them in a straight-sided dish so they can't escape.

You don't need to steel yourself to handle living larvae. If the thought makes you cringe, use dried or roasted critters instead. Birds recognize them quickly because they look like the caterpillars and grubs they find so appealing.

You can buy other foods made with bugs, too, including suet blocks and hamburger-like nuggets that use insects as a main ingredient. Makers of molded treats are getting on the bandwagon, too, and insects in pellets are even showing up in birdseed mixes. Look for them at your bird store, or see this book's Resources section for suppliers.

Block the Big Guys

If starlings move in to gobble your expensive goodies, lower the lid on your dome feeder to exclude the larger birds. Or serve your buggy treats in a bluebird feeder, which smaller birds can enter as they would a birdhouse in order to get to the food. Starlings can't squeeze through the hole, so you won't go broke filling their bellies.

Serving Insect Foods

Insect foods can cost a pretty penny, so use your noggin when you decide which ones to add to your menu. Buy a small quantity, until you see how well your birds take to it. And keep in mind, to attract the uncommon birds, you'll need to offer the food in feeders that they can use.

If you're offering them up for the first time, use a highly visible feeder so the birds can spot them. I buy plain mealworms, waxworms, and other larvae, as well as the hamburger-like or bite-size nuggets, which I serve in a dish or a dome feeder, since that's where my bluebirds, orioles, catbirds, waxwings, and wrens prefer to eat. I've also spotted warblers, kinglets, and titmice snitching a bite from these feeders.

New foods that include insects are coming onto the market all the time, but so far, I haven't found one that rivals Nuts 'n' Bugs, a semi-solid treat that birds absolutely adore. To accommodate the woodpeckers, nuthatches, and other agile types, I stuff it into the holes of a log feeder. I also fill a dome feeder with chunks and crumbs of the stuff for bluebirds, wrens, catbirds, and others, and I put some in a low tray for the robins.

Mealworms, Waxworms, and Other Larvae

Mealworms were such an instant hit with "good birds" when the wrigglers first came onto the market a few years ago that they immediately became a must-have item for anyone who wants to attract bluebirds, orioles, tanagers, wrens, thrushes, warblers, and other special birds. Most of our favorite old friends love them, too, especially chickadees, titmice, and woodpeckers.

It's really fun to serve a food that birds so obviously enjoy. I dole out the worms in small amounts, and birds quickly learned which dish they're in. When I come out to restock the feeder, titmice and Carolina wrens often hang around hopefully.

You can buy live or roasted mealworms at bird shops, pet stores, bait shops, or by mail. Roasted or dead worms are much easier to deal with than live worms. They come packed in a small plastic container, and you can simply pour out a helping at feeding time. Refrigerate the container to keep them fresh.

Dead worms are popular with birds, but live worms are irresistible. Live worms that arrive via mail-order are packed in crumpled newspaper in a box; put the box in your refrigerator for a few hours to slow them down, and then shake them off into a plastic shoebox-size container. Do this job outside, so stray worms don't go flying.

You'll need to feed your live worms so they don't go dormant. Once you have them corralled in the plastic box, pour in about an inch of old-fashioned oatmeal (not the quick-cooking kind) for every 1,000 worms. Add a few slices of carrot for moisture.

Other kinds of larvae, including waxworms and wireworms, have entered the bird food picture. My birds love them all, and so will yours.

INSECTS AU NATUREL

Even when your feeders are full to the brim with the very best foods you can buy, they can't compare to natural foods. Especially bugs.

Want proof? Think about how your birds use your feeders. They're not there nonstop, from sunup 'til sundown. Instead, they fly in, stay for a while, and then return to foraging the usual way. No matter how proud we are of our nice little setups, we're just a way station on their rounds.

Working with black-capped chickadees over several years, University of Wisconsin researchers Margaret Brittingham and Stanley Temple proved the point. The little birds got only about 20 percent of their daily food intake from feeders—and 80 percent of their food from natural sources.

For many birds, most of that natural food is insects. Ever notice how feeder traffic drops off in late spring to early summer? One of the biggest reasons is because insects are burgeoning then, and birds find easy pickin's everywhere they look. Summer is prime time for family life, too, and the main food for nestlings is, you guessed it, insects.

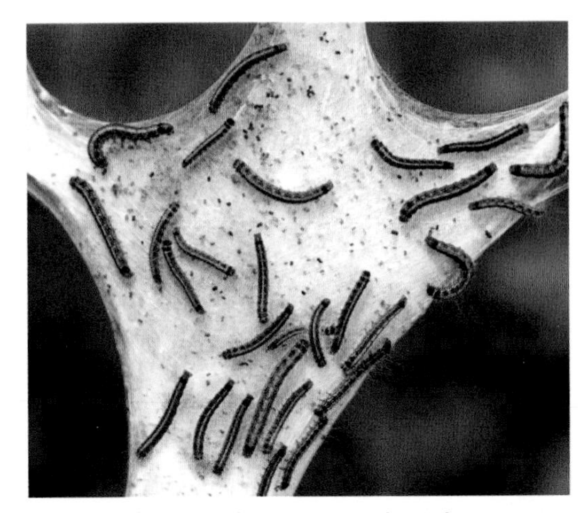

Instead of reaching for the pesticide to destroy eastern tent caterpillars, let nuthatches, cuckoos, blue jays, orioles, and other birds do the job for you. A yard that's alive with insects is also alive with birds.

Go Ahead, Get Bugged

If you want to see lots of birds in your backyard year-round, make your place inviting to bugs. Don't worry, you'll probably never notice the population boost in creepy crawlies. But your birds will.

First, stop killing insects. Learn to live with caterpillars, beetles, and even some aphids, instead of reaching for pesticides at the first sign of them.

Save your pesticides (organic only, please!), like Bt, for plants that you eat, and stop using them on your ornamental plants, trees, or lawn. Bt kills all of the leaf-eating caterpillars on a plant, so you'll be wiping out all kinds of tidbits that birds enjoy. If you're using the milky spore bacterium as a biological control against Japanese beetles—stop! It kills *all* of the grubs in the soil, including those of native beetles. Flickers and starlings eat a lot of grubs, and thrushes, robins, and many other birds depend on beetles.

The worst backyard pesticides, from a bird's-eye view, are products that treat the whole yard. They wipe out just about everything, which means there are few adult insects for birds to seek out in summer, and hardly any eggs, larvae, or cocoons in fall and winter. Instead of fogging or dusting your yard with killer chemicals, spray yourself with repellent. You'll find more info about the effects of chemical sprays on birds in the Pesticides entry.

Next, plant native trees, shrubs, vines, and flowers. Insects are already adapted to using these plants, so they'll quickly take up residence. And because they've had time to work out their differences, you'll rarely see a native plant severely affected by insects—unless the bugs come from elsewhere. (Japanese beetles, anyone?) More plants mean more insects, so squeeze

Solve Problems sans Pesticides

When you do get an infestation of insects—and you will—you can take care of it without resorting to pesticides, organic or otherwise. Pick off tomato hornworms by hand, and toss them on your walk for robins to eat. Tap Japanese beetles into a jar of soapy water. Spray aphids away with a blast from the hose, or clip off infested plant stems and dispose of them in the trash.

in vegetation wherever you can. Birds will be glad for the extra cover, too.

And for the icing on the cake, attract some pretty insects—butterflies. Add host plants and butterfly flowers, and keep planting natives; many of them serve as food for butterfly caterpillars.

When your yard is alive with insects, you've helped restore the natural balance that's so vital to birds. More birds will visit your yard to forage in all seasons of the year. Birds may even choose it as a homesite, thanks to the abundance of natural food for their nestlings.

INTRODUCING NEW FOODS

Birds can be worse than 3-year-olds when it comes to trying a new food. They'll eat around it without giving it a second glance unless you employ a few tricks to make it more appealing. No, you won't need to play "Open wide, here comes the airplane!" Just give the new food better visibility, or serve it in a familiar feeder.

If you're trying a new seed mix, simply replace your regular mix. Your feathered friends will quickly accept the new offering. If it's a single kind of seed, such as safflower or canola seed, mixing a handful with their regular feed may do the trick. If it doesn't, you may have to make them sit at the table until they clean their plate. Oh, wait, sorry, bad idea . . . sort of. What I do is empty a feeder that they're already accustomed to, and put only the new seed in place. Once they try it, they'll be like Mikey from the old TV commercials: "He likes it!" Then you can mix it with your regular offering, and it won't be ignored.

Getting seed-eating birds to accept a new food is child's play compared to tempting the soft-food and fruit eaters like wrens, bluebirds, or robins to try your feeder for the first time. With these birds, visibility and accessibility are the keys, plus a little subterfuge if needed.

Start by choosing a feeder that will allow them to easily see the food, and also accommodate their perching style of dining. That may be all you need, since these birds are becoming more accustomed to visiting feeding stations. Robins and thrushes often adopt a low feeder more easily than one at waist height or higher.

If your delicious mealworms, bird dough, and other soft foods are still spurned, you can try my last-ditch trick. I simply set up a temporary feeder where the birds I want are likely to gather—near the hedge for wrens and catbirds, the compost pile for robins, the berry bushes for thrushes, and the cherry tree for waxwings.

Once birds try a bite, they'll be hooked. And because birds are rapidly adapting to feeders, you may get takers for your new foods in just a matter of days.

New to oriole feeding? Start with half an orange, which orioles recognize quickly as food, stuck securely in a visible location.

JAMS AND JELLIES

Not all birds are blessed with taste receptors for sweetness. Chickens, for example, could care less whether their grain is sweetened or not because they can't taste it. Birds that eat fruit and nectar, on the other hand, are well aware when they hit the jackpot—they're wired to be sensitive to sweetness.

We have plenty of sweetness receptors ourselves, so all of the fruits that taste great to us also taste great to the birds that are attracted by sweet, ripe fruit. Orioles, tanagers, rose-breasted grosbeaks, waxwings, robins, wrens, catbirds, and bluebirds, among others, have a definite predilection for sweet fruit.

What's even sweeter than fruit off the tree? Fruit in a jar!

Jams and jellies are extremely tempting to fruit-loving birds. Orioles love grape jelly. They also love strawberry jam, fig preserves, orange marmalade, and every other jam, jelly, or preserves I've put in their feeder. So do tanagers. Both the western tanagers I hosted in Washington State, as vivid as living flames, and my scarlet tanagers in Indiana come for the treat.

Many oriole feeders include a little platform where you can put a glob of jelly. A custard cup or a deep jar lid will work, too—any container that holds a couple of tablespoons of the sweet stuff and allows a bird to perch on its rim. Or you can wedge a recycled yogurt or pudding cup into a tree crotch, and fill it with jelly for orioles, tanagers, and other sweet-fruit eaters.

All in the Timing

Sticky-sweet jellies and jams are a spring or wintertime treat for your birds. Offer these foods when orioles are migrating in May and for as long as they frequent your feeder. When wasps, bees, or ants get too pesky, remove the feeder. Serve jelly again after cold weather comes, for waxwings, wrens, robins, varied thrushes, and other birds that like a little something sweet. Here's an interesting thing—robins usually aren't very interested in jelly in spring and summer when earthworms and insects abound. Come fall and winter, though, robins become fruitivores, and they'll happily eat jelly once they find your feeder.

When grape jelly begins to attract wasps, switch to suet and bird doughs to keep your Baltimore oriole coming back.

HOW-TO Jelly Jar Feeder

Turn a jar of jelly into a feeder with this easy DIY project. It works great for serving orioles and tanagers, and other fruit eaters may try it, too. Just be sure to keep the lid on the jar until you hang the feeder.

6-inch length of wooden dowel, ⅛ to ¼ inch in diameter
Pocketknife
Floral wire
Wire cutter
Small jar of jelly, jam, or preserves, any kind

1. Make a notch in the center of the dowel by cutting out a small, shallow V with a pocketknife.

2. Wrap a length of floral wire tightly around the dowel at the notch, making several passes so that the wire is tightly attached to the dowel.

3. Holding the dowel horizontally to one side of the jar, just below the lid, continue wrapping the same piece of wire around the jar, just below the lid. Make several passes and keep the wire tight, so that it holds the dowel securely to the jar.

4. Twist the ends of the wire together to secure them. The dowel will be the perch for your jelly feeder.

5. Slip another piece of wire under the wrapped wire, opposite the dowel. Twist together the ends into a loop for hanging.

6. Hang the jelly jar feeder from a shepherd's hook or a tree branch, and remove the lid. The weight of the jar will cause it to hang at an angle, and orioles will have easy access from the perch.

JUNCOS AND TOWHEES

The arrival of juncos is one of my favorite times of the year. As soon as the little gray birds show up, I know the busy winter season has really kicked into gear. At first, only a few of these small "snowbirds" come to pick through the seeds, but soon their friends will be joining them, making a twittering flock of 20 or more birds that stick around until dandelion time.

Juncos are ground feeders by nature, so they usually hang out underneath the feeders where other birds drop seeds, keeping company with native sparrows. But they'll make the hop to a higher tray feeder, too.

Easy to Please

Juncos and towhees are easy to please at the feeder. Millet is their first choice of seed, although they may also eat black oil sunflower and nibble on niger. Since these birds are most comfortable eating at ground level, serve their seed in a low tray feeder or scatter a modest amount directly on the ground.

Scatter a bit of seed on the ground for an eastern towhee, but be sparing: Leftovers may lure rodents.

Towhees share those habits, but they're much less abundant than juncos. One or two is the usual count. If you live near woods, you may draw a few more, especially during snowstorms.

You can count on hosting juncos, but towhees aren't a given, even though they're year-round birds for all but the northern third of the country. For one thing, there are a lot fewer of them than juncos. Plus, they seem perfectly content to stay in the brush along a woods' edge rather than to seek out a feeder.

Still, if you live near their natural woodsy habitat and offer plenty of sheltering cover in your yard, you may attract a bird or two as a regular. And, if you live near their natural nesting habitat, you might even tempt them into raising a family in your yard.

Both juncos and towhees eat a multitude of weed and flower seeds. To give them a natural place to forage, see the entry Birdseed Gardens to get ideas for tempting plants that will provide a rich supply of seeds that they can scratch for all winter.

JUNK FOOD

High in fat and salt, junk food like corn chips, cupcakes, and other all-too-tempting snacks can really pack on the pounds. I try to avoid the impulse to buy, but every so often a bag of junk manages to find its way into my pantry cabinet. That's okay with my jays and starlings, because they get the stale leftovers in the bottom of the bag.

Even the "snowbird" or dark-eyed junco, a winter friend for many of us, will nibble on crushed corn chips or other junk food.

An occasional serving of leftover junk food won't harm your birds. But you won't get many

Betcha Can't Eat Just One

Junk food can come in handy now and then. It's a good way to keep your food hogs occupied elsewhere while other birds eat your normal offerings at the feeder. Just scatter whatever junk food you've found onto the lawn, and watch the fun begin. Starlings, house sparrows, jays, grackles, mockingbirds, and magpies, if you happen to have them, will soon swoop in to see what's on the table.

You can also use potato chips, corn chips, and other dry junk food as an emergency feeder food if you get caught short of seed during a winter storm. Crush the stuff and feed it dry to seed eaters, or mix it with peanut butter to appeal to chickadees, titmice, nuthatches, wrens, and woodpeckers.

Distract—or attract—the bold black-billed magpie by tossing some junk food out in your yard.

takers, either. Finches, cardinals, woodpeckers, and most other backyard birds naturally prefer a healthier diet of seeds and suet, with a side of insects or soft food.

Opportunistic birds, however—think "pests"—will readily gobble up any snacks you care to share. They're already accustomed to eating junk food, because they find it in Dumpsters and on the street. For them, I like to put the stuff out as is, without crumbling it into smaller bits, so the birds feel as if they've snatched a real prize. You'll notice that whichever birds manage to grab a piece will rapidly fly away so they don't have to share!

K/L

KILLDEER

One of the earliest spring migrants, the dapper, long-legged killdeer looks like it'd be right at home in the company of shorebirds. That's the group of birds it belongs to, and many killdeers do scour mudflats and shorelines right along with their close cousins, the plovers.

But unlike its relatives, who are rarely far away from water, the killdeer is also perfectly content to raise its family and find its food far from water.

You won't see a killdeer at your feeder, but if you have a large lawn or a pasture, you're likely to spot this interesting bird scooting around after the grasshoppers, beetles, and other insects it fills its belly with. The birds may also patrol the muddy edges of a pond or creek to nab dragonflies, frogs, and even crayfish. Paved parking lots are another favorite hangout, particularly at night, when killdeers may collect there to catch insects drawn to the lights.

A killdeer may even take up residence at your place if you have a gravel lane, a good-size gravel driveway, or a big gravel parking area at your place where it can lay its eggs. The bird simply scrapes out a small depression in the gravel or along a roadside and deposits its well-camouflaged speckled eggs right on the spot. Like other shorebirds, a killdeer's chicks are "precocious"—they can skedaddle about like fuzzy golfballs just a few minutes after they hatch.

It's easy to identify a killdeer by looks alone, thanks to that dramatic two-band necklace. Its style of locomotion is just as distinctive: The bird runs several steps, stops and bobs, runs some more, bobs, and so on.

It's All an Act

How can you tell if you're near a killdeer nest? Just watch for the famous "broken wing" routine that killdeers use to divert attention from their eggs or young.

First, the bird flies a short distance, uttering loud cries. If that doesn't work, and the blundering human or predator is still too near the family, the parent bird will suddenly flounder around on the ground, with one wing pitifully dragging.

It's a great ruse, and most of us fall for the act. We slowly approach the "hurt" bird, to see what's the matter. As soon as we're far enough from the family, the parent miraculously recovers and flies away.

Where'd He Go?

A killdeer is surprisingly hard to see from a distance, despite its snowy breast and bold necklace. But the loud voice of the bird is a good giveaway—and it seems they can't remain silent for long! To spot a killdeer, just listen for the telltale "Kill-eee! Kill-eee!" as the bird flies here and there.

The killdeer ranges across the entire country. In fall, northern birds retreat to the southern half of the United States, where they can still forage when snow and ice cover their summer homeland.

Listen for migrating killdeers overhead in early spring and fall; they're hard to miss when the small flock goes crying through the sky. Oldtimers knew the killdeer as the "killdee," which comes mighty close to the sound of their call. The birds travel both during the day and at night.

LAYERED LOOK

What's under that shade tree in your backyard? Probably lawn, or maybe a circle of impatiens or hostas. It may look pretty, but it's no great shakes as far as birds are concerned.

Foraging places at various heights, from mulch to treetops, are the natural arrangement of the forest. Boost your bird population by planting in layers to mimic the effect.

Instead of planting a ho-hum flowerbed around your tree, why not go for multilevel marketing (MLM)—it's a guaranteed winner!

No, we're not talking about Amway. We're talking about marketing your yard to birds with multiple levels of plants: tall trees, shorter trees, shrubs, flowers or foliage plants, and groundcovers, all stacked one over the other in the same space.

It's the way Mother Nature plants her forests, and it works wonders in our backyards for nurturing woodland birds. It may tempt towhees, tanagers, wood warblers, thrushes, and other birds of the forest into calling your yard home, or at least stopping in to rest a spell.

More Plants = More Birds

You can fit a lot more plants into a small space by arranging them in layers. Birds will have more vegetation to forage in, and they'll feel more at ease because they can move naturally from one level to the next, just as they do in the wild.

Think of multilevel plants as a vertical travel

corridor, as well as a way to provide habitat for birds that prefer different levels. Orioles, tanagers, and other birds that spend most of their time in the treetops can easily drop down from your big old maple to a shorter dogwood, say, and then to your feeder. Lower-level birds, such as catbirds and thrashers, can skulk in a vine, then a shrub, before reaching the eats. Carolina wrens and robins can pick through the mulch for insects before they hop to a low shrub and then move to the feeder.

Planting in layers means there's plenty of room for everybody, whether they're looking for food, scouting for bugs, or seeking a nest site. I like to use native plants, so my end result looks as if it's part of the natural surroundings beyond my yard. It makes the space more alluring to birds than if the same plants were dotted about here and there.

Understory trees, which naturally grow beneath mature oaks, maples, and other deciduous trees, are the key to a layered planting to attract forest birds. They bridge the gap between the high canopy and shorter plants below.

In your own backyard, you can pick from hundreds of excellent candidates for your understory. Flowering dogwood, redbud, American holly, and shadblow, all hardy to at least Zone 5, are widely adaptable small trees that thrive in shade and attract birds.

Ready for the lower layer of your multilevel marketing plan? Now you have even more choices, because dozens of shrubs with bird appeal thrive in shade.

In my yard, it's mainly American spice bush (*Lindera benzoin*), American hazel (*Corylus americana*), and native hydrangea (*Hydrangea arborescens*), just like in the nearby woods. The first two attract birds with berries and nuts; the hydrangea supplies cover and shreds of bark for nesting. All support a flourishing community of insects, judging by how thoroughly and frequently the birds examine them.

For other ideas, try a native plant nursery or catalog; all native shrubs are useful to birds in one way or another. Or browse the "shrubs for shade" section of your local nursery, and choose your favorites.

Finally, it's time for the finishing touches on your MLM scheme: the impatiens and hostas you started out with around that tree. Give them some ferns or other plants for company, if you like, and move them to a more pleasing place. Spread a mulch of chopped leaves or shredded bark throughout your new garden to give robins and sparrows something to scratch in, and stand back. The birds will be checking it out before you know it.

Bird-Supplied Seedlings

In a forest, the understory layer is filled with young trees of all ages, from seedlings to saplings. Trees will sprout in the mulch of your layered garden, too, because birds will "drop" seeds of whatever they've been eating as they digest the edible parts. Seedling trees are speedy growers, as much as 2 to 3 feet a year, and it's fun to watch them get bigger year by year. So let a few of the baby trees grow, and you'll soon have an understory of plants that are guaranteed to be bird favorites—after all, birds are the ones who planted them!

LOG FEEDERS

One of the oldest kinds of feeder around, the hanging log feeder has stood the test of time. It's a simple thing: a piece of log with tea-light-size holes drilled into it to hold high-fat foods and with an eye hook to hang it by. The "log" is a skinny one, about 3 to 4 inches in diameter and maybe a foot long, with the bark still on it.

Store-bought log feeders have holes that are drilled all the way through, so that you can insert packaged suet plugs into the holes. These feeders are usually made of finished lumber, not natural tree branches.

My birds have tested both kinds, and their reviews are unanimous: A homely natural log feeder wins hands down over the fancified models.

The bark makes it easy for any bird to get a grip. Holes that go only partway through make it easy to refill, and food won't get wasted in the middle, where it's out of reach. You can hang the log vertically, for clinging chickadees, titmice, nuthatches, and woodpeckers. Or hang it horizontally, for bluebirds, orioles, robins, catbirds, wrens, and other perching birds.

Filling the Gap

If you plan to use homemade spreads or soft foods to fill your store-bought log feeder, put a plug in the center of each drilled-through hole to prevent waste, make the food more accessible, and make the feeder easier to refill. Measure the diameter of the log, and subtract 2 inches. Cut a section that length from a wooden dowel the same diameter as the hole. Sand the sides of the dowel to make it a hair smaller than the hole, so you can insert it without it sliding all the way through. Push the dowel in, leaving 1 inch of space on each end. That'll give you an inch-deep cup on each side of the log, instead of a bottomless pit. Repeat the trick for the other holes.

Holes or Cups?

Log feeders with holes drilled all the way through are convenient if you're using packaged suet plugs. At least the first time, that is. Refills can be annoying, and stuffing your own foods into the holes is even messier.

Many plugs are in edible casings, like sausages. But "edible" doesn't mean the birds will eat them. My chickadees and other birds pecked out the soft filling and left the papery casings in the holes.

And the birds couldn't reach the stuff in the middle of the drilled-through holes. So I ended up having to poke out the remains of each plug and casing before I could slide in a new one.

When I switched to homemade foods, the job got even more frustrating, because I had to finagle the stuff into the holes without pushing it out the other side.

As far as convenience goes, I find that it's way easier to spread suet or peanut butter into tea-light-size holes than it is to fiddle with plugs and their remains. But it's hard to find a feeder with these food-holding recesses instead of holes drilled all the way through. So I asked a tool-savvy friend to try his hand. He used a 1¼-inch spade bit on his

A log feeder is the perfect match for the cute little red-breasted nuthatch's feeding style.

electric drill to whiz through the job, and made three feeders to give away in less than an hour. If you have a DIY bent, you can easily do the same. A spade bit is wide and flat at its business end rather than cylindrical, with a short, pointed tip that holds the bit in place while you work. You can buy one for a few dollars at any hardware store.

If you want to get even simpler, forget the holes altogether, and just hang a section of log all by itself. Insert a couple of eye hooks in its ends to hang it horizontally, or screw a single one into one end for a vertical feeder, and attach a wire or chain to hang it. Then, just spread some peanut butter, solidified meat drippings, or lard onto the rough bark, and let your birds work away at it.

LOG-FEEDER FILLER

2½ cups regular oatmeal, not instant

¾ cup lard or solidified meat drippings (bacon fat works great)

½ cup peanut butter

¼ cup chopped peanuts or sunflower chips

Mix the ingredients, and fill the holes or cups of your log feeder. Store any extra mixture in your fridge in a tightly covered container; it'll keep for at least a month. In winter, I mix up double or triple batches and store them on my closed, unheated back porch, so I have plenty on hand whenever I need to refill the feeders.

MEAT GRINDER

From what I've observed, birds have a natural inclination to investigate anything that looks like a caterpillar or worm. They're quick to investigate packaged foods that look like bits of hamburger, and mealworms are a fast favorite.

Bite-size bits, which you can read about in the entry by that name, are another big hit at the feeder. I've noticed that my birds simply can't get enough suet when I serve it chopped into bits. Even juncos, native sparrows, cardinals, and other birds we usually don't think of as suet eaters will gobble it up when it's in a feeder they can access.

In winter, when the demand for high-fat foods cranks into high gear, I start cranking, too—with an old-fashioned metal meat grinder. It turns out bite-size pieces of suet and wiggly "worms" way faster than I can chop by hand.

Thank goodness they're still making those sturdy devices (ask at a rural supply store). I clamp mine to my kitchen table, put in chunks of fat and other goodies, and crank out some superlative bird treats.

El Cheapo fat trimmings from the butcher are the base of my recipes. I throw in some nuts, dried fruit, sunflower chips, or anything else that

Use an old-fashioned meat grinder to process chunks of fat from the butcher and other foods into bite-size bits.

Free Up the Fat

Suet and other fats have a nasty habit of clogging up the works in kitchen appliances, including small food processors and choppers. To make it easier for your machine to do the job without having to stop and clean out the clogs, just spray the blades with nonstick cooking spray. If you don't have a grinder or chopper, make friends with the folks at a small butcher shop—they may be willing to grind fat trimmings for you.

looks good, even hamburger. The grinder mixes it all together.

What comes out looks like the output of a pasta machine or a PlayDoh extruder—or the skinny snakes of clay I used to make in kindergarten. A few quick strokes with a sharp knife, and I have hundreds of fatty bits that my birds go wild for.

MEATY BONES

When my old dog left his big soup bone lying in the yard, birds moved in on it fast. Starlings were the first to pounce upon the treasure, while a robin peered with interest from under a nearby bush. Hmm—could a big meaty bone hold promise as bird food?

It sure can. The marrow inside a bone is premium bird food, ultra high in fat and protein, and any shreds of meat or fat clinging to the bone are fair game, too. I'm a bona fide bone collector now, asking for them from friends, as well as saving my own in a freezer container.

The only problem with bones is that they're not exactly handsome yard ornaments. I don't worry about that in times of dire need, such as when a snowstorm descends. Then, I simply toss the bones out for birds to help themselves.

Hanging a soup bone looks intentional, at least, instead of like forgotten trash. So I often use twine to suspend a meaty bone from a shepherd's hook. To deter starlings but allow chickadees, titmice, wrens, and other small birds to get in at the marrow, stick the bone inside a caged feeder.

The Marvels of Marrow

Bone marrow is a premium bird food, especially in winter when your friends need the extra fat. Large beef bones are easiest to scavenge marrow from, so ask for them at the meat department, and have them split for easy access. You can serve marrow raw or cooked. Use it as you would any soft fat, such as lard or bacon drippings: Smear it on bark, stuff it into a log feeder, or add it to your homemade bird doughs and other soft foods.

MILLET AND MILO

The two M-word seeds, which sound sort of similar, couldn't be more different. Millet is a can't-miss feeder food across the country. Milo is spurned by nearly all feeder birds in the eastern two-thirds of the country, although it's popular with birds in some parts of the West.

Millet is a standard for bird feeding, so it's included in just about every mix on store shelves. The tiny round seed is usually tan, but it may also be reddish brown, depending on which type is used in the mix.

There's no need to look for unusual varieties.

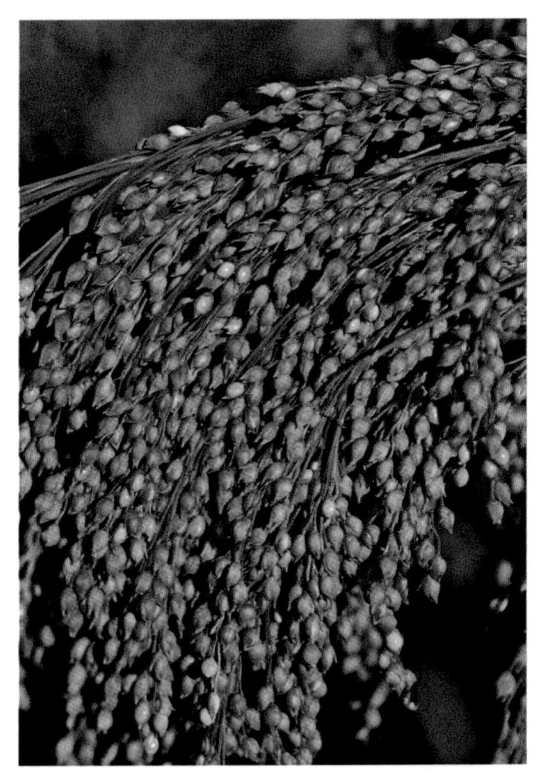

Grassy shoots springing up in the debris beneath your feeders? Let a few mature into handsome sprays of millet seeds that birds can pluck right from the plant when it ripens.

Birds prefer the white proso millet, a pale tan seed that's widely available. I often wonder if other millets are added to seed mixes just to make them look pretty, because the red or deep gold millet seeds often remain in the feeder until after the white millet has disappeared. Of course, you can always try other millets just to see how your birds like them.

Which birds eat millet?

Juncos, towhees, finches, buntings, varied thrushes, blackbirds, grackles, cowbirds, and sparrows, both native and not, are the most devoted customers. Indigo buntings actually prefer it to niger.

Tanagers, which are beginning to learn that bird feeders mean food, will eat millet, too, when they stop in on spring migration. And if the seed is mixed with fats, as is often the case with packaged suet blocks, it'll go down the hatch of just about any bird in your backyard, including bluebirds, woodpeckers, and robins.

It's not how many kinds of birds eat millet that make it a must at the feeder—it's that those birds show up in large numbers. It takes a lot of seed to keep them happy.

Millet is a dense seed: A 50-pound sack is about half the size of a 50-pound sack of sunflower. A pound goes a long way, because most of the weight is in the seed, not the shells. It's one of the best buys out there, when it comes to birdseed.

Milo is a round, dull red seed, about twice the size of millet. It's the seed of sorghum, a stout grass with a whisk broom spray of seeds at the top of the stalk.

If you live anywhere but the West, you've

Read the Seed

Seed mix makers sell their products across the country, so milo is often included even if you live where birds turn up their beaks at it. If you don't live in the West, especially the Southwest, get in the habit of looking at the mix and reading the list of ingredients to judge how much wasted seed will be left in your feeders. The contents of a mix are listed in descending order of proportion in the bag; for you non-Westerners, millet, not milo, should be up near the top.

Indigo buntings begin molting on their wintering grounds. Offer a tube of white proso millet, and you can get an up-close view of the changes. It takes 2 years for a young male to achieve its full blue color.

probably seen milo lying forlornly in the bottom of your feeder after the birds have cleaned out all the seeds they like.

Bird lovers in the West have a completely different opinion of milo than those east of the Rockies. Western birds, including curve-billed thrashers, elegant Steller's jays, white-crowned sparrows, and coveys of cute-as-a-button quail, think that milo is simply marvelous. (Interestingly, white-crowned sparrows east of the Rockies ignore it.) Much to my surprise, the Steller's jays at my previous home in Washington State actually preferred it to sunflower seeds (but not to peanuts!).

For these birds and other western species, milo isn't a seed of last resort: It's a real treat. In the Southwest, it's a preferred food at feeders, attracting Gambel's quail, thrashers, California towhees, and native sparrows.

Milo is popular in wild game plantings across the country because it's sought by pheasants,

Round, dull red milo seeds are a waste in birdseed mixes in the eastern half of the US, but in the West, milo is relished by quail and native sparrows. This dapper fellow is a Gambel's quail.

wild turkeys, doves, and quail. In farm fields, milo also attracts cowbirds, house sparrows, and massive flocks of blackbirds.

The same birds will eat it at the feeder, if they happen to visit your yard—unless there's something better on the menu.

Like us, birds eat the foods they like best first. Except in the West, milo usually isn't on that list. If you're not running a game farm, and you don't live in the West, don't bother with milo. Your birds will find plenty of foods they like better at your feeders.

MOCKINGBIRDS AND MIMIC THRUSHES

Mockingbirds and their relatives, the thrashers and gray catbird, have a special talent: They can mimic other sounds. The birds have their own lovely musical song, usually with repeated phrases, but they also spend hours singing a remix of other birds' repertoires. The mockingbird is the champ, and when mine gets going, I like to keep count of how many different bird songs he mixes in. Usually it's at least six.

Dense shrubs or a hedge may tempt a gray catbird into making its well-hidden home deep in the bushes. Provide a ready supply of fruit and suet and other soft foods, and a birdbath to splash in, and you've covered all the bases for the family.

Mockingbirds adopted backyards and feeders long ago, and other members of the family are learning fast.

Not that long ago, seeing a gray catbird or brown thrasher in winter was so unusual, the sighting was noted on birding hotlines. But these days, more of them seem to be sticking around all winter instead of heading south. Is it global warming or good food? No one knows.

The mocker is a real bully in the backyard. Once the bird lays claim to your feeder, it'll vigorously discourage any other birds from eating there. And I do mean vigorously—this bird is notorious for dive-bombing cats and humans

A Bird in the Bush

Creating habitat in your yard can pay off fast when it comes to mimic thrushes. If you offer the dense cover they prefer, you may attract catbirds or thrashers looking to raise a family. They'll often move into a hedge or bramble patch or an arbor of grapes or honeysuckle, both to build their nests and to hang out all year.

around its nesting area, and it does the same to feeder visitors.

Mimic thrushes will eat seeds at the feeder, but soft foods and fruit are the way to win their hearts. Mealworms and other insect foods, plus anything that's heavy on suet, peanut butter, or other fats, are high on their list. So are fresh fruit, dried fruit, and foods that include them.

Except for the mockingbird, who has quite the show-off streak, these birds like to lay low. To attract them to your yard, give them a thicket or a dense tangle of vines where they can skulk. And plant fruits and berries to tempt the birds to your backyard. "People fruits" like strawberries, blueberries, and grapes are guaranteed to please. Expand your offerings with small trees with berries, such as mountain ash, red hawthorn, and shadblow, among many others.

MOLDED TREATS

I'm always charmed by the molded birdseed ornaments that started showing up in catalogs several years ago. Hearts, stars, mini wreaths, and even little cabins—they're simply adorable. When I saw a little snowman made out of birdseed, I decided I had to try making a molded ornament myself.

After all, how hard can it be to shape some birdseed into a wreath or a snowman and give it a cheerful red ribbon to hang it by? All I had to do was figure out how to keep it "glued" together.

Rain, Rain, Go Away

Protect your molded treats from the rain, because they'll disintegrate if they get soaking wet. If you live in a cold winter area, no need to worry: They'll hold up just fine to snow. But if winter rains are in the offing, either hang your ornaments under a porch roof or tie them among the branches of an evergreen in your yard where they'll be out of the weather.

Peering at the fine print on one of those bigger birdseed bells that have been around for about as long as I can remember, I learned that the only ingredient besides birdseed was gelatin. That had to be the glue.

I mixed up a packet, poured it in a spray bottle, spread seed on a cookie sheet, and spritzed it down. After just a couple of spritzes, the spray top was clogged. Rinse and repeat. And so on, and so on, until I got so frustrated, I simply poured the stuff all over the seed.

The gelatin did hold the seed together, sort of. But it never dried. My charming ornaments were more like a bunch of gooey lumps. Obviously it was time to get crafty.

I started by researching glue. The stuff that makes old-fashioned, time-tested "hide glue" stick, I found out, is animal collagen—and that's exactly what's in gelatin. My box of Knox is just a food-grade version of hide glue; it's made from animal skin and bones. And heat helps it get sticky.

So I tried again, heating some unflavored gelatin and water on the stove. Wow, did it smell bad. But it sure was sticky. It did a great job of gluing the birdseed to the stove, the bowl, and my hands,

which I was using to smash the stuff into molds. Eventually I got the recipe right, and now I love to make molded ornaments for Christmas gifts.

Here's the recipe I use now, and my birds say it's a good one.

MOLDED BIRD TREATS

This recipe makes enough for 1 wreath mold or about 15 to 20 cookie-cutter molds. Prepare the molds before you start: Set the cookie cutters closely on a wax-paper-lined cookie sheet, and spray the molds' insides with nonstick cooking spray. If you're making the wreath, grease the inside of the Bundt pan thoroughly.

1½ cups water, plus another
½ cup water
1 ounce (4 packets) unflavored gelatin (that's a whole box of Knox)
5 cups black oil sunflower seeds
1 cup sunflower chips
1 cup pumpkin seeds (save them from Halloween!)
1 cup dried cranberries
Cookie cutters (outline-type metal, without handles, at least ½ inch deep, enough to fill a cookie sheet) or Bundt cake pan or wreath mold
Cookie sheet
Wax paper
Nonstick cooking spray
Ribbon or raffia for hanging

1. Boil 1½ cups of water in a small saucepan.
2. Meanwhile, pour ½ cup of cold water into a large, heat-proof bowl. Stir in the gelatin, and let it sit for about 1 minute.
3. Add the boiling water, stirring. Continue to stir until all the gelatin dissolves, about 2 to 3 minutes.
4. Stir in all the seeds and berries until they're coated with gelatin and the mixture sticks together. Let it sit for a few minutes, and stir again.
5. If you're making the wreath, scoop the mixture into the Bundt pan or wreath mold. Refrigerate, uncovered, for at least 3 hours or overnight. Let it warm to room temperature, and then invert it and tap the bottom until the wreath slides out. Set it on a rack in a dry place for about 3 days to harden completely.
6. If you're making the ornaments, spoon the mix evenly into the cookie cutters, and firm it into the molds with the back of a spoon. With a pencil, poke a hole into the top of each ornament for hanging. Set the tray in a warm, dry place for about 2 days, until the ornaments are hardened and completely dried. Remove from the cookie cutter molds, and tie on bright pieces of ribbon or raffia for hanging.

Use a Bundt cake pan to mold a birdseed wreath for a festive outdoor treat in a sheltered place.

MULTIPLE BROODS

Very few birds lay only two eggs. Most lay about four to six, but many birds up the ante even further. Robins lay four eggs; cedar waxwings, four or five; house wrens, six or seven; chickadees, six to eight; kinglets, eight or nine; and bobwhites, more than a dozen.

And our birds aren't raising only one family a year. They're doing it two, three, four, or even eight times annually, depending on their species.

Even cedar waxwings, which wait until summer fruits begin to ripen before they get started raising a family, often raise two broods. Mourning doves, which nest year-round in mild climates and from February through October in colder ones, manage to squeeze in as many as 10 broods, about one cycle a month.

So why aren't there tons of birds weighing down the trees and eating us out of house and home?

Taking a Toll

Birds lead a hard life. Not all of their babies make it out of the nest—or even out of the egg—thanks to predators like snakes, cats, jays, and 'coons. Fledglings face a gauntlet of cats and

Birds that nest on the ground, like the lark bunting of western grasslands or our backyard song sparrow, are sitting ducks to predators. Most hide their nests near a camouflaging plant clump, which also offers some protection from the weather.

other dangers. Once young birds take flight, they come up against windows, cell phone towers, hawks, and lots of other dangers. Habitat destruction, weather, and pesticides cull their ranks, too.

Now that many bird species are in decline, anything we can do to boost their survival rate is vital, even if there is a lot of extra work required. We can add high-energy soft foods at our feeders to nourish parents and young; provide crushed eggshells and eggs as food for their special nutritional needs; and make sure our birdbaths are clean and filled. Most important: Keep our cats inside! Birds that nest on the ground are particularly vulnerable to predators, and the ravages of cats are part of the reason many of those birds are in decline.

When a bird nest fails—perhaps it falls out of a tree in a storm, or gets ripped apart by a 'coon—the parents will begin building a replacement almost instantly. With all those broods to raise amid all those dangers, nest building is likely to be going on in your neighborhood anytime from February through August (year-round, in mild areas). So don't forget to put out a supply of nesting materials, for your own pleasure in watching your birds use them, as well as to make life a little easier for them. You'll find lots of ideas in the entry Fluff and Fibers. And keep your birdbath full and fresh, too.

The Home-Supply Store

Nearly all birds build a new nest for each set of babies. So keep your nesting materials ready right through late summer. Refresh your collection as birds snitch pieces of fibers and fluff for their nests, so that there's always a tempting supply. Watch for birds tugging at the twine you used to tie up your garden plants, too: It's a clue that there's a housing boom going on somewhere near you.

Family Matters

Two or three batches of babies are the norm for most backyard birds. Many species begin the process in April or May, and they stop nesting in time for the last batch to be on their own by the time fall rolls around.

Considering that it takes about 6 weeks to 2 months from the selection of the nest site to the last caretaking duties after the young birds are out of the nest, you can see why birds are so busy during the breeding season. There's not much time to hang out at the feeder when hungry mouths need to be fed every few minutes.

NATIVE OR NOT?

Often, something sounds like such a good idea that we think it must be true, and we never bother to question it. Native plants for birds is one of those ideas.

"Native" plants are those that originally grew in the wild places around your house—the kind of natural habitat that used to exist where your home now stands. It's a loose term because it can also include plants native to your county, to your state, or to your general region. There are thousands of plants native to the Midwest, for instance, but only a fraction of them are native to the county I live in, and even fewer would have grown where my home now stands.

No matter what boundaries are drawn to define exactly which plants are native, the word itself is a hot button for a lot of folks. Native, good; nonnative, bad—that's the party line for many people, including some experts.

I've always been a gardener as well as a naturalist, so I don't follow the crowd on this issue. I've grown thousands of different plants in my half-century of digging in the dirt, and in my travels, I've observed how birds use countless natives *and* nonnatives in wild places, in gardens, and everywhere else plants grow. I've always been a huge advocate of native plants, but for me, it's not "nuthin' but native."

What I've seen with my own eyes is that birds use nonnatives just as eagerly as natives when these plants have something to offer. Summer fruit, fall berries, winter seeds, a sturdy branch to support a nest, a battalion of caterpillars—if birds can take advantage of it, they will. In fact, that's why many nonnatives have spread so far, so fast: Birds carried their seeds. Why should we scorn a mulberry tree, say, even if it's 1,000 miles from its native home? Wherever that mulberry is, fruit-eating birds will find it.

If you think only native plants attract birds, check out a mulberry tree full of ripe fruit. Whether it's native to Asia, like this white mulberry, or the eastern US, like our own red, it'll be swarming with birds of a dozen species or more—no matter where it's growing.

All Natives Are Good for Birds

This part of the conventional wisdom is absolutely true. Every native plant in America is somehow closely connected to the birds that live in that area. It may be by a direct link, like the red blossoms of wild columbines that bloom just as hummingbirds are migrating north. Or it may be a few steps removed, like an oak tree that nourishes a crop of caterpillars to stuff down a nestling's gullet.

As we talked about in the entry Habitat Destruction, disturbing Nature's complex web has repercussions we can't even imagine. But the web is already losing a few strands, due to our own impact. And others are getting shaky because of the effects of climate change.

As the weather changes, for example, the caterpillars on that oak may be hatching earlier, which may affect the survival of the nestlings that depend on them. For centuries, insects and birds have been pretty well synchronized, with bugs booming just when birds need them most. That's changing fast, though, and who knows what tomorrow may bring.

The gleaming red berries of spice bush (*Lindera benzoin*) attract all species of thrushes, including bluebirds. It's native to woodlands from Texas to the Atlantic Ocean, from Florida into Canada.

It's still a good idea to include as many locally native plants in your backyard as you can. The birds in your region already know how to make use of them. Those with the most direct value to birds are shrubs and trees, so they're a great place to begin when planting for birds.

You'll find many native plant suggestions throughout this book, but you can't go wrong by starting with a native oak or maple. Every bit of these trees is useful to birds.

- Their flowers attract insects for warblers, vireos, flycatchers, and others.
- Their leaves and bark host a plethora of insects, including many kinds of those vital caterpillars, for many birds, including tanagers, orioles, vireos, and warblers.
- Their seeds offer food in fall and winter for woodpeckers, chickadees, nuthatches, cardinals, juncos, and wild turkeys, to name a few of the scores of species that depend on them.
- Their branches are sought for nest sites by robins, jays, tanagers, vireos, grosbeaks, and more.
- And their dropped, dead leaves nourish beetles, worms, snails, slugs, and other smaller members of the big interconnected web, for feeding thrushes, thrashers, towhees, and other low-level birds.

Nonnatives Aren't Bad

I'm baffled by the idea that nonnatives don't have as much value to birds as natives. Surely those naysayers have seen cedar waxwings descend on fruit orchards? Or white-crowned sparrows and

indigo buntings stretching to reach dandelion seeds? Or red-winged blackbirds and bobolinks feasting in grain fields? None of those plants are native to America, and all of them, along with thousands of other nonnatives, are eagerly exploited by birds.

European weeds, for instance, are one of the main resources in fall and winter for finches, buntings, native sparrows, and juncos. Dandelions, lamb's-quarters, burdock, chicory, chickweed, foxtail grass, cranesbill—not a one was here before Europeans came, but birds gobble all of them by the gazillions.

The only drawback I can see is that most plants that aren't native to America don't host the caterpillars of American butterflies and moths. But that's easy to address: Just include some native host plants in your yard, and you'll still have room for your—and your birds'—favorite nonnatives. Azaleas, anyone?

I'm using the broadest definition of native in these cases—native to America—and even still, birds make good use of the plants. If we narrow the definition, to, say, plants native to the lower Midwest, we've got another problem.

Birds move around. My winter goldfinches may have come from nesting grounds in Michigan. My summer oriole may winter in Florida. My hummingbirds may end up in Guatemala.

Should I add orange hawkweed for seeds for my finches? A potted orange tree for my orioles? A banana tree for hummingbird flowers?

Or, since birds stop to eat all along their travels, shouldn't I consider any of the tens of thousands of native plants that grow between here and there?

When it comes to natives-only for hummingbirds, the whole idea seems silly. Yes, native

Native and nonnative seeds alike are eagerly eaten by the American tree sparrow and other small birds.

Cannas and nasturtiums both hail from Central and South America, in some cases where North American hummingbirds hang out in winter. They're not native to our gardens, but hummers don't mind a bit.

Seek and You Shall Find

There's another big advantage to using locally native plants in your backyard: You can often get them for free! When I spot a roadwork sign or another project that looks like it's going to be uprooting plants, I just stop and ask if I can dig. I've never been turned down. To fill in the rest, I ask friends who own wild land if I can dig some plants. Of course, you can also buy plants that are native to your area at plant sales or through local or mail-order nurseries like those listed in the Resources section on page 300.

columbines, red-flowering currant, and wild azaleas are timed to their migration—but hummers no longer depend on flowers alone, now that we put out feeders. Besides, countless nonnative flowers offer nectar that nourishes hummers.

I think I'll just keep doing what I always have—letting the birds tell me which plants they like best. Theirs is the only seal of approval I need, and they give me that by gracing my yard—filled with natives and nonnatives alike—with their presence.

Natives at Risk

Some native plants are in trouble, thanks to climate change or because of shifts in insects and diseases.

As the number and size of wildfires increase, trees and other native plants get hammered.

Our natural landscape can change fast because of the ravages of insects, diseases, and other factors. Once solid green with conifers, this Rocky Mountain hillside has been decimated by the bark or pine beetle.

Worsening floods and concentrated deluges and blizzards in other regions kill off still more. And higher temperatures, along with more frequent and severe drought, take out native plants, too.

Then there are the new pests and diseases that are attacking native plants. The demise of the great American chestnut and American elm are low points of the past couple of centuries, and now the process seems to be speeding up.

More native trees may soon be shuffling off the stage. Oaks are under attack in the West from Sudden Oak Death, a fast-spreading pathogen; hemlocks are suffering from wooly adelgids in New England; ash trees are dying from the spread of the emerald ash borer; spruces, firs, and other conifers are being decimated by a host of diseases and insects, turning entire mountainsides from living green to dead brown.

And it's not only trees. Native plants of all kinds, from the tallest redwoods to Gulf Coast red bay to ground-hugging trailing arbutus, are facing tough times. Nature is rearranging herself, and our birds can't count on some of the plants they once did.

That's another reason why I defend the use of nonnative plants in our backyards. A diversity of plants is a good way to hedge our bets. Even if my native shadblow goes belly-up, I'll still have the nonnative sour cherry for the waxwings and thrushes.

NECTAR

Next time you mix up a batch of sugar water for your nectar feeders, try a taste yourself. Whether you're making the 1 part sugar to 4 parts water solution that hummers prefer or the 1 to 6 ratio for orioles, you'll find the mix deliciously sweet.

Even a sip of honeysuckle nectar doesn't tickle my sweet tooth like that sugar water. Natural nectar varies hugely in its sugar content, but most plants don't come close to the sweetness of the stuff in our feeders. Plants vary widely in their production of nectar, and the nectar itself changes with the age of the flower, the time of day, the weather, pollination, and other influences.

Nectar is nothing more than a bribe. Plants produce it to reward their pollinators so that insects seek it out.

Some plants have taken it even further and evolved a tricky way of making sure they attract a lot of pollinators: Their nectar is sweeter than most others' around them. Himalayan impatiens, which you can read about in the Impatiens entry, is one of those sneaky characters. That's one of the reasons it's landed on invasive plants lists: By distracting pollinators from native plants, it's made sure its multitude of flowers gets fertilized, and every one of them scatters seeds that ensure its position.

Have you ever noticed how frequently different hummingbirds or butterflies visit the same flower? You'd think the blossom would be drained dry by the time the second or third hummer gets there, but, no, the birds still hover and sip. That's a neat trick, too: Flowers actually increase their nectar production during pollination, just to make sure the blossom is visited often enough to ensure fertilization.

White sugar contains only one kind of sugar: sucrose. But flower nectar can include more than a dozen different kinds. Sucrose, glucose, and fructose are the most prevalent. Amino acids, the building blocks of protein, are in natural nectar, too—all 20 of them.

Nectar can be quite a stew, but hummers and orioles have simplified the situation: They seek out the flowers in which sucrose is the main component of the nectar, just as it is in our feeders.

Sugar and Only Sugar

White sugar and water are all you need in your nectar feeder. Nothing else is necessary, and some additions may be harmful.

Brown sugar, raw sugar, and turbinado sugar contain iron, and when the birds drain your feeder, they're getting much more than they would from sipping at flowers. It can have ill effects on their health, so skip the "healthy" sugars and use refined white instead.

Honey has been implicated in the growth of a fungus in hummingbirds, so steer clear of this sweetener. There's another drawback, too—honeybees visit flowers that are high in glucose, fructose, and other sugars that hummers aren't as fond of. If you use it to sweeten your nectar, you may lose your bird customers to the feeder down the block or to the flowers in your garden.

Don't use dyes, which aren't necessary. And read the labels on instant nectar packages to make sure they don't contain additives or preservatives. There's no research on how they affect hummers, but it's better not to gamble. Save the instant nectar for when you want to draw hummers to your vacation campsite—an occasional taste should be safe.

Nutrition boosters aren't necessary, either. It may look like your birds spend all day satisfying their sweet tooth, but they're really eating lots of little insects in between visits. They'll get plenty of nourishing food naturally.

Now here's a sneaky plant—statuesque *Impatiens glandulifera,* a garden plant that has become invasive in some regions. Its nectar is so sweet that insects and hummers forsake other flowers to focus on its blossoms. No insects or hummingbirds means no pollination, and that spells trouble for competing plants.

Making and Storing Nectar

I've cut my feeder refills down to a 6-minute science. Here's how I do it.

QUICK NECTAR

1 cup water

½ cup white sugar

6 ice cubes

1. Microwave water in a 4-cup Pyrex measuring cup for about 4 minutes so it's hot enough to melt sugar.
2. Meanwhile, clean your nectar feeder.
3. Carefully remove the hot water from the microwave, and slowly pour in the sugar. Stir until it's completely dissolved.
4. Add six ice cubes—the equivalent of 1 cup of water—and stir to cool the mixture. Test the temperature by putting a few drops on your inner wrist, just to make sure it's not hot.
5. Refill your feeder.

When the busy season hits in late summer, I have another trick to make refills even easier: a sugar syrup. Cooks call it a simple syrup, and that it is. You can store it indefinitely in the fridge.

Here's how to make it and how to use it.

SIMPLE SYRUP

1 cup water

2 cups white sugar

1. Bring the water to a boil in a medium saucepan.
2. Turn off the burner but keep the pan in place. Stir in the sugar, and keep stirring until it's completely dissolved.
3. Once the sugar is dissolved, remove the pan from the heat, cover it, and let it cool completely.
4. Store in your refrigerator in a glass jar with a tight-fitting lid.

To use the simple syrup for your nectar feeders, mix it with water in approximately a 1:4 or 1:6 syrup to water ratio. You don't need to be right on the nose with the ratio—a little more or less sweet will still have hummingbirds buzzing your feeder in droves.

For hummingbird feeders, I stir ¼ cup of syrup into just under 1 cup of water. For oriole feeders, which have a larger reservoir than many of those made for hummers, I mix ⅓ cup of syrup with just under 2 cups of water. Adjust the amounts proportionately, depending on how much liquid your feeder holds.

Sweeten the Deal

As hummingbirds change their habits, more migrants are now showing up much later than usual at feeders in fall. To give them an extra boost of energy, switch to a stronger solution of nectar for fall feeding. Use 1 part sugar to 3 parts water after September. As cold weather sets in, you can go even more concentrated: 1 part sugar to 2 parts water. The sweeter solution will resist freezing in case the temperature drops, so you can keep the feeder up as long as you like, just in case any stragglers pass your way. And be sure to take a close look at those late birds: Sometimes they're unusual species that may be trying out a new route.

NEST MATERIALS

I love to look at bird nests in natural history museums, where I can compare them side by side. First I play a little game with myself and with the builders of the nests: I don't let myself look at the tags that identify which birds built them. Instead, I peer at the nest and see what I can see.

Every nest is a work of art, and every nest tells a story. When it comes to making use of the materials around them, birds are incredibly resourceful. They recycle all sorts of natural materials into their nests, depending on what's available in their neighborhood.

If the nest I'm looking at includes hemlock needles, I can practically smell the damp, spicy scent of a northern forest. Tendrils of Spanish moss, and I see moonlight on black swamp water in my mind's eye, and hear the bellows of alligators. Tufts of airy cattail fluff? Marsh bird, for sure.

Nests come in all shapes and sizes, made of materials from the bird's breeding territory. A gawky flamingo makes its mud nest just as carefully as any backyard robin and cares for its chicks with just as much devotion.

Every species has its preferences. The shape and style of nest, the site that's chosen, as well as the materials the bird uses, are all particular to its species.

It's hard to identify many of the materials in a nest without removing it from its site and taking it apart—but that's illegal, according to the Migratory Bird Treaty Act of 1918, which was passed to protect birds from nest collectors, egg collectors, and feather hunters. Still, it's nice to know that each bird's little home includes bits and pieces of the world around it.

Master Class

I gave up after my very first DIY experience with basket making. It looked so easy in the book. But once I got my materials laid out, I soon discovered I just didn't have the patience for the job. Not to mention the dexterity. Those doggone strips were going in every direction except the way I wanted them.

Nest-building birds have me beat by a mile. Using only their beaks, they spend hours fashioning a strong little home that stands up to wind and rain. Whether they're working with twigs, bark, or fibers, they interweave the materials so that the nest will support the weight of the young and the parent.

Twigs are the building material of choice for blue jays, mourning doves, and many other birds. Lengths of grapevine and other vines and strips of bark are woven in to help the twigs stay together.

The fabulous cradle of the Altamira oriole of the Rio Grande valley, hung from a branch tip or utility wire, takes 3 weeks to construct.

Strong, pliable plant fibers are put to good use, too, in many nests, especially those of orioles, warblers, vireos, flycatchers, phoebes, sparrows, waxwings, and good old robins. Native sparrows, juncos, blackbirds, meadowlarks, and dozens of other species depend on strands of dry grass, while others strip fibers from Indian hemp and other wild plants.

Chipping sparrows, warbling vireos, and other birds add long strands of horsehair to the mix, weaving it into the inner circle of lining. Spider silk is often used to bind a nest together.

Fluff makes a soft, insulating lining for many birds, including most of the fiber-using birds, plus chickadees, titmice, kinglets, nuthatches, wrens, and a slew of others. The American goldfinch uses cattail fluff and thistledown, the blue-gray gnatcatcher collects fluffy oak catkins, Bell's vireo adds soft cocoons, and the eastern phoebe is a big fan of moss. Several species, such as the tufted titmouse and the black-throated green warbler, use fur to soften their homes.

Grow Your Own Cotton

Cultivate a few plants of cotton in your flower garden, and you can have the fun of watching chickadees, goldfinches, and other fluff lovers pluck at the white fibers for their nests. Cotton's easy to grow, but you need a growing season at least 5 months long. Work some composted manure into the soil for extra fertility, and plant the seeds (see Resources) in groups of three in late spring, after the soil has warmed. Here's the unusual part: Be sparing with water. Don't water the seeds or seedlings until about 5 weeks after they've sprouted. About 4 months after planting, stop watering. The plants will drop their leaves, and the bolls will split, revealing the cotton. Pluck the cotton and keep it inside until nesting season next year. I like to let some of it stay on the plant; even though weatherworn, it'll still be gathered by birds in spring.

NEST SITES

Nesting birds are one of the great benefits of building your backyard habitat. When you add plants that make your yard resemble the natural areas around you, you greatly boost your chances of coaxing birds to expand to nest sites in your own yard.

Additional cover is always appealing to nesting birds, so simply increasing the number of trees and shrubs will improve your yard's appeal, too. Hedges make ideal nest sites for backyard birds.

Common backyard birds that already nest in typical yards will take up residence in existing shrubs and trees, whether they're native or not. Robins often choose a flowering shrub, such as a lilac or a mock orange, or the branch of a backyard dogwood or maple. Jays nest higher, in both conifers and deciduous trees. Cardinals go for rose bushes, catbirds and thrashers for bramble patches or tangled vines. On the ground, you may stumble upon a song sparrow nest tucked into your strawberry patch or groundcover.

If you live in the desert or chaparral, use native plants in your yard to satisfy your birds' needs. Many of your birds have specialized habits, and using natives makes it easy to coax them in.

Birdhouses will attract cavity-nesting birds, including chickadees, titmice, nuthatches, woodpeckers, and maybe even bluebirds. The prothonotary warbler, a bird of cypress sloughs, bogs, and wet bottomlands near rivers, also nests in cavities, but unless your house is on stilts in a swamp, you're not likely to attract this

All birds are secretive around their nests, but the blue jay may win the prize: It's as quiet as a mouse near home, with nary a rowdy shriek to give the location away.

pretty yellow bird. For more suggestions on attracting birds with nest boxes, see the Birdhouses entry.

A nectar feeder may be an incentive to house-shopping hummingbirds. All birds choose homesites with abundant food, and hummers seem to have zeroed in on feeders as a source they can rely on.

Birds are remarkably secretive around their nests. More than once, I've completely overlooked a jay's nest until the fledglings showed up at my feet. Birds don't want to advertise the presence of their helpless families to predators. So the female bird sits tight, even if you walk by at arm's length. Parents feeding young often approach their nest by a circuitous route.

It takes quite a bit of time and a certain amount of exertion for birds to collect the makings of their nests. So you're highly likely to see such activity once you start looking.

If you've put out nest materials, keep an eye out for any takers. Watch for birds tugging at the dried leaves of your ornamental grasses or the dead stems of your garden flowers. You may spot a bird collecting dead leaves or moss, too, or stripping bark or tendrils from a vine.

Keep Out!

The most important thing you can do to attract nesting birds to your yard is to give them some privacy. If you avoid using some areas of your yard, a pair of birds just may move in. Stay away from your hedge, your bramble patch, and any dense groups of shrubs. Avoid walking through naturalistic plantings, and minimize your fiddling in the flowerbed. And pay attention to your birds—when you see a bird carrying a stick or other nesting material, watch where it goes. Then keep away, no matter how tempting it is to spy. Once birds raise a successful brood, they're likely to return to the same area next year.

And next time you see a bird carrying a caterpillar, pay close attention to where it goes. You're likely to lose the bird the first few times, but eventually you'll find out exactly which spot it's calling Home Sweet Home.

NIGER

We all know that sunflower seeds sprout with a vengeance under a feeder, as do grassy millet and milo.

But have you ever wondered why niger seed never seems to crop up?

It's been sterilized, that's why: heated to kill the germinating part of the seed.

Niger wasn't always called niger. When it was first introduced to bird feeders about 35 years ago, it was called thistle seed.

Goldfinches have a real weakness for niger (or nyjer, as it's sometimes spelled to prevent mispronunciation), and that's how this seed came to be known as thistle. These little birds are so well known as thistle eaters that their German name is *distelfink*, "thistle finch."

Niger seeds are heated to prevent sprouting, but occasionally one manages to germinate. Pretty yellow flowers jam-packed with tiny seeds will result, if you don't weed it out.

That may have sounded like a good marketing idea, but it backfired. Who would want to risk a crop of thistles under the feeder?

And niger (*Guizotia abyssinica*, botanically speaking) isn't a thistle at all. It's a daisy. No spiny leaves or stem, no puff of down, no aggressively spreading roots—just a pretty branching plant covered in yellow daisies late in the season.

When bird lovers squawked about thistles, distributors soon spread the word that the seed was sterilized so it wouldn't sprout.

Heating the seed to kill the sprout inside isn't done to placate buyers—that was just a happy coincidence. It was done to prevent foreign weed seeds from causing problems in America.

Nearly all of the niger we pour into our tube feeders is brought in from Africa and Asia, where it's cultivated as a vital cash crop and as a human food. Niger, a native of Ethiopia, India, and other hot spots, needs a long growing season. North American birdseed-growing regions, including Canada and North Dakota, aren't a good match.

After the USDA discovered that shipments were contaminated with seeds of some notorious weeds, including a particularly nasty dodder, sterilizing was the only way to go.

Dripping with Oil

Niger seeds seem dry as a bone, but inside, these mighty mites are rich in oil. In its homelands, the seeds are pressed to yield cooking oil and used in all kinds of foods as a crunchy, nutritious addition.

At the feeder, it's finches that are the main customers for your niger seed: goldfinches, purple finches, house finches, Cassin's finches, and their close relatives, the buntings and pine siskins. Lots of other birds would eat it, too—if they only had the chance.

Since nearly all of us use niger in tube feeders, the doves, quail, towhees, and other ground-feeding birds that also enjoy the oily seeds have to scrounge up the stuff that drops. They aren't able to cling to the tubes.

Other seed eaters, including cardinals and grosbeaks, prefer more bang for their bites. They ignore the niger and go for bigger, meatier seeds, such as sunflower.

Niger will be a year-round attraction in your backyard. Traffic will drop off in summer and peak in spring and fall, when migrating finches settle in.

NIGER SOCK

Niger socks are a great invention, but they're not exactly photogenic. No matter how many handsome feeders you have around, it's the sagging white sock that will draw the eye like an old rag hanging on your shepherd's hook.

High visibility is an advantage when you want to attract birds to a new feeder setup, so if you're just getting started, a white niger sock will be great advertising. But if birds have already found your feeders, you don't need to spotlight the sock; the presence of any birds at all will draw others to your yard.

Niger socks cost $5 to $10 apiece, without seed. That's not a bad price. But until manufacturers start offering them in more discreet colors, I'm making my own.

HOW-TO Sock It to Me

All you need to make your own niger sock is about ¼ yard of perforated nylon fabric, such as the kind used in sports jerseys; choose one with very small holes. I use black fabric, so it doesn't stand out.

- Perforated fabric, about ¼ yard
- Scissors
- Needle and thread
- Safety pin
- Woven drawstring cord, about 18 inches long
- Niger seed

Five minutes of sewing, and you've got yourself a niger sock.

1. Cut a piece of fabric in a rectangle about 6 inches by 12 inches. A longer sock will accommodate more birds, but it will soon go limp at the top as birds empty the seeds.

2. To make a channel for the drawstring you'll be adding, fold down one of the short sides about 1 inch, and stitch along the edge of the fabric.

3. Fold the fabric in half the long way. Stitch a seam across the bottom and up the side, stopping at the stitches of the drawstring channel.

4. Turn the sock right side out, so the seams are on the inside. Attach a safety pin to one end of the drawstring, and insert it through the channel.

5. Fill with niger, tighten the cord, and hang your pennywise feeder.

NIGHT MOVES

It's strange to think about songbirds flying at night, but most of our American birds do just that at migration time. The behavior may have evolved as a way for them to evade day-flying hawks that could pick them off during their travels.

Tilt an ear to the sky in spring and fall, and you may catch the call notes of wood warblers, thrushes, tanagers, and many other birds filtering down from the heavens. I make it a point to spend time bird-watching by the full moon during these periods, because, with binoculars, I can catch the silhouetted shapes as they cross the glowing moon.

Night travel has become dangerous for birds because we've put obstacles in their path. Collisions with satellite towers, wind turbines, and tall buildings kill countless birds every year. No one really knows the grim total, but those who monitor some of these obstacles report a heavy toll that may range into the hundreds of millions.

The lights on tall buildings are a deadly attraction for birds that migrate at night. They draw birds toward the buildings, and broken necks are often the result.

Some cities have adopted a policy of turning off their buildings' lights at night. "Lights Out Twin Cities," a project of St. Paul/Minneapolis Audubon groups, is just one of the many efforts aimed at helping migrating birds make it through the night. Dozens of buildings in the area, including banks, offices, and libraries, now make a point of turning out their lights during migration season. Indianapolis, Boston, Chicago, New York, and many other cities are part of the lights-out-for-birds movement, which has been proven to reduce bird deaths.

NIGHT SONGS

It's not unusual, but it's definitely odd to hear a bird sing at night. Mockingbirds are famous for their moonlight serenades. Other mimic thrushes, such as catbirds and thrashers, may hold forth in the dark hours. Thrushes, including our common robin, also occasionally sing at night. Except for mockingbirds, which can go on, and on, and on—Hey, pipe down, will you? I'm trying to sleep!—most birds give only a short performance before they go back to sleep.

Many birds let loose with a quick burst of song when they're disturbed while sleeping. Nesting season is usually when you'll hear these quick protests from your backyard birds, because that's when predators are seeking bird nests.

If you hear a sudden short song—usually just a few seconds—from a song sparrow or other bird in your backyard, it may have just lost its eggs or even its own life to a nighttime stalker. At other times of year, the brief outburst may indicate a predator, or it may have been caused by nothing more than a roosting companion jostling the singer in its sleep.

NIGHT WATCH

Bird-watching is mostly a daytime activity, but there's plenty going on at night, too. I've gotten into the habit of stepping outside a few times at night to keep tabs on what's going on. Often I'll hear a brief snatch of birdsong when a roosting songbird is disturbed. Sometimes I'll catch the faint calls of birds migrating overhead. And, regularly, I listen to the doings of the owls that patrol my neighborhood.

You never know what you'll see when you investigate the nighttime world of birds. One late night, I happened to be outside when a white cat crossing the parking lot of the nursing home across the street caught my eye. I could see the cat was watching something intently. As my eyes adjusted, I realized it must be stalking a mouse that had come to nibble on the birdseed scattered on the paving. Just at that instant, a great horned owl swooped in, snatched the cat by the back of the neck, and flapped away, hardly breaking stride. I could see the white body dangling from its clutches as the big bird made its way to the big trees in a nearby park.

Even a city backyard may get a nighttime visit from an owl. Usually, they're looking for rodents. If your feeding station attracts mice or rabbits, the animals may become a meal when the sensitive ears of an owl catch the sound of scurrying feet.

Owls are a big reason why backyard birds seek protected places at night. Getting eaten is a constant concern for birds, even at night when they're sound asleep. Hawks may be gone with the setting sun, but owls, snakes, cats, raccoons, and other predators are now on the prowl.

Invite Nesting Backyard Owls

Screech owls are chubby little guys, only 8 to 9 inches tall. They've adapted well to using our backyards as habitat, and they're usually quick to adopt a nest box that's just their size. Build or buy one with an entrance hole that's 3 inches in diameter, and mount it as high as you can reach—at least 10 feet, and as much as 30 feet, above the ground. These little predator owls will do a swell job of controlling any mice that may scurry around your feeders at night.

Screech owls patrol both cities and countryside at night. So do much larger great horned owls, barn owls, and barred owls. They're looking for mice and other rodents, but they'll nab sleeping birds, too, if they happen upon them.

NUT BUTTERS

The supposed danger of feeding birds pure peanut butter is a myth that simply refuses to die. I wish it would, because there's nothing better than peanut butter when it comes to attracting birds. It's safe, it's cheap, it's easy, and it works like a charm. The tiny bites that chickadees, Carolina wrens, and other birds take will not gum up their beaks or throats.

I spread peanut butter—yes, straight from the jar—onto my trees and onto my feeders. Served straight, the high-fat food is like manna to chickadees, titmice, nuthatches, woodpeckers, brown creepers, house wrens, Carolina wrens, kinglets, warblers, and others. Even ground-level juncos and sparrows enjoy it, if they can reach it—which is why, in cold weather, I also spread peanut butter at the bottom of the wooden post supporting my big tray feeder, where these birds quickly find it.

Mix in a little cornmeal, oatmeal, or other stiffeners to your peanut butter, and the list of birds you'll entice gets even longer. The possibilities include all of the birds listed above, plus bluebirds, thrushes, catbirds, mockingbirds, brown thrashers, rose-breasted grosbeaks, red-winged blackbirds, grackles, orioles, and house finches. Am I forgetting anybody? Maybe, so spread some peanut butter treats and see for yourself. You'll find some of my favorite recipes in the entries Doughs and Peanut Butter Treats.

Almond, cashew, hazel, and other nut butters work just as well at attracting birds, but they

Stain Guard

Nut butters are extra oily, and they'll leave a dark grease stain on any absorbent surface. Any bits of nut butter that birds drop, or the oil that may drip in warm weather, will leave a lasting stain on wood and pavement. The grease stain won't harm a living tree, so if you don't mind a dark spot, you can spread peanut butter right on the tree's bark. But do keep nut butters and nut butter feeders away from porch posts, decks, sidewalks, and patio pavers, where they can make a mess.

The beguiling brown creeper is a tiny bird with a big appetite for peanut butter, suet, and other soft foods. It'll nibble the stuff right off the bark of a tree or from a feeder.

usually cost a lot more. They're fun to experiment with, although I don't find them any better at bringing in birds than good old PB.

Stock up on peanut butter, and other nut butters if you like, whenever you see them on sale. An unopened jar stays good for a long time. If you buy the giant economy size jar of peanut butter, store it in your fridge instead of your cabinet. If you don't refrigerate it, its oil can go rancid long before you get to the bottom of the jar.

NUT FEEDERS AND NUTS

Birds are simply nuts about nuts. Nuts are one of the most alluring foods you can offer at your feeders. High in fat and protein, nuts are premium food for a whole slew of birds—easily a hundred different species will chow down on them, given the chance.

Jays are fondest of nuts in the shell, because their instincts drive them to cache the food or bury it. They're so addicted to peanuts that you can even hand tame these birds with the nuts as a bribe. Larger woodpeckers take nuts in the shell, too, carrying them off to hammer open.

Other birds don't have as powerful a beak as jays and big woodpeckers, so they'll take their nuts already shelled, thank you. Chickadees, titmice, nuthatches, and smaller downy woodpeckers eagerly peck at large pieces of nuts, but they also have a habit of carrying off their prize to finish eating elsewhere. To keep them in view, serve larger pieces of nuts in a wire nut feeder, from which they can only extricate one small piece at a time.

Chopped nuts are a huge hit with lots of perching birds, including bluebirds, thrushes, wrens, catbirds, native sparrows, and juncos. Serve them in a mealworm feeder, a tray, or a domed feeder.

All of the soft-food eaters in your backyard, including tanagers and orioles, will relish a taste of nuts if you mix them with suet or other fats in a bird dough or other recipe.

Birds will eagerly eat any kind of chopped nut. Unfamiliar whole nuts, like cashews and shelled almonds, may baffle them. I once scattered

The Holy Grail of the woodpecker clan, the giant pileated 'pecker is showing up in more and more backyards. Serve nuts in a sturdy, open tray to tickle the fancy of this fabulous bird. Suet will entice it, too.

blanched, sliced almonds in my seed tray, thinking I was giving my birds a special treat, only to have them be completely spurned. But once I put the nuts into my usual wire-cylinder nut feeders, the birds quickly began pecking at them. (See Brazil Nuts for more on exotic nut appeal.)

Stocking Up on Nuts

Peanuts are the best buy, by a mile. All of the nut-eating birds find them irresistible. Even some birds that don't usually seek nuts love peanuts—like cardinals, for instance. When I spilled peanuts on my brick patio while filling a feeder, cardinals scavenged for days, searching out every stray in the cracks of the bricks and under the patio furniture.

Peanuts are "ground nuts," legumes that grow underground. They form under the soil in a fascinating process called pegging, in which the stalks of the aboveground flowers turn downward after pollination, going into the soil where the "nuts" form. You can see for yourself by planting your own—if you have a long, hot growing season that gives them the 5 months that the plants need to mature.

Walnuts, almonds, pistachios, and all other nuts are tree nuts. Tree nuts can cost a pretty penny to buy—$12 a pound for pecans is the going rate at my supermarket. Wait for sales, which often run during the prime baking season from Thanksgiving through Christmas, and then stock up.

The closer to the source you get, the less nuts cost. Buy them from a grower if you can, or at a farmers' market. Or, to cut your costs down to nothing, pick them yourself. Wild nuts grow in every part of the country—pecans in the Southeast and lower Midwest, black walnuts in New England and the Midwest, hickories from the Plains eastward, hazels in the Northwest, backyard almonds and pistachios in California. Just look around and see what you can find.

Keep your nuts in the freezer to prevent them from turning bitter and rancid when the fat content spoils. They'll last for at least a year—and then you can replenish your supply at the next Christmas baking sale.

A Little Dab'll Do Ya

To get the most out of nuts, use them sparingly. A scattering of peanuts or walnut halves will disappear from your feeder in minutes, as birds snatch them up and carry them away. But a handful of chopped nuts among your usual seed mix will allow many more birds to have a taste, and it'll take longer for them to pick the pieces out of the mix. Grinding your nuts into meal makes them go even further. Just a few tablespoons of nut meal in a recipe will make birds flock to the treat.

NUTS ABOUT TANAGERS

1 cup crunchy peanut butter

1 cup lard

2 cups oatmeal, not instant

2 cups cornmeal

½ cup white flour

½ cup ground walnuts or pecans

1. Melt the peanut butter and lard in a saucepan over low heat.
2. Stir in the oatmeal, cornmeal, flour, and ground nuts.
3. Spoon the mixture onto a jelly-roll pan or a cookie sheet with a rim, and put it in the refrigerator to harden.
4. Cut the mixture into blocks to fit a suet feeder, or into chunks to fill a tray, dome, or log feeder. You can also spoon the mix into a mold, such as the recycled tray from a suet block or a muffin tin. Your wrens, catbirds, thrushes, bluebirds, woodpeckers, chickadees, and titmice will enjoy this treat, too.

TANAGER TREAT

Tanagers and warblers are extra fond of the recipe below, so mix up a batch during spring and fall, when the birds are passing through your region.

1 cup lard (not shortening)
1 cup white flour
2 cups quick cook oats
2 cups cornmeal

Melt the lard over low heat. Stir in the other ingredients to make a crumbly dough. Serve in an accessible feeder, such as a tray or mealworm dish.

NUTHATCHES AND CREEPERS

Nuthatches and creepers don't belong to the same bird family, but they often share space on the same tree. While the nuthatch travels the trunk going from top to bottom, the creeper spirals upward. They're both scouting for insects and insect eggs hidden in the bark.

Because these birds are so adept at clinging, they often eat from the same feeders, too. Nuts and fat are the preferred foods of these birds. Nuthatches are fond of sunflower seeds, too, but the creeper beak isn't built for cracking tough seeds, so this bird prefers hulled sunflower seeds or chips.

Soft foods are also a boon to these birds. Anything with peanut butter or suet in it is an instant hit. And if it also has nuts ... well, these birds can't resist. You'll find tempting recipes throughout this book, including in the entries Doughs, Nuts, and Peanut Butter Treats. Your mealworm feeder will get plenty of use by these birds, too.

Home Sweet Home

To attract a nesting nuthatch to your yard, put up a birdhouse. Mount the box on a tree, about 4 to 10 feet from the ground. Nuthatches prefer a shady site for nesting, which can also help deter house sparrows that might otherwise adopt the box. Choose a box with an entrance hole of about 1¼ to 1⅜ inches for the white-breasted nuthatch. Smaller red-breasted, brown-headed, or pygmy nuthatches will do just fine in a birdhouse made for chickadees with an entrance hole of 1⅛ inches. Don't get your heart set on a certain pair of tenants; part of the fun of putting up birdhouses is seeing who will claim the box.

ORANGES AND GRAPEFRUITS

Citrus fruit is the lure for spring orioles and tanagers, so be ready when they arrive in late April to May. Orioles have learned to recognize orange halves as food, and these birds will quickly adopt the feeder. Tanagers are close behind on the learning curve, so you can expect to see them eventually, too.

Most woodpeckers enjoy a taste of something sweet and juicy now and then. Natural sap and nectar feeders will do the trick, but oranges are a big inducement, too. This is an acorn woodpecker, better known for stashing acorns in holes like marbles in a Chinese checkers board.

Lots of other eager beaks will enjoy your halved oranges and grapefruits, as well. Mockingbirds, robins, and starlings have been fond of them for a long time. In fact, I call oranges and grapefruits my "robin savers"—when a snow or ice storm hits, they're the first thing I put out for the loyal robins that flock to my backyard.

More recently, woodpeckers, especially the red-bellied, have begun seeking them out at the feeder. Tanagers, thrashers, and house finches have also learned that citrus fruit is good to eat.

Serve your citrus in any feeder that will hold the fruit securely, or set the halves right on the ground for robins.

Birds Say No to Mold

Birds don't like rotten fruit any better than you do. Feed them the pick of the crop, not that moldy, mushy orange that's been hiding in your refrigerator for months. Fruit eaters can taste the difference, and if they learn to associate your feeder with bad fruit, they may not make a return trip when you put a better one out.

ORIOLES

Of all things bright and beautiful, orioles are right at the top of the list. Dressed in glorious orange or glowing yellow, these birds are talented as well as beautiful. Their melodic voices are clear as a bell, with a loud, whistled tune that seems to say "Look at me!"

Orioles are headline news in today's bird-feeding world: They've become regulars at backyard feeders. Once they find yours—and they will—they're likely to visit daily, especially in spring.

These gorgeous birds are fruit eaters, insect devourers, and nectar lovers. They'll use a hummingbird feeder, but you can give them their own, with a less sweet mix (1 part sugar to 6 parts water), a bigger reservoir, and sturdier perches. Now that orioles are visiting our backyards, you'll also find other feeders tailored to their needs, such as dishes of various types for jellies and jams, fruit feeders, and multipurpose feeders. Turn to the entries Jams and Jellies and Nectar for more advice on feeding your beautiful friends.

Orioles and oranges are a natural match, and not only in color. These birds love fruit, and oranges are high on the list, whether they're in a feeder or on a tree. Our friend here is a northern oriole, but all of his relatives eat oranges, too.

Water, Water, Everywhere

When it comes to keeping clean, orioles are as addicted to bathing as Howard Hughes was. Maybe it's all that sticky fruit they favor? Whatever the reason, a freshly filled birdbath is a must for orioles. They'll quickly accept the classic pedestal style, or you can add a fountain or mister to any bath for extra enticement. Just be sure the water is clean and the basin is free of algae; orioles are fussy about where they dip their pretty feathers.

Soft foods also attract orioles, so start stirring up doughs, peanut butter treats, and other goodies from the recipes in this book. Mealworms and other larvae are hugely popular, too. Or you can buy commercial blocks and pellets that include the fats, fruits, and insects they adore.

Trees are what you need to attract a nesting pair. They're partial to tall, spreading trees, so they can hang their cradle way out on a limb where predators will have a hard time getting to it.

Even if your backyard isn't graced by a mature tree, you can still attract orioles. Plant sweet fruits to gain their favor, such as cherries, mulberries, grapes, and figs. Fresh fruit of various kinds is welcome at the feeder, too, as backyard orioles branch out beyond oranges. You'll find suggestions in the Fresh Fruit entry.

Natural Nectar

All orioles make frequent visits to flowers to drink nectar in their tropical vacation grounds

HOW-TO Citrus Feeder

I'm not much of a carpenter, but even I can knock this feeder together in a few minutes. All it takes is a piece of scrap wood plus eye hooks, wire for hanging, and two big nails—one to spear the fruit and one to serve as a perch.

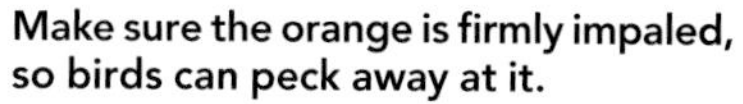

Make sure the orange is firmly impaled, so birds can peck away at it.

1 piece scrap wood, 2 × 4, about 6 inches long
2 eye hooks
2 20d nails (20-penny, which are 4 inches long)
Floral wire, about 18 inches long
Orange half

1. Screw the eye hooks into the top end of the board, centered and about 2 inches apart.

2. Measure and mark spots for the nails. Hammer one into the front center of the board and offset the other about 1 inch from the bottom edge and 1 inch from a side edge.

3. Double the floral wire and run it through the eye hooks, twisting the ends together. This will be your hanger.

4. Push an orange half cut side out onto the center nail, and hang the feeder. Now comes the hard part: Being patient until the birds find it!

during winter. But when they're visiting us, it's the western species and the orchard oriole that are most visibly focused on flowers.

Flowering trees and plants with tall spikes of flowers, such as agave, are what they prefer. They home in on red or orange-red, although they also visit flowers of other colors.

It's hard to tell exactly what an oriole is eating when it's in a flowering tree, unless it has its head stuck in a blossom. Orioles are attracted to fruit trees and crabapples in bloom, and I've seen these birds at Chinese chestnuts, too—but are they eating insects or sipping nectar? It's almost impossible to tell.

As for perennials, I've never seen a Baltimore oriole pay any attention to my red-hot poker flowers at all here in the Midwest or East. But when I added the plant to my Northwest garden, the flowers quickly attracted a Bullock's oriole, the Baltimore's western counterpart, who nipped off the blossoms one by one.

Coral trees (*Erythrina* spp.), often planted as street trees or landscaping in places with mild climates, are magnets for nectar-loving orioles. The orchard oriole is the main pollinator of one coral tree species, *E. fusca,* which has rusty red flowers that are the exact color of the bird's feathers.

PEANUT BUTTER TREATS

Peanut butter attracts so many birds that I find it fun to keep a running list. So far, I have more than 60 species on my "life list" of backyard peanut butter fans, ranging from chickadees to ravens.

That's a cumulative list from my backyard feeders in Pennsylvania, Indiana, and the Northwest, plus camping trips to many states (yes, I take along bird treats even on vacation!). But your number will be a big one wherever you live. In the 3 years I've been back in New Harmony, Indiana, my peanut butter treats have attracted nearly 40 kinds of birds.

Not bad for a homely little nut.

Know Your Peanut Butter

Cooking for birds is more like flying by the seat of your pants than mastering the art of French cooking: You'll often need to adjust the recipe depending on the consistency or moisture content of your ingredients. Peanut butter is one of the main wild cards, because its consistency varies depending on which brand you buy. Adjust the recipe's other ingredients according to the oiliness of your peanut butter. To judge the texture of your mixture, form it into a ball in your hands—if it sticks like glue to your fingers, add more dry stuff; if it falls apart into dusty crumbs, give it another glob of peanut butter.

Peanuts took a long road to get into that jar most of us have on the shelf. They became popular in this country by way of Africa, even though the plants are native from Mexico to South America. Early Portuguese explorers carried the nuts from Brazil to Africa, where they soon became a staple.

The Miracle Food

Peanuts came back to America with the slave trade. Known as goober peas, the nutritious food was soon being grown in Virginia and in other slave states.

When I was in grade school, I was riveted by a biography of George Washington Carver, the ground-breaking scientist, inventor, and educator. Hoping to better the lives of poor farmers, he became a tireless advocate for peanuts as an excellent homegrown food and a better crop than cotton.

He passed out recipes for 105 tasty dishes, and he came up with nearly 100 products that could be made from peanuts, ranging from cosmetics and dyes to paint and nitroglycerin.

Talk about sustainable agriculture—this guy had the right idea way before anyone else. In 1941, *Time* magazine called him the "Black Leonardo," likening him to da Vinci.

Too bad backyard bird feeding wasn't in business when Carver was around, or he could have added even more uses and recipes to his repertoire. You'll have to do your own experimenting, by using some of my fave concoctions as a starting point. But the same principle applies: When it comes to peanuts, the possibilities are endless.

SIMPLE SPREAD

2 cups peanut butter

$1\frac{1}{2}$ cups cornmeal

Mix thoroughly. Spread directly on tree bark or bark feeders to serve chickadees, nuthatches, woodpeckers, and many other clinging birds.

QUICK CRUMBLE

2 cups peanut butter

3 cups cornmeal

Measure the peanut butter into a large bowl. Using an electric mixer, beat in the cornmeal while pouring it in a slow stream. Serve the crumbles to catbirds, wrens, thrashers, thrushes, grosbeaks, orioles, and other perching birds in a tray feeder, mealworm feeder, or, in small quantities, directly on the ground. Fill the holes of a log feeder for clinging birds such as chickadees and titmice.

COAXER FOR COLORFUL BIRDS

1 cup peanut butter

1 cup lard or suet

2 to 3 cups cornmeal

1 cup hulled sunflower seed

1 cup dried, chopped raisins, berries, apples, or other fruit

Combine the peanut butter and lard or suet, using an electric mixer. Beat in the cornmeal while pouring it slowly into the bowl, and mix in the other ingredients. Mold into cakes or serve as crumbles in an accessible feeder to delight orioles, tanagers, waxwings, and bluebirds.

PILEATED PLEASER

2 cups peanut butter

1 cup lard or suet

3 cups oatmeal, not instant

1 cup cornmeal

1 cup chopped nuts, any kind

1 cup hulled sunflower seeds

Mix this recipe in the biggest bowl you have—it makes a lot. Combine the peanut butter and lard, and then slowly beat in the oatmeal and cornmeal. Mix in the nuts and seeds. Mold into blocks to fit your pileated suet feeder. This treat will attract other woodpeckers, too.

PERCHES

Whenever I'm out watching birds in the wild, I can often guess just where a restless bird will land next. Birds like a lookout when they pause between flights, so they often land on the very top of shrubs or small trees—or even at the tippy-top of big trees or utility poles.

Adding more places to sit down for a spell will encourage birds to linger in your yard, and they'll be in easy view, instead of up in the trees. Once you notice which perches your birds use, get in the habit of scanning them every time you step outside. You'll get to know your birds and their

Put Down the Pruners

Don't be too quick with the pruners when you spy a dead branch on one of your small trees or shrubs. The dead sticks often become popular resting places for birds as they move about the yard, especially if the twigs stick up above the rest of the foliage. Birds particularly use them in summer, when foliage obscures the living branches. In winter, any skinny twig is fair game.

A vermilion flycatcher could be your reward for not removing dead branches if you live in the Southwest, from Texas to California. If not, look for one of the olive-green species in your flycatcher-friendly yard.

habits better, and you may get a view of a bird you don't normally see.

Hummingbirds are one of the main reasons I make sure my yard has lots of perches. Hummers need thin twigs to get a grip on, so my young trees, fruit trees, and open shrubs are favored resting places.

Birds with bigger feet like to land on my arbor—the tallest element in the yard, not counting the trees overhead. It's a popular landing site for orioles, robins, tanagers, and many other birds.

A yard with only shade trees and flowerbeds doesn't offer many mid-height possibilities for birds to take a rest. You can remedy the situation by adding small flowering trees to your flowerbed, such as crabapples or dwarf fruit trees. Or you can stick in a shepherd's hook here and there to supply a much appreciated perch.

PESTICIDES

Birds got some great news in May, 2009, when the US Environmental Protection Agency (EPA) announced its decision to ban all uses of the highly toxic pesticide carbofuran on food crops. This deadly poison has caused the deaths of millions of birds since its introduction in 1967, including bald eagles as well as countless songbirds. A single grain of the granular form, used until several years ago, was powerful enough to kill a bird. The grains looked a lot like seeds, and birds pecked them up quickly, flew away, and dropped dead. If a flock of mallards settled in a carbofuran-treated alfalfa field to feed, 92 percent of the flock would quickly die, according to the EPA's own calculations. The results would be just as bad for native sparrows or finches working through a carbofuran-treated field of strawberries.

Carbofuran, which is still not off the market, isn't the only bad actor. Forty or so pesticides

Pesticides kill thousands of birds a year, as well as the insects that they're targeted for. Farmland birds like this red-winged blackbird comprise the highest numbers of casualties.

still used in the United States have caused significant die-offs of birds, and no doubt will again. In most cases, the pesticides were used completely legally.

In a 1992 *BioScience* article, researchers estimated that more than 670 million birds are directly exposed to pesticides every year—and that about 10 percent of them die as a result. That's 67 million birds, in case you're counting.

That ghastly total doesn't include the untold millions of birds that suffer harmful effects, not sudden death. Reproductive problems, deformities, cancers—it's the same list of dangers that we ourselves face from some of these products.

Get Educated

There are safe alternatives to toxic pesticides in your backyard. Don't expose your birds—or yourself—to risky chemicals. To make a difference in the bigger picture, consider joining the not-for-profit American Bird Conservancy (ABC), which works hard to do exactly what its name implies. The ABC's Pesticides and Birds Campaign is an active effort aimed at reducing the risk to wild birds. You can read about it at www.abcbirds.org/abcprograms/policy/pesticides/index.html.

With birds on the decline, getting rid of our most harmful pesticides is a must. Joining organized groups that are bringing the issue to light is a good way to begin making a difference. But here's an even better one: If all of us 46 million US bird lovers bought organic products, the demand for chemical pesticides would sink like a stone, and farmland that's safe for birds would increase. Why not start with buying organic strawberries today?

PHOEBES AND FLYCATCHERS

Poor flycatchers—they hardly get any notice in the backyard, even though they're just as interesting as other birds. Blame it on their natural habits: These birds are retiring types, who spend a lot of time sitting and waiting until an insect flies along. And since most of these birds are drab green, it's hard to see them among the leaves. Only the brilliant vermilion flycatcher of the Southwest is a real standout.

A few flycatchers do attract our attention. These are the feisty members of the clan, the so-called tyrant flycatchers. Bigger than their quiet cousins, they're also a lot louder, a lot more active, and a lot more aggressive. You can't overlook an eastern or western kingbird, a great crested flycatcher, or a western sulphur-bellied flycatcher, or, least of all, a scissor-tailed flycatcher when it goes on the attack. These birds vigorously defend their territories, driving off anything they consider a threat, whether it's a snake, a cat, or you yourself.

As for phoebes, they're drab birds, too, with reserved manners. I have a soft spot for them, though, because they're one of the first migrants to return in spring. I'm always pleased to hear that first buzzy *fee-bee*—wow, it's really spring!

Not a standout or a showoff, the trusting eastern phoebe often nests right on our own dwellings.

Flycatchers at Home

If great crested flycatchers are in your neighborhood, they may quickly adopt a birdhouse. (Sulphur-bellied flycatchers also use nest boxes; the others aren't cavity nesters.) These birds actually have benefited from the fragmentation of forests, because they prefer to live in openings or woods' edges rather than deep among the trees. You'll need a deep nesting box with a 1¾-inch entrance hole for these birds. Although they often perch on the very top of trees, they nest relatively low, usually at heights ranging from 5 to 20 feet. Mount your box on a tree, and keep your fingers crossed.

Phoebes and flycatchers are big insect eaters, and some of them gobble down fruit, too. They're not regulars at the feeder—yet. But I have hosted my first kingbirds and great cresteds at the mealworm dish, and I suspect they'll be coming back. Flying insects are the main part of their diet, so a butterfly garden is a good attraction.

Another reason to be fond of phoebes is that they often nest right on our own houses. A ledge over a window suits them to a T, or you can nail up a shallow shelf under an overhanging eave. They often return to the same nest site year after year. Put out fresh green moss among your nest material offerings, and your phoebe may take it for its nest.

PINECONES

Pinecones (including fir cones, spruce cones, hemlock cones, and all other conifer cones) are such a vital food source for birds of northern conifer forests that when there's a lean year, the birds "irrupt," heading south to welcoming feeders and other food sources. If you see crossbills at your feeder—and you don't live in the Far North where these birds are regulars—you can bet it's a bad year for cones.

HOW-TO Pinecone & Birdseed Wreath

You can spread a lot of peanut butter over and between the scaly layers of a pinecone. And you may have—pinecone feeders are popular projects with kids' groups and Scouts. Here's the upscale version of those familiar rolled-in-birdseed treats.

Small wire wreath form
Pinecones
Florists' wire
Chunky peanut butter or lard
Finely chopped or ground walnuts or pecans
Sunflower chips
Raffia (optional)

1. Wire the cones to the wreath, overlapping them as you go.

2. Spread the front of the cones with peanut butter. Work the fat between their scales, and apply an outer coating about ⅛-inch thick.

3. Pour the nuts and sunflower chips into a pie pan, platter, or other container that is large enough to accommodate the wreath, and mix together.

4. Press the wreath into the mixture, so that the goodies are pressed into the fat.

5. Loop several strands of raffia or florists' wire through the wreath, and hang it where it will be shielded from rain. Got a garden shed? Hang it on an outside wall under an overhang.

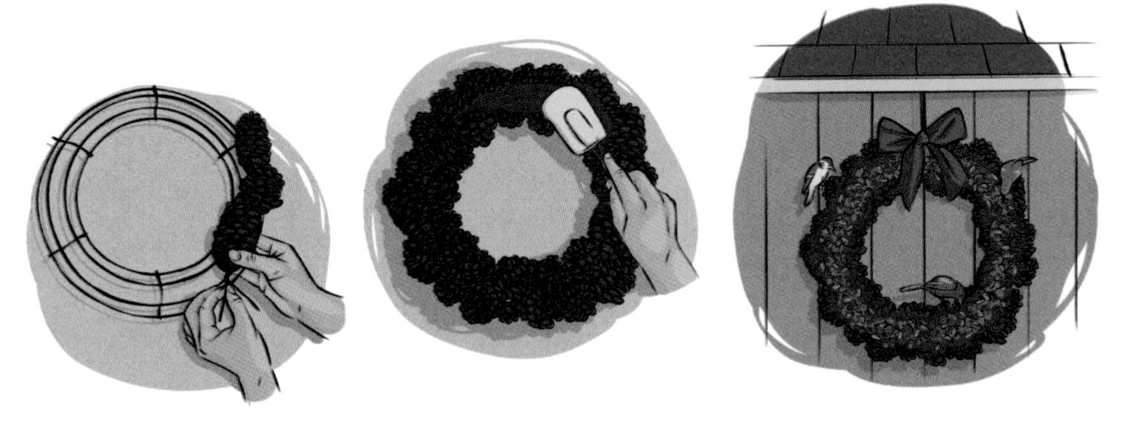

Super-Size It

For a one-of-a-kind pinecone feeder, use one of the enormous cones from the sugar pine, a Western species whose cones can reach 18 inches long. Depending on the size of the cone, you may be able to spread more than 2 cups of lard or other fat between the scales. Keep some of the rows of woody scales free of fat, so your birds can use them as perches as they nibble their way around the monster cone. Slide a piece of florists' wire under the top layer of scales for hanging.

Pinyon jays are a Southwestern species that depends on the seeds inside pinecones. In their case, the plump nuggets we call pine nuts are their prize inside the cones of pinyon pines. You can read more about northern birds and pinyon jays, and their dependence on pinecones, in "A Whole New World," on page 1.

Pinecones are sought by birds of all areas, so be sure to include some conifers in your backyard habitat. Young trees quickly reach bearing age, and chickadees, nuthatches, and other birds will be on the cones before you know it, pecking out the bounty of nutritious seeds tucked among the scales.

POPULATION DECLINE

When I was growing up, the call of the northern bobwhite was a common part of the background soundtrack whenever I walked the fields in eastern Pennsylvania. Whistling back was fun, and I loved getting a glimpse of a mama bobwhite with a whole line of babies running after her.

A couple of years ago, when I went back to visit, I didn't hear a single bobwhite. Most of the farms where I'd walked are gone now, turned into subdivisions. And the farm fields that are still there are way bigger than they used to be. The sheltering brush and hedgerows where I used to spend hours watching birds have been cleaned out to squeeze in another few rows of corn.

"Clean farming" has destroyed so much habitat in the northern bobwhite's wide range that the species has dropped like a rock—down 75 percent in the last 20 years.

Habitat destruction is one of the biggest obstacles our birds face and is the main reason for the dramatic decline in the numbers of some species. So why don't we just stop destroying their habitat?

Because there's 6.7 billion of us on Earth, at last count.

Feeding us, housing us, and making the things we use, from toilet paper to fast-food hamburgers, require a lot of room and a lot of resources.

Our birds can't adjust fast enough to keep up with habitat decimation. Other factors, including fragmentation, pesticides, and climate change, are also sending their numbers into a free fall.

Birds in Trouble

Almost a third of the 654 bird species in the continental US is declining in numbers, some dramatically (by as much as 85 percent), others less steeply (by half or less). If you've been watching birds for a while, you'll find that many of them are familiar faces.

For a full account of what's going on with bird numbers, see the comprehensive and sobering *US State of the Birds* report (2009), a joint effort of many conservation groups, scientific institutions, and the US government.

Here's a sampling of the many birds whose populations are declining noticeably; there are many, many others on the list.

Desert and Arid-Land Birds

Bendire's thrasher
Elf owl
Golden-cheeked warbler
Greater sage grouse
Gunnison sage grouse
Le Conte's thrasher
Scaled quail

It's Up to Us

With a downslide like this in bird populations, there's no time to waste. Nearly a third of our bird species, the "canaries in the coal mine," are singing for their lives, even those whose numbers appear secure today. So, add your voice to conservation groups, and keep nurturing the birds in your backyard. We bird lovers are 46 million strong. And we have success stories to point to already, like the bald eagle, the wild turkey, and the wetland birds that made a comeback when we changed our ways. We *can* make a difference.

Nest boxes can help the chestnut-backed chickadee of western coastal and northwestern forests recover from loss of habitat in its breeding areas.

Grassland Birds

- Bobolinks (once so plentiful they were killed by the millions by rice farmers in Louisiana)
- Henslow's sparrow
- Meadowlarks (both eastern and western species)
- Northern bobwhite
- Short-eared owl

A flock of bobolinks in breeding plumage is quite a sight when they flutter about with black and white feathers flashing. Like many other birds, they've suffered a noticeable decline in recent years.

Forest Birds

- Brown-headed nuthatch
- Eastern towhee
- Eastern wood-pewee
- Field warbler
- Prairie warbler
- Red-cockaded woodpecker
- Whippoorwill
- Wood thrush

Western Forest Birds

- Cassin's finch
- Chestnut-backed chickadee
- Lewis's woodpecker
- Oak titmouse
- Pinyon jay
- Rufous hummingbird
- Varied thrush

Northern (Boreal) Forest Birds

- Blackpoll warbler
- Cape May warbler
- Connecticut warbler
- Evening grosbeak
- Pine siskin
- White-winged crossbill

Urban Birds

Nearly all year-round birds of cities and towns are in good shape, because they've already adapted to making use of our backyards and feeders—*mi casa, su casa.* Instead, it's the birds we tend to see when they're passing through to homelands in other habitats, like those listed above and many others, that are in decline.

PREDATORS

Predators are a fact of life when your yard is alive with birds. You're likely to be visited by hawks, owls, raccoons, skunks, opossums, and other animals seeking a meal, in any season. Nesting time will bring even more predators on the prowl, because there's more "food" awaiting—parent birds sitting on eggs, eggs themselves, and of course tender baby birds, a favorite meal for any meat eater than can grab it.

There's not much you can do to keep these creatures away. But you can take steps to help keep your birds safer, and give them a better chance at survival.

Protective Cover

When your yard has plenty of shrubs, trees, and other places for birds to make a getaway, they may be able to escape the clutches of a determined hawk, owl, or even a cat. And when you give your birds sheltered access routes of plants, so that they can approach your feeder safely, you help them evade predators, too (see the entry Access Routes for details).

Think about how many birds your own cat kills—that you know of—then multiply that by millions of cats, and you have an idea of how huge an impact the feline factor is on our feathered friends. Have a cat? Keep it indoors.

Prickly plants deter predators in a big way, even at night. Be sure to include roses, hollies, junipers, and other "Ouch!" plants in your yard.

Protective Devices

Dealing with a neighbor's straying cats is a touchy subject, so I started using the Scarecrow, a glorified sprinkler contraption. Poke it into the ground, attach it to your garden hose, and you're good to go. When an animal sets off the battery-operated motion sensor, the device lets loose with a blast of water that sends the cat, skunk, or 'coon skedaddling. The Scarecrow costs about $80, but it has saved my birds and my neighbor relations, and that's no small potatoes. It's on duty day and night, too, so it also repels nest predators. The only trick? Be sure to switch off the water before you refill your feeders!

To protect birds nesting in a birdhouse, attach a predator guard tube at the entrance hole. The guard increases the distance a raccoon, possum, or cat has to stretch its arm into the nest box and may be enough to keep the family safe. You'll find the guards at bird supply shops.

For extra insurance, nail a wide band of sheet metal to your tree or use a conical shield on poles to block snakes, 'coons, and other predators from climbing to the nest.

Some suppliers also sell chemical repellents, ultrasonic devices, and even plants that are supposed to keep cats away. Read the customer reviews before you buy any of these so-called repellents. Some of them are nothing but snake-oil schemes or only mildly effective.

Q/R/S

QUAIL

Sorry, my fellow bird lovers in the eastern half of the country, we're out of luck: The only quail we have is the northern bobwhite, and it rarely comes to backyards.

Nope, it's the western part of the country that gets to enjoy the most adorable birds you could ever dream up. Quail are undeniably cute, with their football-shaped bodies and the bobbing topknots that some species sport on their heads. California quail and Gambel's quail have adapted well to backyards, and other species may come have a look-see, too.

Quail travel, feed, and sleep in companionable groups called coveys. They eat seeds and insects, nip at fruits, and take tastes of vegetation, like the chicken whose relative they are. At the feeder, they're easy to please—a scattering of millet and milo right on the ground or in a low tray will keep them pecking happily.

Water Music

Quail are easily attracted by water. Even those that are well adapted to their desert life will go out of their way to visit a reliable source of fresh water. Set up a ground-level birdbath for them, or consider a larger, naturalistic faux-stone bath with shallow pools where several birds can drink at once. Or just let the birds fly up to your pedestal birdbath; they're perfectly able to do so. If you haven't hosted quail before, try a solar fountain to catch their ear. Once the birds find your bath, they're likely to follow a regular routine for their visits, arriving for a drink in the morning and before bed.

RANGE SHIFTS

The rufous hummingbird, a coppery mite with a blazing orange throat, was once a rarity anywhere east of the western Plains. And in winter, it completely disappeared from the United States, because it vacationed in northwestern and central Mexico.

Yet starting in the 1970s, the rufous hummer has been showing up with increasing frequency all across the country during spring and summer. By 1998, there was "a large and rapidly increasing number of Rufous Hummingbirds wintering in the southeastern United States," as researchers Hill, Sargent, and Sargent reported in *The Auk*.

The pygmy nuthatch is packing its bags and moving north. Climate change has caused it to depart from a large part of its usual wintering grounds in New Mexico in favor of new digs up to 300 miles farther north.

My 1987 edition of the National Geographic Society field guide to North American birds shows that the rufous hummer appears in winter only on the Gulf Coast. Nowadays, this bird is a winter regular northward all the way to Tennessee. I even hosted a male for a few months in the dead of winter here in southern Indiana.

Could it have been drawn inland by following a tempting trail of red plastic feeders? Maybe so, although there seems to be no way to ever know for sure. We can collect more circumstantial evidence from researchers Hill, Sargent, and Sargent: They note an interesting distribution of those wintering hummers, with "clumps" of birds in certain areas—maybe where there's an abundance of feeders?

Other hummingbird species are also on the move, though not nearly to the extent of the rufous. (The total sightings of these other strays are usually only in the double digits, compared to thousands of rufous reports.)

Climate Change Causes Shifts

As for non-hummingbird species, their changes in range are because of climate change, scientists say. A 2008 report by Greg Butcher, the director of bird conservation at the Audubon Society, took a look at 305 widespread North American bird species and discovered that more than 50 percent of them have expanded the boundary of their range to the north—and disappeared from the more southern parts of their range.

That's a huge overall shift, and it has nothing to do with backyard feeders. The pygmy nuthatches that once wintered in New Mexico, for example, have shifted their range 265 miles to the north, and their population in the state has declined by 90 percent.

A large study of northeastern birds by SUNY College of Environmental Science and Forestry in 2009 revealed the same conclusion: Birds are on the move as climate change takes hold. The ranges of northeastern birds are moving northward. "Their southern range boundaries are actually moving northward as well, and at a much faster clip," reported Dr. Benjamin Zuckerberg, the study's lead researcher.

Except perhaps in the case of hummingbirds, the trend we're seeing is part of a much, much bigger picture—and it's only just begun. You never know who might turn up in your bird-friendly yard tomorrow. The picture is definitely changing.

ROBINS AND THRUSHES

The American robin has always been a beloved harbinger of spring. But once the thrill wears off, the birds become just part of the background for most people.

Not any longer. The robin is one of the birds that has been adapting to bird feeders in recent years, and that puts a whole new spin on things. Suddenly, the bird feels like our new best friend. Hi, Mr. Robin, here, have some mealworms!

Soft foods are a big reason why robins and even a few thrushes are taking an interest in our feeders. These birds, like the bluebirds they're related to, aren't much interested in seeds. But insect foods, suet doughs, fruity treats, and soft bite-size bits and nuggets—now we're talking!

To attract robins to your feeders—and thrushes to your yard—add berry bushes and other fruiting plants. Choose small fruits that the birds can gulp down in one bite, such as blueberries, shadblow, and elderberries. That's their preferred way of eating, although these birds will also peck at larger fruits, including apples, oranges, and grapefruits.

Be sure to include some native plants with berries that ripen in late summer to early fall, to catch the attention of thrushes and robins on migration. You'll find some ideal candidates in the entry Best of the Berries and adaptable American native plants in the entry Fats and Oils (yes, that's right, and you'll see why when you read that entry). Or check a native plant catalog or nursery to find berry bushes that are native to your area.

Freshen Those Feathers

Thrushes—and that includes robins and bluebirds—love a good splashy bath. The forest thrushes that are just beginning to investigate our backyards are most comfortable using a ground-level bath. In spring and fall, when these birds stop in my yard during migration, I set up a mister over a big clay saucer on the ground as extra incentive. So far, three of the five species of forest thrushes that pass through my region have taken me up on the invitation. And I even got an unexpected guest: a varied thrush from the West, which I've now seen 2 years in a row with a flock of migrating robins.

ROOSTING SITES

When bedtime rolls around, birds seek out hiding places that will shield them from predators. Trees and tall shrubs with dense branches, and thick tangles of vines, are favored sleeping spots for many backyard birds. The vegetation helps discourage their enemies, especially if it's prickly.

Thick foliage also blocks the wind and rain, and it creates niches that help hold heat. In winter, short-needled evergreens are popular hideouts for birds that roost together, such as white-throated sparrows.

Very few birds sleep on the ground, even if they

spend most of their time there during the day. A sleeping bird on the ground is a sitting duck for any predator that may happen upon it.

Native sparrows and juncos perch relatively low, but they try to get at least 3 feet off the ground. Doves and wild turkeys, also ground-feeding birds, sleep high in trees. Most birds settle in for the night somewhere between 4 and 20 feet above the ground.

If I had to vote for the best roosting plant for backyard birds, I'd give a great big thumbs-up to juniper. The foliage is thick and stiff, so it discourages climbing cats, 'coons, and possums. Junipers come in all shapes and sizes, but for sleeping quarters, the tall forms are the best. Junipers have other assets that birds appreciate: They offer berries in fall and winter for waxwings, bluebirds, Townsend's solitaire, and yellow-rumped warblers, and they attract insects, including caterpillars, for birds to feed upon.

For guaranteed bird appeal, plant a juniper that's native to your area. Several species of these rugged evergreens grow in various regions across the country. In the eastern half, it's the tightly erect eastern red cedar (*Juniperus virginiana*); in the West, look for Rocky Mountain juniper (*J. scopulorum*), western juniper (*J. occidentalis*), Utah juniper (*J. osteospermum*), California juniper (*J. californica*), and other species. Ask at your local nursery or check a native plant supplier, like those in the Resources section.

In one of my former yards, a 10-foot eastern red cedar (*J. virginiana*) sheltered at least a dozen birds every night, and in winter, its branches hid whole flocks of mixed sparrows and juncos, plus a handful of cardinals and doves.

The Telltale Tail

Cavity-nesting birds look for holes in trees, empty birdhouses, or roosting boxes to sleep in, especially in winter. Holing up overnight is why titmice and other birds sometimes show up at the feeder with bent tail feathers on a winter morning. When you see bent feathers, you know the bird spent the night in tight quarters, with its tail pressed against the wall. To give your bluebirds, chickadees, titmice, or Carolina wrens a snug place to sleep on cold nights, put up a roosting box, which you can buy at any bird supply shop or build yourself. The box looks like a simple wooden birdhouse, except that the entrance is near the bottom and there are pegs inside for perching.

ROSE-BREASTED GROSBEAK

Here's the best "bouquet" a mother could ever ask for on her special day—the rose-breasted grosbeak, which in my neck of the woods often arrives at my feeder on Mother's Day.

This striking bird is a relative newcomer to feeding stations. The first one I saw at a feeder was in my mother's yard some 20 years ago, but it wasn't until about a decade later that my own feeder was honored with a visit.

Today, you can count on rose-breasted grosbeaks at the feeder if you live within their range. At my place, they usually visit for several weeks in spring when they stop during migration or until they find mates and retreat to nesting grounds.

Sunflower seeds are all a rose-breasted grosbeak asks for at a feeding station. A generous helping will keep the birds content. But have fun experimenting, too, because these birds are learning to try our other foods and feeders, too.

Mealworms and other insect foods, as well as accessible soft foods like doughs, fruit, and nuggets, may tickle their fancy. I've even seen a "rosie" stealing sips from my hummingbird feeder.

Get Cracking with Safflower Seed

Want to steal the rose-breasted grosbeaks from your neighbor's feeder? Serve them safflower seeds. The tough white shells are no problem for the birds' stout beaks. And inside is an incredibly oil-rich seed meat that the rose-breasted grosbeaks of my acquaintance utterly adore. Try serving them yourself and see.

SALT

Ever notice all the birds alongside a road after a snow? Some are picking up exposed seeds, but many are after the salt used to de-ice the road.

Most of the real salt fiends belong to the Finch family—goldfinches, purple finches, siskins, crossbills, grosbeaks, and cardinals. They'll eat it from roadsides, barnyards, and even bricks.

That same taste for salt spelled doom for the passenger pigeons and bright green-and-yellow Carolina parakeets that once roamed the eastern half of the country. "Market hunters" set up nets at natural salt licks. "When enough birds are gathered upon the beds to make a profitable throw, the net flies over in an instant, while in its meshes struggle hundreds of unwilling prisoners," wrote W.B. Gershon in 1907.

There's a "salt lick" right in my small town: the brick sidewalk right outside the post office. I first discovered it when I had to step around a squirrel that was busy licking a white splotch on the brick.

Now, town squirrels are pretty tame, but this guy was extreme. "What's he eating?" I wondered, so I wet my finger, dabbed it on the white stuff, and took a taste. Salt!

Aha. Now I knew why I'd often seen house finches on the sidewalk, and the occasional bunch of pine siskins or evening grosbeaks.

To set up your own salt lick, just put out a plain salt block from a farm store. You'll see mourning doves, squirrels, lots of pretty finches and grosbeaks, and all kinds of other birds at it.

Weed Killer at Work

Salt stunts or kills most plants, and when your salt block gets rained on, it'll create a dead zone under and around it. I put that effect to work for me by setting my salt block right on my brick patio. The birds eagerly visit it there, and as far as it killing plants—well, that's less weeding between the bricks for me!

SAP SIPPERS

Yes, Virginia, there really is a yellow-bellied sapsucker. And a red-breasted, a red-naped, and a Williamson's sapsucker. All of them drill rows of closely spaced holes in trees to create a "sap works" that they visit over and over, often for years.

Sap is a tree's lifeblood, and a hole in a tree usually closes over fast as the tree stanches the flow. But the holes that sapsuckers drill stay moist. Not enough to harm the tree, but just enough so that the sapsucker doesn't have to redrill its works.

Why? So far, the best guess is that sapsucker spit contains an anticoagulant that keeps the sap from hardening up completely.

Whatever the reason, sapsucker works are vital to hummingbirds during a cold snap. Flower nectar may stop as blossoms get nipped by frost, but the tree sap keeps on flowing.

Sap also nourishes hummingbirds returning to their more northern haunts in spring, when flowers are few. They depend on sapsucker workings for natural sugar-water feeders. And hummingbird migration coincides perfectly with the peak of sapsucker activity. Neat how that works, isn't it?

Other birds sip sap, too. Last winter, when I was tapping a sugar maple to make syrup, a red-bellied woodpecker often perched on my bucket and drank the sap right out of the spout. Other woodpeckers, warblers, titmice, and chickadees sip sap, too. Many birds visit sapsucker works to collect insects that are attracted by the sweet stuff, too.

The Sap Is Running

Late winter to very early spring, when the days are bright and sunny and the nights still cold but not frigid, is when tree sap starts running. Look for sap-sipping birds then, often at dripping icicles that form where a twig has snapped and sap has leaked out. And don't forget to watch for the sapsucker itself—this bird is among the earliest spring migrants. Keep an eye out for those trademark rows of holes, and look for the bird in the vicinity.

SEASONAL SURPRISES

Bird surprises are the norm in spring and fall, when migrants are moving around. A hospitable yard may entice a bird that doesn't nest or winter in your area to alight and stay a while during its travels. Wood warblers are one of those treats for many of us—even if only a few species of warblers nest in your region, dozens of species may show up on a late April day.

Winter blizzards may also bring unusual birds to your backyard. I live in farming country, but my house is a good 2 miles from the closest field, and my yard looks nothing like grassland. So I was mighty surprised to find meadowlarks, horned larks, and sparrowlike dickcissels hungrily gobbling seed at my feeders the day after a snowstorm. They stayed for several days, until the snow began to melt, and then returned to their fields.

In summer and fall, the powerful winds of hurricanes or tornados can sweep birds along in their path. Hurricanes are so well known for shoving birds way off course that some birders hurry to the area to see what rarities have blown in on the wind.

Strong winds in winter can have the same effect. When a cold blue norther howled down from Canada one year, it brought a twittering flock of hoary redpolls to my feeder, even though it wasn't an irruption year (when pinecones are scarce and northern birds move south en masse).

Anytime a seasonal storm goes through, I keep an eye on my feeders and the birds in my backyard. You never know who might turn up.

Stock the Pantry for Surprise Guests

Since there's no way of telling just who might be showing up in your yard, you'll want to have food on hand to satisfy any kind of bird. Mealworms are always a safe choice, as far as soft foods go; even if the hungry birds have never visited a feeder before, they'll recognize the mealworms as something they can eat.

SEED MIXES

There are seed mixes, and then there are seed mixes. In most cases, you get what you pay for.

"One size fits most" is a claim I've learned to be leery of, whether we're talking about T-shirts, panty hose, or birdseed. Oh, sure, the shirt or tights may cover the intended parts, but chances are the clothes won't be the most comfy fit. I'll be tucking in the billowing waist, pulling up the sagging ankles, or yanking at the elastic. And if they really don't fit my "most," I'll be peeling them off as soon as I can, in favor of something more my size.

Targeted birdseed mixes, on the other hand, are like tailor-made clothes: They fit the intended purpose to a T. These are premium mixes that cost more than the bags of cheap stuff, and in most cases, they're worth it.

Come One, Come All

Inexpensive seed mixes are "One size fits most." Many of them are filled with seeds that birds will eat—but which they don't prefer. The ingredients are likely to be heavy on cracked corn and have a good amount of milo, oats, or wheat kernels in the mix.

These are fillers that take up space, but don't add much bird value. Although grains are eagerly eaten by quail, pheasants, wild turkeys, and doves, they also attract hordes of house sparrows, starlings, and blackbirds, which most of us consider less desirable. And if you live in the eastern two-thirds of the country, the milo will probably go uneaten.

There'll be some millet in these mixes, too, and probably a light scattering of sunflower seeds. When you figure the cost per pound, and subtract the fillers, you'll see it makes more sense to buy millet and sunflower separately and mix them yourself, without the "fillers" that will attract birds you don't want.

You will find a few high-quality all-purpose mixes. They'll be heavy on millet, and they'll include a generous helping of sunflower seeds and perhaps hulled chips. Safflower and niger

Tailored for a Perfect Fit

The kind of feeder you choose determines who eats your seed mixes. Select a feeder that's tailored to the feeding habits of the birds you want to attract, and, just as important, that keeps out the birds you don't want. When I spread a premium woodpecker mix in a tray feeder, I got lots of house sparrows and a cardinal. When I offered the same mix in a sunflower tube feeder, chickadees and titmice were the main customers. When I put the mix in a wire mesh nut feeder that flickers, red-bellied, downy, and hairy woodpeckers were already accustomed to visiting, I had a waiting line—and woodpecker wars!

may be in the mix, too. Some may have cracked corn, because cardinals eat it, but the bits and pieces won't make up more than a small fraction of the mix.

Read the list of ingredients before you buy an all-purpose mix. If it includes the seeds that are already staples at your feeder (sunflower, millet, niger) and perhaps a few treats, it'll work fine. If it's heavy on fillers, just say no. The only exception: If you live in the West, where milo is a favored food, then go for the grain.

Tailor-Made Mixes

Finch mixes have been around for years, and they work wonderfully at attracting the birds they're intended for. You can read more about them in the entry Finches and Finch Mix.

No-waste (or waste-free) mixes have been around for a while, too. If you feed birds on your deck, patio, or balcony, or if you simply don't like the messy shells around a bird feeder, give these mixes a try. They use hulled seeds and shelled nuts, so that birds eat every bit. Lyric Delite, for instance, includes an appealing mix of hulled sunflowers, hulled pumpkin seeds, tree nuts, and peanuts. You won't see any shells beneath your feeders, and you won't see any sprouts, either, because the seeds can't germinate without shells.

Other than finches, though, many of our favorite birds haven't had their own mixes until recent years.

Finally, seed mix makers wised up, no doubt because of the huge potential buying crowd of feeder keepers.

Now, you'll find several brands of tailor-made mixes on the shelves, and more hitting the market every year. Manufacturers are still fiddling with the concept, and I expect there'll be more fine-tuning, more competing products, and, as always, the unscrupulous bag of "special" mix that's heavily padded with fillers.

Just looking at the labels is enough to make your mouth water—for birds, that is. You'll find cardinal and chickadee mix, woodpecker and nuthatch mix, "colorful birds" mix, and others that feature the birds most of us like best.

The makers have done their homework. These seed mixes are chock-full of ingredients that will attract the birds you want, and plenty of them. The price tag is higher for these premium products, but the payoff will have you smiling.

So far, the premium mixes have lived up to their labels. I've tried a number of these products, and—important point!—when I put them in an appropriate feeder, most of them have been terrific at attracting the birds they're intended for.

It's tremendously satisfying to pour out a seed mix and see peanuts, sunflower chips, fruit bits, safflower seeds, bird nuggets, and other premium ingredients, instead of being disappointed by how much cheap cracked corn is in the mix.

Keep in mind that there's a lot of overlap among birds, as far as which foods they eat. You'll attract the birds the label says the mix is intended for, but you're likely to attract others, too. As long as the birds that have a taste for those premium ingredients can access your feeder, you may get some takers you didn't expect.

SHADE-GROWN COFFEE

Imagine you've been going to the same winter vacation spot for years. It's a popular camping place in the foothills of the mountains, where the climate is mild and there's plenty of shade and privacy, thanks to the trees and bushes between you and your neighbors. And the self-serve snack bars are not to be believed—they're everywhere, jam-packed with all your favorites, and all you have to do is help yourself.

All day long, it's visit with your friends, have a snack, sit in the shade, have a snack, take a dip in the pool, have a snack, check out the waterfall, have another snack ... sounds like heaven, doesn't it?

This is coffee. Lots of coffee. Only coffee. It replaced the Central American rain forest here that once sheltered dozens of bird species, including many of our summer friends.

Birds of Shade-Grown Coffee Farms

Shade-grown coffee farms are vital islands of survival for more than 50 American birds. Many of our flycatchers, vireos, wood warblers, tanagers, and orioles visit or winter on these farms.

Here, in the order you'll find them in the Sibley field guide, are just some of the birds that will sing your praises for making the switch to shade-grown coffee.

- American kestrel
- Ruby-throated hummingbird
- Willow flycatcher
- Western kingbird
- Red-eyed vireo
- Warbling vireo
- Yellow-throated vireo
- Violet-green swallow
- Cliff swallow
- Barn swallow
- Blue-gray gnatcatcher
- Wood thrush
- Swainson's thrush
- Yellow warbler, Blackburnian warbler, and 20 other species of wood warblers
- Summer tanager
- Western tanager
- Rose-breasted grosbeak
- Indigo bunting
- Painted bunting
- Baltimore oriole

The red-eyed vireo, only a hundred years ago one of the most abundant birds of eastern forests, finds winter shelter on shade-grown coffee farms.

Raise a cup of shade-grown java to the rose-breasted grosbeak, another species that winters on the bird-friendly coffee plantations of Central America.

Now imagine that the campground gets a new owner. Bulldozers come in and scrape off all the trees and bushes—and the snack bars, too. New campsites are laid out in rows, with no privacy whatsoever, and suddenly the predators—there are all kinds of scary creatures that can eat you in this campground—can see you plain as day. You manage to find some food, but it sure gives you a bellyache, and your neighbors are dropping like flies.

That's what happened in Central and South America when the coffee boom that started in the Pacific Northwest spread across the United States.

The Price of Coffee

In order to supply all those millions of cups of java we were clamoring for, hundreds of thousands of acres—right in the heart of wintering bird habitat—were stripped of forest.

What went in instead was a monoculture crop of coffee, grown in the sun. Pesticides are dumped on the closely managed bushes regularly.

Insects vanished. And tanagers, yellow warblers, ovenbirds, thrushes, and dozens of others that had been using the area for millennia—our winter vacationers—disappeared.

Uh-oh. Will we have to give up that fresh-brewed mug (or two, or three) of morning coffee that we like so much?

Nope. There's a better solution: We can drink shade-grown coffee instead and help birds at the same time.

Shade-grown coffee farms look very much like their natural surroundings, with a diverse, layered habitat of trees, shrubs, and other plants. They're alive with birds, insects, and other creatures. These farms are havens for American migrants, as well as for tropical residents like toucans and hummingbirds. Our birds cram into these farms when they fly south in fall, because the feast they expect is waiting for them.

The Seal of Approval

When you buy shade-grown coffee, be sure to look for a seal from a reputable conservation group, such as the Rainforest Alliance, or the "Bird Friendly" seal of the Smithsonian Migratory Bird Center. Some unscrupulous growers leave a few isolated trees standing and slap the word "shade" on their packaged coffee. Make sure the coffee you buy says "organic" on the label, too. Serve it proudly to your friends and family, and spread the word. Our birds need all the help we can give them.

Make the Change

It's hard to believe, but making the switch to organic shade-grown coffee is one of the biggest things we can do for these birds. Why? Because so many of us drink coffee. If we all switch to shade-grown, what a difference it would make.

Today, it's much easier to find shade-grown coffee than ever before, and the price has come down considerably. You'll still pay more per pound than regular coffee, but the price is worth it. Nothing like sipping my coffee on a May morning while a tanager sings from the tree in my backyard. I always figure he's reminding me we're all in this together.

SISKINS

I met my first pine siskins nearly 30 years ago in Boot Hill cemetery, of all places. I was bent over, peering at tombstones for famous names from Wild West days, when I heard a bright, clear bird-call that sounded exactly like the querying chirp of the canaries my mother used to keep.

Thinking that somebody's pet must have flown the coop, I straightened up slowly and looked toward the sound. Nothing there but a small, non-descript brown bird swinging on a dead weed.

Some birders have a special name for birds like that. They call them "LBBs," or "little brown birds." Without fancy feathers, they often don't rate a second glance.

Siskins are easy to overlook, because they're such nondescript birds. Light brown with faintly streaky breasts and a small splash of yellow, they fade into the background—until they open their mouths. What comes out of that little pointy beak is a loud, chirpy call note that sounds just like my mother's old canaries. But there's no melodious canary song to follow. Instead, siskins hold forth with a series of slurred, wheezy buzzes.

Niger seed and black oil sunflower will get their attention at the feeder, where they show up in gangs to eat alongside their goldfinch cousins. You may spot siskins plucking the seeds out of your pinecones, the food that gives them their name, or gleaning seeds from your garden.

Weeds You Want

All of our gardens are of course perfectly weeded, but if you should happen to overlook a sneaky plant of lamb's-quarters or ragweed, just think of it as siskin food. Plants with multitudes of small, oil-rich seeds—which include many of our most common weeds—are a huge hit with tiny siskins. If you tolerate a few of their favorite weeds in your yard, you'll be able to get a close-up look at their outstanding acrobatic skills. Siskins are smaller than chickadees, but their weight is enough to tip a weed's stem toward the ground. They often hang upside down while cracking seeds at the tip of the stem.

SMART STORAGE

Seeds, grains, nuts, corncobs, and other "dry" feeder items are great food not only for birds. Tiny weevils, meal moths, and other pesky insects like to eat them, too. So do mice and, perish the thought, rats. Molds and bacteria thrive on them, too, when they get moist.

To keep your dry foods safe, store them in metal cans with tight-fitting lids. Galvanized metal trash pails are just the ticket. You can buy the pails and lids in several sizes, including 6 gallon, 10 gallon, 20 gallon, and even 30 gallon monsters.

If your feeder setup is modest, one 10-gallon can, or even a 6-gallon, may be all you need to store your small amount of seed. I feed a lot of birds at a lot of feeders, so I use a variety of sizes to separate my bird foods for easy access.

- The 20-gallon pail holds black oil sunflower seeds, which I buy by the sack whenever they're on sale at a bargain price. I empty the sacks into the can, so that all I have to do is lift the lid and scoop out the seed when I refill the feeders every morning. I often keep a small sack of safflower seed on top of the sunflowers, because I like to mix the two in some feeders, for chickadees, cardinals, and rose-breasted grosbeaks.
- I use two 10-gallon pails for small, dense seeds: millet in one, niger in the other. Each can accommodates at least 25 pounds of little tan or black seeds. I empty the seed sacks into the cans, lay a scoop on top of the seed, and these mainstays are ready when I need them for daily refills.
- I use another 10-gallon can to hold special seed mixes, keeping them in their individual bags. Since I serve them in selective feeders that suit only the birds that like them best, I don't go through these nearly as fast as I do the basics.

If you notice tiny moths fluttering around your birdseed or other bird foods, buy sticky traps to take care of the problem. These critters are most likely meal or flour moths, whose larvae chew into seeds and nuts, turning them into dusty, cobwebby droppings. You can buy moth traps in discount or hardware stores; look for them near the mousetraps.

Speaking of mice, keep the area around your seed cans clean and tidy to prevent attracting them. Sweep or vacuum up any spills right away. Use metal cans so mice can't chew their way into your stored seed. And remember to keep the lids tightly closed—some of these little guys are good climbers, and they can wiggle through surprisingly small spaces.

Don't keep extra suet blocks or other soft foods with your seed. Put them in the fridge instead, or for longer storage, in the freezer. Fat can turn rancid quickly, so store your suet, lard, and homemade or store-bought bird foods made with these or other fats in cold storage. Keep nut oils and nut butters in the refrigerator. Store blocks, doughs, nuggets, and other high-fat foods, including homemade peanut butter treats, in your freezer. The fats and oils will stay fresh for months.

Look Right Here

Instead of mixing bite-size bits, nuggets, and other soft foods in with my regular seed offerings, I serve my special foods and homemade concoctions in three separate feeders. My birds soon become accustomed to checking there for their treats. One feeder is a domed type, so I can lower the lid to keep out piggy starlings. Another sticks to a window, which also helps to keep feeder hogs away. The third is a log feeder, hung horizontally so that both clinging and perching birds can use it. Come winter, though, when it feels good to nurture any bird, I make big batches of soft foods to crumble in the come-one, come-all tray feeders, both high and low. I even serve small amounts right on the ground, where robins come hopping to see what's for dinner this time.

SOFT FOODS

As more and more bird feeders dot the land, a big shift in behavior has begun to take place among wild birds.

Rose-breasted grosbeaks and indigo buntings, once a rare sight at feeders, were seduced by our handouts years ago, and are now a common sight in spring.

Both these birds are seed eaters. But rosies also eat fruit, and they're quickly learning to gobble the newest trend at feeders: soft foods.

Soft foods are a real revolution in bird feeding. Thanks to convenient, commercially available foods, many new species of birds are turning up at our feeders.

Have your everyday chickadees and cardinals had some unusual company lately? Bluebirds, catbirds, thrashers, orioles, warblers, wrens, thrushes, robins, waxwings, and others, once rarely seen at feeders, are quickly becoming everyday visitors.

They've learned to associate our backyard feeders with food. That's a great big leap for a bird brain. And it's great news for us, because now we don't have to wait years to attract a gray catbird to a tempting dish—it may take only days. Thanks to soft foods, the birds are learning to recognize feeding stations as a reliable source of their kind of food.

By offering the soft foods these special birds prefer, instead of only a scattering of ho-hum seeds, you, too, can join the revolution. The more of us there are feeding soft foods, the more likely that birds will make the connection.

SONGBIRDS

"Songbirds" is another name for *passerines,* which means "perching birds." This gigantic group of birds includes more than half of the bird species in the world. Think of a robin or a sparrow, and you've got the idea: These are perching birds, with legs and feet built for closing on a branch or other perch. Three toes front, one toe back, is the arrangement. All of the toes join the leg at the same level, and there's no webbing between them.

Even if the bird spends very little time actually perched, it still is classified as a passerine if its toes are arranged right. Swallows are passerines. So are nuthatches. But not woodpeckers: They have two toes front, two in back.

All of the best singers belong to the passerines. But "songbirds" is a misnomer for many members of this group. Although they all vocalize, and I'm sure their sounds are sweet to the ears of their own kind, it's hard to think of, say, a creaking grackle or a monotone-trill junco as a songbird.

Super Singers

The best singers by far are the thrushes, at least in my opinion. Their voices are hauntingly beautiful, with a fluting timbre that sends chills up my spine. Robins are our most common thrush, so I'm really glad that they're plentiful—their voices fill the spring and summer mornings with song.

Some of the grosbeaks (including the cardinal), wrens, and sparrows are masterful singers, too. Finches and buntings, mockingbirds and other mimic thrushes, and vireos delight the ear, as well. Whoever named wood warblers, though, was pretty far off the mark—most of these birds have high, thin voices with a rapid-fire delivery, instead of the languid, melodious fluting of a thrush.

With so many good singers, we can all have our favorites, just like we do in our music collections at home.

Birding by Ear

Learning the songs and calls of your backyard birds is like learning to interpret a new language. You won't need to speak it yourself, but you can listen in as your backyard birds communicate with each other.

When you hear a song, look around and find the singer. Learning whose voice is whose lets you get an instant inventory of which birds are around, just by listening.

I learned my first birdcalls at my mother's knee. "Hear that thrasher?" she'd say. "He sure sounds happy." Or, "Listen to that blue jay, he's mad about something."

Birds save their full-blown songs for breeding season, so April through June are when you'll hear the most variety. Males are the vocalists, and they're tireless singers. Starting before dawn, a song sparrow, for instance, repeats his song every 8 seconds, more than 2,000 times a day.

SPARROWS, NATIVE

Let me admit right away, I have a soft spot for sparrows. These unassuming little guys delight me when they peck and scratch at the feeder or in the yard, or when I hear their pretty songs in spring.

But I think the main reason I'm fond of them is because they're such a challenge to identify when I'm out exploring. So when the birds show up in my yard, it's satisfying to remember how hard I worked to peg them in the wild.

Identifying a sparrow is trickier than figuring out most birds. Many bird-watchers don't even bother; they just call them "LBBs"—little brown birds. Some have tails edged with white, some have stripes on their heads, some have caps, some have wing bars, but it's tricky to spot the details when the birds are in the brush. To make the challenge even tougher, native sparrows hang out in groups of mixed species.

Most folks pay little attention to the native sparrows that flit about our fields and brush. Still, each species plays an important role in the web of life. This is the grasshopper sparrow, named for its insectlike trill.

Sociable Sparrows

Look for the largest number of native sparrows at your feeders from fall through early spring. With dozens of species covering the country, you're likely to see several different kinds. Sparrows are ground feeders, so they often forage beneath the feeders rather than in them. Let your gardens stand in winter, and you'll find sparrows hopping about among the dead stems, looking for seeds. Any overlooked weed will also be a bonanza to these small seed eaters.

At the feeder, though, it's a different story. Once you get familiar with your usual sparrows—which'll probably include song sparrows, chipping sparrows, white-throated sparrows, and golden-crowned or white-crowned sparrows—it's a lot easier to notice when a stranger shows up in their midst. Who's that bird? Out comes the field guide.

Unlike the imported house sparrow, which you can read about in the entry by that name, native sparrows are terrific feeder guests and welcome backyard residents. Millet is all you need to keep them satisfied. They'll also eagerly peck at cracked corn, chick scratch feed, and other grains, and they may eat finely chopped suet or other soft foods in winter. All species welcome a birdbath or a mister.

SQUIRRELS

Face it—if you feed birds, you're probably going to attract squirrels. Squirrels are plentiful in most parts of the country, and they'll soon find your feeder.

Birds are loath to approach a feeder that has a squirrel munching contentedly in the middle of it. And munch they do. Not only will squirrels clean you out of bird food, they'll also deter the birds from visiting. Just about all feeder foods are fair game, as long as the squirrel can figure out a way to get at the goodies.

Larger nest boxes, such as those for flickers or screech owls, are often taken over by squirrels for their own cozy homes. The animals will chew around an entrance hole to enlarge it. To prevent the problem, mount a metal guard plate over the entrance. You can buy a squirrel guard at bird supply shops and online, or you can use a big, sturdy metal washer from the hardware store. The washers have holes of different sizes; choose one that matches the entrance hole of your birdhouse. A few short screws, and not even squirrel teeth will be able to enlarge the entryway.

Putting up squirrel feeders for cobs of corn or peanuts in the shell can help keep squirrels away from your feeders. If the bushytails are a big problem, buy squirrel-proof feeders, like those described in the entry Anti-Pest Feeders.

A burgeoning population of squirrels spells trouble for backyard birds. These interesting animals are natural predators of bird eggs and nestlings, so you may want to think twice about putting up feeders especially for them. If you bar them from the bird food and eliminate peanut boxes and other temptations, they just might move elsewhere.

STARLINGS

Do you scorn starlings? You're not alone. Most folks despise these birds.

Starlings are noisy birds, squeaking and squabbling, and they hang around in a bunch, gobbling up suet, peanut butter, and other expensive treats in no time flat. They're messy, too, because their diet of mostly soft foods leads to big, splashy droppings that go splat on our cars. And they have a knack for finding any hole in our house siding where they can get in to raise a big, loud, messy family.

Worst of all, say a lot of people, starlings are the reason some of our other birds are declining, because they steal their nesting holes.

Hold it right there!

I'll agree that starlings are messy (but not ugly—I love their starry winter plumage). And they definitely like to eat.

But starlings aren't the reason other bird species are declining.

A 2003 study looked at the effects of starlings on 27 different species of cavity-nesting birds. The researchers concluded that only sapsuckers suffered because of starlings. The other 26 species raised a family just fine, even after starlings snitched one of their holes.

So who is to blame for the dramatic drop in songbirds and other species?

A thumbprint smudge? Smoke in the sky? Nope—a massive flock of starlings flying in close synchronization. The sight is a celebrated event in some European countries.

A Friend Indeed

Next time you stop to smell your roses, thank your starlings. The grubs of rose-eating Japanese beetles are one of their favorite foods. When a flock of starlings waddles about on your lawn, probing with their beaks, grubs are what they're after. That's why I keep a decoy feeder just for starlings—I appreciate their role in keeping nature in balance in my backyard world.

We are. We cut down dead trees in our backyards and orchards, instead of letting the dead limbs become bird homes for cavity nesters. We replace wooden fence posts on pastures with metal ones, and bluebirds go homeless.

In the bigger picture, we chop up the forests, so that 'coons and 'possums can get in and eat bird eggs, and cowbirds can parasitize nests. We let our cats stray, so they can wreak havoc on nesting birds. We buy beef and wood and coffee from Central and South America, so habitat for wintering birds disappears there, too.

If we'd keep our cats indoors instead of letting them roam, we'd save way more songbirds than if we shipped starlings back to England. Which might not be such a bad idea, because starlings recently landed on England's endangered list—their numbers have plummeted by more than 80 percent since 1964.

"We have long suspected, and the research confirms, that the decline of starlings is closely related to changes in agricultural practice, such as the increased use of pesticides and the loss of pasture and unimproved grassland which has reduced food sources available to birds," reported Michael Meacher, former UK environment minister, in a 2009 article in the *Guardian* newspaper.

Starlings and house sparrows are beloved birds in England, and both species are in serious trouble. Preservation efforts are underway.

The Good Side of Starlings

Starlings may not be drop-dead gorgeous on the ground, but they're breathtaking in flight. The birds move in synchronization, like iron filings pulled by a magnet.

"Bird watchers are being invited to marvel at the wonder of up to 45,000 starlings swooping over the Sussex coast every evening at dusk," began a BBC feature in the fall of 2009.

The Danes, too, flock to see the phenomenal flocks. When a million birds gather on the coast of their country, they call it the "Black Sun."

Unfortunately, starlings adore soft foods, and keeping them from gobbling your offerings can be difficult. A close-fitting dome, a too-small entrance hole, or a weighted feeder will bar them. But it'll also keep out other, desirable birds. And when times are really tough, as during a snowstorm, the clever starlings may quickly outwit "starling-proof" feeders. A decoy feeder that draws starlings away from your other feeders is an alternative; see the entry Decoy Feeders to learn how to set one up.

Not only will starlings take over birdhouses, they'll weasel their way into holes in your siding or soffits to nest inside the wall. As soon as you spot starlings taking an interest in your house, find the weak spot and make repairs lickety-split.

SUET AND SUET FEEDERS

Talk about a convenience food—suet blocks are the best thing since sliced bread. Remove the wrapper, slide the block into a cage, and presto, chickadees, titmice, nuthatches, woodpeckers, and lots of other birds arrive like magic.

Suet is smooth, white fat from the loin and kidney areas of an animal, and birds love it (just as they do the other fats you'll find in the entry Fats and Oils). But suet blocks aren't just fat. Most of them have seeds and grains added to the suet, supposedly to make them more appealing to birds.

Maybe I'm too suspicious, but I suspect it's because those ingredients are cheaper than suet. Adding them to the block fills up a lot of space, so less fat is needed. The cracked corn and seeds in the block will also attract gangs of house sparrows and squirrels, which don't frequent plain suet blocks.

On the other hand, I've been delighted with the Oregon Suet Block, enriched only with insects. It's been given the seal of approval by my tanagers, wrens, warblers, and other less common birds, as well as by the usual crop of chickadees and other familiar friends. Squirrels and sparrows don't touch it.

It's nearly impossible to keep a determined starling away from suet, but an upside-down feeder gives a downy woodpecker and other suet lovers a fighting chance to grab a few bites of fat.

Overflow Crowd

In winter, when suet is in high demand, it's nice to have several suet feeders to handle the crowd. For a quick homemade suet feeder, just fill a plastic mesh bag with chunks of suet or beef fat trimmings. Recycled bags from onions, potatoes, or flower bulbs work great. Just fill it with the fat, tie it shut at the top, and hang it for your suet lovers.

Before I buy a suet block with extra "attractions," I read the label. You'll be surprised at how misleading they can be. A block that was called something like Peanut Treat, for instance, had mostly cracked corn. The peanut part of the treat? That was peanut flavoring, not any nuts themselves.

Still, no matter how aggravated I get at manufacturers that try to pull the wool over our eyes, I still buy plenty of suet blocks. Mostly, I buy plain suet blocks, which are getting harder to find. But no matter what's in the block, you'll still get lots of bird fun for only a buck or two—and priceless convenience.

Suet Feeders

An inexpensive wire cage works great for a suet feeder—unless you're plagued with starlings, which can scarf down the whole block in a day or two.

Hanging wire cages also make it hard for the newer birds that are frequenting our feeders to get a bite. Perching birds like orioles, tanagers, catbirds, and others find it more difficult to get a grip than acrobatic chickadees. But as these birds learn to associate the cage with food, even they can master the swinging setup.

Mounting the cage to a board or buying a feeder with a mounted suet holder works better for perching birds. It's also an improvement for

HOW-TO A-Tisket, A-Tasket . . .

. . . A chickadee basket! Mini suet baskets are charming and useful. Decorate them with red bows, and you have a perfect gift for your bird-loving friends. You can find the baskets at craft stores for about 50 cents or less, or by the bag.

1 suet block, plain if possible
Aluminum foil
4 to 5 mini baskets, about 3 inches in diameter
1 cup sunflower chips
½ cup chopped peanuts
Floral wire or raffia
Narrow red ribbon, optional

1. Break the suet block into four pieces and melt it in the microwave or in a saucepan over low heat. In my microwave, it takes about 2 minutes on high to melt a plain block, but your microwave may vary.

Mini suet baskets are perfect for chickadees.

2. Meanwhile, make a "nest" of crumpled aluminum foil for each basket. Use the foil to support the baskets in an upright position on a cookie sheet.

3. Remove the melted suet from the microwave. Let it cool, stirring occasionally, until it begins to thicken. Stir in the sunflower chips and peanuts.

4. Spoon the mixture into the baskets, dividing it evenly among them.

5. Refrigerate the tray for at least 2 hours or overnight, until the suet is hardened.

6. Attach a loop of floral wire or raffia for hanging, and tie a small red ribbon on the handle, if you like.

large woodpeckers, including the pileated, which can prop their tails against the board to help support them while they eat.

The design still won't deter starlings, though. For that, you can try an upside-down suet feeder, in which the block is held horizontally beneath a roof. It'll slow the starlings down, but it's not starling-proof. Determined birds can still get at the fat. To thwart them entirely, you'll need a suet cage inside a larger cage. The openings in the outer cage allow smaller birds to enter, but keep out starlings and squirrels. Be sure the suet holder inside the cage doesn't rest against the outer bars; if it does, starlings will happily peck away at the all-too-tempting fat.

SUMMER SLOWDOWN

No matter how many good things you put out at your feeders, it's natural to see a dramatic drop-off in backyard birds in late spring or early summer.

The crowds that visited from fall through spring are now dispersed to nesting grounds, so there aren't as many birds in the area. Now that it's time for family life, the birds that remain to nest in your area are looking for insects, the food of choice at this time of year. Parent birds may still drop in to fill up on feeder foods, but until their fledglings leave the nest, you won't see them as often as you did before. They won't linger, either—with the kids waiting at home, their visits will be grab-and-go.

You can take a break from bird feeding in summer if you like, or you can keep the buffet going year-round. Any birds that are nesting in your backyard or nearby will appreciate having a reliable food source near at hand. Cut down on the amount you put out, so that it stays fresh.

Hummingbirds dwindle in summer, too, for the same reasons. Once the family leaves the nest, though, they'll be back, with the youngsters in tow. Reduce the amount of nectar in your feeders when the traffic drops off, but keep your feeder in place—the hummers may still be visiting even if you never catch them in the act.

You're likely to see more customers at your birdbath than at your feeders in summer, so keep it brimming with fresh, clean water. Now's the time to consider beefing up your attraction with a mister or fountain, which'll really bring in the birds on hot summer days.

Wild fruit ripens in summer, drawing more birds away from your backyard. Instead of losing your friends, why not plant some blueberries, elderberries, cherries, or other fruits to keep them close to home?

Summer Nectar Needs

If you have even a single hummer visiting your feeder in summer, you probably have a nesting pair nearby. For these birds, your nectar feeder is even more important now; it may have been the reason they nested nearby to begin with. Make sure you have hummingbird flowers to fill in the gap if you go on vacation, or ask a neighbor to keep your feeder filled.

SUNFLOWERS

Every time I drive past acres of farm fields crowded with smiling sunflowers, I wonder, "How in the world do they keep the birds out of them?" Turns out that sunflower farmers around the world ask themselves the same thing. Timely cutting is key, notes one farmers' guide: As soon as the backs of the sunflower heads turn brown, an indicator that the seeds are ripe, the grower should jump to it. Crop loss increases with every day the flowers are left standing.

In Australia, where massive flocks of cockatoos, numbering in the thousands, wander the

HOW-TO Sunflower Faces

Ripe sunflower head, stem removed
Several "fingers" of millet, available at pet shops
Ornamental grass seedheads
Foxtail grass seedheads (reserve 1 for "nose")
Strawflowers
Quick-drying glue
Floral wire
Over-the-door wreath hook

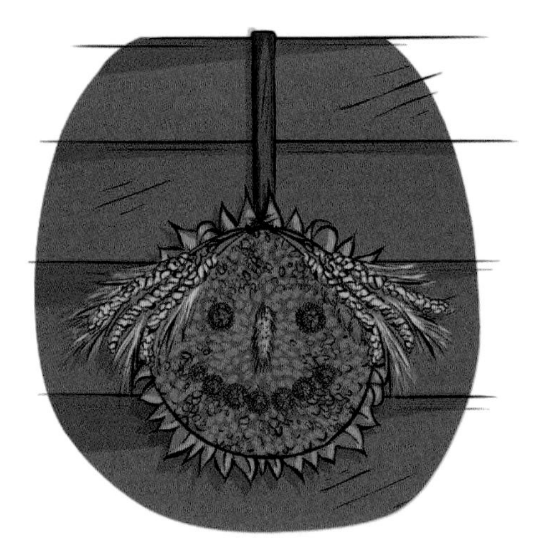

Make your birds a smiling seed face.

1. To fashion the "hair" for your sunflower face, make two small, similar bouquets of millet, ornamental grass seedheads, and foxtail grass seedheads, and wrap the stem ends with floral wire to hold them together. Leave about 8 inches of wire free at the end of each bundle.

2. To attach the hair, set one bundle on top of the sunflower face toward the right, and poke the end of the wire through the rim of the sunflower. Repeat with the second bundle on the left. Twist the wires together so the hair stays in place at the center "part" where the bundles touch.

3. Glue on strawflowers for eyes and mouth.

4. Glue a foxtail grass seedhead (no stem) above the mouth, vertically, to create the nose.

5. Hang the wreath on your fence, gate, or garden shed to attract the birds.

fields, the answer isn't easy: Decoy crops, which are successful in oats and other grain plantings, don't work with sunflowers. Why? "The main problem is rendering the main crop less attractive than the decoy," explained Australian researcher Mary Bomford at a conference at the University of Nebraska in 1992.

In other words, some birds love sunflower seeds so much, it's difficult to find something they like better.

We already know that at the feeder. And the same is true in the garden. I've seen chickadees, titmice, nuthatches, goldfinches, jays, cardinals, woodpeckers, and many other birds working on sunflowers as they stand. No cockatoos yet, but I'm waiting.

Head Start

Harvest some of your homegrown sunflower seedheads so you can enjoy watching birds pluck out the seeds in close view. Leave a piece of stem attached to the seedhead, so that you can wrap it with twine for hanging. The bird bouquet will add a homey touch on fence or lamppost.

Couldn't Be Easier

Sunflowers sprout so easily and grow so quickly that you've probably already had a crop—every spring. Seeds dropped by birds germinate fast and furious after winter, as well as throughout the year, whenever there's a rain.

I let a lot of these volunteers grow. It's just birdseed on the stem, after all, and even the puny little heads on overcrowded plants attract finches and other birds to the feast.

Sunflowers sprout elsewhere in our yards, too, wherever jays tucked a gulletful of seeds into the soil or mulch. These birds have a penchant for planting, and they only retrieve a fraction of the seeds, nuts, or acorns they stick undercover for safekeeping. If you've ever wondered why little clusters of sunflower seedlings sprout here and there in your yard or gardens, now you know—it's jays that deserve the thanks.

Twenty years ago, the only sunflowers for the garden were the typical mammoth type, and a branching, small-flowered whitish variety. Then the country-style decorating craze hit, and a fad for sunflowers was born.

These days, you'll find varieties in dozens of sizes, colors, and forms. Some are shaggy, some humongous, some full-size flowers on knee-high plants. All of them are simple to grow, and all are welcomed by birds, as soon as the seeds ripen.

All you need is a patch of soil in full sun. Poke the seeds into the ground, cover them up, give them a drink, and before long, your feeders-on-a-stem will be reaching for the stars.

T/U/V

TRANSLATING BIRD LANGUAGE

Birds have a whole vocabulary of songs and calls, but you don't need to know their language to grasp the point they're trying to get across. The more you listen to your birds, the more you'll understand them.

Think of that robin in your backyard. You've heard all three of his main types of vocalizations, though the bird may be such a part of the background that you haven't really listened to him. Here's what he's been saying.

- **I'm king of all I survey.** Your robin greets the day with song, and he keeps it up, off and on, all day long during nesting season. The song is a long, lovely, lilting tune that sounds something like *cheerily, cheer up, cheer up, cheerily, cheer up.* It's one of the prettiest birdsongs in the backyard and a major part of the dawn chorus at most of our homes. Male birds sing around the perimeter of their nesting territory, so if a bird is perched and singing in your yard, at least part of your yard has been claimed—and may hold a nest.
- **Could be trouble . . .** This is an early warning sign that the robin is uneasy. It's a simple, one syllable *chuck* or *yeep*. The robin may repeat it, while flicking its wings and tail nervously.
- **It *is* trouble!** No doubt about it, your robin is saying something is seriously wrong. This call is a fast, harsh, repeated *chirr chirr CHIRR CHIRR* that gets louder as it goes on. Often, the bird utters this call when it's chasing off a predator or another male that dared trespass into its nesting territory.
- **I love you.** When they're courting or singing to their partners, male birds and sometimes

Warning Signs

Alarm calls are sharp and sudden, no matter which bird is sounding the alert. Once you start listening, you'll be able to hear the panic or scolding in the voice. When you hear an alarm call, pay attention: You may be getting close to a nest, or there may be a predator around that you can help the bird fend off. If other birds join in and add their voices to the alarm, you can tell they're banding together against a serious threat—usually a snake, crow, or owl. Check out the commotion: Your appearance may scare off the stalker.

females occasionally sing a "whisper song": a quiet, intimate piece of music that's utterly romantic. The song has a whispery quality to it, sounding something like *hissalee, hissalee.* Consider yourself extra lucky if you get to hear a bird's whisper song; usually, it's delivered in private.

- **Hey, guys, I'm here, too.** When a flock of robins is feeding, you may hear the birds keeping in touch with each other by uttering a thin, high-pitched note that sounds a lot like that of a cedar waxwing. Robins also use this call in flight, maybe as a way to keep track of each other.

Other birds have their own versions of these kinds of calls. Not all species sing a whisper song or use a contact note, but you'll definitely hear territorial songs, call notes, and alarm calls from every bird within earshot, once you start listening.

Learn to recognize the calls of baby birds, too: a rhythmic cheeping, very faint when birds are newly hatched, but getting louder day by day.

UMAMI

Sweet, salty, sour, bitter . . . and umami. Umami? Yes, there are five, not four, distinct types of flavors in our sense of taste.

The fifth flavor has only recently been recognized, although it was first discovered a century ago. Back then, a Japanese researcher, trying to figure out what it was about seaweed broth that tasted so good, isolated the molecule responsible—it was glutamate. Does that word sound familiar? We know it better as monosodium glutamate (MSG).

The taste of foods that contain glutamate is now called umami, which means "savory" in Japanese.

Foods that taste umami (boy, doesn't that sound odd) have a rich, satisfying flavor.

Meat is umami. Crab and lobster, umami. Seaweed broth? Umami. Soy sauce? Anchovies? Parmesan cheese? Gouda? Iberian ham? You guessed it, all umami. Even ripe tomatoes taste umami (which makes the name 'Beefsteak' not far off the mark).

Umami foods are high in protein, of which glutamate is a building block. When something makes us lick our lips at the delicious flavor—not quite sweet, not quite salty; why, it must be umami!—we're responding to the protein in it. No wonder these foods make us feel so satisfied.

It wasn't until 2000, almost a hundred years

Finding the Fat

The science of taste still has a long way to go. Kirk Klasing, an animal nutritionist at the University of California–Davis, suspects that birds also have a receptor for fat—and I'd say that the circumstantial evidence sure agrees. Just think of all the birds that enjoy high-fat suet at our feeders. Knowing about umami makes me want to experiment—maybe my bluebirds and rose-breasted grosbeaks would enjoy some bread soaked in high-protein seaweed broth?

after glutamate was isolated, that our taste receptors that connect to umami were identified. And, guess what—birds have them, too!

Kirk Klasing, an animal nutrition expert at the University of California–Davis, recently discovered that birds can taste umami. And seeds that are high in protein are nearly always high in fat, as well. So the birds' sense of taste leads them to foods that will fuel them through a long migration or keep them warm on a cold winter night.

All those dogwood berries and other native fall berries that birds devour during migration? All the poison ivy berries they gulp down in winter? Now we know why birds seek them out: They're unmistakably umami.

VOLUNTEER PLANTS

Birds are a great source of free plants. Every year, young trees, vines, and shrubs will sprout in your yard from the seeds that pass undigested through their bodies after the birds have chowed down on berries. My yard is full of seedling redbuds, for instance, which were "planted" by chickadees that ate their seeds elsewhere. I have some dogwood seedlings, too, plus sassafras, holly, Virginia creeper, bittersweet, and way more hackberry trees than I could ever need.

You can count on these volunteer seedlings to grow into plants favored by birds, or birds wouldn't have eaten the berries or seeds that spread them. I transplant my baby trees in fall to the locations where I want them, and they grow fast—2 to 3 feet a year. It takes about 7 years for a dogwood to flower, but the time slips by surprisingly fast.

Some bird-planted volunteers aren't exactly my cup of tea, even though I love birds and plants. I yank out the poison ivy, most of the pokeweed and wild river grape, the giant ragweed, and the wintercreeper seedlings.

Wherever you live, you're going to find the same situation: volunteer plants that were sown in your yard by the birds. Start looking for them, and learn to identify them when they're young. Then you can move them to better locations in your yard, where they will grow to supply bird-approved berries in a few years.

Moving Time

Transplant seedling trees in mid-fall, before they lose their leaves. The soil will still be warm enough to encourage good root growth before the ground freezes. Lift the plants with a shovel, keeping as much soil on the roots as you can. Water them thoroughly after you move them, and let fall leaves pile up around your little nursery for insulation over winter.

W/X/Y/Z

WAXWINGS

If you had asked me just a few years ago whether cedar waxwings would ever be feeder birds, I'd have said "No way!" Oops, guess again. The birds are now visiting not only my feeder, but others across the country.

Waxwings are still unusual guests, and I still feel honored every time they deign to drop in. But I'm guessing that in a few years, most of us will be delighting in these fabulous, sleek birds right in our own backyards.

Waxwings have always been quick to come for fruit and juicy berries, which is one of the reasons I lugged in five—count 'em, five—big clumps of shadblow trees (*Amelanchier arborea*) to my yard. Shadblows, also known as Juneberries and serviceberries, are American natives that have clusters of sweet, blueberry-like fruits, and waxwings can't resist.

Cherry trees are their other top fave, so I planted two of those, too. Natural fruit is always a sure way to lure waxwings, but now these birds are branching out.

It was an oriole feeder that turned the tide at my place. The multi-purpose feeder was freshly stocked with orange halves, grape jelly, and a handful of mealworms when a small flock of waxwings happened to come by on one of their neighborhood patrols. I'm not sure exactly what it was that caught their eye, but soon they were alighting in the tree above the feeder. I could hardly believe my eyes when the bravest bird fluttered down to the feeder, looked brightly at the different foods, and dipped its beak into the grape jelly.

That was all it took to break the ice, and before long more birds in the flock were taking turns getting a bite to eat. Before long, though, as if someone had turned a switch, the flock up and left, moving on to the next fast-food fly-thru.

Cedar waxwings are the birds most of us see, with the similar, bigger Bohemian waxwings usually staying in the North. Both types are gorgeous creatures, with sleek feathers in subtle colors, a backswept crest, and a dramatic black mask. It's a picture-perfect outfit, especially with that little zingy red touch on their

How Sweet It Is

Sweet, juicy fruits are the way to win a waxwing's favor, on plants, that is. So far, the birds seem to be mostly interested in jelly and mealworms at my feeders, although they've also sampled a fruity bird dough I made with chopped fresh apples, raisins, peanut butter, and suet.

wings. The red is actual wax, and why it's there, no one knows. Whatever the reason, it sure is pretty.

The birds, which hang out in groups of a dozen or more, are opportunistic feeders. They range about widely, looking for good feeding opportunities for the flock. When they spy a fruit tree or a creek where insects are rising off the water, they settle in and gorge themselves. Then it's on to the next.

WEED SEEDS

Sometimes I wonder what native sparrows, juncos, and finches ate before European weeds covered our country. These birds, and others, eat what must be tons of seeds of dandelions, chickweed, chicory, filaree, lamb's-quarters, pigweed, and every other weed that came to America after 1492.

Weeds are an important source of food for all sparrows, juncos, buntings, finches, cardinals, towhees, meadowlarks, horned larks, and other seed eaters. More than a third of the diet of lazuli buntings, for instance, is weed seeds. Horned larks are partial to filaree; western towhee species like tarweed; vesper sparrows zero in on chickweed; goldfinches love thistle; and dandelions are a magnet for white-crowned sparrows, indigo buntings, and goldfinches. The list goes on and on.

Not all of the weed seeds that birds eat get digested. Some pass through whole, and disperse the weeds to new places. I seem to be always weeding out giant ragweed from around my open tray feeder. That's the feeder my cardinals like best. Guess which weed seed cardinals favor? Giant ragweed, of course.

Ornamental Weeds

Lamb's-quarters (*Chenopodium album*) is a weed, but since it's edible, you can find seed for selected strains, including colorful 'Fire Red' or 'Magenta Spreen'. Whether you grow the green weedy type or the salad greens, lamb's-quarters is an interesting addition to your flowerbed. Combine it with bright red or mixed color zinnias, cosmos, and other exuberant annuals for an unusual and handsome combination. The dense, nubbly seedheads are ornamental, and the myriad of seeds will nourish native sparrows, juncos, and other seed eaters all winter long.

Arching foxtail grass lends grace to casual flowerbeds and supplies zillions of seeds for fall and winter foraging. This common weed is actually a millet.

WINDOW BOXES

Window boxes offer the potential of bringing birds right up to the other side of the glass. Fill the boxes with hummingbird-attracting flowers in spring and summer. Fuchsias, bright-colored geraniums, scented geraniums, 'Gartenmeister' impatiens, and salvias are good choices for a window box, and hummingbirds will soon be visiting their flowers. Tuck small nectar feeders on short stakes among the plants to up the ante and encourage the birds to linger.

Cut back or remove the plants in fall, and transform your window boxes into winter bird feeders. You can sprinkle seed and other treats right on the soil to coax birds up to your window. This is a good opportunity to try a premium seed mix for chickadees and cardinals, or to make your own out of sunflower seed, sunflower chips, and safflower. Add a few peanuts in the shell to tempt jays, too.

Birds at the Window

Instead of using birdseed in your bare winter window boxes, you can stick branches of holly, winterberry, western toyon, and other berried shrubs into them. Insert the stems into the soil as far as you can, so that the branches are firmly anchored. Robins, mockingbirds, waxwings, and other fruit eaters may come to pluck the berries off the boughs.

WINDOWS

Sooner or later, you're going to hear the heartbreaking *thump* of a bird hitting the glass, especially if you have large windows or patio doors. Birds don't see windows as a danger, and that's the problem. The reflection of your yard or the sky on the glass fools them into thinking there's no barrier.

When I lived in a house with a plate glass window on one side, I heard that dreadful thump at least once every few days. Migration season was the worst; then, collisions were a daily occurrence until I covered the window.

No one really knows how many birds break their necks on windows every year, but biologist Dan Klem of Muhlenberg College, in Allentown, Pennsylvania, one of the top researchers into the

If a bird decides your window is his rival, cover the glass, or lay a rubber snake on the sill to scare him off.

problem, estimates it may kill 100 million birds annually in North America.

Bird Protectors

To protect the birds from crashing into your windows, you'll need to put something on the outside of the glass, not the inside, because it's the reflection that's the problem.

Decals work, a little. But unless you plaster your window with them, there will still be large areas of glass left uncovered. For better protection, try one of these methods. You'll find the products at bird supply stores or craft shops. Or check the Resources section near the back of this book.

First Aid for Victims

Not all collisions result in death, so don't dawdle when you hear that thump. A bird on the ground is highly vulnerable to predators. Go outside and look for the victim, who will usually be near the base of the wall, sitting stunned.

A bird that has just run smack into a window may look like it's on death's door. It will be wobbly and weak, and often its feathers will be puffed up. No matter how sad the bird looks, it's worth

Protecting Birds at Your Windows

These solutions should save your birds from broken necks. Compare the convenience and the costs to choose a method for making your windows bird-safe.

PRODUCT	COMMENTS
Fiberglass screen for the outside of the window	Available in several sizes that you cut for a custom fit, these screens are framed top and bottom for a tidy look. You'll be able to see through them, just as you do with a regular window screen. Prices start at about $20.
Removable nonreflective vinyl film	This material, which won't block your view, sticks to the outside of the window. A roll that will fit a sliding patio door costs about $35 to $40.
Frosted-glass window film	Apply this product to the outside, not the inside, of your window to eliminate the reflection. Your view won't be as clear, but you'll still be able to see the light. A roll about 26 inches wide by 5 feet long costs about $16.
Decals	Widely available, stick-on decals break up the reflection. But they still leave big parts of the window unprotected. A hawk decal may fool birds into keeping their distance.
Glass paint	Easy to apply, transparent, and relatively inexpensive. Look for glass paint at art supply stores and craft shops.
Poster paint	Inexpensive but not see-through, poster paints or tempera paints let you apply your own reflection-busters to the glass instead of buying decals.

HOW-TO Safety Screen

Hang this screen on the outside of your window to prevent collisions. It'll also discourage birds from attacking their own reflections. This is a simple project, but you'll need a helper to handle the slippery and sticky materials.

Fiberglass window screening (sold by the roll at hardware and home supply stores)
Measuring tape
Scissors
2-inch wide waterproof tape, in black or a color that blends with your house
An awl or other tool for poking holes
4 suction-cup hooks

1. Measure your window. Subtract 3 inches from the height and 4 inches from the width, and cut a piece of window screening to those dimensions.

2. Have a helper hold the end of the tape while you measure and cut a piece to the width of your screen. Working carefully so the tape stays flat and doesn't stick to itself, lay it sticky side up on a flat work surface.

3. With your helper, carefully align and press the top edge of the screen onto the bottom inch of the tape along its width.

4. Fold the tape over the screen so that it forms a tidy edge.

5. Repeat the tape treatment on the bottom edge of the screen.

A simple outside screen will head off many bird collisions at your windows.

6. Poke a hole in each of the four corners of the screen, so that you can hang it on the hooks. Make the hole through the tape about 2 inches in from the sides of the screen.

7. Measure the distance between the holes, and attach the suction-cup hooks accordingly to the top of your window. Attach the lower hooks about a half-inch higher than the actual measurement, so that there's a little slack in the screen.

8. Mount the screen on the hooks.

giving it a chance at rescue. You'll be amazed at how often the worst-looking "hopeless cases" recover.

Put the bird in a shoe box lined with crumpled tissues, and cover the box with a dish towel while you poke air holes in the lid. Replace the towel with the lid, and let the bird recuperate for an hour or so indoors. Then carry the box outside, and check the bird. Usually, the victim has recovered by then, and it'll quickly fly away.

WOOD WARBLERS

Tiny, active birds, wood warblers flit through the treetops and shrubs in search of insects, their main food. A handful of the more than 50 North American species nests in backyards, but you're likely to see many more kinds passing through your place during migration.

Or maybe not. Wood warblers are among the birds that are dropping fast in numbers, because of habitat destruction, fragmentation, pesticides, and increased predation by cowbirds. Twenty years ago, I used to make a game out of seeing how many species I could spot each April, and for years I managed to tick off every one on my regional list—more than 40 different warblers. Nowadays, I'm lucky to spot a dozen species in spring.

There's a bright note here, though: Wood warblers are learning to adapt to our backyards, occasionally for nesting, but more often for food and water. Spring and fall migration, which peak in late April and September for most of us, is when you'll see the most warblers in your yard. Some species hang around all winter,

After foraging at the flowers of your spring-blooming trees during migration, this male Cape May warbler and other wood warbler species may make the jump to your feeder.

It's a Cling Thing

Warblers are agile birds that can easily cling to wire feeders. A simple suet cage makes a good holder for suet blocks and other high-fat offerings. Use a wire mesh feeder or nut feeder for homemade bird doughs, bite-size bits, and other high-fat enticements. Invest in a feeder with a suet cage inside another cage, too, so these small birds can eat without having to compete with larger birds at your other feeder.

including the yellow-rumped Audubon's and myrtle warblers.

Orange-crowned warblers, Cape May warblers, and others visit nectar feeders. Yellow-rumped warblers have been visitors at suet feeders for a few years, and pine warblers and black-throated blues have now joined them as feeder regulars. Other species may show up at any time.

What's made the difference? Soft foods and mealworms. Insect-eating birds are crazy about suet and peanut butter, as well as high-fat foods that include those ingredients. A dish of mealworms gets their attention, too.

Yellow-rumped warblers, one of the most abundant species, love the berries of junipers and bayberry. And all warblers are attracted by the sound of water. Even if they're not yet ready to sample your food, they'll appreciate a shower in your mister.

WOODPECKERS

If you ever want proof that more and more birds are adapting to backyard feeders, put up a pileated woodpecker suet feeder. This heavy-duty wooden model holds the suet securely and gives the giant bird a comfortable place to support its heavy body while it chews the fat. I live quite a ways from the woods, but this bird of the forest regularly makes the journey to my backyard.

Suet is the standard for woodpeckers, but branch out with other soft foods, too. Woodpeckers like them all, whether it's a homemade batch of peanut butter dough, a mesh bag of fat scraps, or store-bought nuggets. Nuts, both peanuts and tree nuts, beckon to these birds, too. Some also eat mealworms. Sunflower seeds and chips are eagerly eaten, and an ear of corn will get takers, too, especially red-headed and red-bellied woodpeckers.

What do all of these foods have in common? Umami, for one thing—the savory flavor that indicates high protein. In these foods, that nourishing protein goes hand in hand with high fat, another must for these birds.

Woodpeckers also eat a lot of fruit, and some have taken to sipping from our nectar feeders. Mix up some fruity recipes for these guys, and you'll satisfy their sweet tooth and their penchant for protein and fat.

Dead-Wood Delights

Dead wood attracts woodpeckers like magic, because it holds the promise of insect larvae. If your yard is short on natural snags, "plant" one! Just haul home a good-size dead limb whenever you spot one, dig a hole about 2 feet deep, and set it in as you would a 4 × 4 post. Smear peanut butter or lard on the snag, and your woodpeckers will soon learn to recognize it as their feeder. For pileated woodpeckers and flickers, add a log to your yard as a horizontal ground-level feeder. Scatter nuts and sunflower seed on top, and spread peanut butter, suet, or other fats on it.

WRENS

I'm starting to feel like a broken record, but the message I'm repeating is great news for us backyard bird lovers: Wrens are another family of birds that's recently learning to come to feeders, and soft foods are the reason why.

To attract house wrens, winter wrens, Carolina wrens, Bewick's wrens, and other species, offer mealworms, suet, and high-fat foods, either homemade or store-bought. Fruity mixes appeal to them, too, so add chopped dried fruit to your suet or peanut butter recipes.

Put up a birdhouse, too. It's a surefire way to make your backyard more appealing to house wrens, and other species may also be interested in the accommodations.

Just Right for Wrens

Wrens seem to be constantly in motion, exploring every nook and cranny for the insects and spiders they crave. These birds can cling to rocks, flutter at walls, hitch across the eaves—and easily access any feeder you put your wren foods in. A simple suet cage works just fine, but, as for other small birds, they'll also appreciate a more protected dining area where they won't be disturbed by bigger birds. I use a domed feeder with the roof lowered to allow only small birds access. Caged feeders that bar bigger birds will do the trick, too.

The itty-bitty winter wren appreciates a handout of suet, mealworms, and other soft foods.

XTRAS

With all of the new birds coming to our backyards, the foods we once thought of as occasional treats have become must-haves in the daily menu. Make sure you keep suet blocks and soft foods such as doughs and nuggets available to satisfy the less common birds at your feeder, as well as the regulars that have quickly learned to love them.

With food needs taken care of, and your birdbath brimming full, you can add extras such as birdhouses, nesting materials, and a mister or fountain. For edible extras, check out the entry Eggs and Eggshells for possibilities in nesting season.

Seed-eating birds have a special organ called the crop above their stomachs. This is where the hard seeds and nuts they eat get ground up before passing through the rest of their digestive systems. The small pieces of grit that birds pick up help the grinding muscles break down their food.

Keep a pile of coarse sand near your feeders, so birds have a handy source for replenishing their supply. Mourning doves are especially attracted to it, but sparrows and juncos help themselves frequently, too, and sometimes an entire flock of evening grosbeaks settles in to eat the sand. You can buy boxed grit at pet shops to use instead of sand, if you'd rather.

Crushed oyster shells are another occasional offering you may want to add. Like eggshells, they supply calcium to female birds during nesting season. Make it easy for the moms, and offer the crushed shells in a small dish or separate feeder, so they don't have to wade through seeds to find it. Look for bagged crushed oyster shells at farm supply stores, where they're stocked for folks who raise chickens.

Spaghetti on the Side

My compost pile has been one of my best bird feeders. When I threw leftover cooked pasta onto the pile, I learned that brown thrashers are quick to snatch it up. Now I offer it at my feeders as well as on the pile. Same with pumpkin and melons—catbirds and thrashers peck out the flesh, and titmice and cardinals enjoy the seeds.

YEAR AFTER YEAR

Birds are creatures of habit. Once they discover a good source of food or an ideal nesting site, they'll return to the same place next year.

If you're late getting your nectar feeder out in spring, you may have seen a newly arrived hummer hovering right where the feeder usually goes. If cardinals choose your climbing rose for their nest, there's a good chance the birds will be back same time next year. If it's not the original pair themselves, their offspring are likely to move in.

John James Audubon proved the point way back in 1803, when he started wondering if the phoebes that returned to a nest site were the same birds. To test his theory, he did a little birdbanding experiment: "When they were about to leave the nest, I fixed a light silver thread to the leg of each, loose enough not to hurt the part, but so fastened that no exertions of theirs could remove it. At the next year's season . . . I had the pleasure of finding two of them had the little ring on the leg."

These kinds of connections are what make our

Creatures of Habit

Consistency works best when you want birds to return to your yard. Whether they're once-a-year visitors or everyday regulars, birds quickly learn to expect the same foods in the same feeders they visited last week—or last year. Pick a place for your feeding station, and keep it there. Then you can add new feeders elsewhere in the yard. Your birds will discover them, too, and return for more of the same.

relationship with our own backyard birds so rewarding. In late winter, you can watch your chickadees or nuthatches start checking out their birdhouse. In March, you can watch for your phoebe, the one that nests on your window ledge. In April, you can greet the orange-crowned warbler that visits each year for a sip of nectar. In May, you can wait for your rose-breasted grosbeaks and buntings to show up for sunflower seeds. And so it goes, all around the year.

ZONES FOR PLANTING

What hardiness zone do you live in? If you're a gardener, you'll have the answer at the tip of your tongue, because your zone number is one of the big criteria for determining whether a plant you're lusting after will survive in your yard.

I'm Zone 6b, thank you very much. But that doesn't mean I don't try out Zone 7 plants. And it doesn't mean every plant rated for Zone 6 will thrive at my place.

Take tall English delphiniums, for instance, those fabulous hybrids that send up flower spikes almost as tall as me, in catch-your-breath blue and romantic pastels. They're hardy in Zones 3 to 8, a nice, wide spread for such a gorgeous plant.

Sure enough, in my Zone 6 eastern Pennsylvania garden, they were the centerpiece, getting bigger and better every year. In my Zone 8 Pacific Northwest garden, they were showstoppers, too, and they kept blooming for months.

But in my Zone 6b southern Indiana garden, they're duds. Giant delphiniums like life on the cool side. No matter how I coddle them, there's simply no way to shield the plants from the humid summer heat that saps their strength. Seedlings rarely come back a second year, and if one does survive long enough to bloom, it's a puny stalk, not a 5-footer.

Those zone ratings are from the USDA's map of hardiness zones, first published in 1960, and still the standard. Plants in catalogs and nurseries are routinely tagged with their zone numbers, so that we can choose plants that will survive in our area.

But the USDA map is based on just one factor: how cold it gets in winter. As my delphiniums tell me every year (yes, I keep trying!), it's not only winter cold that determines whether a plant will thrive. Good growth depends on summer heat, humidity, water, wind, soil, and the length of the growing season, too.

Another climate zone map, created by Sunset Books, takes most elements of climate and conditions into consideration. Originally for Western gardeners, the Sunset map has been expanded to cover the entire country. Unfortunately, though, it's still the USDA zone numbers that most plants carry on nursery labels and in reference books.

Another drawback to the USDA zones is that the map hasn't been updated since 1990. In the past 20 years, there've been some big changes climate-wise.

For a dramatic look at the differences, check out the comparison between the national Arbor Day Foundation's map of 2006, created by analyzing newer data, and the USDA map; you can see the differences for yourself at www.arborday.org/media/map_change.cfm. My southwestern Indiana yard is no longer Zone 6b, according to the Arbor Day map; I've made the leap to Zone 7.

Zone numbers are a great place to start when it comes to choosing plants. But they're not foolproof. No matter which zone map you follow, keep in mind that it's based on averages of weather data. An unusually harsh winter can take its toll, no matter what zone the map says you're in.

Resources

Bird Food and Feeders

The seeds and soft foods mentioned in this book are widely available at discount stores, farm stores, and bird supply stores. You'll find a selection of feeders at these places, too, along with some birdbaths, including classic concrete or pottery pedestal models, and usually some birdhouses, too. Ask about anti-pest models, if problem animals like bear, deer, squirrels, or other critters are scarfing down your birdseed.If you can't find what you're looking for locally, or if you just want to explore the wide world of bird supplies, check out online and mail-order sources. Here's a small sampling of the many suppliers for backyard birds.

Hurley-Byrd
462 Williams Cross Way
Fairmont, WV 26554
877-363-0199
www.hurleybyrd.com

You'll find only feeders at this source; no foods, houses, or baths. But what feeders they are—their beautiful, simple lines and natural wood make them the standout among all of the fussy, fancy, too-small feeders on the market. Crafted of clear-grade western cedar, they're built to last. You'll find a variety of sizes and styles, all designed for the way birds like to eat. And you can even buy your deer a feeder of their own at this source, which makes heavy-duty feeders and troughs for your larger wild friends.

Duncraft
102 Fisherville Road
Concord, NH 03303
888-879-5095
www.Duncraft.com

An extensive selection of foods, including mealworms; many feeders and poles; well-made birdhouses; birdbaths and misters are all offered. Duncraft sells one of the best birdbaths I've ever used—a naturalistic faux-rocky pool that warblers, tanagers, thrushes, and other forest birds take to as if was the real thing. You'll find many anti-pest feeders such as the Feeder Hut Pest Proof Feeder in Duncraft's catalog, too.

BestNest
4000 McMann Road
Cincinnati, OH 45245
877-562-1818 or 513-232-4225
www.BestNest.com

Lots of bird foods, feeders (including anti-pest styles), houses, and birdbaths, plus ladybug houses, arbors, and other fun additions to your bird-friendly backyard can be found here. Best Nest has a big selection of appealing "human style" birdhouses—you'll find everything from a Nantucket Cape Cod to a cozy cottage. I prefer the uncluttered look of unadorned nest boxes, but these make pretty yard accents, even if they don't get any tenants.

Bird-House-Bath.com (online only)
www.bird-house-bath.com

This Web site offers all kinds of foods—plus an unbelievable selection of artsy feeders and birdbaths to drool over, as well as the usual types. I fell in love with the sculptured pair of cupped hands that proffers a handful of seed, but at more than $300 . . . well, that would buy a whole lotta birdseed instead.

Wild Birding World
The Kayes Group, Inc.
PO Box 3326
Mesquite, NV 89027
702-726-2604
www.wildbirdingworld.com

No bird foods or baths at this source, but a wide variety of birdhouses and feeders. Look for a window feeder that's worth putting on your wish list—a good-size, see-through model that attaches to your window with suction cups so you can watch the birds right on the other side of the glass.

Canary Seed

For small amounts of packaged canary seed, check the caged birds section of your local pet store. You can also find it online at:

Alta Loma Seed
909-717-5802
www.altalomaseed.com

This small, family-owned company sells canary seed alone and in mixes, as well as other wild birdseeds.

Doctors Foster and Smith
2253 Air Park Road
PO Box 100
Rhinelander, WI 54501
800-443-1160
www.drsfostersmith.com

This company specializes in foods for both caged and wild birds, offered in separate catalogs. You can buy canary seed alone, in 5- or 10-pound bags, on its Web site.

Hot-Pepper-Treated Seed

Ask your bird supply store for treated seed, or check online sources, such as:

Cole's Wild Bird Products Co.
PO Box 2227
Kennesaw, GA 30156
877-426-8882
www.coleswildbird.com

The Hot Meats line includes hulled sunflower seeds; suet blocks; and a cardinal blend with safflower. The company also sells bottled Flaming Squirrel Seed Sauce, so you can treat your own bird foods to repel squirrels. You'll find other premium seed mixes and foods on this site, too.

Squirrel Free, Inc.
255 Great Arrow Avenue
Buffalo, NY 14207
888-636-1477
www.hotbirdseed.com

This wholesale company experiments with treated seed and sells its products through retailers. Visit its Web site to learn about the research that's gone into its products and to find a list of retailers in your area.

Hummingbird Feeders

Nectar feeders are widely available at the same places that sell feeders for other birds. If you are looking for a particular model, such as the wasp-discouraging Perky Pet "Our Best" Model 209, ask for it by name at your local bird supply shop. If they don't have it in stock, they may be able to order it for you. Or do an online search for the feeder you want, to find suppliers. Here are two places you can find the Perky Pet "Our Best" model:

Pet Mountain
1-888-373-8686
http://www.petmountain.com/product/bird-feeders/107692/perky-pet—our-best-feeder-30-oz.html

Amazon.com
http://www.amazon.com/Perky-Pet-209-Hummingbird-capacity/dp/B00004RA8P/ref=sr_1_1?ie=UTF8&s=garden&qid=1271014874&sr=1-1

Insect Foods

Oregon Feeder Insects
866-641-8938
www.oregonfeederinsects.com

This small company began in 1984 with its first product, the Oregon Suet Block. The suet is blended with insects (particularly house flies, raised for this purpose), and it's irresistible to wrens, catbirds, thrashers, bluebirds, brown creepers, and many other birds. Other varieties of suet are available, too, as well as Bug'Mmms, a bagged mix of seed enriched with insects. You may also be able to find the Oregon Suet Block at pet stores; it's popular with caged birds, too.

Birdbaths, Fountains, and Misters

Many of the previously mentioned sources for bird foods and supplies also carry birdbaths, misters, and other water devices. You can also check the following suppliers for your backyard water needs:

Birdbaths.com (online only)
Hayneedle, Inc.
12720 I Street, Suite 200
Omaha, NE 68137
888-880-4884 or 866-579-5182
www.birdbaths.com

This Web site provides many styles of birdbaths and other ways to offer water to your birds, including baths with built-in solar fountains.

Gardener's Supply Company
128 Intervale Road
Burlington VT 05401
888-833-1412 or 800-876-5520
www.gardeners.com

If you want more bugs, butterflies, and birds, and a chemical-free yard, this company offers a wide range of garden tools and supplies, birdbaths, and other temptations, from practical to pretty. You'll also find more garden hoses and nozzles than you ever knew existed, plus a good selection of baths and solar fountains.

Motion-Activated Cat Chaser

To find a device that hooks up to your hose to deter cats and other trespassers with a sudden blast of water, check bird supply stores, well-stocked garden centers, mail-order sources such as those listed above, or suppliers such as these.

Biocontrol Network
5116 Williamsburg Road
Brentwood, TN 37027
800-441-2847
www.biconet.com

Contech Enterprises Inc.
Unit 115–19 Dallas Road
Victoria, BC V8V 5A6
Canada
800-767-8658 (toll free in North America)
www.contech-inc.com/products/scarecrow/
www.amazon.com/Contech-Electronics-CRO101-Scarecrow-Motion-Activated/dp/B000071NUS

SafePetProducts.com
KMP Products LLC
1060 Zygmunt Circle
Westmont, IL 60559
888-977-7387
www.safepetproducts.com

Shade-Grown Coffee

Look for organic shade-grown coffee in your supermarket, coffee shop, or other local specialty stores. Or check this Web site for a list of outlets: www.shadecoffee.org/shadecoffee/

Window Treatments

Pebeo paint is available at art supply shops, including Dick Blick stores, and online at www.dickblick.com/products/pebeo-vitrea-160/.

For screening that goes on the outside of your windows, check:

Birdscreen
2469 Hammertown Road
Narvon, PA 17555-9730
717-445-9609
www.birdscreen.com

For frosted glass film, both plain and patterned, and other vinyl window film, check:

CollidEscape
722 Walsh Road
Madison, WI 53714-1370
866-533-2841, Ext.103
www.collidescape.citymax.com

Glass Décor and More (online only)
http://www.glassdecorandmore.com/cgi-bin/category.cgi?category=frosted_film

Planting for Birds

Agastache

If you can't find warm-colored agastache plants at your local nursery or garden center, you'll find a whole garden's worth of fabulous varieties in the High Country Gardens catalog. This was the first mail-order company to come up with adaptable hummingbird-beloved agastaches for the home garden. The beautiful catalog is a feast of hummingbird plants and other interesting natives.

High Country Gardens
2902 Rufina Street
Santa Fe, NM 87507
800-925-9387
www.highcountrygardens.com

Impatiens

For out-of-the-ordinary impatiens varieties, as well as hundreds of other beautiful and unusual flowers to drool over, check specialty flower catalogs, such as:

Annie's Annuals
Annie's Annuals & Perennials, LLC
801 Chesley Avenue
Richmond, CA 94801
888-266-4370
www.anniesannuals.com

Annie's online catalog is an education in rare and unusual flowers, including many fascinating species of impatiens. Annie's sells started plants by mail-order during the growing season. The selection varies from week to week, but there's always something that'll make your mouth water.

Thompson & Morgan Seedsmen, Inc.
220 Faraday Avenue
Jackson, NJ 08527-5073
800-274-7333
www.tmseeds.com

This company offers seeds for thousands of varieties of uncommon flowers, including impatiens and many others.

Native Plants

It's much easier to find native plants these days than it once was. Start by asking your local nursery for native junipers, oaks, shrubs such as spice bush or arrow-wood, or whatever other natives you're looking for. If you have a nursery that specializes in native plants in your area, check it out. Ask for whatever it is you want; if it's not in stock, the owners may be able to acquire it. And just asking for a plant creates a demand that savvy nursery owners will pay attention to.

Independently owned nurseries are the best bet. Native plants—the same plants that are common as dirt in wild places—are often hard to find at garden centers. When I do manage to find a few, they're often priced higher than common ornamentals, probably because there's a smaller demand for them. But even the garden centers of big-box stores are beginning to stock some native species—and the more often native plants are requested by their customers, the more likely that stock will increase.

Another good place to find natives is at plant sales. I keep an eye on my newspaper in spring, looking for plant sales by garden clubs, plant conservation groups, native plant societies, and other organizations that may have interesting native plants for sale—usually at bargain prices.

The Internet has been a boon for finding mail-order sources for unusual plants. Not so long ago, only a handful of nurseries specialized in native plants; today, there are scores of them, in every area of the country. Just do a search for "native plant nursery [your state]" and see what turns up.

To find out what kind of experiences others have had with the company you're considering buying from, you can read reviews by actual customers on the Web site Garden Watchdog at davesgarden.com/gwd/. This site provides a great service, acting as a sort of Better Business Bureau for mail-order gardeners.

If you can't find natives nearby, check mail-order or online sources, such as these.

All Native Garden Center
300 Center Road
Fort Myers, FL 33907
239-939-9663
www.nolawn.com

Here are fabulous plants with tropical flair and natives that can take heat and dry spells. More than 200 native Florida species of plants are offered, many of them superb for hummingbirds and songbirds. This garden center doesn't offer mail-order services currently, so you Floridians are the luckiest shoppers. If you live in the region, it's worth the drive.

Blake Nursery
316 Otter Creek Road
Big Timber, MT 59011
406-932-4195
www.blakenursery.com

This nursery specializes in plants for western gardens, including a terrific selection of hardy Montana natives that will thrive elsewhere in the West, too—or give that western touch to an eastern garden.

Digging Dog Nursery
PO Box 471
Albion, CA 95410
707-937-1130
www.diggingdog.com

Get ready to fall in love with hummingbirds—this nursery has so many plants that hummers adore, you can fill your yard and your neighbor's with great finds. You'll also discover other interesting perennials, including native plants for songbirds. Specializes in plants for the Southwest, but many of these beauties will thrive elsewhere, too.

Forestfarm
990 Tetherow Road
Williams, OR 97544
541-846-7269
www.forestfarm.com

Plant addicts, beware: One look at Forestfarm's chunky, jam-packed catalog and you'll be hooked. There's an unbelievably vast selection of thousands of plants, including natives from across America. I've been thrilled every time with their superior size and vigor.

Hamilton's Native Nursery and Seed Farm
16786 Brown Road
Elk Creek, MO 65464
417-967-2190
www.hamiltonseed.com

This company offers seeds and plants for native grasses, prairie flowers, native shrubs and trees, and other great finds.

For Further Reading

All of the scientific facts and data in this book about declining bird populations, climate change, pesticides, habitat destruction, and other issues are from original source materials.

For a broad view of the problems, see:

The State of the Birds, United States of America (US Government, 2009) This massive report, issued by the federal government, draws on research and cooperation from the Nature Conservancy, the US Fish and Wildlife Service, National Audubon Society, the Cornell Lab of Ornithology, the American Bird Conservancy, the Association of Fish and Wildlife Agencies, and other organizations.

http://www.stateofthebirds.org/2009

The State of the Birds, 2010 Report on Climate Change (US Government, 2010) Building on the original 2009 report, which took a frank look at the current state of American birds, this detailed report examines the ways in which climate change is affecting birds and makes careful predictions about what the future may hold.

http://www.stateofthebirds.org

Birds and Climate Change: Ecological Disruption in Motion (National Audubon Society, 2009) Another comprehensive report, focusing on the effects of climate change on American birds.

http://birdsandclimate.audubon.org

Global Climate Change Impacts in the United States (US Government; Cambridge University Press, New York, June 2009) Science-based information on climate change effects on weather, water, air quality, and other aspects that are vital to all living things on earth.

http://www.globalchange.gov/publications/reports/scientific-assessments/us-impacts

For more about other facts and figures in this book or for a deeper look at certain topics that refer to these sources, read:

1915 Annual Report of the State Board of Agriculture, Massachusetts. Boston: Wright & Potter Printing Co., State Printers, 1916.

Adam, David. "Where have all our birds gone?" *Guardian*, May 25, 2009.

Brennan, Leonard A. "How Can We Reverse the Northern Bobwhite Population Decline?" *Wildlife Society Bulletin* 19 (1991): 544–55.

Brittingham, M. C., and S. A. Temple. "Does Winter Bird Feeding Promote Dependency?" *Journal of Field Ornithology* 63 (1992), no. 2: 190–94.

———. "Impacts of Supplemental Feeding on Survival Rates of Black-Capped Chickadees." *Ecology* 69 (1988): 581–89.

Chaudhari, Nirupa, et al. "L Glutamate Receptor Identified as Taste Receptor of Umami." *Journal of Neurology* 247 (May 2000): 5.

Deis, R. D. "Is Bird Feeding a No No?" *Defenders of Wildlife* 57 (1982): 17–18.

Desrochers, André. "Morphological response of songbirds to 100 years of landscape change in North America," *Ecology* (February 1, 2010).

Egan, Erica, and Margaret C. Brittingham. "Winter Survival Rates of a Southern Population of Black-Capped Chickadees." *The Wilson Bulletin* 106, no. 3(1994): 514–21.

Gibson, Arthur. "Why Do Our Hummingbirds Hum?" *Newsletter of the UCLA Mildred E. Mathias Botanical Garden* 3 (Summer 2000): 3.

Hammerson, Geoffrey A. *Connecticut Wildlife: Biodiversity, Natural History, and Conservation.* Lebanon, NH: University Press of New England, 2004.

Healey, Sean P. "The Effect of a Teak (*Tectona grandis*) Plantation on the Establishment of Native Species in an Abandoned Pasture in Costa Rica." *Forest Ecology and Management* 176 (2003):497–507.

Hill, Geoffrey E., Robert R. Sargent, and Martha B. Sargent. "Recent Change in the Winter Distribution of Rufous Hummingbirds." *The Auk* 115, no. 1(1998): 240–45.

Johnson, Robert A., Mary F. Willson, et al. "Nutritional Values of Wild Fruits and Consumption by Migrant Frugivorous Birds." *Ecology* 66, no. 3(1985): 819–27.

Kare, Morely. *The Chemical Senses of Birds.* University of Nebraska, 1970.

Koenig, Walter D. "European Starlings and Their Effect on Native Cavity-Nesting Birds." *Conservation Biology* 17, no. 4 (August 2003): 1134–40.

Macphail, Euan M. *The Neuroscience of Animal Intelligence: From the Seahare to the Seahorse.* Columbia University Press, 1993.

Pimentel, David, H. Acquay, et al. "The Environmental and Economic Costs of Pesticide Use." *BioScience* 42 (1992): 750–60.

San Gabriel, Ana, Takami Maekawa, et al. "Metabotropic Glutamate Receptor Type 1 in Taste Tissue." *American Journal of Clinical Nutrition* 90, no. 3(2009): 743S–46S.

Sterba, James B. "Crying Fowl: Feeding Wild Birds May Harm Them and Environment." *Wall Street Journal*, December 27, 2002.

Stiles, E. W. "The Influence of Pulp Lipids on Fruit Preference by Birds." *Vegetatio* 107/108(1993): 227–35.

Vander Wall, Stephen B. *Food Hoarding in Animals.* Chicago: University of Chicago Press, 1990.

Vyas, N. B. "Factors Influencing Estimation of Pesticide-Related Wildlife Mortality." *Toxicology and Industrial Health* 15(1999): 186–91.

Zuckerberg, Benjamin, Anne M. Woods, and William F. Porter. "Poleward Shifts in Breeding Bird Distributions in New York State." *Global Change Biology* 15, no. 8(2009): 1866–83(18).

Photo Credits

© R. Curtis/Vireo: 6, 23, 52, 88, 95, 125, 148, 149, 204, 206, 207, 292
© G. Bailey/Vireo: 7
© Mark Gibson/Visuals Unlimited, Inc.: 9
© J. Heidecker/Vireo: 11
© J. Hunter/Vireo: 14
© Steve Maslowski/Visuals Unlimited, Inc.: Cover, 18, 28, 30, 34, 41, 55, 59, 60, 67, 75, 92, 106, 157, 200, 218, 222, 240, 260, 268, 268, 277
© A. Morris/Vireo: 19, 214, 294
© Bradley Mitchell/Visuals Unlimited, Inc.: 21
© W. Greene/Vireo: 24, 138
© Paul Debois/Gap Photo/Visuals Unlimited, Inc.: 26
© Juliette Wade/Gap Photo/Visuals Unlimited, Inc.: 27
© John Glover/Gap Photo/Visuals Unlimited, Inc.: 33
© R & S Day/Vireo: 37, 69, 118, 208
© G. Bartley/Vireo: 44
© G. McElroy/Vireo: 45, 85, 134
© Jonathan Buckley/Gap Photo/Visuals Unlimited, Inc.: 50
© Elke Borkowski/Gap Photo/Visuals Unlimited, Inc.: 52
© Charles Melton/Visuals Unlimited, Inc.: 53, 187, 192, 245
© J. Turner MD/Vireo: 56
© Zara Napier/Gap Photo/Visuals Unlimited, Inc.: 63, 66, 179
© S. Greer/Vireo: 65
© Tom Edwards/Visuals Unlimited, Inc.: 66
© Claire Davies/Gap Photo/Visuals Unlimited, Inc.: 69
© James Hager/Getty Images: 73
© Derrick Ditchburn/Visuals Unlimited: 76 bottom
© M. Tekulsky/Vireo: 76 top
© Dick Keen/Visuals Unlimited, Inc.: 80
© Bill Beatty/Visuals Unlimited, Inc.: 83, 210
© Wally Eberhart/Visuals Unlimited, Inc.: 84, 202
© Joe McDonald/Visuals Unlimited, Inc.: 87, 89, 91, 218, 239, 250, 273
© Mike Powell/Getty Images: 94
© Leroy Simon/Visuals Unlimited, Inc.: 97, 167
© Brian E. Small/Vireo: 97
© Matthew Bartmann: 99, 199
© B. Steele/Vireo: 103, 146, 171, 227
© Marilyn Angel Wynn/Nativestock.com/Getty Images: 104
© William Thomas Cain/Getty Images: 105
© Adam Jones/Visuals Unlimited, Inc.: 109, 232, 246
© Rose Nicholson: 113, 168, 288
© Robert Domm/Visuals Unlimited, Inc.: 116
© Roger Cole/Visuals Unlimited, Inc.: 120
© R & N Bowers/Vireo: 126 top, 252
© Michael Durham/Visuals Unlimited, Inc.: 126 bottom
© John Cornell/Visuals Unlimited, Inc.: 128, 241
© K. Schafer/Vireo: 138
© Arthur Morris/Visuals Unlimited, Inc.: 141, 176, 186
© Rob & Ann Simpson/Visuals Unlimited, Inc.: 144
© S. Fried/Vireo: 152
© Robert Servranckx/Visuals Unlimited, Inc.: 161
© M. Hyett/Vireo: 164, 194
© Mark Carwardine/Visuals Unlimited, Inc.: 170
© Jack Ballard/Visuals Unlimited, Inc.: 174
© F. Truslow/Vireo: 177, 219
© Richard Bloom/Gap Photo/Visuals Unlimited, Inc.: 191
© Dr. John D. Cunningham/Visuals Unlimited, Inc.: 196, 228, 251
© Graham Strong/Gap Photo/Visuals Unlimited, Inc.: 198
© T. Vezo/Vireo: 203, 244
© K. A. Niya/Vireo: 206
© Inga Spence/Visuals Unlimited, Inc.: 217, 267
© Corbis: 224
© Dr. William Weber/Visuals Unlimited, Inc.: 225
© Sally Roth: 226
© J S Sira/Gap Photo/Visuals Unlimited, Inc.: 227
© S & O/Gap Photo/Visuals Unlimited, Inc.: 230
© G. Lasley/Visuals Unlimited, Inc.: 233
© John & Barbara Gerlach/Visuals Unlimited, Inc.: 234, 256
© Nigel Cattlin/Visuals Unlimited, Inc.: 236
© P. Latourrette/Vireo: 255
© Fritz Polking/Visuals Unlimited, Inc.: 257
© Tim Zurowski/Getty Images: Back cover top, 259
© Ashley Cooper/Visuals Unlimited, Inc.: 275
© Danita Delimont/Getty Images: 282
© Laurie Neish/Vireo: Back cover bottom, 286
© Doug Weschler/Vireo: 289

Index

Boldface page numbers indicate photographs or illustrations. Underscored references indicate boxed text, charts, and graphs.

C

USDA Plant Hardiness Zone Map

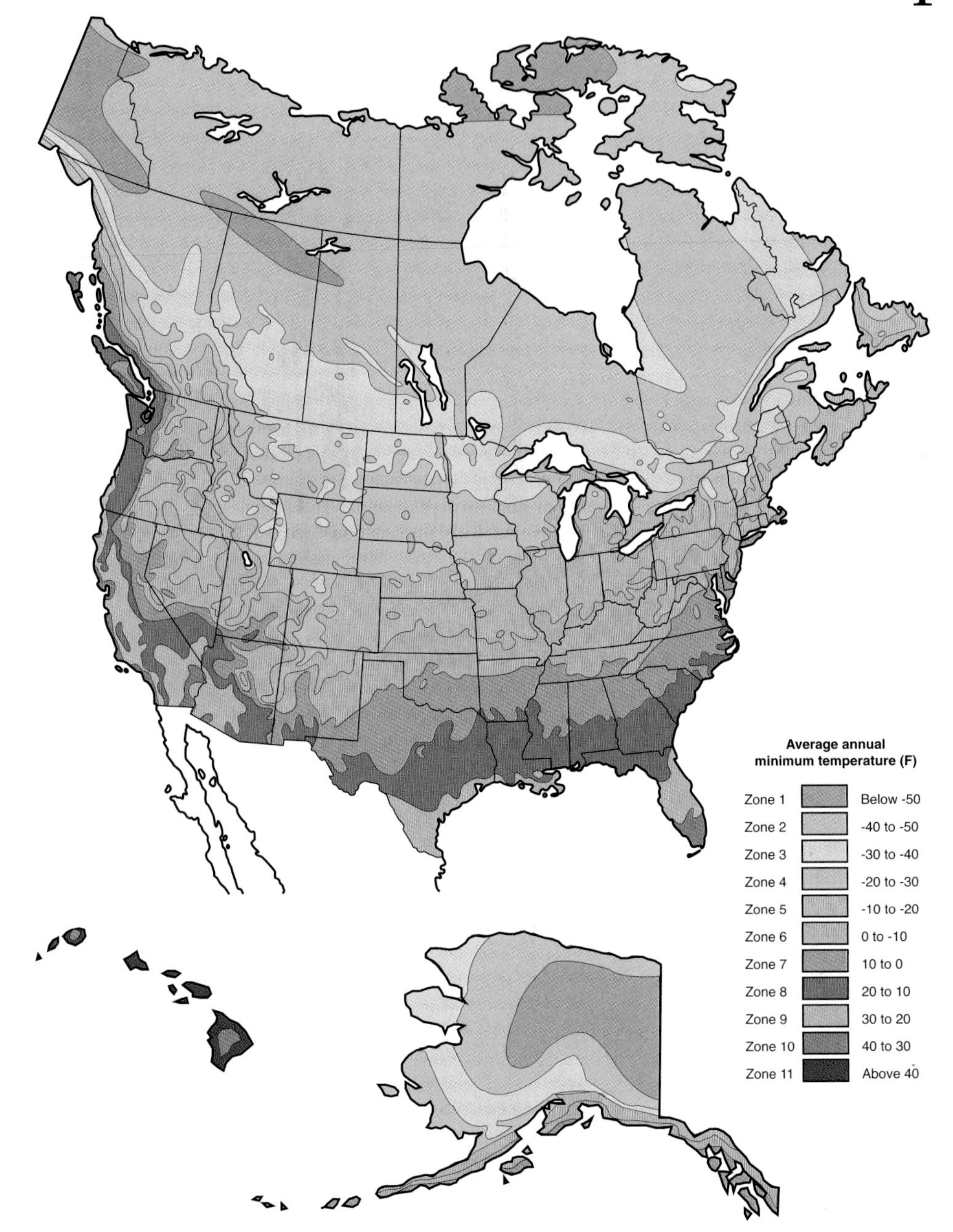

This map is recognized as the best indicator of minimum temperatures available. Look at the map to find your area, then match its pattern to the key at right. When you've found your pattern, the key will tell you what hardiness zone you live in. Remember that the map is a general guide; your particular conditions may vary.